ALL IN A DAY'S WORK

Dorothy Gardner

MINERVA PRESS
LONDON
MONTREUX   LOS ANGELES   SYDNEY

ISBN 1 86106 395 4

First Published 1997 by
MINERVA PRESS
195 Knightsbridge
LONDON SW7 1RE

2nd Impression 1997

Printed in Great Britain by
Antony Rowe Ltd, Chippenham, Wiltshire

To Betty

ALL IN A DAY'S WORK

From DOROTHY.

All my Love. XXX

I write under my Christian names my novel should help to pass the time while you are getting better.

Introduction

The United Kingdom

Far to the north of the kingdom, in the year 1926, a baby girl was born in the City of Edinburgh. Round about the same time a princess was born in the City of London.

As they grew into their teen years, the kingdom was plunged into war. Food and clothing was rationed, and the allowance of hot water in the bath was six inches to conserve fuel.

When the girl from the north reached the age of seventeen and a half years, she volunteered to work on the land to help feed her war-weary nation.

The princess joined the Auxiliary Territorial Army on her eighteenth birthday. She drove, and worked on army vehicles as a mechanic.

Everyone knows and loves the story of Princess Elizabeth's part in helping to win the war.

Jaqueline, the girl from the north, now tells the story of her war effort working on the land, while the skies over Europe rang with the sound of battle. Hers was the world of neatly dressed girls who worked in the shops and offices of Edinburgh's West End. On week days Jaqueline travelled by early morning train from the suburbs to The Caledonian Station in Princess Street. She would pause for a moment, while crossing the West End, to watch the early morning mists rise from the castle that had stood on its mighty rock since the eleventh century.

No matter how far she roamed to achieve her ambitions, when the world was once more at peace, this was her city, and she would always return to the place of her birth.

Part One
Earlson Farm, 1943

Chapter One

While the bedroom fire glowed warmly, I lounged on the soft rug staring dreamily into tiny flames that licked their way round shiny black coal.

"It's little more than a week before you join us in the fields, Jaqueline," said my sister, pulling on her new pyjamas, "then you really will know what hard work is all about."

I felt slightly ruffled by her remark, and answered,

"I'm not going into the fields, I'm going to be a poultry maid."

"It doesn't make any difference," she replied, "farm workers don't have any time for make-up or well-manicured, long nails. You'll find it quite a change from pushing a pen or dressing a window. You should have waited to join the WRNS as you planned at the beginning of the war."

Still feeling ruffled by her attitude, I moved back from the increasing heat of the fire and answered indignantly,

"But Mum said the war would be over if I waited another six months. And there's never going to be another war,"

"Yes, she said the same to me, Jaqueline. Don't you remember? I would have waited for my eighteenth birthday to join the WAAFS. You know, the more I think about it, the more I realise Mum's desperate to keep us near home. She couldn't, if we were in the forces." I was much too busy thinking of life on the farm and newly hatched chickens to bother about what seemed like unimportant details; I could hardly wait to get into the riding breeches and short coat that all land-girls wore.

Her eyes dancing with mischief, my sister continued,

"Would you like to come to a barn dance on the estate next weekend? It would give you the opportunity of meeting the kind of people you will be working with as a land-girl."

I sat up to watch her parading in front of the bedroom mirror, my interest aroused by something different.

"Yes, I would," I answered. "But what, exactly, is a barn dance?"

"Just what it suggests. A dance held in a barn. You might say, it's the equivalent of the *Palais de Dance* country style."

As I tried to picture the relationship between a barn for storing hay and the local *Palais de Dance*, she lifted her brush and ran it through her auburn hair.

"Do you think I look better in *your* new pyjamas, or my own?" she asked.

"You definitely suit the mustard and brown, Margaret, they go well with your colouring; but I'm sticking to my own choice of navy and white. You can always borrow them occasionally," I answered, having ended up with second choice on many occasions.

She was quiet for a while, rolling her hair into little curls and pinning them flat round her head.

"Jaqueline," her voice was thoughtful when she spoke again, "I haven't told Mum and Dad about the German prisoners of war working in the next field to us." She looked vexed as she turned towards me. "Do you think I should? I don't want to worry them."

Prisoners of war were something to be afraid of, so I replied as lightheartedly as I could.

"I don't know, Margaret. They can't do anything about it. Come to think of it, Dad must know what the Germans are like being a veteran of the Fourteen-Eighteen War, and I don't suppose they had any more say in the matter than we did. I mean, about going to war."

Crossing the room she sat down on the rug beside me in front of the warm fire.

"Yes," she said quietly, "you know, I hated these prisoners at first, because they started the war. But some of them really do look so like Dad, tall and straight with the same thick, blond hair. They don't seem like foreigners at all, until they start clicking their heels and bowing as we leave the field."

I watched the flames dance over the glowing coals, amused by what she had said.

"Do they really click their heels and bow?"

"Yes," she answered, smiling.

"How many are there?"

"Usually ten, with two armed guards."

A hint of anxiety had replaced the smile in her brown eyes, so again I tried to allay her fears:

"Forget it, Margaret. I've got one clothing coupon left now, after using five for pyjamas. I wonder if Mum has an odd one? I could do with a new pair of gloves."

While the sirens wailed in the distance, we sat hugging our knees dressed in our new pyjamas. Suddenly there was a knock on the bedroom door and my father called out,

"Stay where you are, girls, until the sirens sound in our area, If they do, we gather under the staircase; the air-raid shelter is up to the knees in water after the heavy rain. Better to die in a warm house, than of pneumonia in the shelter."

"Yes, Dad," I answered.

And my father returned to the window of the darkened hall where he could watch the shadowy forms of approaching bombers. Then as an afterthought, he called out:

"Switch off your bedroom lights, the fire glow will be enough while they are directly above us. We can't be too careful, there could be an odd chink of light showing through the black-out curtains."

As the enemy planes passed over in waves of throbbing sound carrying their heavy load of destruction towards the River Forth, my sense of danger told me we should be doing something to ward off the threat that hovered above us, or be more afraid while we waited. However, my father's dry sense of humour with its own brand of reasoning left us unafraid, and we continued our interrupted conversation.

"You seldom talk about your work in the fields, Margaret."

"I prefer to forget it at the weekend. It's so hard stooping for several hours working across a large field planting or weeding. Only the company of friends makes it bearable."

For the first time in my life, I saw utter despondency cross my sister's pert, pretty little face and I felt concern for her.

"But, Margaret, can't you stand up and stretch occasionally?"

"The foreman doesn't like it. If we do, he swears and complains about the soft folk from the city. I often wish I was back behind the cash desk."

She shrugged her shoulders and stretched her arms, then continued in a brighter voice:

"I keep repeating to myself, 'a Girl Guide smiles and sings under all difficulties'," then she threw back her head and a light laugh escaped her lips. "Hark at me, Soldiers are dying on the battlefields. Ships are blown up every day and sailors drown, and planes are shot out of the skies. What have I got to complain about?"

We sat silently watching the flames vanish from the coals leaving a soft red glow. Then a thunderous explosion roared through the quiet of the night and the earth seemed to vibrate. We fled from the bedroom and ran to the safety of the staircase as the house shuddered.

My brother's face was ashen, and my father stretched out his arms to encircle the group as we huddled together. Gradually the distant rumbling died away and tears began to run down my mother's face.

"It's all our fault, we should never have allowed it to happen again."

I looked at my mother, aghast at what she had said.

"Why is it your fault?" I asked.

"Your mother means that it is the fault of our generation to have allowed another war to happen," said my father quietly.

"Nonsense," I exploded. "It's people who are greedy for power and money that start wars, It isn't your fault."

"Make a pot of tea, girls, and I'll have some before I report to the first aid post." A smile flickered in his eyes as he spoke.

The droning of the bomber planes moved slowly westwards, while the activity of making and drinking tea had brought back a happier atmosphere to the house.

"I don't know what could have caused such a thunderous explosion," my father said, thoughtfully stirring his tea. "Is there any sugar left, Dora?"

"No, it's finished until I collect the rations on Monday," my mother replied.

"They certainly emptied their bombs somewhere near, I'd better get up to the first aid post and find out." And he pushed his arms into his coat before making a final statement. "You may as well all go to bed, because when the bombers make their way back over our area they'll be empty. But keep the lights off, just in case." Then he hurried out of the house closing the door quietly behind him.

"I'll wash up the cups, Jaqueline. And no more tears, Mum. Stop torturing yourself over something that has always been way beyond your control." A hint of authority had crept into my sister's voice,

"Alex, better get into bed – you'll be working all weekend and you need your sleep."

As they walked from the warm kitchen into the hall, I could hear my brother saying,

"Dad and you have done well enough working all your lives to raise the three of us. The responsibility is ours now. Goodnight, Mum."

"Goodnight, Alex," she replied quietly.

When their bedroom doors had closed, my sister's indignation rose, her eyes were angry but her voice was quiet as she spoke.

"I think it's scandalous having a sixteen year old boy working on huge destroyers in the Forth; and yet, he seems to love engines. I suppose it's quite an adventure at his age. I almost died when I looked into his room; all these sheets of paper spread over the floor and his motor bike completely taken apart, how will he ever get it together again? Mum must be mad to allow it, she can't even get in to make his bed."

Glancing at the hard calluses on the palms of her hands as she dried them, she added,

"I suppose you get accustomed to anything after a while."

We switched off the kitchen light and moved into the hall.

"How do you manage with no electricity or gas on these isolated farms, Margaret?"

"It's amazing how pleasant candle-light or paraffin lamps can be, and eating breakfast in a large kitchen with a glowing range really is something special." She smiled and her anger was gone.

We chatted on after climbing into bed and reached the conclusion that we were molly-coddled-suburbans. I was dozing with the all-clear ringing in my ears, when my sister spoke again.

"Are you asleep, Jaqueline?"

"Not yet," I murmured.

"Then listen to some good advice. If the work is too heavy for you, don't do it. Mary is having trouble carrying her baby due to straining herself badly when she was in the Land Army. She's been in hospital for six weeks now, because of continuous bleeding."

"Dad's back," I said, sitting up quickly.

Several minutes elapsed before he knocked on the bedroom door.

"Can I come in, girls?"

"Yes, Dad."

14

We were suddenly wide awake, anxious to hear what had happened.

"Nothing was dropped in our area, but a land mine exploded in the Port of Leith just a few miles down the coast. Goodnight, girls."

"Goodnight, Dad."

And when the door closed we settled down to sleep.

On Sunday evening, with the weekend nearly over, I went to see my sister off at the bus station. As the bus moved slowly out, she called from the platform,

"I'll see you at the bus stop outside the estate entrance on Friday, Jaqueline, Remember, second stop after the harbour, take the five thirty and we'll be waiting to collect you for the barn dance."

I waved as the bus gathered speed and suddenly I felt very proud of my hard-working sister. Her hat was worn at a rakish angle with the brim swept up at both sides transforming it into a tricorn; her coat had been shortened to achieve the appearance that was necessary to her fashion-conscious mind. The result of these minor adjustments had brought out the personality of the wearer of this otherwise mass-produced uniform.

The bus merged into the constant flow of traffic and, as I turned to make my way home, my thoughts were already a week ahead picturing the poultry farm and fluffy, yellow chickens. At last I would be helping to win the war that had started in my fourteenth year.

Chapter Two

The following Friday, after a thirty mile journey by S.M.T. bus, I arrived at the estate situated on the Firth of Forth where my sister worked as a land-girl. A groan went up from the girls who waited when I alighted at the entrance.

"Oh! Margaret, Didn't you tell her what to wear for a barn dance?"

My sister smiled, looking at my slim skirted dress and high heeled shoes, she answered,

"Too late to do anything about it now, let's go,"

We passed through the impressive entrance gates of the estate turning right on to a well worn path, and as we walked, she introduced me to her friends.

"Meet Melissa, Mildred and Margie, the three lumberjills. This is my sister, Jaqueline."

I kept stumbling into deep ruts made by tractor wheels on the path, while I shook hands with each of the girls. Melissa stretched out a hand laughing as she caught my elbow.

"Walk on the raised part in the middle where the grass is, it won't be so hard on your shoes," she said.

"Hiking boots would have been better." And I grabbed her shoulder to steady myself, while I enquired, "How far is it?"

"The barn is just a hundred yards along this path," and as Melissa spoke the large wooden barn with its corrugated iron roof came into view.

As we drew nearer I could see that one end was completely open to the weather and inside, bales of straw were stacked up to the roof along the walls. The centre had been cleared and long tables set up at the far end.

"That's the bar for the men," said Margie, pointing to a makeshift bar on the left as we entered the barn. "Tea is being served for the ladies at the top end."

The men clustered round the bar as we passed, draining pints of beer in little more than two prolonged gulps. They all wore spotless white open-necked shirts and seemed to be oblivious to everything but their beer.

We made our way down to the long tables where rows of cups adorned with pink roses sat on gold-edged saucers, set out on a stiffly starched cloth of white damask. A young woman with vivid red hair stood serving tea from a polished copper urn, while grannies, mothers and daughters sat in groups chatting to the tinkle of their teacups. Lively children crawled under the tables or darted roundabout as the mood took them.

The drone of men's voices coming from the makeshift bar was occasionally broken by loud outbursts of laughter that would gradually settle down to a contented hum.

I gazed round the very basic surroundings for an evening of dancing: the cement floor, the glowing paraffin lamps suspended from the rafters, and the glint of gold as the flickering of the lamps danced along the bales of straw.

Reaching into a pram that stood behind the tea-table the pretty young woman who had poured our tea lifted a wailing baby.

"You're staring, Jaqueline," my sister whispered and she nudged my arm.

"Oh! Sorry, but it is an unusual baby," I answered quietly, and we moved towards more of her friends.

"Meet the twins, Trudy and Penny, both are land-girls but you might not believe it looking at their breeches."

Everyone in the group was wearing the fine gabardine riding breeches issued to lumberjills.

"Are you allowed to swap breeches?" I asked.

"Not officially, but we do it, because the cord breeches are warmer for working in and the gabardine go very well with silk blouses for dress wear, as you can see." And Melissa flicked back her long, dark hair to show an emerald green, silk blouse daringly unbuttoned low at the neck; a leather belt accentuated her tiny waist.

"Yes, they are very nice," I admitted, but my admiring gaze soon returned to the unusually beautiful baby not far from her.

Noticing my interest in the baby, Melissa spoke again.

"That was quite a story while it lasted," she began, "the mother claimed she had been raped, and since her only alternative was to be mutilated by a knife, she submitted to her attacker. Look, over there by the tables, you can pick out her children quite easily, they are the two with red hair just like her own. Her husband is the fair man with the accordion."

Margie broke in at this point of the conversation with a look of disgust on her face.

"And would you believe it, Jaqueline, When the woman told the police what had happened to her, they shrugged and put it all down to a lively imagination. Aren't they detestable, They were more interested in their tea break being disturbed than in the woman's complaint."

Having expressed the disgust she felt, Margie left Melissa to continue the story.

''We have three black lumberjacks helping to clear the new nursery area on the estate, and when they were questioned by the police, they all denied the raped woman's accusation completely."

"You can hardly put the baby down to a vivid imagination, one of them must have been guilty," I said indignantly, looking again at the beautiful blending of two races.

The baby's skin was dusky, and soft golden hair curled round its head; the large, dark eyes that looked back at me were wide and innocent and made me feel disconcerted by their calm purity.

"Not only that," Melissa was saying, "it was particularly distressing to the other women in the community, as the law seemed to have lost interest by the time the child was born."

Resentment was rising inside me as the story unfolded and I interrupted her:

"It could have happened to any one of you; didn't they make a charge against the accused?"

"No," she replied.

"But if they don't enforce the law to protect women, it could happen again."

Melissa glanced at Mildred and I saw the flicker of a smile pass between them before Mildred spoke.

"There are other ways to deal with what they call 'a bad egg' in a close community like this," she said quietly, "the men don't say much, but wife beaters and those who batter children are dealt with in their own way, and that would include men who interfere with their womenfolk. We have never been allowed to work on our own since the rape."

Our conversation came to an abrupt end as the two accordions playing in the background switched to a lively reel. All of a sudden I found myself desperately trying to keep my feet on the floor. My partner, who had simply grunted at my elbow and steered me into position, wore a set, determined look on his face. The perspiration was glistening on his brow as he whirled me round faster and faster. Then the next man grabbed my arm to pull me round in the opposite direction; I could see sparks jumping out from under my partner's boots as he struck the concrete floor to keep him turning.

The pace of the dancing was an unbelievable contrast to the modern waltz, or the quick-quick-slow ballroom dancing I was used to in the Edinburgh ballrooms; it left me gasping for breath and I felt sure Victor Sylvester had never been heard of in this part of the country.

The reel ended just as suddenly as it had started and I was left sagging against a cool bale of straw at the side of the barn, the floor and the paraffin lamps spun before my glazed eyes while the girls clustered round.

"What do you think of country dancing, Jaqueline?" they chorused.

Between short, quick gasps I managed to answer,

"You're not going to tell me this is Scottish country dancing as taught in school."

"It is, you know," the twins insisted. "With a few extra turns thrown in for good measure and, of course, speeded up a bit."

Through the happy laughter and chatter that followed I caught Melissa's eye.

"You didn't finish the story, Melissa, how was the 'bad egg' dealt with?" I asked.

"Well," she began, lowering her dark lashes and flicking back her long hair, "one of the lumberjacks had a nasty accident after the baby was born: they found him lying in the place where the young woman had been raped."

Eager to say her piece Margie broke into the story.

"The locals say it's a sad business," her hand rose nervously to her boyish haircut before she continued, "but rape is something he can never be accused of since the accident."

I was still looking at her and while she fingered the buttons at the neck of her rose silk blouse the meaning of her words began to sink in. Then a male voice rang out,

"Take your partners for Strip the Willow,"

I felt myself shudder at the sordid justice that had been carried out on the rapist. He had behaved like an animal and they had dealt with him as they did the animals in the fields. Had it been any more painful than giving birth, I wondered?

There was a shuffling of feet on my left and I looked round to find one of nature's inspired creations, who was blushing to the roots of his thick, dark hair.

"Would you partner me for this dance, Miss?"

I smiled, dazzled by such perfection, and taking my hand in his he led me on to the crowded floor.

"Stand with the ladies," he said.

We took up our positions at the end of a set with ladies on one side and gentlemen on the other. A quick check was made to form sets of eight, while bagpipes tuned-up at the open end of the barn; there was a tortured moan as the pipes wailed up to full pitch and we were off.

My partner linked his arm through mine and whirled me round for a count of eight, then I was whirling right down between the couples as each brawny arm reached out to dance with me. Between dancing with each male, I turned to whirl with my partner as he moved down the line of ladies.

The men, white shirts soaked with perspiration, had rolled up their sleeves to expose bulging biceps. Most of them wore braces, and a broad leather belt at their waist; short leggings encased their dark trousers at the ankles. On their feet they wore the same hob-nailed boots that were worn in the fields, but the boots had been polished until the toe-caps shone. I shuddered as I glanced down at my toeless shoes.

Having finished the set I found myself standing still while the farm worker's daughters danced past in their full-skirted, colourful dresses. They were void of make-up, but freshly washed, shining hair had lent a glow to their faces that make-up could never have achieved.

We were gradually moving back up the set dancing with each couple in turn; it should finish now, I thought, but my partner swung towards me and the pace of the music quickened.

"I can't last another minute," I gasped, as my two feet threatened to leave the floor at the same time. It was like the sun after rain when my partner smiled down at me.

"Why, you're doing just fine," his soft voice drawled.

Quite unexpectedly the bagpipes droned to a discordant halt and it was all over. While the barn spun hazily, I searched for the sign 'Ladies' and making straight for this sanctuary, sank down on to a chair in the improvised boudoir with a sigh of relief.

Ladies didn't just glow at a barn dance I decided, dabbing my forehead with a handkerchief, and to use face powder was a complete waste of time. A plank across a hole, a mound of soil and a shovel caught my eye; the floor beneath my feet was grass.

Having cooled down considerably I opened the door to step back into the scene of refreshments and glowing, happy faces.

"Over here, Jaqueline," yelled the twins and I weaved my way through the happy throng carrying groaning trays from the buffet.

"Bales are all we have to sit on, so make yourself comfortable and we'll introduce you to the lads."

I smiled and nodded as they reeled off the name of each girl's partner.

"And this is Joe, Joe, meet, Jaqueline."

Joe, who would have delighted the eye of Michaelangelo, dazzled me with another devastating grin as he shook my hand.

"You're a grand dancer to be from Edinburgh," he said.

Still dazed, I accepted his remark as a compliment; but on reflection I questioned it. He put his hands on my waist and lifted me effortlessly on to an up-ended bale of straw.

"Your sister tells me you're a land-girl?" he was saying.

"I will be on Monday."

With my feet well above floor level he looked me up and down.

"You're better up there where we can see eye to eye," he said, still grinning. "Now, what makes you think you can do a man's work?"

"They wouldn't have asked us to do it if they thought we couldn't," I replied, smiling into his eyes.

He placed a laden tray of food on the bale beside me, then passed a cup of tea.

"Did you have a medical for the Land Army?" he asked.

"No, but you have to be over five feet two inches in height or they turn you down."

"I guess you just made it," he replied and busied himself with the food while he waited for my reaction.

I felt slightly nettled by his attitude when he continued,

"You're not made for heavy work so you shouldn't have joined."

"I'm too young for the forces. I had no choice." And then I added, "How tall are you? And why are you not in the forces?"

"I'm a foot taller than you are, And I will be in the army next month, when I'm old enough," he said quietly. "That makes us about the same age, doesn't it?"

The manliness radiated from this healthy young farm worker as he towered in front of me and I felt like a helpless female.

Then his friend called out,

"How can a Macleod be wearing Royal Stuart tartan braces?"

Unabashed by his friend's remark, Joe stood to his full height, raised his hands above his head and clapping slowly made a full turn, Spanish style, to show off his tartan braces. I felt the laughter bubble up inside me as I watched the naturalness of this unaffected, young man.

"Does your sister cook pastries as well as your mother, Joe?" his friend continued.

"Why don't you ask for the next dance, then you can ask her yourself."

Joe gave his friend a hearty slap on the shoulder and it toppled him over between the bales; as he struggled to rise I heard a new voice ringing clearly above the merriment that the scene had caused.

The farmer, who was a titled gentleman, had dropped in on the festivities to pay his respects. He seemed to know every worker on his large estate by their first names and as the welfare of their families was discussed his cultured tones rang clearly above the soft dialect of the workers.

An appreciative murmur ran through the gathering when the offering of some delectable pastries arrived from the big house; and when an enquiry was made as to the health of her ladyship, the cultured voice, considerably softened, replied,

"My dear lady wife should be out and about again in a few days."

The loud wailing of the bagpipes tuning-up for the next reel echoed through the barn, drowning out any further attempt at conversation and food was forgotten as couples formed sets in the centre of the concrete floor.

Refreshed by the strong tea I was lured once more by Joe's smile. We danced and whirled to the lively music of the pipes and I never really knew where I was until placed back on the spot from which I had been taken. I felt sticky all over and longed to kick off the high-heeled shoes from my aching feet. However, the agony was to be endured until the bagpipes groaned to a final halt.

When the dancing came to an end, in one last wild reel, a hush descended on the gathering and with heads bowed we stood blissfully silent while the national anthem played. The last note had barely died away when a great surge of activity began. The men dismantled the long, trestle tables and heavy bales were effortlessly stacked. The glowing lamps were quickly lowered from the rafters and their golden light extinguished.

Amid a chorus of goodnights we climbed into the farm van to be driven to the lodge where the girls lived on the estate. The retreating barn stood dark and silent, but my thoughts were full of the evening that had been, and blissfully unaware of the hard labour that was to begin soon, following the weekend.

The lodge was cosy and as I kicked off my shoes with a sigh of relief, the twins spoke in one voice.

"Did you enjoy your first barn dance, Jaqueline?"

"Yes, it was an education, but if you work as hard as you dance I'll never survive."

We fell on to our beds amid peals of laughter as the tall, fair-haired Mildred drifted across the room looking utterly feminine in a chiffon nightie.

"When do you start in your first post as a poultry maid, Jaqueline?" she asked.

"I report on Monday," I said, beginning to wonder what lay ahead of me.

"Lights out, girls," Mildred lifted the paraffin lamp from the hook it was suspended on, turned it down and blew out the last of the flickering flame, then crossed to the window and opened the black-out curtains.

Trudy's voice spoke quietly from the next bed as I settled my head on the soft, feather pillow.

"Best of luck to you, Jaqueline. But remember to take it easy with the strenuous work until you become accustomed to it."

"Thank you, I'll remember, goodnight, Trudy."

As I drifted into a heavy sleep I could hear her voice echoing inside my head, "remember to take it easy... until you become accustomed...".

Chapter Three

At just seventeen and a half years of age, I was on my way to my first post as a land-girl: at long last I would be playing an active part in helping to win the war that now raged into its fourth year across Europe.

As the bus made its way out of Edinburgh, past the airport, the Guide law kept running through my thoughts, 'I promise upon my honour, to do my duty to God and the King, to help other people at all times and obey the Guide law'. Having been programmed in that inspired institution I was full of noble aspirations towards the task that lay ahead of me; and as the countryside rushed past the windows of the speeding bus, an old woman seated beside me heaved her two shopping bags from the floor.

"This is my stop, ring the bell, would you?" she said, looking at me with a face flushed by her exertions as she struggled up from the seat. I rose and rang the bell, steadying her with one hand until the bus stopped.

Having dropped one of its passengers in what seemed like the middle of nowhere, the bus continued on its way and I settled down to wondering what my work would be like: feeding poultry, egg collecting, then travelling home by bus in the evening.

"Earlson Farm, Miss, This is your stop." His lilting dialect, untouched by the city, was absorbed by my mind as the bus came to a halt at the roadside, where the conductor pointed to a muddy path.

"Take this path for about two hundred yards; that collection of timber buildings you can just make out is the farm."

I thanked him as I stepped awkwardly down from the bus in my stiff new uniform.

"'s pleasure, Miss," he replied, pushing the bell to signal the driver.

Left alone as the bus moved away I looked across the flat, uninteresting countryside that stretched for miles; its bareness was broken only by an odd tree standing in the surrounding fields. Nothing resembled the colourful, story-book image of a farm, bred into town people like me.

With a pang of uncertainty growing inside me, I started down the muddy path that lead to the farm and as I walked, in my heavy, unbending shoes, I became increasingly aware of the great change in my working life. No longer would I step from the train at eight a.m. and walk sedately across Edinburgh's West End in dainty, high-heeled shoes, stopping for a few moments to watch the morning mists rise from the castle.

The clumsiness of pulling each foot from the mud as I squelched my way down the path, and the stiffness of my new uniform, made me long for a freshly ironed silk blouse and a neat skirt.

What I was approaching looked like a set of factory units, and stopping to push my foot back into my shoe without the need to untie the lace, I was swamped by mud and disappointment. Then I came in sight of two men in an open shed deftly stretching the necks of hens across their knees and giving a sharp tug; they plucked and hung up the birds with effortless ease as I approached.

"Excuse me, I called, "can you direct me to the farmhouse, please?"

They looked up and smiled:

"You'll be the new land-girl, Jim's expecting you, Do you see the white-washed cottage at the top of the path?" I nodded. "That's the farmhouse."

His voice was soft and unhurried, and yet his hands flew across the bird stripping it of its plumage before it had ceased to twitch. I turned and hurried along the path not wanting to see his hand reach into the crate for his next victim.

The dust and feathers had wafted into my face and I took out my handkerchief to dust them away before I reached the cottage door. Just as I raised my hand to knock the sound of booted feet on the path made me turn and I looked round at a tall, lean man: he smiled and the laughter lines round his blue eyes deepened.

"I'm your foreman, Jim," he said, shaking my hand vigorously, "you'll be Jaqueline,"

"Yes, I'm pleased to meet you."

The smile lingered in his eyes making me feel inadequate and I was reminded of Joe, at the barn dance, saying 'and what makes you think you can do a man's work?'.

The feeling of inadequacy grew as he placed an arm round my shoulders and guided me as if I were a child.

"Come this way and meet Peggy, she's the daughter of the village blacksmith. You can learn a lot from her, but just go easy and watch what she does, you'll soon pick up the routine. Oh! and never try to pull a loaded cart by yourself. Just wait for someone to help you, Kerry is always somewhere around."

We had turned down a broad, concrete path with long, creasoted buildings on either side of it; the buildings were well spaced with short grass growing between them. At the bottom of the path I could see a stream with a boundary hedge behind it. The overall impression was one of tidy neatness. We had almost reached the second to last building on the right when its sliding door opened and a girl of about my own age stepped out on to the path; in front of her she carried a large, shallow basket brimful of eggs.

"Mornin', Peggy. This is the new land-girl, Jaqueline."

When she smiled the colour in her cheeks glowed as on the face of a child and she gripped my hand even harder than the foreman had done.

"Well, I'll leave you to get on with it, girls," Jim drawled softly, and turning he walked back up the broad, concrete path.

"I'm just on my way to the egg store, Jaqueline, so come with me and I'll show you round the farm. Is this your first post?"

"Yes," I replied, and the feeling of inadequacy began to slip away.

"Seems a pity to spoil these beautiful hands," Peggy said, smiling and pointing to the last building nearest the stream. "Oh! yes, that will be your battery," she added after a moment's reflection.

We turned up the path passing four more identical batteries where we came to a slightly smaller building and Peggy stopped.

"This is the incubator house where we have lunch." And pulling along the sliding door she called, "Jane, come and meet Jaqueline, our latest recruit,"

The fair-haired girl closed the door of the incubator before turning round, and then stepped forward and offered her hand.

"Welcome to slavery, Jaqueline, You'll be joining us here for lunch. This is the only civilised place on the farm."

The last of my wilting confidence vanished on seeing Jane's pale face blending into her beige shirt; she was just as town bred as I was, I decided when shaking hands, and looked equally incapable of manual work.

"See you lunch-time, Jane," Peggy said, and we stepped out on to the path closing the sliding door and turning to the creosoted building directly opposite.

Unlike the others this building was raised from the ground with four steps leading up to it.

"Maureen is in charge of the day-old-chicks and the young birds up to a month old," said Peggy. Still clutching her heavy basket she climbed the four wooden steps motioning me to follow.

On one side the interior was sectioned off into compartments with wire netting, and daylight poured in through the large windows. The side at which we had entered was a narrow corridor running the full length of the building.

"I'm with the day-old-chicks," a voice called, and a slim, dark-haired girl appeared from one of the compartments.

The air in the unit was warm and smelled of paraffin.

"Jaqueline's arrived," called Peggy, moving towards the girl.

"That's a relief," the girl replied, "Peggy's hard pushed since Ruth had to give up."

I was already beginning to feel that I belonged amongst these girls and their easy conversation.

"Pleased to meet you, Maureen," I said pleasantly. "But why did Ruth have to give up?"

"Overdid the hard work, so break yourself in easily; we're not all Amazons like Peggy."

A smile flitted across Maureen's composed face as she looked at the broad-shouldered, lean-hipped girl who was a few inches taller than we were.

"We're on our way to the egg store, I want to show Jaqueline how the daily quota for the egg pool is worked out. See you at lunch, Maureen," and a slightly embarrassed Peggy hurried out of the brooder house to avoid a conversation that might sound like a compliment to herself.

I was impatient to see the battery of hens I would be responsible for and as we made our way back from the egg store I quickened my steps.

"It's just a case of being sensible when it comes to heavy work; there's always someone within calling distance if you need help, so don't be a martyr like Ruth," Peggy said.

We had reached the battery that was to be my responsibility, and when Peggy pushed along the sliding door I had my first impression of a battery of hens. The din was deafening and as we walked down the centre aisle it increased, I shouted to Peggy above the noise of the complaining birds:

"Is it always like this?"

"No," she shouted back, "only before feeding time, you'll get used to it, Hang up your coat on that peg."

I took off my Land Army coat with its heavy blanket lining and immediately felt a stone lighter.

"Show me how to feed them," I yelled, "for the sake of some peace and quiet,"

We began by pushing a square, wooden box, which ran on castors, down to the end of the battery.

"Do you think you could lift one of these sacks?" Peggy grinned widely as she spoke. "It's the hens' staple diet, called balancer meal."

"I doubt it," I replied, "how much does it weigh?"

Peggy was thoroughly enjoying herself as she watched me touch it with a well-manicured hand.

"It weighs one and a quarter hundredweights." I could see her sizing me up as she spoke and as if she had reached a decision she began, "Right, grip a top corner with your right hand, like this. Now, Grab the bottom corner with your left. Tighten all your muscles before you take the strain, and up with it on to the bin," she commanded.

My side of the sack stayed exactly where it was with the first couple of tries; but after several attempts I managed to lift it off the floor at the same time as Peggy.

"I'm more like a hindrance than a help," I puffed, as the meal ran from the sack into the bin billowing up around us until we were covered in the sand-coloured powder that drifted everywhere.

"You'll think nothing of it by the end of the month." And lifting a tin of white grit Peggy hung it on the side of the box on wheels.

The hens were in individual cages of fifteen to a row and three cages high. With a back to back arrangement this gave a solid block of ninety cages.

"How many birds are in here?" I asked, lifting down a hopper and filling it with meal plus a handful of grit as Peggy was doing.

"Six hundred and thirty at present." And her blue eyes sparkled as she added, "But, when the eight blocks are full you will have a total of seven hundred and twenty hens."

It was only necessary to turn on the taps at the end of each block to fill the water troughs running along the front of the cages.

"What's that fishy smell?" I enquired.

"Cod liver oil. Smells a bit, but it keeps the birds healthy mixed in with their meal. It'll be lunch-time before you get round all the birds, so I'll see you in the incubator house, Jaqueline."

Peggy hurried off to finish her own work and I continued along the gangway that ran right round between the eight blocks and the battery walls. The noise had gradually become easier on the ears as I filled each hopper and by the time I was finished the uproar had dwindled to an odd little clucking noise as each hen settled down after feeding.

"Hello there, it's lunch-time," I hurried towards the door and a voice that was new to me. "I'm Kerry," she said, and the smile lingered in her large, brown eyes. Her handshake was light and brief. "Do you take tea or coffee?" she asked politely.

"Tea, please, and I'm Jaqueline."

I was aware of Kerry studying my face when she spoke again:

"Peggy gave a good description of you," she began, "a mop of gold hair, dark lashes and blueish-green eyes."

I smiled at the candid statement of this girl with sleek, raven hair, she wore it in a chignon at the nape of her neck.

"I'm just going up to the farmhouse kitchen to make the tea and coffee, don't be too long or it will be cold, Jaqueline."

A few minutes after Kerry had gone I closed the battery door on my contented hens and headed for the incubator house. A tall, thin, elegant girl greeted me when I stepped through its open doorway.

"I'm Alison, I work with the field hens. I'm pleased to meet you, Jaqueline."

Alison looked aloof, but pleasant, as she helped pass the tea and coffee from the tray Kerry had brought; then we sat down on empty crates in the cosy atmosphere of the incubator house to eat our packed lunches.

"Your friend from the government will be here tomorrow, Jane," said Alison airily, "and since you're the only one who has spoken to him, tell us what colour his eyes are."

A titter of amusement ran round the girls.

"I can't say I've ever noticed," Jane answered ruefully.

"What about his face? Describe him to us," encouraged Alison.

Jane looked at her demurely:

"Well," she said, "he's rather stodgy faced, a bit blue round the chin, slightly thin on top and greyish at the temples; I suppose you might say, a carbon copy of one of His Majesty's civil servants. He doesn't say anything. Just grunts when he arrives and when he's finished, puts on his coat, turns up his collar, pulls down his hat and grunts as he leaves."

We were hardly able to eat our sandwiches for giggling at Jane's description.

"What about you, Maureen? Can *you* describe him?" said Kerry, "after all, when he's finished sexing the day-old-chicks you collect them."

Maureen launched into her description of the man who came to the farm once a month to sex the newly hatched chickens:

"All I ever see of him is a dark overcoat, a black hat, the black briefcase that he picks up as he hurries past me, and on a wet day – a black umbrella!" Maureen raised her hands in defeat. "No chance of romance with the elite when you've opted for work on the land."

Peggy, who had been listening quietly, chimed in:

"There's more to him than that!" she said, running her hand over her short, coppery curls. "He wears a watch, because he looks at it as he picks his way carefully across the yard holding up his collar to pass the midden, then he vanishes into the incubator house without saying a word to anyone."

The colour of the man's eyes was still a mystery and after the hilarity had died down, Kerry spoke.

"He's terrified of us, and who wouldn't be! Can you imagine what we look like to a civil servant, wading through the slop in the midden and standing in line to brush off the fleas after emptying a load?"

She lifted the tray, shaking her head and smiling as we passed the cups.

"He certainly doesn't approve of farm workers. Coming to work on the land gives you a whole new outlook on how people judge people," said Jane.

We walked down the path towards the batteries, having collected the baskets from the egg store, and my mind was still turning over the lunch-time conversation. What had the midden to do with a poultry maid, I thought when Peggy's voice broke into my thoughts:

"Remember to put a tick at a.m. or p.m. on the correct day, Jaqueline. The card below each cage is for recording the amount of eggs a hen lays during one month. Any hen that stops laying goes to the plucking shed."

I pushed open my battery door and a chorus of clucks rose from the hens.

"Will you do me a favour, Jaqueline?" Peggy asked.

"Yes," I replied instantly.

"Will you put a tick on Henrietta's card every other day; I don't want her to go to the plucker's shed." Then opening the door of a cage on the bottom row, she continued, "Here she is, I don't know the breed, but she's beautiful; there's only one of her on the whole farm."

While Peggy was singing her praises, Henrietta stepped out on to her egg tray and fluttered daintily to the floor. She preened herself and turning her head to the side looked at me haughtily with a bright, dark eye.

"She hasn't laid an egg for months and if you don't put a tick Jim will take her to the plucking shed." She looked quite downcast as her eyes followed the hen across the floor.

"But, Peggy, she's only a hen!" And I couldn't keep the smile off my face when she answered.

"Yes, I know, but I can't bear the thought of it; you see, she was always in my battery until they brought in the young pullets."

Henrietta's feathers had a silky sheen and they lay smoothly in varying shades of grey. Her comb and wattles were dainty and of a rich cyclamen colour, and as she walked, her legs seemed longer than the average hens and were a shiny black right down to her grey claws.

We began by collecting the eggs and Henrietta tailed along behind making soft, little burring noises in her throat. Before we left for the egg store, with our laden baskets, Henrietta was told to go back to her cage and to my amazement, she did, fluffing up her pale grey, black-edged bustle as she balanced on the egg tray before entering her cage.

I was gazing with pride on the two hundred and three eggs that filled my basket, when an idea occurred to me.

"How much does a hen cost if it has stopped laying?" I asked.

"About ten shillings from the plucker's shed," Peggy replied, glancing at me.

"Then stop marking Henrietta's chart and buy her – you could keep her in your garden."

"Now, why didn't I think of that!" she exclaimed, giving me a friendly pat on the back that almost knocked me off my feet.

Steadying my basket to control the wobble threatening my lovely eggs, I suddenly found myself being hauled off the path on to the grass.

"Look out for the eggs, Jaqueline!"

From the side of my eye I caught sight of a black and white calf charging down the path with its head lowered, and Peggy went on,

"It's Buttercup, she's a menace when you're carrying a basket of eggs."

Buttercup charged past and then she slithered to a stop.

"She's absolutely spoiled by all of us and that includes Jim," said Peggy, pushing the playful calf away from her basket. "Oh! while I remember, Jaqueline, wear your drill cloth coat and dungarees tomorrow; and also your boots and leggings, you'll need them for the midden."

We were just entering the egg store and I felt my chin stiffen with indignation; what had a midden to do with a land-girl? But then, I had a lot to learn about life on the farm and the next five months were to indoctrinate me into work with poultry that had never been mentioned in story-books: my only guide to work on the farm.

Chapter Four

The following morning, dressed in full working outfit of a fawn drill cloth coat, dungarees, black leather boots and webbing leggings, I started work in earnest at eight o'clock.

"Slide the boxes in at the end of the belts like this," Jim was saying, "make sure they're not sticking, or they won't come out when they're full. Now! Push the handle into the socket here, then wind nice and easy; there's plenty of leverage with a big handle like this."

I stood watching as the belt moved along with each turn of the handle.

"Right," he said, "we're barely a third of the way along and the box is full, so we empty it into the cart and replace it to take the rest of the muck."

I watched with disgust as the foul smelling, sticky mess dropped from the belt into the box. Jim lifted it with ease, carried it to the door and tipped it into the cart that stood outside on the path.

"That's all there is to it," he said casually, "do you think you'll be able to manage?"

"Oh! yes, I'll manage," I said, pulling on my working gloves, and I turned my face to the side as I took the box from him. The smell rising from it was revolting and I could see an amused look in his eyes, which had the effect of instantly crushing what confidence I had.

When he had gone I slid the box in at the and of the belt, put my hands on the handle and pulled, but nothing happened, the handle stayed exactly where it was as Jim had left it just over the top on the downward pull. All the tugging, jumping and swinging on the stubborn handle made not the slightest bit of difference, and I was furious, because I couldn't get started to the morning's work. After a few abortive attempts I was forced to go next door for help.

"No wonder you couldn't move it; the belts on this block haven't been cleared for three days and Jim knows that. The muck's dried out like cement just where you're stuck." Peggy lifted the hose as she spoke, "Turn on the water just a little and then turn it off as soon as I say stop." Directing the flow of water along the belt she suddenly held up her hand. "Now, try giving the handle a turn!"

The mess that had jammed beneath the cages slowly moved along and I heaved a sigh of relief.

"Thanks, Peggy, I thought I would never get started!"

"Bigoted sense of humour, Jim's got. You would think he would try to make it as easy as possible for new girls." And she walked out of the battery with a bewildered look on her face.

I staggered to and from the cart taking smaller and smaller loads and by the time the cart was full I was leaning on the end of it exhausted.

"Tea break," called Peggy, striding towards me carrying a flask. "It's such a lovely day – let's sit on the grass. On second thoughts, by the look of you, you had better lie down for five minutes before we have tea." Then she laughed and shook her head. "You're all the same when you first start and some never make it, like Ruth; after a month she had to give up."

I left the support of the cart on trembling legs and flopped down on the grass.

"I can't see how I'll ever be any different," I said, but the heavy, leaden feeling gradually lifted from my limbs as I lay face down on the sweet smelling grass.

"Right, Jaqueline, you'll just have time to drink your tea before we head for the midden," and Peggy handed me the cup of steaming tea as she continued. "Ten minutes break makes all the difference between collapsing on the job or being able to finish a morning's work. Are you ready?"

"Yes, sir!" I touched my forehead in mock salute and started to get up, when Peggy's hand shot out giving me a playful push that knocked me flat on my back.

"When I'm able to stand up to your playful pats, Peggy," I said, brushing the odd bit of grass from my clothes, "I will have passed fitness test grade one."

She had taken up her stance between the handles of the cart, and lectured on,

"Now, push from the back, Jaqueline."

Once the cart had started to move the momentum carried it along the path easily.

"Don't stop now, Jaqueline, push it right into the middle of the midden."

I had hesitated at the open end of the midden wall and was loathe to go a step further.

"Push!" yelled Peggy, so I pushed holding my breath.

In front of us and on either side the foul smelling mass was piled up to four feet in height, and I stared in disbelief at the army of fleas advancing up my leggings. Horrified, I dashed out of the midden.

"You'll get accustomed to it," called Peggy, "they seldom jump higher than the knees!" And she shovelled dutifully in the middle of the fly-infested, stinking mass around her.

"I won't, you know!" I answered in a voice that shook.

"You will, just takes a little time," said Jim from behind me and he strode over with a shovel to join Peggy in the centre of the midden.

A few minutes later, having calmed down to a more rational way of thinking because the fleas had stayed below my knees, I picked my way cautiously over to where they shovelled.

"That's a good girl!" said Jim, handing me the shovel, "and it smells like ashes of roses after a while." The irritating smile was there in his eyes and his voice was as soft as a whisper.

I shovelled like mad, then rushed from the midden to fill my lungs with fresh air.

"Come on, Jaqueline, you'll never get it done at this rate," called Jim from the byre, "just ignore the smell."

I walked back into the midden desperately trying to use Jim's advice, and shovelled submissively; until a wave of brown, strawy sludge started sliding towards my boots.

"Right," said Peggy, "they're hosing out the byres, let's get out of here!"

There was no way out but to wade through the oncoming sludge. Appalled at the thought of falling, I pulled each boot from the slurping mess that washed up to my ankles, slipping and slithering in my haste to escape the unbearable stench.

"There's a hand brush on the wall to brush off the fleas," said Peggy casually, "then wipe your boots in the long grass."

Having hauled the empty cart from the midden without my help, Peggy was already wiping her boots in the long, lush grass that flourished outside the midden walls, so I joined her as if it was all in a day's work.

The webbing leggings with four buckles belted tightly over the top of our boots, reaching to just below the knee, they kept the bottom of our dungarees clean protecting us from the invasion of fleas. I brushed obediently, watching the moving black mass fall from my leggings and vanish into the grass.

Chapter Five

By the end of the first week I was caught up in the hustle and bustle of mass-produced eggs and found myself hurrying about the farm as everyone else did. The eggs were graded in the egg store to be collected by the large van from the government egg pool.

The farmer, a slim, mild man of average height, moved quietly about his well-managed farm in a fawn drill cloth coat. He was kind, and seemed well pleased with the activity surrounding him.

Monday morning was to find me in a state of exasperation as I struggled to move a belt without resorting to the use of the hose; I had learned that water made the muck messier and heavier.

"Hang on, Jaqueline." I looked up to see Kerry's happy face peeping round the edge of the door as she called breezily, "You need a second handle with someone on the other side of the block, that'll soon shift it."

Our art student, Kerry, tended to drift around the farm offering help and advice to all. She had plucked out her natural eyebrows and hard black lines had been pencilled on; the end result gave the appearance of a very surprised, and pretty, brown-eyed doll.

Within seconds she had borrowed a handle from Peggy, and stationed herself on the opposite side of the block.

"See how easy it becomes with someone helping," she crooned in her soft voice as we wound in the stubborn belt.

All at once the peaceful sound of dozing hens and the creaking belt was shattered. Clatter! Bang! It was like a bull in a china shop; Buttercup was making her way up the centre aisle towards Kerry; feeding boxes crashed to the floor and the dozing hens flew into a state of panic.

Alarmed by the chorus of squawking hens, the lumbering young calf tried to turn and flee. Eggs were dropping to the concrete floor and meal poured from the feeding boxes, spilling over the broken eggs.

"I'll hold her head, if you run round and grab her from the rear, Jaqueline!" I dashed round the block and grabbed the only part I could: the tail.

"We can't turn her round, it's too narrow, Kerry – let's try backing her up gently!"

Buttercup's legs shot out and just missed me as she bucked.

"Take her right up to the end of the battery – it's the only place we can turn her round," I shouted above the din.

Dust and feathers floated everywhere as the panic-stricken hens squawked and flapped in their tiny cages.

"Wait, Kerry," I almost screamed, "hold her till I collect the eggs!" and I hurried ahead collecting the eggs to avoid any further drop in production.

The frisky calf was alarmed by the close proximity of so many hens, and it was all Kerry could do to keep her calm enough to reach the top end of the battery without wrecking the place. Once at the top she had to be turned round and led back to the sliding door through which she had entered; the narrow back door was not wide enough for the fat little calf.

I went outside to remove all the shutters on both sides of the battery and let the wind blow out the dust and feathers while cooling down my poor agitated hens.

Kerry, having led the instigator of all the trouble through the sliding door, stood smiling and hugging her all the time cooing, "Poor little Buttercup". My poor hens were panting like marathon runners in their tiny cages and the only consolation I could give them was the cool air blowing through the battery.

While I set about cleaning up the mess, Kerry wandered off oblivious of the chaos she and Buttercup had left behind. I hosed and brushed the centre aisle humming a tune as I worked, unaware that Earlson Farm was only a training ground for what the future held in store. Surrounded by town-bred girls of my own age, in a small, well-run farm, was something I would remember in the months to come.

Chapter Six

I was quite surprised and pleased when Maureen, who kept herself to herself more than the others, walked into my battery one morning.

"Would you like to join us in the haymaking tomorrow, Jaqueline?" she asked.

"Haymaking? Where?"

"In the large field at the back of the farmhouse, everyone's going to join in, to lift the hay while it's dry."

"Count me in then, Maureen, it'll make a pleasant change from the daily routine."

"Don't start clearing your belts in the morning, let them lie for a day or two. Hope the weather stays good," Maureen went on, "I'm looking forward to it!"

Her dark, curly hair bounced on her shoulders as she moved towards the door, and I turned back to collecting the eggs. The thought of Maureen's perfectly applied make-up made me smile, she never seemed to get grubby like I did.

"See you lunch-time to work out the details," she called, and I turned my head to reply.

"Ouch!" I dropped the egg I had just lifted from a tray, as dark blood oozed from the back of my hand.

Maureen, who had reached the door, turned round.

"What is it?" she asked.

"I've been pecked," and I held up my hand as blood dripped to the floor.

"Looks nasty, you had better go up to the plucking shed, they keep the first aid box there."

As we walked up the path together, Maureen chatted away,

"You can hardly blame the poor birds becoming nasty, seeing their eggs taken away from them every day; they must get the urge to hatch a brood at some time or another."

"Yes, although I hadn't given it much thought, it's not natural to keep them in a small cage all their lives," I agreed, as Maureen climbed the steps to her brooder house.

I pulled my handkerchief tighter round my hand and hurried on to the plucking shed.

"Ripped quite a hole in you, didn't it?" the plucker said, removing the handkerchief. "Take a seat on the stool and I'll fetch the first aid box."

When he returned with the box he was grinning from ear to ear, and opening a bottle of iodine, he said,

"This'll hurt a bit." He poured the iodine straight onto the wound and I winced. "Trying to make a meal of you," he said, as the iodine ran off the side of my hand.

The other man kept on with his work, wringing the hens' necks and plucking them with remarkable speed.

"Got to keep the wounds covered up when you're working with poultry or animals," he remarked, "old Eb died, went all stiff."

The down from the plucking floated onto my hand while he spoke, and I blew it off. He pulled another bird from the crate and placed its neck across his knee, and then paused,

"Keep the dirt out and keep the plaster dry."

I gave another puff at my hand before his grinning friend applied the plaster, then I watched him grip the bird as it waited for death on his knee. I had become so accustomed to the sharp tug and the twitching of the lifeless body, but this time the bird fell from his knee and the head came away in his hand. The headless body ran around the shed, then dropped and lay twitching at my feet. I stared, absolutely shaken. Feeling nauseated, I rose from the stool and hurried back to my battery without saying a word of thanks.

Chapter Seven

We had all gathered in a group at the top of the broad path on the following morning, to collect our hay forks.

"You all got one, girls?" drawled Jim, his smiling eyes roaming over us, "then follow me!"

Behind the farmhouse was a neatly laid out vegetable garden, where the farmer's wife was busily hanging out a row of snowy white, babies' nappies.

"Stop for some pancakes at the tea break, girls," she called, as we passed through a gate into the large field.

Her eyes shone with pleasure when she spoke; or, was it the same smile of amusement that I detected in Jim's eyes. It suddenly came home to me that none of the farm workers took the land-girls seriously, and when I looked round the group I realised why.

Mothers, who were accustomed to seeing their daughters turned out to perfection for work in the city, were still as meticulous over fawn dungarees, jackets and beige shirts. Everyone of us showed not a crumple or a crease, with collars flat and not a hair out of place, and every pair of boots gleamed black and shiny.

The tall, slender Fiona was already in the field waiting with her pony and cart, the ends of her green chiffon scarf trailing elegantly over one shoulder.

"This is how it's done, girls!" Jim's face was wreathed in smiles as we draped ourselves along the side of the cart to watch.

His lean muscular body swung into action, but as the first and second bundles of hay came flying towards us we dashed out of the way to let them fall neatly onto the cart. Busily flicking the odd piece of hay from my fresh clothing, I heard Jim call me,

"Come on, Jaqueline, up on the cart and place the bundles neatly in rows as I toss them."

I climbed on to the cart and stood ready.

"Catch it!" Jim shouted.

I stuck out the hay fork and missed, but the bundle caught me squarely in the chest, I wobbled on the cart as the pony moved and fell over the side clutching the bundle of hay.

Jim was laughing heartily and the girls tittered as I scrambled back onto the cart. When the next bundle flew towards me I was ready; I caught it on the fork and ducked letting the second one sail over my head. I managed to keep it up for a few minutes, catching what I could and dodging the rest.

Jim stopped abruptly, the smile never leaving his face, then he said,

"I think you've got the idea, girls, so pile the cart as high as you can and take it to the haystack that's been started over there in the corner of the field."

Left to get on with it we moved slowly over the field lifting the dried out bundles and piling them as high as possible on the wobbly cart; then Peggy stuck her fork into the load to steady her side, and called to me:

"Lie flat on the top to steady it, Jaqueline, before we start making our way to the corner of the field!"

I flattened myself out on top of the hay and closed my eyes, barely aware of it clinging all over my clean clothes. The sun shone down from a clear, blue sky and the cart swayed slowly along; I filled my lungs again and again with the freshness that engulfed me. This is the life I was thinking, when Peggy's voice rudely interrupted.

"Right, Jaqueline, we're here, start unloading at this side."

I struggled to my feet on the yielding mound of hay and tossed down the bundles enjoying every minute of haymaking.

The haystack was growing nicely after our second load had been added to it, but then Maureen, who had been on top of the load, started to sneeze. At first we hardly noticed it, but as the sneezes persisted we all made various suggestions.

"Try holding your breath, Maureen." She held her breath then sneezed. "Now, take a deep breath." Maureen took a deep breath and sneezed several times.

I could see Jim striding towards us from the corner of my eye.

"Hey there, girls, this is not a discussion group! What's up?"

"It's Maureen, she can't stop sneezing," we called out.

He came across shaking out a large, clean handkerchief.

"Cover your mouth and nose with this; you must be allergic to the smell of freshly cut hay."

Maureen covered the lower part of her face, and looked at him through watery eyes, gasping,

"Oh! doe! Ab I? Ad I did so wat to joid id!"

"Off you go to the farmhouse and ask for a real hot cup of tea. That should help; and keep away from the field," he added firmly, putting his arm across her shoulders as she started another fit of sneezing.

Buttercup, the calf, had quietly followed Jim into the field and stood nibbling the stubble as we piled the hay on to our third load; each time we were managing to pile it a bit higher.

"That's high enough," called Peggy, flattening herself out on top.

I could see Buttercup moving towards us, and digging our forks into the sides of the high, wobbly load we started towards the corner of the field. But the calf pawed the ground daintily, lowered her head and charged straight at the pony.

"Get her out of here!" screamed Fiona, hanging on to the nervous pony, but the stricken animal reared and fled across the field.

I put my hands over my eyes as the load toppled with Peggy somewhere inside. Having terrified the pony and sent the tall, slender Fiona charging after it, Buttercup turned her attention to the haystack we had been building.

"Get her out of the field," yelled Fiona, "before she does any more damage."

But it was already too late; Buttercup charged at the haystack, backed up shaking her head, and charged again. Peggy crawled from the hay on hands and knees just as Jane and I leapt into action.

I could hear Jim's loud laughter as we advanced with our hay forks at the ready, handles pointing forward, but Buttercup lowered her head and charged.

"This way, girls!" Jim shouted, and we turned and ran for the open gate. "Don't be too hard on her, she's just playful."

We glared at him and raced for the gate with Buttercup charging behind.

The farmer's wife stood beside Jim, her face glowing, and as Jane and I hurriedly closed the gate on the calf, she said,

"I hadn't realised just how big she has grown, she could give you quite a bump."

"Let her enjoy herself while she can," said Jim, and I felt my mouth drop open, "she'll be going to visit the bull soon enough." And then he turned away with a grin on his face that stretched from ear to ear, while we turned to look at the devastation in our field.

"She tends to be a bit jealous of anything you're doing," he said, leading Buttercup from the field, "but don't take it too badly, girls, building a haystack takes quite a bit of practice, at least a day or two!"

Standing outside the closed gate with her nose pushing its way through the bars Buttercup mooed sorrowfully, as only Buttercup could.

Kerry had just appeared at the back door of the farmhouse with a tray of steaming cups, and her gaze immediately fell upon the calf mooing plaintively outside the gate.

"Poor little Buttercup!" she exclaimed as she approached, then she placed the tray on the ground and wrapped her arms round the neck of the naughty calf.

I watched Kerry croon and hug for just a moment, then I stuck my fork into one of the bundles that lay by the battered haystack and felt a strong inclination to gnash my teeth.

Chapter Eight

I had worked at Earlson Farm for some time before I realised that Kerry was not just a teenager like the rest of us, but a woman in her mid-twenties.

She lived in a little cottage just a stone's throw from the farm; in fact, the only access to her cottage was through the farm and across three stout planks that bridged the boundary stream. Kerry's tiny white home stood on a slight rise and was almost hidden from sight by rambling roses, giant sunflowers, and hollyhocks in every hue as they burst into flower.

We pulled on our coats that evening and headed up the path, then stopped to watch Kerry painting one of the farm cats. She had set up her easel on the main path, and the likeness of the large, untamed cat sitting just in front of the boundary stream was slowly taking shape on her canvas.

Big Tam, as the girls called him, was a shaggy blue Persian with a heavy ruff framing his snub-nosed face. He never came near enough to be fondled, as the other cats did, but stayed his distance and studied us with round, amber eyes.

Kerry's raven hair was tightly drawn back into a chignon and tied with a large floppy bow of pastel pink silk. She wore an artist's smock in a drab green colour, and although it seemed casual, the colours had been well chosen to set off her sleek, dark hair.

While her brush moved across the canvas, she spoke softly to the untamed aristocrat who was the subject of her painting.

Reluctantly, we turned up the path waving to Peggy as she climbed the stile and headed across the fields towards the village, leaving Kerry completely absorbed in her painting.

"Has anyone ever stroked Big Tam?" I asked, as we walked.

"Not that I know of," replied Jane, keeping her eyes on the deeply rutted path, "he keeps his distance."

"The nearest you'll ever get to him," chimed in Maureen, "is in the meal shed, when he sits waiting to catch the mice as we lift the sacks."

After a few moments of concentration, while she picked her way along the path, she went on dramatically, "His large, fluffy paw comes down on the little mouse pinning it to the floor and covering it completely; except for the tail sticking out you wouldn't know there was a little creature there."

Jane gave a shudder as she took up the tale,

"I wouldn't like to be the mouse! Tam grips it between his teeth keeping his body low, so that his long, fluffy coat trails on the ground; then he backs away growling in the back of his throat, his amber eyes blazing with rage."

"I wouldn't want his dinner," said Fiona calmly, "but I wouldn't like to try and take it away from him."

I could see the bus approaching as the girls discussed Tam.

"Come on, girls! Hurry, or we'll miss the bus!" And I ran up the path waving for it to stop.

We were a grubby but dignified bunch as we stepped onto the single deck bus, and I had noticed that it was becoming increasingly difficult to get the bus to stop for us.

"Thank goodness it stopped! I hate having to walk to the terminus, it must be all of three miles from here," said Fiona, lowering herself sedately into a seat.

"Would you mind moving to the back of the bus, please?"

We all looked up at the conductor.

"Please, girls! There's plenty of room at the back," he almost begged.

We rose and moved to the back, with Fiona whispering as she sat down again,

"Do you have the feeling of not being welcome?"

I felt the laughter bubbling up inside me and whispered back,

"You mean that feeling of being a parasite?"

"Precisely!" Fiona replied, her eyes dancing with fun.

Although we had changed from drill cloth coats to dress coats and from boots to shoes, the distinct odour of hens permeated the local bus. This might have been excusable, but the odd hen flea was not.

"Yes, I think we all feel it," said Maureen, as we settled into our seats.

Having been too young for the forces, we had volunteered for the important task – as it had been put to us at Land Army Headquarters – of helping to feed our war-weary nation. Unfortunately, the nation seemed to have no time for weary, hen-flea-ridden land-girls, and the back of the bus was not far enough away to please them.

My ears burned as I listened to the rude remarks of the passengers, and I felt compelled to say in a clear voice,

"If these passengers are a sample of the British public, then I wish we had left them to starve!"

Having said my piece I straightened my shoulders with rebellion, until I realised I had spoken out against people older than myself and I blushed. But why should they make us feel awful with their rude remarks, because of the work we had volunteered to do?

Maureen's raised voice snapped me out of my misgivings:

"If it wasn't for noble creatures like us," she said, for all the bus to hear, "these hypocrites wouldn't have an egg ration! If they expect to eat eggs, they should be made to muck out their own hens!"

Her well-modulated voice could be heard clearly by all the passengers, and we had to suppress our glee when an awkward silence descended upon them all.

From the impeccable elegance of clothing that our previous occupations had demanded, and the respect we had known, we were now being ridiculed and shunned.

A profound silence still reigned throughout the bus, so I glanced along the profiles of my fellow workers: the face of our Biology student, Jane, was calm and unconcerned; Maureen's dark curls touched on her shoulders and her expression was just as it would have been behind the reception desk. I leaned forward a little to look at Fiona seated against the window and felt the urge to smile; the expression on her face was one of refined boredom. Her slightly tip-tilted nose completed the picture of a model posing for the camera; she was a natural for her chosen profession.

The bus had already covered the three miles to the terminus, and the passengers were filing out, when Jane said:

"It's just not good enough, we must do something about this tomorrow."

The next morning everyone's mind was on the transport problem, but we were too busy to say more than a couple of words on the subject. It wasn't until midday, when we gathered in the incubator house for lunch, that the humiliating experience of the previous day could be discussed. No one had yet opened the subject as the tea and coffee was passed round, but I knew we were all quietly determined to do something about our lot.

Suddenly the door opened, and before Jim could step inside we all started to speak.

"Hold it, girls!" he said, backing away with his hands up. "Let's hear you one at a time."

Maureen's precise consonants were even more distinct as the words poured from her lips.

"The bus is refusing to stop and pick us up in the evening because of hen fleas. We had to walk to the terminus twice this week and the situation isn't going to improve."

Having launched her attack, Maureen waited for his reply which came in the usual casual drawl,

"Hen fleas don't live for more than an hour on humans."

"That's long enough for the bus passengers!" said Fiona primly.

"But it's only a short walk to the terminus," Jim replied, "not much more than a mile."

We all gasped and stared at him.

"We're talking about the measured mile, not a country mile," I said, determined to make the point, "I don't get home till nine o'clock at night if I miss my connection! And it's all of three miles to the terminus."

"Okay, girls," he drawled, leaning easily on the door post, "I'll see what I can do."

Touched by our plight the farmer's wife started driving us to the bus terminus in her tiny van; we were packed in like sardines but enjoyed every minute of the three mile trip, having developed an irrepressible sense of humour towards our lot in the Land Army.

As we separated to board the various buses that would take us to the part of the city where we lived, the smell of hens became less obvious, and the pall of cigarette smoke that hung in the upper deck of any city bus blanketed the odour and anaesthetised the fleas.

Chapter Nine

None of us could have anticipated the sudden change that was about to take place at Earlson Farm on that raw, eventful day. Maureen had called me as I passed her brooder house.

"Jaqueline, can you spare a minute?"

"Surely," I replied, putting down my basket and walking up the steps to her spotless rearing unit.

I followed her past the wired compartments that housed the day-old-chicks, wishing that I was in charge of the fluffy, yellow, cheeping bundles.

"Would you say the three-week-old birds look poorly?" she asked.

"Yes – it could be the change in the weather, they might have a chill."

"I'd better find Jim," Maureen replied, a worried frown creasing her smooth forehead, "although it may be nothing at all."

She hurried off in search of the foreman and I made my way back to my battery; but just as I reached the door, I heard a low, growling noise and a large, black and white cat rushed past me on the path.

Before I could open the door, Big Tam came bounding along in that peculiar, slightly sideways, powerful lope. His stride seemed almost leisurely as he gained on the fleeing cat, and then pounced.

The quiet air was suddenly rent with screeches while they rolled and clawed; Tam sat up on his haunches and with a mighty paw walloped the intruder, sending him fleeing towards the barn, his ears flattened on to his head. Tam stayed where he was on the other side of the path and licked his paw.

Down by the boundary stream, I could see a very ordinary, thin, motley cat cleaning herself and then she turned up the path. It was only when she turned that I saw a collection of kittens move out from the overgrown grass and dart after her.

Fascinated by their playfulness, I watched and was ready to throw my heavy basket at Tam if he should attack them. The first kitten to follow the mother was a little ginger cat, and the thought crossed my mind that ginger cats were always male.

The two that came next trotted playfully together, one was as black and shiny as jet, while the other, a slightly smaller kitten, had the distinct markings of the Tabby.

The last one to fall in line, and I thought it completed the family, was white with no markings of any kind.

Then the overgrown grass moved and I saw it; a pair of golden eyes glowed in the round, fluffy face and before it stepped from the grass it hissed and spat. I stayed perfectly still as it came slinking from cover with its blue-black fluff trailing on the path.

The procession moved past me towards Tam, but I was still ready to do battle if it should become necessary, so I waited.

Unperturbed by the large cat sitting at the side of the path the motley cat walked on with her kittens; but as the wild bundle of fluff drew level with the only cat that could have sired it, it stiffened its fluffy tail until it stood straight up on end, quivered for a second, arched its back and pranced sideways, challenging Big Tam.

I laughed with delight, for as soon as the fluffy bundle stiffened and spat at Tam, it fled to the front of the parade and shot under the mother cat.

Big Tam sat silently watching the antics of his exact miniature as it walked along hugging its mother's side. When they had all passed Tam moved down the path, gathered speed, and leapt the boundary stream vanishing into the scrub beyond.

The next day was to bring the news, confirmed by the vet, that coccidiosis was rampant among the poultry. The disease swept right through the farm and by the end of the week Maureen's young birds were dropping dead where they stood. We could do nothing but watch and clean up the mess as each battery was cleared and fumigated.

Preparations were already going ahead to switch from poultry to pigs; it would be a year, the farmer said, before poultry could again be introduced into Earlson Farm.

Long before any sign of the disease had become apparent, I had stopped putting a tick on Henrietta's chart, and as a result I had had to watch carefully each time Jim came to collect the doomed non-layers.

"Good afternoon, Jaqueline."

"Good afternoon, Jim," I replied with a smile, brushing the water through the battery doorway as I hosed the floor.

Jim carried in a crate and placed it on the clean floor, and started going systematically along the hens' charts.

"I see this one doesn't get a tick since you took over the battery, Jaqueline," and thrusting his hand into Henrietta's cage, he continued, "had my doubts about it for months, vents too narrow to be a layer."

I was shocked by the suddenness of seeing Henrietta dropped into the crate. Frantically I swept the last of the water out of the doorway.

"I'll just give the brush to Peggy, Jim, she's waiting for it." And I dashed along to the next battery.

The door was wide open, but there was no sign of Peggy, but as I turned to leave I saw her coming down the path.

"Peggy, Peggy, Jim's taken Henrietta!"

Her rosy cheeks blanched and she hurried into her battery without saying a word.

Quickly I returned to my battery to answer the usual string of questions I would be asked while Jim thrust his hand into the cages and the doomed birds squawked.

Only a couple of weeks later, when all the girls were invited to Peggy's house on her birthday, did I see Henrietta scratching in a flower-filled garden.

"She's started to lay eggs again!" said Peggy, hurrying to the kitchen to show off Henrietta's three, very white eggs. "I always knew hens shouldn't be kept in batteries. And Henrietta's proof of it."

No longer in need of poultry maids, the farmer called us together to ask if we would like to stay on and rear pigs. Jim, who had been hovering in the background with the usual smile in his eyes, invited us to see the converted battery which was now a very modern piggery.

However, when he pushed along the sliding doors, the first whiff of pig almost bowled us over; making us realise that he was asking too much, and that the fields were to be preferred.

"You'll soon get accustomed to it, girls!" he drawled, radiating charm with his dimpled smile as he lounged by the door post.

No one answered; we were all thinking of the midden on a hot day, and of being banished even from the city buses.

"Did I hear you mention ashes of roses, Jim? Or would it be orchids this time?" I said, smiling to break the wrathful silence that hung over the girls.

All his smiling encouragement fell on deaf ears; we stood looking sympathetically but resolutely back at him.

"If they want to eat bacon, Jim, they will have to raise the pigs themselves." As she spoke, Fiona's smile was as charming as Jim's, while I imagined the bus passengers' reaction to the foul smell of pigs.

The innocent, earnest, city girls who had volunteered for life on the farm had been bruised by the callous remarks of their fellow humans and nothing could now induce them to accept work that would banish them to the order of the untouchables.

We waited politely to hear Jim's final plea, then each shook him by the hand, smiling with an amused smile.

Strangely enough, Kerry wandered into the piggery, fell in love with the greedy, fat little piglets, and crooned over the revolting, pink and black sow who lay on her side happily grunting over Kerry's cooing conversation.

She took on the job of looking after the piglets who trotted behind her down the long aisle in the middle of the piggery. They would nibble at her wellington boots, and squeal out complaints when she closed them in the pen.

On that day we left Earlson Farm for the last time to go our separate ways. Ten forlorn little faces peered over the low wall in the piggery, their short legs propping them up as they waited to chase after the beloved Kerry, who saw beauty in all God's creatures.

We stepped out of the tiny farm van and stretched, waving happily to the farmer's wife as she drove off towards the farm. Then we shook hands and each one boarded her bus; words were few, but their warm smiles were indelibly etched in my memory.

I stood alone in the descending evening mist; they seemed to have scattered like leaves in the wind, but I felt no sadness. I would soon be eighteen and life was full of adventure; the bus drew alongside, and as I climbed to the upper deck the future glowed bright and full of promise.

What would my next post be like? And where would they send me? Earlson was already receding into the past, and I sat looking through the blue haze of cigarette smoke conjuring up pictures of life on the farm. But all of them were like the colourful story-book version with none of the hard labour involved, and I knew I was deluding no one but myself.

The bus sped on its way, and I closed my eyes to find a soft lavender glow spreading through my mind, soothing and settling. I would accept whatever tomorrow was to bring. Life had become a series of adventures.

Part Two

Burnsyde Farm, Summer 1943

Chapter Ten

The supervisor sat behind her desk at Land Army Headquarters, and I waited to hear what she had to say. "There's something here that might interest you, my dear." She looked at me, "Jaqueline, isn't it?"

"Yes," I replied.

She paused, glancing at some notes on a pad, then looking up across the half spectacles perched on her nose, she continued, "I see you have almost six months experience in poultry to your credit. Would you like to live on a farm in the West Country?"

"Yes, I think so," I said hesitantly, and she lowered her eyes, then went on checking her notes.

"It says here: they have hot water on tap in the bathroom, but no electricity. It's entirely up to you, there are plenty of other posts available." Her face puckered into a smile as she finished.

I had never lived away from home before and hesitated to make the decision.

"The name of the farm is Burnsyde, Jaqueline, and, of course, you would be treated like one of the family. Have you been to the West Country before?" She studied me across her spectacles waiting for my answer.

"I've never been further than Stirling Castle, and that area is beautiful."

"Yes, it is," she replied, "and you would find the West Country warmer than the east coast."

She had not offered me anything else, so I decided to take the plunge. "Yes, I think I would like to work at Burnsyde," I said recklessly.

"Then it's settled! Here are the details of buses available; I see there is one direct, but it stops at every village on the way. Hmm!" she studied the paper. "The entrance to the farm is not visible from the road, so have a chat with the conductor when you board the bus."

She ran quickly through the rest of the details before saying,

"They will be expecting you on Sunday evening to start work on Monday morning, the farmer will deduct board and keep from your wages and give you the remainder. Goodbye, dear." Then she smiled and called out, "Next please!"

I felt more than a little agitated when I boarded the bus on Sunday afternoon; leaving home for the first time to live with complete strangers was not easy to accept, and I would miss the company of the girls I had worked with at Earlson.

The conductor took my half-crown.

"A single to Burnsyde Farm, please," I said, "and could you let me know when I get there?"

"'s about two hours run from here and we'll be stopping all along the way," he answered chattily, giving me my ticket and change, "but I'll let you know!"

The countryside was becoming greener and more hilly with each stop, and I kept glancing at my watch or dozing in the warmth of the bus.

After some time, I looked up as the conductor collected another fare and he silently mouthed the words, "not yet". We went up and over another hill, then travelled alongside a river for a short time.

As the river meandered away to the left the driver dropped to a lower gear and again the bus started to climb.

"Burnsyde Farm, miss! We're here!"

I couldn't see anything but overgrown greenery and high overhanging trees until we stopped opposite the entrance to Burnsyde.

"Best o' luck, miss!"

"Thank you." I smiled and as soon as my feet had touched the ground he pressed the bell and the bus moved on up the hill.

Before walking in under the canopy of trees, I looked across to the far side of the road at the tall, dark conifers of an impenetrable fir plantation. Already I was fascinated by my new surroundings.

The overhanging trees stopped abruptly just a few yards in from the road, at the open entrance gates of Burnsyde. A steep drive, edged with flowering shrubs, stretched ahead and as I walked up I was listening to the hum of honey bees hovering above a cascade of glowing flowers.

A light air rustled the leaves of a giant, copper beech tree standing on the left at the top of the drive, and when I reached it, the ground then levelled out to a broad gravel area which lay to the back of a graceful white house.

I stopped in amazement to look at the paradise that spread itself before me: colourful flower beds clustered round the side and the front of the house, but the main entrance was to the back and had three wide, rounded steps up to a double oak door.

I felt a surge of pleasure as my eyes followed the sweep of the gravel area; it widened, continuing round to the garages and barn which, I later learned, had been stables.

Opposite the main door lay several acres of lush green grass, this was to become known to me as the lower field. Beyond the lush grass the hills rose sharply, their tops were capped in mist.

Reluctant to let my presence be known, just yet, I walked along to the wide yard in front of the garages and turning to the right looked up through a long avenue of aspen trees that fringed the side of the lower field and curved gently into a dip in the hills.

Having taken in the whole picture of this little Eden, I slowly walked up the rounded steps and pulled the black, wrought-iron bell. I could hear it ringing loudly inside the house.

I waited, then the door opened and a sharp pair of hazel eyes took in every detail of my appearance within an instant.

"I think you were expecting me, I'm Jaqueline," I said quietly.

After a quick, hard handshake, she answered in a hoarse voice,

"Come in, you will address me as Miss Gillian!"

The tall, lean, jodhpur-wearing female, who had peered round the edge of the door before opening it fully, led me across the polished hall to a thickly carpeted staircase. We went up and round the staircase which opened on to a broad landing, turned left, past the open door of a bathroom, and entered a small, white painted bedroom.

"This will be your room," her voice was deep and hoarse as she spoke, "unpack! Use the bathroom next door!" She ran her finger along the mantelpiece before continuing. "When you are ready, come down to the dining-room which is on your right at the foot of the stairs."

My small L-shaped room could just accommodate the single bed and the dressing table that stood in front of the window. There was a mantelpiece over a blocked-up fireplace, and a heavy brass fender edged the blue-tiled hearth. The bed lay in a recess opposite the fireplace, and I could see no form of heating; it felt cold, and because of the all-over white paper and paint, it looked cold.

Miss Gillian, looking frigid and aloof, turned out of the room and strode towards the landing and my thoughts instantly fled to the large, comfortable, pink and blue bedroom I shared with my sister at home.

Having emptied the contents of my suitcase into the four deep drawers of the dressing table, I leant over it, opened the white net curtains and pulled down the top sash of the window to let the warm outside air filter through.

The bathroom I had been told to use next door had a large, white bath which seemed to be sunk several inches into the floor, and there was plenty of hot water on tap.

Having met Miss Gillian and her lofty manners, I was anxious to meet the other members of the family I was to live with. There was no wardrobe so I hung my coat on a hook behind the door, tidied my hair, and walked along to the wide landing above the hall, wondering what lay in store for me.

The evening sun streamed through the tall, staircase window picking out gold motifs on the pale green wallpaper; an aura of comfort and wealth was everywhere, except in my little white room.

As I started down the thickly carpeted stairs and passed the rich, red velvet curtains that framed the tall window, I was tempted to touch them, but thinking better of it, I contented myself by sliding my hand down the dark polished wood of the banister.

Feeling at ease in this beautiful house, I made my way down to the first door on the right at the foot of the stairs. A flutter of excitement ran through me as I knocked; what kind of people waited behind the door, and were they all like Miss Gillian?

I felt an age had passed and then a man's voice called out,

"Come in!"

I turned the handle, thinking he had sounded slightly bored, then I pushed open the door and four pairs of eyes looked towards me.

Miss Gillian was seated on a chair with her jodhpured legs apart and her bony hands gripped the edge of the seat between her legs.

"This is Jaqueline," she said in her hoarse voice, and I could just detect the trace of a smile as she turned to the white-haired lady standing near her. "Meet my sister, Miss June."

A pink flush spread over the smiling face of Miss June and she came towards me offering her hand.

"I *am* pleased to meet you, Jaqueline, welcome to Burnsyde."

Then she turned to the dark-haired man who stood with his hands behind his back in front of the large open fireplace; when he smiled his dark eyes glowed with pleasure – or was it the amusement caused by the spotless appearance of a land-girl?

Abruptly the man stepped forward and shook my hand heartily, while Miss June spoke in a quiet voice.

"Meet my brother William, Jaqueline."

He gave a slight bow and his smiling eyes roamed over my immaculate uniform.

"Welcome to the family," he said, releasing my hand; I smiled.

On a beige satin sofa by the glowing log fire sat a dignified old lady; she had been quietly watching the introductions and looked the picture of refinement in a black, moir-silk dress that reached the tip of her shoe.

Because the old lady was rather deaf, Mr William had to shout to introduce me.

"This is Mother! And we are very proud of her eighty-one years!"

The plump old lady wore her white hair plaited on top of her head, and when she raised her ear horn for the second time, Mr William shouted even louder,

"This is the land-girl we applied for, Mother!"

Mother straightened her back and a dainty hand fingered her hair; then looking at me doubtfully, she addressed her son,

"Do you think she will be strong enough? She's rather small."

"Why, of course, Mother," bellowed Mr William, "after all, she is a land-girl!"

The statement startled me; I felt like a horse must feel being sized-up before purchase, and almost wondered if they would open my mouth to examine my teeth.

It was while I stood there, feeling embarrassed under Miss Gillian's stony stare and the sizing-up of Mother and Mr William, that Miss June quietly walked towards the dining-room table and motioned me to follow.

"My apologies for my family," she murmured.

The large mahogany table was set for five, with heat-proof mats and silver cutlery; neatly arranged at one end were the serving spoons.

"I always sit at this end of the table to serve the food," the soft voice went on, "if you take the seat at the side there you can assist me by stacking the empty dishes on the trolley."

Then Miss June turned towards her sister who had been watching us and a silent signal passed between them. Quickly Miss Gillian rose to her feet and broke into the loud discussion that was still going on between mother and son.

"June will be serving supper in a few moments, Mother."

Mr William looked up.

"Supper, Mother!" he said. "Let me take your arm, we seem to be sitting down to supper early tonight," his masculine voice echoed round the spacious room.

"Don't treat me like an invalid, William! Give me my stick, I can manage perfectly well!"

The hands on the dining-room clock read six thirty by the time the two sisters carried in the evening meal.

"Don't fuss, William! Just push in my chair a little," Mother was saying.

When Mr William had made his mother comfortable, Miss June passed warm plates generously covered by large, fluffy omelettes and decorated with crunchy lettuce and tomatoes.

"Toast, Mother?" As she spoke Miss Gillian passed a silver toast rack stacked with tiny triangles of toast. Then she stared straight across at me.

"Toast!" she said irritably, and her obvious dislike hardened her features.

"No, thank you," I replied, wondering why I had got off to such a bad start with this woman.

"Tea, Jaqueline?" Miss June asked, smiling as she filled the dainty china cups.

"Yes, please," I said, watching her pass each cup on its fluted saucer carefully up the table.

The contrast between the two sisters was amazing; I wanted to be happy in this house, but the displeasure on Miss Gillian's face disturbed me.

The rest of the family were enjoying their supper.

"We always have high tea for supper," Miss June informed me, "and dinner is at midday. In the afternoon around three thirty, we have afternoon tea; so come to the back kitchen at that time with Sean. Oh! and there's a cup of tea at ten a.m."

I pricked up my ears at the name Sean, it immediately conjured up the picture of a farm worker similar to the foreman, Jim, at Earlson; I would not be working alone.

While the teacups passed back and forth for refilling, I was silently guessing the ages of the family and enjoying the delicate omelette; there was no shortage of eggs on a poultry farm.

Miss June would be in her middle fifties, I thought, and I placed Miss Gillian in her late forties. Mr William passed his plate for a second omelette, while I studied him.

"Penny for your thoughts, Jaqueline?" he said suddenly, suppressing a grin.

I almost dropped my cup in embarrassment, and caught unawares answered in confusion,

"I was trying to guess your age."

Mr William took a penny from his pocket and tossed it onto my side plate, where it spun for a moment and then clattered to a stop.

"Whatever are you doing, William?" Mother sat rigid waiting for an answer.

"Jaqueline wants to know what age I am," he said loudly.

Mother's face was suddenly lit up, and she looked at me coyly while she tucked away a stray wisp of hair.

"Oh! William is the baby of the family, – I have another son who comes in between Gillian and June."

I glanced at the baby of the family, trying hard not to smile, but his eyes were glued to his plate; he must have been about thirty-seven, I decided.

So I had come to stay with a middle-aged family and their very bright, genteel mother of eighty-one.

"I'll have another piece of toast, June."

"Yes, Mother."

Miss June made to rise from the table.

"Oh! Is there none left?"

"I'm afraid not, Mother, but it won't take a minute to make more."

"No, no, if it's finished, I won't bother."

Miss June sat down and lifted her teacup.

"Oh! I do wish I had just another nibble of toast!" Mother complained.

The two sisters looked at each other, and Miss Gillian rose, striding quickly out of the room. In a very short time she was back with some toast, and placing it by her mother's plate she sat down to continue her meal.

"Oh! you shouldn't have bothered, Gillian. But I *will* have another piece. William, do you want some?"

"Yes, Mother." And quickly he spread the toast, devouring it within seconds.

I had already stacked some dishes on the trolley beside me, when Mother rose from the table.

"*We* will attend to the washing up, Jaqueline. Go and sit opposite Mother by the fire," Miss June said softly but firmly. "Have you any knitting or sewing to do?"

"Yes, I have some embroidery."

"Then fetch it and I'll see it later."

Obediently I went upstairs as the trolley was trundled through the hall to the kitchen. Mr William, who had helped his mother to the sofa, was seated behind his newspaper by a small, round table.

When I took the chair opposite Mother by the fire, she smiled.

"What is it you are embroidering, dear?"

"A flower on the pocket of my dress," I answered.

"Very commendable, and very pretty too!" she said, smiling.

The room was quiet and only the crackling of the logs in the fire disturbed the peace while Mother dozed. Then I became aware of Mr William's eyes looking over the top of his newspaper; he smiled and the newspaper rose to cover his face completely.

Coming out of her doze with a start Mother straightened her back and began to question me:

"What age are you, dear?"

"I'll soon be eighteen."

"And how long have you been a land-girl?"

"Almost six months."

I noticed that her ear horn lay on the sofa beside her, and that she didn't seem to need it when I spoke. She looked over my uniformed appearance and asked,

"What did you do before becoming a land-girl, dear?"

"I was a manageress trainee and went to business classes on Tuesdays and Thursdays."

"Mmm!"

Mother was turning over my answer in her mind, when the door opened and Miss Gillian sauntered into the room, she slumped into an armchair and stared fixedly at the fire.

Miss June came a few minutes later and seated herself at the dining-room table with her work basket.

"Come over here, Jaqueline, and let me see your embroidery."

Gathering up my dress and threads I joined her at the table, relieved to escape Mother's questioning.

"Did you make this dress?" Miss June looked at me enquiringly.

"Yes."

"It's beautifully done and the embroidered flower makes it quite a classic. When I'm finished with the mending I'll show you the tapestry I'm working on."

She suddenly seemed much younger while we talked and stitched, and by nine o'clock Mr William stopped the loud conversation he had been having with Mother. The old lady yawned, and as she covered her mouth with a dainty hand the rings on her fingers sparkled.

"I think I'll go to bed, Gillian," she said fretfully.

Miss Gillian came to life, and rose energetically from the depths of her chair to take her mother's arm.

"I don't know how you two can sew, you'll damage your eyes, June, in this light." The old lady had paused by the table while she spoke, "William, it's time to light the lamp."

"Yes, Mother." He folded his paper and placed it on the round table, and reached across to the radio to switch it on. The nine o'clock news had just started; instantly I saw Mother stiffen and her skirts rustled as she turned round.

"You know how I detest all this nonsense about war, William, have the grace to switch it off until I am out of the room!" Mother turned again towards the door, holding Miss Gillian's arm, and her voice rang imperiously,

"If men must have wars, I don't want to hear about them!"

Rising from his comfortable leather chair Mr William switched the radio off, and lifted a highly polished, brass lamp from where it stood on the sideboard, placing it on the end of the table he began to pump it furiously.

"Has the spare battery been charged, June?" he asked, "the radio sounds weak."

"Yes, William, it has, as always."

The daylight was fading fast, and I watched with interest as the opaque ball of glass was lifted from the lamp to light it.

"The matches, June, where are the matches?"

"You'll find them in the end drawer of the sideboard where they always are, William."

It was incredible to watch him put a match to this out-moded form of lighting, and when the mantle glowed he replaced the ball of glass.

My curiosity had got the better of me and I said on the impulse,

"We have electricity at home. Why don't you have it at Burnsyde?"

"Too expensive to install," he replied briefly, and crossed the room to switch on the news.

I suddenly felt tired as the news ended; I had forgotten about the war in these last few hours, with no sirens wailing as they did in the city suburbs.

"Goodnight, Miss June, Mr William," I said, rising from the table.   "I want to get up early in the morning."

"Goodnight, Jaqueline," they both answered, smiling.

"Oh! breakfast is at seven thirty," Miss June added.

As I climbed the stairs in this beautiful house I felt that a new phase in my life was about to begin.

Chapter Eleven

My first morning at Burnsyde dawned bright and sunny. I was awake at six thirty and the clinical appearance of my room seemed softer in the morning light.

The household was already busy, and the smell of bacon and eggs drifted up from the kitchen as I opened the bathroom door. I felt hungry and eager to get out to my new surroundings, which looked almost too picturesque to be a commercial egg and poultry producing farm.

Having dressed in the usual working clothes of fawn dungarees and belted jacket, I carried my shining black boots downstairs as it would have been a violation to walk on the beautiful carpeted staircase wearing them.

The dining-room door was open when I laid my boots at the foot of the stairs, and Mr William's voice called out,

"Good morning, Jaqueline, did you sleep well?"

"Yes, thank you, Mr William," I replied, smiling as I entered the dining-room.

Miss June was already serving breakfast at the end of the table and the pink in her cheeks deepened when she indicated the chair nearest her, beside the trolley. I scarcely heard her soft good morning as she continued to address me.

"Will you have some porridge?"

"No, thank you, I never eat porridge," I replied quietly.

While Miss June filled my teacup, Mr William remarked from the head of the table,

"I thought all true Scots ate porridge?" He glanced at me, then spooned the sugar over his well-filled plate.

"A true Scot takes salt on his porridge," I replied and he spluttered with laughter before answering,

"You certainly caught me out this time, Jaqueline, first round to you!"

Miss June was tittering with amusement, when Miss Gillian turned from the far window where she had been standing so still, that I was taken by surprise. She had not been amused, and taking her seat opposite me at the table, the whites of her eyes reddened. Glaring across, she asked,

"Do you eat bacon and eggs?" The hoarse voice sounded furious.

"Yes, please, Miss Gillian," I answered quietly.

Two eggs and several rashers of bacon were piled onto a plate and passed to me, and I had to restrain myself from commenting on rationing.

Last night the omelette I had eaten at supper must have been made with three eggs, and this morning I was looking at two fried eggs on my plate. In these two meals alone, I had a week's ration for a family of five.

I felt guilty consuming so much rationed food, and yet Mr William passed his plate for a second helping and Miss Gillian considered more bacon, having wiped her plate clean.

Feeling pleasantly stuffed on the hearty breakfast I had eaten, I listened while the day's programme was outlined.

"I'll take these pullets along to Bob's place and stay for lunch with the family. They asked me to try and coax Mother along, but she finds the journey too tiring." Mr William looked vague as he finished speaking. "Oh! before I go I had better show Jaqueline round the farm. Feeling fit this morning, Jaqueline?"

"Yes, Mr William, I'm ready," and folding my napkin I rolled it up and pushed it into its silver ring before leaving the table.

Miss Gillian sat glumly staring at the empty plates, while her sister sipped a freshly poured cup of tea.

"I'll clear the table, Gillian, if you take Mother her breakfast."

Quickly I followed my new employer from the dining-room, leaving the two sisters to their daily chores.

"Don't forget to pick up your boots, Jaqueline!"

I whirled round to pick up the boots I had almost forgotten, then tailed after Mr William through to the back kitchen.

"You can leave your indoor shoes here, all the boots and wellingtons are kept on that wall," he said, pointing to a slightly recessed section of wall on the left.

The back kitchen was austere, with white-washed walls, a scrubbed, wooden table, half a dozen chairs with rush seats, and two wooden benches along the walls. On either side of the door that led into the main kitchen, stood deep, double sinks. Everything was clean and tidy.

Mr William had selected a pair of boots and seated himself on one of the benches. He pulled off his shoes without untying the laces.

"You shouldn't do that, it spoils your shoes," I remarked, pulling on my boots at the end of the bench.

"Ha, ha, ha!" he laughed, pushing his feet into the boots. "Bullying me already, Jaqueline?"

I felt myself blushing. I had caused quite a bit of hilarity at the table over the porridge, unintentionally, and now my frank statement on untied laces had produced another outburst of laughter.

The door leading to the yard was slightly ajar, when, without warning, it was pushed open banging against the wall and a large, golden labrador blundered in. It made straight for Mr William, licking at his hands and face and as he rose, the wagging tail flicked the leg of a chair sending it spinning across the floor.

"I'm up against four females now and even the dog is a bitch!" He smiled while he patted the excited animal. "Out, Belle! Out!" he said loudly when the swinging tail threatened another chair, and gripping her collar he led her through the open doorway.

Hurriedly, I finished tying my laces and followed them out to the yard. The sun was bright, and from where we stood, I could see it filtering through the trees into the long avenue that led towards the hills.

"The high field is on the side of the hill at the end of the avenue of aspens," he walked forward, still speaking, and pointed towards the lush green grass facing the entrance to the back of the house. "That is the lower field; we rear the chicks in these rows of brooders to the front. The hen houses laid out towards the back of the field are for the mature birds, there are twenty-four of them!"

Glancing thoughtfully up at the fine mist drifting over the hilltop, he continued"

"It'll be a fine day today, and hot! The birds need watering every day, start with the brooders first and then water the hen houses."

As we stood in the early morning sun, I noticed that he was only a few inches taller than I was, and yet in the house his dark good looks seemed to loom over me.

"Cleaning out the hen houses is rather like painting the Forth Bridge, Jaqueline," he glanced at me sympathetically, "you get to the last house and then go straight back to the beginning. Eggs are collected twice a day," he added as an afterthought.

We turned to walk back across the yard, which was edged on two sides by the garages, incubator house and the meal barn.

"The burn that runs down the side of the lower field is piped under the yard and comes out just here," his hand indicated a gentle, green slope I had noticed on my arrival. Then the tone of his voice changed, taking on a coldness, and he waved his hand over the stream towards a walled garden. "That is the kitchen garden, and you are not allowed in there!"

I made no answer, and only glanced at the high, brick wall of the garden and the solid wooden doors set in its centre; the garden lay about a hundred yards beyond the sparkling stream.

A movement by the entrance to the barn had caught my eye, and looking across I saw a tall, slim boy quietly observing us. He wore a leather jerkin and tight-fitting moleskins; the lank, brownish-fair hair above his tanned face was just a few shades lighter than his clothing.

Mr William had also become aware of the boy.

"Good morning, Sean," he said, "this is the new land-girl, Jaqueline, take her with you today and show her what has to be done."

I walked over to where Sean stood and shook hands, while Mr William turned towards the garages, and was immediately struck by the half-closed, keen, blue eyes that surveyed me from his lofty height.

In complete silence we loaded a one-wheeled barrow with peat-moss and some tools, and set off up the long avenue of trees that led to the high field.

Sean was very quiet as we worked together scraping and cleaning each hen house floor; a grunt, or a couple of words seemed to be the sum total of his vocabulary. About an hour had passed and my mind was full of questions; how could anyone be so quiet for so long when only their hands worked?

Thinking I had waited long enough, I said quietly,

"Can I ask what age you are, Sean?"

"You can," he answered, "I'm seventeen and a half. And you?"

"Almost eighteen."

A long silence followed my answer and I could see that he was annoyed, probably because I was older than him by a few months.

Boys tended to be bumptious if you were a little older or more clever; unless, of course, they were trying to be charming. Finding myself completely ignored I went on with my work.

On the way back to the peat-moss shed, I was offered a ride in the barrow.

"It's empty!" he said nonchalantly. "You may as well sit in it and I'll push."

For the first time since I had met him that morning, he was smiling and his whole attitude had changed.

"Won't I be too heavy?" I asked.

"No," he said scornfully, "you're not more than a hundred and twenty pounds!"

Weary from the morning's work I quickly settled myself in the barrow, my feet dangling near its one wheel. The sunbeams were filtering through the glorious avenue of aspen trees that stretched ahead, dancing on the path and playing across my eyes. Suddenly life was wonderful and I was pleased to think that he could do more than just grunt.

We rounded a curve in the shaded avenue and there was the incubator house straight ahead at the far side of the yard. At the end of the trees, on my right, I could see the edge of the peat-moss shed; I now had a fair picture of the farm lay-out.

Swoosh! I shot straight out of the barrow taken completely by surprise, and landed head first in the steamy mess of a small tip. My tall, slim work-mate walked on wheeling the barrow without a backward glance.

Hurriedly, I scrambled out of the assortment of tin cans and fermenting vegetables that had come from the kitchen, and was making my way towards the peat-moss shed, when Miss Gillian came striding out of the incubator house.

"You don't have to use your head to clean the floors!" she said scathingly, giving me a withering look. "What on earth have you been doing?"

I hesitated for a moment before answering.

"I slipped and fell in the small rubbish tip."

It went against the grain to lie, but I had chosen the least complicated way out of an awkward situation.

"Go and clean yourself up before dinner!" And with a final glare she strode towards the back kitchen, so I followed.

The clock was chiming twelve thirty when I entered the dining-room and took my place at the table.

"Which piece would you prefer, Mother?" shouted Mr William, sharpening the knife expertly and cutting into the meat. The slices fell away under each cut, and Mother said, pointing daintily,

"I prefer it a little more rare, William, nearer the bone if you please, and I'll have a good piece of crackling with it today."

Three thick slices were placed on the plate and passed to the fresh-complexioned old lady. Then the other plates were generously covered and passed down the table.

"You don't have to go without soup just because we have finished ours, Jaqueline," Miss June spoke softly beside me.

"The main course will be more than enough," I replied, my mind on the packed lunches at Earlson Farm.

Miss Gillian's long arm paused above a dish piled high with large potatoes cooked in their jackets.

"One or two potatoes?" she asked, her eyes gleaming with impatience.

"One please," I answered, and she placed an enormous potato on my side plate.

"Veg, Jaqueline?" Miss June's face glowed with pleasure as she held the dish towards me.

It was almost as though we were whispering, while the rest of the family talked loudly and kept refilling their plates.

"I was expecting you at ten o'clock for a cup of tea, Jaqueline. Don't you think you need a little refreshment mid-morning?"

"Yes, I do, but Sean sneered when I mentioned tea, so I just went on with my work."

"Oh! But you mustn't do as Sean does," she said kindly.

Mr William was again slicing into the meat as he spoke,

"What about you, Jaqueline, more meat?"

"No, thank you," I replied, "I've had plenty."

From across the table Miss Gillian glared.

"Eat up! No time for dainty appetites when it comes to eating," she said gruffly, "if you work hard you need to eat well."

Miss June carried in the sweet while I busied myself stacking plates on the trolley beside me.

"Queen of Puddings today, I hope, June?" said Mother, tidying her napkin.

"No, Mother, Apple Charlotte."

Miss June piled the pudding into the sweet dishes and passed them up the table.

"Just a little, Miss June," I said, aware of the hazel eyes opposite piercing through me.

The sweet melted deliciously on the tongue, and I felt like a contented cat as I placed my spoon in the empty plate. In the meantime, Mr William and Miss Gillian devoured their second helpings; and I wondered how Miss June had time to eat, since she had spent most of her time fetching food from the kitchen, or serving it at the table.

Having eaten more than I should, I excused myself from the table and escaped upstairs to groan for a few minutes flat out on my bed. It was years since I had seen so much food, and my stomach had shrunk since the beginning of the war. I was now paying the price of over-indulgence.

As I lay there, my bloated tummy began to ease and I was seized by an impulse to see more of the house and its surroundings. I could hear the family still chatting round the dining-room table when I reached the foot of the staircase, so I crossed the hall and went out by the main door.

It was warm outside and I walked along to the shade of the giant copper beech tree where the air felt cool and refreshing. A lacework of black painted wood edged the gently sloping roof of the lovely house, and the windows were wide and glazed with diamond shaped leaded panes.

Farmers, I thought as I stood there, don't go in for beautiful houses like this; and my eyes travelled over the carpet of colour that lay to the front of the house and the breathtaking view of the valley below.

Then I noticed a tall tower standing to the far side of the garden overlooking the valley, it was built of stone blocks and the top of it was much higher than the ridge of the house roof. I felt it must have stood there long before the house came into being.

The crunch of shoes on the steep drive broke into my thoughts, and I turned to see Sean making his way up the slope pushing a bicycle.

"Hello, Sean." He grinned. "Can you tell me what that tower is for?"

"You're not mad at me after this morning?" he asked, looking keenly into my eyes.

"What good would it do me?" I answered coolly. "I'll just put it down to the hazards of working with a person like you. Now, tell me, what is the tower for?"

"It's a look-out tower," he said, still watching my face. Then he added quietly, "It has a ghost."

I walked with Sean towards the garages eager to hear more about the tower, but just as he stood his bike against the wall, Mr William stepped from the side door of the house carrying a cricket bat in his hand.

"Catch!" he called out, and I leapt and caught the hard ball as it sailed above my head. "Do you play cricket?"

I rubbed my stinging hand down my side.

"No," I answered, "rounders!"

"Good! Then you can field for Sean."

As I pulled on my working gloves, I could see an expression of utter contempt crossing Sean's face. The cricket ball left his hand, speeding low and fast towards Mr William, smacked into the bat and shot towards me; but I had learned to catch the hard way with my brother and his friends, and each time the ball hit the bat my hands were in the right place at the right time.

Sean's face became cold and distant as the ball continued to slam into the leather palms of my working gloves, so I stayed as far away from him as I could to avoid the steely look in his eyes.

Suddenly, Mr William threw down the bat and laughed uproariously.

"I would never have believed it, that'll teach me to judge by appearances," he said, and added, "I would have missed this if the car hadn't packed up on me this morning!" And picking up his bat he walked away shaking his head and smiling.

I was disgusted at the way Sean ignored me while working side by side all afternoon, and when I could contain my disgust no longer, I turned on him.

"You're in the pet because I caught every ball that came my way when you were bowling for Mr William, aren't you!" I snapped at him. "Why don't you grow up?"

He made no reply, but looked at me sideways with his slanting eyes.

"Would you rather I pretended to be a helpless female?" I looked straight into his eyes, but they remained very blue and hostile, and still he said nothing.

Picking up my tools I walked on to the next hen house to work alone, but all the time I was wondering why a tall, athletic young man, of nearly my own age, could be so childish.

I finished my lonely working day at five thirty, in time to clean up and change for supper, having missed the afternoon cup of tea. It was nice to slip into a straight, navy skirt and silk blouse and find I could still get my feet into court shoes after spending the day in boots.

My next thought was to write home and give my parents a rough idea of what the farm was like, and what kind of people I was living with. Sitting on my bed busily writing, my mind kept drifting to the tower that looked out over the valley to the green hills beyond.

Sean had mentioned a ghost, and the thought of what it might be intrigued me: was it male, female, or something more frightening like the kind the imagination creates? But how would I ever find out if he sulked all the time?

It was just before seven when I finished my letter and made my way down to the dining-room to find the family seated around the table talking. Miss June was already serving the meal and everyone glanced, smiled and went on with their conversation as I took my seat.

"Do you think you will enjoy working at Burnsyde, Jaqueline?" Miss June's quiet voice was suddenly drowned as Mr William spoke.

"No, Mother, the car won't be fixed till tomorrow, so I can't see Bob until the weekend, and I'm afraid he can't bring the family over, they're much too busy at this time of year."

"Yes, I suppose you're right, William," said Mother, "but I hardly ever see the family," she smiled delicately, "and I won't be here for ever."

On hearing the pathetic statement coming from her mother's lips, Miss June called out:

"Can you manage a little more, Mother?"

"What was that, June?"

"Can you manage a little more, Mother?" shouted Mr William.

"You don't have to shout, William, I'm not deaf!" said Mother, changing her ear horn from one ear to the other as she answered Miss June. "Yes, I will, just a morsel, June." And Miss Gillian passed her mother's plate.

The delicately flavoured egg soufflé was just beginning to sag on my plate as I scooped up the last of it.

"Jaqueline," Miss June said softly, "more?"

"That was delicious, Miss June." And I held out my plate for more.

I was wondering if I should ask about the tower, when Miss June spoke again.

"We're having coffee this evening, Jaqueline, so keep Mother company until we finish the washing-up."

I busied myself clearing the last of the dishes on to the trolley, while Mr William helped Mother from the table.

"Don't fuss, William, I'm not incapable of reaching the sofa." She waved his hand away, seated herself on the sofa, and tidied her dress, arranging it round her until she was satisfied. "I think I'm coming down with a slight chill, I feel rather feverish." And taking a wisp of a lace handkerchief from her sleeve she gently pressed it to her brow.

All activity stopped instantly, and Mr William was first to speak.

"Then you must go to bed, Mother."

"Yes, I think I will."

Everyone made a move towards the sofa, but Mother raised her hand and she looked magnificent as she said,

"Now don't smother me! Gillian, may I have your arm, please?"

I could see the hint of a flush in her unlined cheeks as she made her way out of the dining-room, leaning lightly on Miss Gillian's arm.

"Where do I post these letters, Miss June?" I asked. She had started to push the laden trolley towards the door.

"Oh! yes, leave them on the hall table and they'll be handed to the postman in the morning when he delivers the mail."

The voices of Miss Gillian and Mother drifted from the landing above the hall, and I placed my letters on the antique, rosewood table by the door; one to my parents and one to my sister at the lodge.

When I returned to the dining-room, Mr William was absorbed in his newspaper; and taking a seat by the window, where I could admire the large open fireplace with its glowing, log fire, I decided to ask about the ghost of the tower.

"What has Sean been telling you?" he said, grinning broadly.

"He just mentioned there was a ghost when I asked about the look-out tower," I replied.

"Then I had better start at the beginning," said Mr William, folding his newspaper and placing it on the round table. "I'm taking you back to the dim, dark ages when the clan chieftain who ruled this part of Caledonia, as it was called in ancient times, decreed that the tower should be built."

His dark eyes shone as he became absorbed in the tale; and it occurred to me as I listened, how handsome he looked for a man who was old enough to be my father.

"When the tower was completed," he said, "the chieftain proclaimed that all the land he could see from the top of the tower would be his domain."

My eyes never left his face until he had finished the romantic story, and I was imagining a vivid picture of the events, when he suddenly said,

"There, have I made it exciting enough for you?"

I must have looked crestfallen when I answered,

"Then you were only making it up as you went along?"

The dining-room door was pushed open as I finished speaking, and Miss Gillian strode in carrying two silver pots. Close behind Miss June followed carrying a tray of small coffee cups and saucers.

"Oh! no! There is a story and there is a ghost!" Mr William was assuring me.

"Have you been telling Jaqueline about the tower?" enquired Miss June, setting out the coffee cups on their dainty saucers. Mr William coughed. "The usual romantic misinterpretation, I suppose, William?" Without waiting for an answer, she continued, "Black or white, Jaqueline? How do you take your coffee?"

"White, thank you," and I rose to collect my cup from the table.

"Stay where you are, William, and Jaqueline will bring your coffee."

Giving Mr William his coffee, I smiled and said,

"I would rather hear the true story, Mr William, because I *am* interested."

Miss Gillian had flopped into a chair and sat puffing clouds of cigarette smoke towards the ceiling; already she had gulped down two small cups of the strong coffee and rose to pour a third.

Miss June set down her cup, and pulling the work basket to the edge of the table she started to speak.

"This house is built on the foundations of the original fort, or castle, that once stood here."

My attention was at once held by her quiet voice.

"The tower was still standing, so Father had it restored to its former glory once the house was completed."

Her voice carried across the quiet of the large room and we all listened intently.

"The clans were still fighting amongst themselves in these heathen times," she paused to thread her needle, "and when the chieftain from the north came over the hills plundering and burning everything in his path, he slew the defenders of the castle and put the family to the sword. All, excepting one!" she glanced at me.

I felt myself give an involuntary shudder, but Miss June calmly stitched and continued with the story.

"The lady of the castle was in the garden when the plunderers swept down, and she fled to the top of the tower to hide."

I waited, tense with excitement, while Miss June moistened a thread between her lips and passed it through the eye of her needle.

"The murdering plunderers filled themselves with food and wine, and as they lay sleeping their chieftain climbed the steps of the tower to view his next prey in the valley below."

I was in agony for the lady hiding in the tower, and only the story teller's voice broke the stillness in the room.

"When the evil chieftain found the lady she had climbed on to the parapet, and as he tore at her clothes to savage her she jumped from the tower to her death."

I felt chilled to the marrow because it had all happened on this spot; and I could see the tower, which looked ghostly in the fading light, from where I sat on the window seat.

Miss June reached for a coffee pot, but both were empty.

"Really, Gillian," she said in exasperation "does anyone want more coffee?"

"No, thank you," I replied, glancing at Mr William and thinking how far from the truth his version of the story had been.

Chapter Twelve

Long before we had even started work on that wet thundery day, I knew it was impossible for me to lift the one-and-a-quarter-hundredweight sacks of meal, but Sean and I had been told to fill the meal bin.

"You lift them like this," Sean said, placing his back against a bulging sack and gripping it at the corners, "then you carry it to the bin and tip it in, and that's all there is to it."

He tipped the contents of the sack over his shoulder while I watched and it poured down into the bin.

"I can't lift a sack of meal, it's too heavy," I said quietly, but he looked at me impatiently.

"Look, I'll show you again," he insisted, then bending forward to support the next bulging sack on his back he walked the few feet to the bin.

On the spur of the moment, I made up my mind to copy his movements exactly; it was only a few feet and I just might make it.

"Yes, you make it look so easy," I said, feeling it was a waste of time to argue.

Gripping the corners of a heavy sack, I pulled and it came forward from a leaning position. Pleased with the first step I put my back against it and pulled again, but it remained where it was as solid as the wall behind it.

"Try again," suggested Sean, chewing on the long piece of straw that dangled from his mouth. Then he strode across with a sneer on his face, "Stiffen your legs and put your back against the sack. Now! Grip the corners!"

He helped to lift the sack onto my back and I staggered a step forward, but then my legs doubled up and I went down in a heap with my burden. Lying beside the half-empty sack with the rest of its contents settling over me, I was furious. Why had I let myself get into this ridiculous situation?

By this time, Sean was perched on the bin chewing thoughtfully on his piece of straw. I stood up, wiping the meal from the back of my neck and shaking it out of my hair.

"I knew perfectly well I couldn't lift one of these sacks," I said loftily. "We were never allowed to lift them at Earlson Farm without help, but at least I tried!"

All he did was to grunt in reply expressing his contempt, so I ignored him, and lifting a shovel I threw the scattered meal into the bin. Realising I had found a method, I pushed at the next bag and let it fall to the floor.

Friendship had been growing steadily between us, but I couldn't understand his attitude towards the female; or was he being antagonistic because I was a stranger to the West Country? I still shovelled slowly into the mound of meal on the floor, and thought again. Perhaps it was something more basic, such as the budding male asserting his superiority over the female?

Impulsively, I stood to my full five feet two inches and looked him straight in the eye as he lounged on the bin.

"It is a known fact that men are stronger than women, but you seem to be unaware of this," I began, but there was no reaction so I plunged on, "it is therefore necessary for the female to develop a high standard of intelligence to combat this defect, if it is a defect. The male, being able to apply brute strength, is less inclined to develop his reasoning."

He continued to chew on the straw with his eyes studying the toe of his boot, but I had satisfied my ego and willingly set about heaving over the next sack, shovelling the scattered contents into the bin and trying to forget he was there.

When I stole a quick glance at Sean, a deep flush had crept over his tanned face and he lifted a hand to push back a lank strand of hair from his brow. I felt my throat go dry, and stepping back I dropped the shovel and ran from the barn.

The sun was pushing long shafts of light earthwards between heavy, black clouds, and the thunder that had roared down from the north was now belching its way gradually into the distance at the far side of the valley.

I slowed my steps aware of a dull ache low down in my body, and headed for the kitchen.

"May I go up to my room for a few minutes, Miss June?" I asked as soon as I entered.

"Certainly, Jaqueline," she glanced at my face enquiringly, smiling. "Just a minute," she said, "step outside and I'll brush the meal from your clothes. I'm beginning to think Gillian is right, really, when she says you stick your head into everything you do! Now you can use this towel to brush it off your face."

As she finished speaking I excused myself and ran upstairs.

I had felt fear when I dashed from the barn, just as I sometimes did when my father's eyes darkened and I became aware of his anger. Another mental note went into my list of undesirable qualities in the male. I would never marry a man I was afraid of.

Struggling back into my dungarees as quickly as possible, I tried to convince myself that this unmentionable curse, referred to in the bible as unclean, was something to be proud of and that without menstruation there would be no future generations.

Some minutes later I was back in the kitchen.

"It's near enough the tea break so I've made a fresh pot, sit down for five minutes, Jaqueline, and have some tea."

Sipping the hot tea I could feel it weaving its way down to the toothache-like pain inside me and I felt colour come back into my face as it eased.

"Have you started a period?" the brisk question came leaving me no time to be embarrassed before I answered, but shame was already flooding through me. I felt unclean, because the scriptures said this of the female.

"Yes, it shouldn't have come until next week," I replied, unable to look at Miss June's face because we were discussing this unmentionable subject.

"Then no heavy lifting today! In fact, you can set the eggs up for testing in the incubator house and it will leave me free for jam making."

I was about to rise and head for the incubator house, when Miss June stopped me.

"Stay where you are," she said, "and have another cup of tea, then tell me how you are getting along with Sean?"

"I think he's a moron," I said bluntly, still feeling apprehensive because I could only retaliate with words against him.

Miss June came across with the teapot and refilling my cup she said:

"You're probably the first career-minded young lady with a will of her own that Sean has come across; he must be feeling completely out of his depth."

"It's more than that," I answered, "it's aggression, because I'm a stranger!"

Her merry tittering tinkled through the kitchen as she listened, then she became thoughtful.

"Jaqueline, I have been given the task of setting up a canteen for a contingent of Polish soldiers; they are to be based in our village while waiting to be called to active duty." She turned back to the sink, but continued to speak. "It has been impossible to enlist the help of any of the village girls, do you think you could help on one night of the week?"

She turned, waiting expectantly.

"What would I have to do?" I asked.

"Help me to serve coffee and cakes, grill sausages and bacon, and help wash-up the dishes."

''Yes, I will," I answered, feeling pleased that she had asked me, "as long as you are going to be there with me!"

"Naturally I will be with you," she said. "Oh! Jaqueline, will you tell Sean to come to the kitchen for tea, if he would like some?"

Without wasting another minute I hurried out through the large, wet blobs that dropped from a thunderous sky, and raced for the barn, but there was no one there; Sean had gone.

My wild dash from the side door to the barn had surprised six large rats scurrying along the rafters above me, so I backed slowly towards the door petrified in case they should fall, and I turned and fled to the incubator house.

Chapter Thirteen

I settled into the family routine, happy in the company of everyone except Miss Gillian. There were times when she would smile, but at that moment she glared at me across the table. I heard Mr William speak and turned my eyes from her baleful stare.

"They need help on the neighbouring farm, Jaqueline, have you ever worked on a combined harvester?"

"No, Mr William, but I don't mind having a try at something different."

Miss June refilled his soup plate and it was passed to Miss Gillian, past Mother to Mr William.

"Thank you, June," he said, placing it carefully on the table mat.

Having started on his second plate of soup he once again looked up and smiled at me.

"Good! I'm sending you and Sean to help with the labour shortage next door. All the young men are taken from the area as soon as they reach call-up age;" he stared blankly down the table while speaking, "there will soon be nothing but old men left, with the exception of men in reserved occupations like myself."

Without really meaning to speak my thoughts aloud, I heard myself say,

"Then Sean will be called-up when he is eighteen just like all the others?"

"Yes," replied Mr William, "just like all the others! He's a bright boy, top in mathematics at the academy; could go a long way if he were given the chance."

On the following morning the tractor was waiting at the foot of the drive and Sean was already sitting beside the driver. I climbed up across Sean's legs, to be wedged between man and boy on a small block of wood.

The tractor trundled up the road and in through the gates of what looked like an endless field of wheat.

"Have you worked on a combined harvester before?" Sean asked.

"No, I can't say I have," I replied carefully to his question.

"Huh, you'll probably be on the chaffing! I'll be feeding-in!" he said, arrogance showing on every feature of his face.

I didn't want him to know that I was completely ignorant of what chaffing, or feeding-in meant, so I remained silent while he jumped down from the tractor. Looking for a foothold, I turned to find the driver offering his hand to help me down.

With one last withering look, Sean climbed to the top of the harvester and stood looking very important, while I waited below.

The rest of the men took up their places at various points of the harvester, and one climbed up to work with Sean as the huge, yellow monster spluttered into life. I watched Sean catch the bundles tossed from a cart below, and his knife flashed in the sun as each bundle fell apart and dropped into the mouth of the hungry machine.

"Lassie, come over here!"

I went to the side of the harvester, where the tractor driver stood, as the first of the chaff came pouring down a chute. It flowed into a sack and just as it threatened to overflow, the driver lifted the sack from the three large hooks on which it hung and replaced it with an empty one.

"That's all you do, remove the full sack and replace it with an empty one. Think you can manage, lass?"

"Yes," I replied, "I think so!"

The first few sacks were fine, but the chaff that had escaped during the removal of a full sack and the replacing of an empty one was gradually creeping up my legs. I bent down to brush it aside, then I gasped in alarm; a waterfall of chaff was suddenly pouring over me.

Blindly I pushed in my hands to remove the overflowing sack from the three hooks, but they were lost somewhere under the river of chaff that flowed into my face.

"Help!" I shouted as the chaff poured into my dungarees, filling up the legs until I was padded solid.

The noise of the machine drowned my voice and the chaff moved on up to my chest, it was now impossible to remove the sack or myself.

"Help!" I screamed.

Two men who were lifting the heavy, metal-bound bales as they fell from the front of the harvester looked up and without a word, walked over, caught me by the shoulders and yanked me out of the chaff before I disappeared from view.

I stood gasping in my stuffed dungarees, while the men moved all the full sacks and swept aside the mound of chaff; then they tore off the sack from the hooks and replaced it with an empty one. Without a look, or a word, they went back to lifting their bales.

I dashed in before the sack overflowed to start again; but it wasn't until I was about to go under for the third time that the harvester stopped, and in the blissful silence of a warm, sunny day, the men lit up their cigarettes.

During the next ten minutes, I took off my leggings to let the chaff run from the bottom of my dungarees, and almost back to normal proportions, I sat down to empty out my boots.

Sean, contemptuous and aloof, was watching from his lofty perch. I tied a piece of string round my waist and buttoned up my shirt at the neck, but I had the feeling that Sean didn't want to know me.

After a well-earned break the combined harvester started up again, and the men sweated and grunted carrying the heavy sacks of grain to the waiting lorry. By noon I had been rescued again, but I had definitely improved.

The reaper and binder worked from the outer edges of the field, drawing gradually nearer to the centre in an encircling movement, until only a small patch of wheat remained. I watched with interest as the men left the harvester and formed a ring around the forlorn patch in a field now reduced to stubble. Then the reaper turned and drove straight through the middle of the patch.

Amidst a chorus of loud whoops and yells, the men threw themselves on the escaping rabbits that had been trapped by the encircling movement of the reaper. They all went home that evening with a pair of rabbits slung over their shoulders.

"Why didn't you catch a rabbit, Sean?" I asked.

"I can catch rabbits anytime," he replied, shrugging his shoulders, and remained silent and moody all the way back to Burnsyde.

The driver turned in at the entrance and we jumped down from his tractor, but while he was reversing out, he called,

"There's another field to cut, lass!   See you in the morning! Goodnight!"

"Goodnight, Jamie!" I called, but Sean had swung his leg over his bike and was already speeding towards the village without a word to either of us.

Chapter Fourteen

"Mmm, Jaqueline," said Mr William at breakfast the next morning, "I want you to give Miss June a hand with the chicks from the incubator today. Miss Gillian will be away for a week, she left last night to help out with the family at my brother's farm; there's been a new addition, a baby daughter," he ended softly.

I had been resigned to the thought of starting on the next field with Sean and the combined harvester; when Mr William's statement came, it sounded like a reprieve to my pricked all over, stinging body. Inwardly I heaved a sigh of relief, and answered,

"Yes, Mr William."

"I know you were doing well on the chaffing, and it takes all you've got to keep up with two men feeding-in up top."

I dismissed the mental picture of being unceremoniously plucked out by the shoulders from the overflowing chaff, and basked in his praise. I could still feel the sting from hundreds of little pricks after last night's hot bath and I winced; it would have been the same today as the chaff found its way inside my shirt and stuffed itself down my dungarees, pricking me all over until I looked like I had a bad case of measles.

After a thoughtful pause, Mr William said,

"My brother has two sons and now the long-awaited daughter has arrived; they must be delighted!" Then he snapped out of his musing. "All good things must come to an end, Jaqueline! We need you to help with the day-old-chicks. Sean will take over the chaffing!"

I smiled with delight as I spread my toast; the high and mighty Sean would be doing the job he had scoffed at.

"Mother will be pleased to have a granddaughter at last!" said Miss June, her face radiant, and I found myself wondering why the two sisters had remained spinsters.

Only one son from this family had married and he now had three children, but Mr William was still young enough to think about marriage.

"May I congratulate you on your new niece."

"Thank you, Jaqueline," they both murmured.

I was stacking the dirty dishes on the trolley, when Miss June rose from the table.

"I've given Mother her breakfast, but the dirty dishes will have to wait this morning; let's get out to the incubator, Jaqueline. The newly hatched chicks won't wait."

Leaving the table uncleared, we headed for the back kitchen where she slipped into a raincoat and green, rubber boots. We hurried across the yard while she chatted on.

"We use a dark cockerel and a white hen for breeding to make sexing the chicks easy. It is a proven poultry breeding fact that the female chick will have the dark colouring of the cockerel and the male chick the light colouring of the hen."

Mr William was already opening the doors of the incubator when Miss June and I hurried into the warm, box-like room adjoining the barn. On the shelves in the incubator stood hundreds of fluffy, yellow chicks, some still struggling out of their shells.

Without wasting a moment Miss June slid out a tray of chicks and carried it to the table.

"Take another tray from the incubator and place it beside this one, Jaqueline. Now, you can see how pale the male chicks are; I want you to pick out all the pale yellow ones and put them into the one tray, and I will take care of the females."

We stood on opposite sides of the table separating the chicks, until each tray was filled with one sex only and all the shells had been removed. In the meantime, Mr William was counting the females and placing their trays back into the incubator.

"Take the trays of males over to the bench beneath the window, Jaqueline," he said, lifting a tray and carrying it across.

I was so happy separating the tiny chickens and helping the odd late-comer to discard its shell. Soon there were several trays lined up beneath the window and I had become aware of a higher note to their cheeping when I carried a tray across. Tiny as they were, they became alarmed by the movement from the table to the bench.

The rich brownish-yellow chickens were cheeping loudly from the incubator and the warm air flowed from the open doors as I carried the last of the males to the bench.

"I think the percentage of females is higher this month, what do you think, William?"

"Yes, June, sixty per cent females," he said briskly.

The fluffy little chickens were clustering round my hands, and when I tapped my fingers on the tray they started to peck. How independent they were in comparison to the offspring of the human.

I helped Mr William double-check the number of males and he entered the details in a notebook. When we had finished he handed me a heavy, woven meal sack and said,

"Fill this sack with the male chicks, Jaqueline, and drown them in the burn!" I must have looked horrified, so he explained, "Cockerels are a dead loss to the farmer, we only select a few for breeding purposes; the rest would eat more than their worth before they were ready for the table and so they go for pig food."

I was in agony as I dropped the warm chirping bundles into the dark depths of the sack; over three hundred of them, but Miss June just smiled and busied herself with the females. I couldn't stop the tears that trickled down my cheeks, and Mr William seemed to be ill at ease.

"Jaqueline, a farmer's wife must learn to do jobs like this, you know. After all, they are only food like the cattle in the fields and the sheep on the hills; and when they go outside to live in the hen houses some of them will become food for the fox or the badger."

I moved to the door with the sack, steeped in despair, avoiding the eyes of the two who were so heartless.

"Use the large, flat stone to hold the sack under, Jaqueline." Mr William's voice sounded so callous above the muffled cheeping of the condemned chicks.

I carried the sack down to the stream and placed it gently on the grass hoping a miracle would happen. Then lifting the heavy, flat stone used for this dreadful deed, I placed it at the water's edge and brushed away the tears.

The pigman, who had come to collect the chicks, seeing the state of misery I had been reduced to, walked down the bank. Lifting the sack he said,

"Let's see it, lass, the quicker it's done the better!"

Then he plunged the sack of tiny, cheeping bundles into the cold water and placed the stone on top of it. Turning abruptly away from the stream, he pointed to the top of the hill and started to speak in his slow, lilting voice; while I stifled a sob.

"The mist is still rising, but you can see the cattle grazing on the skyline up there, 'tis going to be a grand day!" he paused to puff at his pipe. "But if the cattle start making their way down to the lower slopes it will rain within the hour."

I listened, dabbing at my eyes with a handkerchief as he spoke. The Rs rolled off his tongue making a grand day seem much more grand. I kept my eyes on the sunlit scene of drifting mist and the grazing cattle; Mr William had said they were only food, like the contents of the sodden sack the pigman now placed in his barrow.

"Sean will bring you down to see the piglets, lass. Wear your heavy boots and leggings, or they will take the toes off you!"

"Thank you," I murmured.

After the pigman had gone, I stood there wishing I had not been so emotional, and how glad I was that Sean had not been there. How he would have sneered. Then with leaden steps I walked into the incubator house. Miss June looked up.

"Do you have a garden at home, Jaqueline?"

"Yes," I answered listlessly.

"Would you have room for a few hens?"

"I think so," I replied, feeling the gloom lift, "ours is a corner garden, so we have more ground than the other houses."

"Then take home a dozen chicks at the weekend; we have hatched a higher percentage this month. Your mother could raise them in a warm kitchen and feed them on household scraps, but she will have to give up her egg ration and apply for balancer meal to feed the growing birds."

Miss June's offer of chickens to take home had dispelled the last of the gloom; my mind raced ahead thinking of the surprise it would be to my parents. It would mean fresh eggs every day, if the chicks survived, and some fat cockerels to help out with the meat situation.

Since the night she had felt feverish Mother had been spending a lot of her time in bed. She had only been downstairs once for the midday meal during the past week. The doctor had called twice and he insisted she stay in bed, even although Mother had declared she was perfectly well. With Miss Gillian away it was easier for Miss

June to keep her in bed. The fire in the sitting-room could be left unlit until suppertime, and there would be no one to keep Mother company if she were downstairs.

Only then did I think about how few people were employed by Mr William. The poultry, the dozen or so cattle, and the sheep that grazed on the hill all had to be tended by someone.

During Miss Gillian's absence Mr William spent his time at the table talking to me, while Miss June served the food and smiled.

"Why did you become a land-girl, Jaqueline?" he asked.

"Because I wanted to take part in the war before it ended."

"Then it wasn't your love of the open air, or raising poultry?"

"No, I would have joined the WRNS, if I had been old enough."

Mr William lifted the sugar bowl, and looking thoughtfully at his porridge, he asked,

"What work did you do before joining the Land Army?"

"I was a manageress trainee, and if I go back to the company I was with, they have promised to make me a manageress on my twenty-first birthday. The trouble is, I really want to travel through Europe and see a bit of the world as soon as the war ends."

His eyes remained focused on his porridge, but when he raised them to answer I could see he was smiling.

"You have great ambitions, Jaqueline. May I ask how you spent your spare time at home?"

"I went dancing with friends, or skating at the ice rink and, of course, swimming; and there's always a good selection of shows to see; Gilbert and Sullivan at the Kings Theatre is my favourite."

"What about the cinema?" he asked.

"Yes, I enjoy all the Hollywood musicals," I replied happily.

There was silence while the empty plates were passed and I stacked them on the trolley, and then he began again.

"What do you think of Sean?" Mr William concentrated on his bacon and eggs as he spoke.

"He's a little immature, and he has no conversation," was all I could say.

"Being a bit hard on him, are you not?" he answered, glancing at me.

Then Miss June's voice broke into the conversation:

"Being a country boy he doesn't have the stimulus of city life, and I think he is shy; but he is very clever!"

Mr William passed his cup for tea, and a grin spread across his face as he helped himself to toast.

"I can see, Jaqueline, nothing less than a prince on a white charger will do!"

I had to think for a moment to grasp his meaning, then I grinned back, and answered,

"No, a prince on a black charger will be good enough!"

Chapter Fifteen

When Miss Gillian returned from her brother's farm she was full of the news of the new baby girl, and the happiness of her sister-in-law at having given birth to a daughter; her face had lost its greyness and her eyes had the lustre of happiness that glowed from within. However, the transformation was short lived and she soon returned to her moody, drab self.

The sister-in-law's two boys were already in their teens and she had almost given up hope of ever producing a daughter; some of her happiness had definitely rubbed-off on Miss Gillian for a short time.

The breakfast conversations changed to what they had been and it was only a couple of days before I was again Miss Gillian's pet hate. Mother, once more, dominated the scene at the midday meal. It had been impossible, with the return of Miss Gillian, to keep her in bed any longer.

When I took my seat at the dinner table, Mother had already been installed and Mr William was wrapping a rug round her legs.

"And I will be heard!" she was saying, "the doctor is a fool, if I were to listen to him I would become bed-bound through lack of exercise, and I need the mental stimulus of conversation with the family!"

Nothing was ever forgotten, because it had to be repeated until Mother was satisfied that she had missed nothing of the conversation.

"Now, tell me again, Gillian, I want to know all about my granddaughter. You say she is fair, so she has taken after father's side of the family; and her eyes are blue, but all babies have blue eyes. They could change colour in a few weeks."

Mother's mind was as alert as it ever had been, and in fact, the stay in bed and no second helpings had done her a lot of good.

"You did say, Gillian, her weight at birth was almost ten pounds?" Miss Gillian grunted and Mother talked on. "Well, I would have expected that, really, because the boys were over nine pounds when they were born. What did you say her exact weight was?

"Nine pounds fifteen ounces, Mother," Miss Gillian said gruffly.

But Mother had not heard her clearly.

"Nine pounds fifteen ounces, Mother," bellowed Mr William.

And I suddenly realised I had been missing the liveliness that Mother's presence created.

Miss Gillian had never been a conversationalist, and any information had to be extracted from her by a series of questions as her eyes roved over the banquets Miss June produced.

"When will the family be visiting? They must know that I can't wait to see my granddaughter. Pass the salt, William!"

"Another potato, Mother?" The potato hovered on the serving spoon as Miss Gillian waited for her reply.

"Yes, I really think I must eat a little more, my clothes are quite hanging on me since the fever." Mother had a delicacy about her manners, when eating food, that belied the amount she consumed.

"A little more meat, Mother?" Mr William lifted a generous slice as he spoke.

"Just a morsel, William." And the slice was placed on her plate.

"Getting back to the family, Mother! There's too much to be done at this time of year, so we will all have to wait, and the baby is too small to travel."

Mr William's voice, which had become quite normal while Mother was absent from the dining-room table, sounded unnecessarily loud; while Miss June and I, once more, seemed to be whispering.

When the sweet arrived it was Mother's favourite and I found myself scraping the last crumb from the dish. I could see how easy it was to become addicted to second helpings.

"I think I must go to bed and rest, Gillian." Mother had yielded to a second helping of Queen of Puddings.

Trays in bed from Miss June must have been like semi-starvation over the past week or so, and from her obvious discomfort I could see Mother was paying the price of over-indulgence. She leaned heavily on Miss Gillian's arm on her way out of the dining-room.

"I didn't realise how weak I still am," she complained, "it's such a relief to have you home again, Gillian."

Chapter Sixteen

The dawn sky was grey and light rain dampened our clothes as we set off for the high field with the loaded barrow.

"Did you know, Sean, that Miss June is organising a canteen for the Polish officers who are to stay in the village?" I queried, "and I'm going to help on Tuesdays."

"My mother wouldn't let my sister help in a canteen," he answered.

"Why not?" I asked, feeling puzzled.

"Because they're foreigners!"

"Foreigners they may be, but they are our allies!"

He looked straight ahead and made no answer, so I probed.

"These officers are only men caught up in war as we are. How would you feel if you were in a foreign country? Wouldn't you like the people to take an interest in you?"

As we approached the first hen house there was still no answer, and I thought: Oh! it's going to be another one of those days.

"Why don't you answer?" I asked.

Silently he selected a key from the bunch he carried, turned it in the lock and pushed open the hen house door.

I stared in horror at the grizzly scene that met our eyes. Dead hens littered the floor, and there was blood and feathers everywhere. The few remaining birds that had survived whatever attacked them were huddled in a corner terrified and bleeding.

"It looks like the work of a badger," said Sean, kneeling to examine the ripped-up floorboards.

"How can you tell?" I asked from the doorway.

"Look at the claw marks; he must be a big fellow to rip out the nesting boxes the way he has."

I picked my way through the dead hens and broken eggs to the surviving birds.

"What can we do for this poor creature?" I asked, picking up a maimed bird.

"Put it outside," he said, still examining the claw marks, and almost muttering to himself, "Mr William is not going to be happy about this."

I carried the hen out to the grass and as I laid it down the third eyelid moved across its undamaged eye, then it stretched its wings and lay still.

"I'll check the other houses," Sean called, "you go and tell Mr William!"

I hurried off down the avenue and caught Mr William just as he was entering the side door with a basket of fresh vegetables.

"Mr William!" I ran towards him. "Mr William!"

"Hello, Jaqueline, what's the panic?"

"A hen house in the upper field has been raided!" I said urgently.

"Just a minute, June's waiting for these."

He hurried in the side door, and as I turned towards the avenue of aspens he dashed out again.

"How bad is it?" he asked, striding up the avenue in his wellington boots.

"There are only six or seven alive and they look in a poor state," I answered, trotting beside him. "Sean says it's the work of a badger digging in and coming up through the floorboards."

"Badgers haven't been seen in these parts for years! How can he be sure it's not foxes?"

"Claw marks," was all I could gasp.

When we reached the high field Sean had already put all the dead birds out on the grass and Mr William stopped and stared.

"I'm not happy about this, not happy at all," he muttered.

Then he looked at the mess of blood, feathers and broken eggs on the hen house floor.

"Pass out the live birds, Sean, and I'll take the ones we can save to the lower field where I can keep an eye on them."

Only four hens went with him to the lower field; the others were quickly put out of their misery with a sharp tug, and laid out on the grass.

"Food," I kept saying to myself, "they are only food!"

Before Mr William left I started throwing sand across the floor and brushing it with the hard brush.

"Put the dead birds into sacks, Sean, and the pigman can collect them. We need nails and a hammer to put back the nesting boxes and the floorboards. Use plenty of sand, Jaqueline."

When they had gone I began to see what Mr William had meant by food for the badger or the fox; but this had not been a meal, it was a massacre.

I was setting the nesting boxes back in place when Sean arrived with a box of tools.

"What will be done to prevent this happening again, Sean?"

"Set traps, because you never can find them during the day."

His answer had come without hesitation as he hammered in a few nails to secure the nesting boxes, and then he turned his attention to the floorboards.

When the job was done we looked proudly round the now empty, spotlessly clean hen house. Suddenly Sean leapt up, caught a cross beam and did several pull-ups.

"Bet you can't do that!" and smiling at me pleasantly as he spoke, I had the feeling of being caught off guard.

"I could," I said rashly, "if I were as tall as you are." But I was not to get out of it so easily.

"Take off your wellington boots and I'll give you a leg up."

I stepped out of my thick-soled, rubber boots aware of some sixth sense telling me not to, and placing a woolly-hosed foot on his clasped hands I was hoisted into the air.

I grasped the beam and was hanging there, pulling hard with little effect, when I realised Sean had gone. In his place, framed in the doorway and wearing blue sweater and jodhpurs, stood Miss Gillian.

"Have you nothing better to do with your time?" Her voice was even more hoarse than usual and she turned away with an outraged expression on her face. My heart sank to my woolly socks and I dropped to the floor.

Instead of two eggs, one rasher of bacon and a few spoonfuls of sugar to sustain me over the weekend, Miss Gillian handed me a single unwrapped egg, as I left to catch the one o'clock bus on Saturday. Holding it in my gloved hand I walked down the drive wondering where to put it, and all the way home in the bus, each time I looked at the egg sitting in the palm of my hand, I thought how childish and silly fully-grown adults could be.

On Monday morning at the breakfast table I heard about the second raid by the badger, this time in the lower field.

"He's come over the hill and is making his way down to the valley. We can't leave it another day. He must be a big fellow to split the floorboards the way he does, and there are signs of foxes stealing hens. I think the lair will be up in the area of the reservoir." Mr William had lost his appetite and left before bacon and eggs could be served.

I was feeling hungry after what had seemed like fasting over the weekend. A feeling of guilt would engulf me, while at home, if my mother gave me any of their weekly rations. Never a crumb was left from the humble portion of cheese per person, or a scraping in the dish from their two ounces of butter. The weekly ration of one egg per person was kept for Sunday breakfast.

My twenty-three inch waist had thickened since accepting the post at Burnsyde, and yet the family complained that I hardly ate anything at all.

At home, my mother spent every moment she could spare doting on the chicks Miss June had given me. They scampered around on fresh newspapers in the bottom of the airing cupboard below the hot water tank. Meanwhile, out in the garden, my father sawed and hammered and a neat hen house was taking shape.

My mind was so full of the events at home over the weekend that I failed to hear Miss June's soft voice as she addressed me:

"Jaqueline, more toast?"

"No, thank you, Miss June. Sorry I didn't hear you the first time. I was thinking about my mother and the chicks."

"Has she had any fatalities?" she asked.

"No, and it's most unlikely! Two of the chicks have had brandy administered to them from an eye dropper. I don't think they would get the chance to die even if they wanted to."

She laughed with delight, but across the table Miss Gillian munched and brooded. Mr William, having reconsidered his hasty exit without bacon and eggs, had returned to fortify himself against the busy morning that lay ahead.

"Never a sign of disturbance or breakages, that's what mystifies me about the rats. How do they take the eggs out of the incubator house?" He set a heaped plate in front of him and stared at it.

"I'll get the men in to put down poison. Jaqueline, I want you to go with Sean this morning, he's setting traps from the lower field to as far up as the reservoir. Don't go any further, or you'll be trespassing."

He started to cut into the bacon on his plate, looking thoughtful, but he stopped, and said,

"Six or eight traps should be sufficient, and tell Sean I want a word with him before he sets out."

"Yes, Mr William," I answered, rising from the table before I was tempted by Miss June to over-indulge.

When I walked into the back kitchen to put my boots on, Sean was there lifting traps from a narrow cupboard behind the back door.

"Hello, Sean."

"Hello, to you too, are you coming with me this morning?"

"Yes, and Mr William wants a word with you before we go."

"That's why I'm here," he said, turning his back on me in his lofty way.

I was still smarting from Miss Gillian's displeasure at finding me hanging from the beam and now, Sean's rude gesture of turning away provoked me.

"You knew Miss Gillian would arrive while I was dangling from the beam on Friday, didn't you, Sean?" He made no answer. I folded my dungarees neatly round the ankles and belted on my leggings. "That's a real mean streak you've got, don't you agree, Sean?"

I could hear Mr William making his way towards the back kitchen.

"Jaqueline," he called, "have you told Sean I want a word with him?"

"Yes, Mr William, he's here."

He strode into the back kitchen, grabbed a pair of boots and pushed his feet into them, discarding one of his slippers in the middle of the floor and the other by the door. While he tied his laces, I picked up the slippers and placed them against the wall.

"It's the way I've been raised," I said, when he grinned at my automatic action.

"You've been picking up slang from too many westerns, Jaqueline." And he laughed as he turned to Sean. "Good, Sean. I see you're taking eight traps."

Sean's face was inscrutable and he leaned on the door post with the traps slung over his shoulder, but I could sense anger in him.

"Did I leave the keys in the door of the incubator house when we checked the eggs?" asked Mr William, patting the pockets of his jacket.

"You did, Mr William," and Sean held out the keys.

"Still can't see how they take the eggs during the night, and the door was locked this morning. As it always is." Mr William frowned as he continued, "I had better get the pest control people here as soon as possible. Right, Sean! It's a perfect day for setting traps, give Jaqueline a bit of instruction as you go along." He smiled. "And see if you can find the lair of the foxes, they may have young."

Chapter Seventeen

The fine sky was azure blue with not a wisp of cloud in sight. We had reached the end of the avenue and started on the long trek up to the reservoir, when I noticed a small, whiskery face peeping from the pocket of Sean's leather jacket.

"You've got an animal in your pocket," I said in surprise.

"It's my ferret," he replied, "it can give you a bad bite, so don't touch it."

The ferret's small face popped in and out of Sean's jacket pocket as we trekked up over the hill. We had almost reached the reservoir when he stopped and laid the traps on the grass.

"Sit on that stone for a few minutes and I'll show you how to catch a rabbit."

After examining several rabbit holes, he took some nets from a small bag he had been carrying and placed them over the holes securing each with pegs. Whistling softly, he took the ferret out of his pocket and gently stroking it put it down one of the holes.

It was just as if I didn't exist while he waited; then he lunged at one of the nets taking hold of the frightened rabbit that had rushed into it.

"What are you going to do with it?" I asked apprehensively.

He made no reply; just took the rabbit out of the net and brought the heel of his hand down on the back of its neck. There was no more struggling, when he placed it on the grass it was quite still.

It had all happened so naturally, there was barely time to realise that what had been alive was now dead within seconds of being caught. Nothing around me had changed; the whisper of a zephyr still played across the grass and the sky remained clear blue. Mother Nature had not wept for the rabbit, and as soon as it was lifeless the apprehension I had been feeling left me.

"What about the ferret?" I asked.

"She'll be here," he answered, picking up the nets and giving a low, soft whistle.

The ferret's head popped out of the hole where the rabbit had been trapped, and with a quick movement of his hand Sean lifted it and put it back into the pocket of his leather jacket.

The air was crystal clear and it was soon apparent, as we scouted round the area, that the foxes lived in these tranquil surroundings. Behind a bush, sitting at the entrance of a fox hole, we found two fluffy grey fox cubs; they rose and made towards us on unsteady legs.

"I don't think they can see properly yet," I said, stooping to lift one as its legs splayed out and it rested on its tummy. But Sean's hand shot out and gripped my arm.

"Don't touch them," he warned, "the vixen will desert her cubs if they smell of humans."

We sat down on the low stone dyke that edged the length of the reservoir.

"It's late in the year to find such young cubs," Sean remarked, gazing into the water thoughtfully. Then he turned and pointed, "We can set a trap over there where the trail narrows between these thick bushes, and another in the scrub below the dyke where the faint trail suggests a watering place."

He sat silent for a while just gazing into the depths of the still, clear water.

"What kind of fish are these?" I asked.

"Carp."

"Can you eat them?"

"*I* wouldn't," he replied bluntly, and started to speak on the subject of fish. "In the river that runs through Avonlea Estate there's salmon. They're much better than these."

"Do you go fishing then?" I prompted, to prevent another long silence.

"No, we go poaching."

"But that's stealing."

"We don't get caught! We've done it since we were old enough to walk."

A hint of boastfulness had crept into Sean's voice and after a short pause he picked up a handful of pebbles.

"The gillie can't be everywhere." With a flick of his wrist each pebble skimmed across the mirror-like surface of the water. "And we usually know where he will be at any given time," he added.

Sean finished setting the traps at selected points of the fox trail, but the idea of the ruthless metal traps worried me.

"I don't like this method at all," I complained.

"It's the only method," he replied.

"And what happens to the cubs if we catch the mother?"

"I would come back and put them to sleep, naturally. It would be cruel to let them die of hunger."

The catching of animals in gin-traps was barbaric to me.

"Isn't there an alternative to this cruelty?" I asked.

"Can you think of another way?" Sean waited for my answer, but I was forced to admit he was right; there was no other way.

On the trek down to the lower field we picked up the remaining four traps from where Sean had left them.

"I check the traps last thing at night and then again at four or five in the morning. Mr William keeps a check during the day; so, between us, we do our best to avoid any unnecessary suffering." He sounded so matter-of-fact.

"I still don't like the thought of killing animals," I murmured.

"But you eat bacon for breakfast, and you have lamb and beef for dinner. You city people are all alike, as long as it's prepared and put in the butcher's window." Sean's voice was full of scorn.

I was reduced to silence and felt ashamed, because I knew he spoke the truth. Did city people close their minds to it?

"Now, let's consider the mind of the animal kingdom. They kill to survive as nature intended. Probably the badger caused a panic in the confined space of the hen house and everything was slaughtered," said Sean shrewdly.

Under the giant copper beech amongst the leaves we finished setting the last trap; the truth was hard to take and I remained silent. Someone had to do the dirty work, I reasoned.

"When we close the hen houses tonight we can make the rounds of the traps," Sean suggested, "but I think it will be morning before anything is caught, or it could be days."

Sean came back to Burnsyde after I had finished supper, and with Mr William's point-two-two rifle resting on his shoulder we set out to check the traps and close the hen house doors.

The hens went into their houses just as daylight was beginning to fade, which meant we could be chasing them in at ten o'clock during the long, light nights of summer.

It was getting dark as we made our way back to the yard having checked every trap and closed every hen house door.

"Do you think there will be many rats in the barn, Sean?"

"Difficult to say," he said, smiling down at me, "probably a few hundred."

I could feel the hair rising at the back of my neck thinking of such a horde, so I shrugged and answered,

"I never see more than six at any one time." And I winced at the thought of them crossing the rafters above me in the barn.

"They stay in hiding when anyone is about, it's quite likely they will be on the move now. We could go round to the back of the egg house, if you like, and watch for a while through the window."

The warmer was on under the racks of eggs being prepared for the incubator and in its faint glow we could see well enough to make out any signs of movement. We waited and watched seeing more detail as our eyes grew accustomed to the gloom.

"What will you do when you're called-up for the forces?" I whispered as we peered through the window.

"I'm not waiting to be called-up, I'll enlist in the air force as soon as I'm old enough," came the whispered reply. "I'm going to be a pilot!"

I felt a twinge of envy, as it was something I would never be able to do because I had been born a woman.

"That will take a few years of training," I said, resigning my envious mind to the role of the interested, or submissive woman.

"Depends on the person. I'm an air force cadet, and I was top in mathematics at the academy. I stand a good chance of being accepted for training," he replied. The arrogance that irritated me was there in his whispering voice.

I stole a glance at his firm jawline and the straight nose silhouetted against the dark sky; he seemed so determined and remote.

There was a faint movement in the gap under the door that led into the barn and our whispering stopped. One greyish rat had appeared closely followed by a shadowy companion; they scurried across to the egg racks as a third made its entrance. What followed would have done credit to any skilled juggler.

Having climbed the rack, the first two rats eased out an egg from the hole it rested in and rolled it to the edge; then the third rat positioned itself directly below the egg, rolling over on to its back. From a height of approximately twenty inches, the egg was dropped on to the feet of the rat who waited motionless on the floor below.

As I watched, my interest grew to admiration. The two rats scrambled down from the rack towards their friend and the egg was lowered gently to the floor, then they rolled it along until it vanished under the door leading to the barn.

We watched, fascinated, all conversation forgotten as the performance was repeated again and again.

"It's getting late," Sean whispered, "and now we know how it's done!"

"I'll leave you to explain what happened in the incubator house tonight, they won't believe me," I said, and turned away.

We walked to the top of the drive where Sean mounted his bike, then he raced down the steep slope,

"I hope your brakes are good," I called.

"They are," he shouted back, slithering to a halt by the entrance gates; then with a wave of his hand he moved into the dense greenery that screened the road from view.

I suddenly felt lonely for all my young friends and turned towards the house. Right at that moment my friends would be queuing for the theatre, or meeting at the coffee shop in Princes Street, while the music drifted up from the bandstand in the gardens below the castle; and, of course, many would be away in the services and their thoughts would be the same as mine.

I sometimes wished I could be back in the business world with my studies and enjoying the social life of the city; but it was too late for regrets.

I had just put my foot on the first step at the main door when it opened and Belle came charging out, Mr William following pulling hard on her lead.

"Has Sean left, Jaqueline?"

"Yes, Mr William, and we checked all the traps when we were locking up."

"Good," he replied as the dog pulled him down the steps.

"Stay, Belle, stay," he said sharply, tugging her to a halt. "The dog will have to be kept on a lead until the traps are lifted, so don't leave any of the house doors open, Jaqueline, close them every time you go out, especially the side door. Gillian and I will check the traps tomorrow night while we are locking up. Goodnight, Jaqueline."

"Goodnight, Mr William," I answered, closing the door behind me.

Chapter Eighteen

The following day Mr William laughed as he listened to Sean.

"Pull my other leg, it's got bells on!" he said.

Sean looked at Mr William stoically, then turned and led the way to the incubator house.

As it was Mr William who locked the door each night, the evidence was there for all to see when he unlocked the door and pushed it open.   A distinct trail in the fine meal that had settled over the floor could be seen running under the door leading to the barn.

"Well! What you have told me is possible, Sean; rats are pretty clever. We had better get that concrete broken up and re-lay it to close the gap below the door."

Although his face remained impassive, the triumph in Sean's eyes was that of the sage looking down on lesser mortals; I had to resist the urge to smile as he glanced at me casually.

On that same day, the pest control men arrived to put down poison for the rats. Mr William, having satisfied himself that enough poison had been used, watched while the men placed several bowls of water on the floor of the barn. The windows were checked, leaving some open, and the doors were locked for the night.

The following morning I stepped through the side door to find a heap of dead rats in the centre of the yard; they lay in all sorts of positions and every now and then a few more would fly out of the barn windows. Sean appeared from the barn carrying a half dozen by their tails, glancing at me he threw the dead rats on to the mound.

"Three hundred up to the present! Want to lend a hand collecting them?" he asked.

"No! I'm busy on the brooders this morning," I answered, hurrying away from the musty smell and the unthinkable idea of touching dead rats.

Quickly I made my way towards the fresh green fragrance of the lower field, and shuddered at the thought of how many rats had been watching me from their hiding places, and yet, I had only seen a few at any one time; but it was enough to make me stay near to the barn door for a quick escape.

The roofs on the low brooders slid along allowing easy access to the chicks. It was pleasant and sunny and I sang to myself as I fussed over the fluffy bundles. In a week or so they would be quite different to the balls of fluff that cheeped in alarm when I pushed along each roof to clean the floors and check the lamps.

I could smell paraffin fumes as I approached brooder six, and when I pushed along the roof the fumes engulfed me. The lamp had gone out during the night and fifty little chicks lay dead from the cold, or the fumes that had risen from the lamp when the flame died. I couldn't help wondering how a fat pair of broody hens would have done the job.

Gently I placed the last of the dead chicks on a sack, then a long, yelping howl rent the air. I ran towards the sound coming from under the giant copper beach at the top of the drive, feeling terrified of what I would find there; it was where we had set the last trap.

Lying on the leaves, that concealed the trap, with its leg cruelly gripped between the teeth was Belle, the large golden labrador belonging to Mr William. I knew I couldn't open the heavy, rusted trap; it had taken Sean more than one try when he set it; so I raced to the back door of the house and called Mr William.

"Who the hell left the main door open!" he roared, and we ran to the beech. "Couldn't you have opened the trap? The longer it's on her leg the more damage will be done!"

"No, it's too stiff!" gasped my panting voice, "and I've never opened one before."

He reached up and wrenched off a length of branch, then placed his heavy boot on the opening mechanism of the trap; slowly it opened and the dog wailed, he applied more pressure and the cruel teeth withdrew from the wounded leg. Mr William pushed the branch between the teeth, and I knelt and lifted the dog's leg from the jaws of the vicious trap.

While the dog lay quite still, its eyes full of pain, Mr William examined the leg.

"Must get her down to the vet; keep an eye on her till I bring the car round, Jaqueline!"

"Yes, Mr William," I answered as he hurried away.

Two days were to pass before the other traps yielded a handsome male badger and the female fox. A lump rose in my throat when my eyes came to rest on the two plump cubs lying beside their mother, their soft furry greyness touching the vivid coat of the red fox.

I lifted my eyes to the top of the hill where the hazy mist drifted, and I thought of the words uttered by the rugged pigman, and the way his soft rolling Rs made a grand day seem much more grand.

Then I became aware of Mr William's voice saying,

"That's enough, lift the rest of the traps." He had become sickened by the sight of death in his yard. "Take the point-two-two with you, Sean, you might need it, and take Jaqueline along."

There was not the slightest whisper of a breeze when we set off up the avenue, and yet the rounded leaves of the aspens trembled and whirled like coins spun on their edge.

"Do you have a boyfriend?" Sean's question came in his usual abrupt way.

"Plenty of boyfriends and girlfriends," I replied.

"I mean, have you a special one?"

"No, I haven't come across anyone special."

I pushed my hands into the pockets of my drill cloth coat eager to hear his next question.

"Has any boy been in love with you?" His eyes were on his feet but he was digging deeper, so I said in a casual tone,

"Do you mean like Andrew White, just before I left school at sixteen?"

"What was he like?" Sean asked, suddenly looking intently at my face.

"Oh! he was all smiles, muscles, and chasing after most of the girls in class."

There was a silence, and again, I waited.

"Would you have married him if he had asked you?"

"He did, and I said no."

"Why?" He had slowed his step and was waiting for my reply.

It was difficult to put into words the yearning I had to do things I dreamed of. My mother had said, 'do something with your life', and the money from her dressmaking had started me off at business school. My father had been against it; in his opinion, educating a woman was money wasted.

I was so deep in thought I had forgotten Sean, until he touched my arm.

"Why?" he repeated, and I answered,

"I couldn't see myself standing at the kitchen sink washing Andrew White's dirty socks for the rest of my life! And that's about all there is to marriage, so I went to business school."

"You might not be asked a second time."

"Should I be worried?" I asked lightly.

Provocation was one of his main weapons against my straightforward thinking and having put it as plainly as I could I refused to be drawn further on the subject.

"Can you use a rifle?" he asked.

"No, I can't."

Then I hurried my steps towards the reservoir to lift the traps before any more animals could be caught. Without warning a tin-can spun on the low dyke of the reservoir and toppled back into the water. I turned quickly to find Sean still looking through the sights of Mr William's gun. His shot had passed me too close for comfort.

"I'm a good shot," he said on seeing my startled expression.

I had to spend the rest of the day with Sean; he looked so pleased with himself, that I had to check the impulse to do the same as he had done with the tin-can. He would be easier to get along with, I decided, if he remained ignorant of the way I handled my brother's air rifle.

Chapter Nineteen

And so it was Wednesday morning already. Monday and Tuesday seemed to have flown past. The misery of traps and dead animals had been forgotten, or put out of my mind, as I hurried to the back kitchen.

What Sean thought of cup-of-tea-time no longer bothered me. I looked forward to ten o'clock, a chat with Miss June and tea. She had been baking this morning and the smell of fresh cakes and scones filled the kitchen.

"It all smells delicious!" I remarked, "but how do you manage to do so well with the sugar ration?"

"There are always people who take sweets for their children instead of sugar, so we take sugar instead of sweets; it balances out and the grocer doesn't mind," explained Miss June.

My eyes wandered over the crisp shortbread and freshly baked scones, and a gorgeous jam and cream sponge.

"Jaqueline, the minister is coming to tea this afternoon, would you like to join us?"

"Oh! yes, I certainly would," I replied, still entranced by the light, fluffy sponge drenched in icing sugar, the jam and fresh cream oozing from its centre.

"Then come in just before the afternoon tea break and change, Mother would never approve of working clothes when the minister comes to tea, and, after all, your sugar ration goes into the making of all these nice things just as ours do."

At 3.15 p.m. the minister arrived, and as he was a very special visitor the table had been laid with extra care. A cream-coloured, lace cloth draped its fragile patterns almost to the floor, and the silver glowed softly among the delectable goodies Miss June had created.

The visitor was a tall, gaunt man in his forties, dressed in black from hat to shoes; the only relief in his sombre dress was the white ministerial collar below his greyish complexion. At the tea-table I was seated directly opposite him, and Miss Gillian now sat on my left facing Mother.

The minister's presence pervaded the room with an unaccustomed air of sadness and, while Miss June poured tea, Mother spoke with a hint of melancholy in her voice,

"He was a very fine man and I do miss him these past eight years." She touched her hair delicately and smoothed the sleeves of her pearl grey silk dress.

Her hearing was good today, or perhaps it was the unusual quietness in the room.

"A very fine man indeed," agreed the minister in reverential tones, "one never ceases to grieve over the dear departed."

I was beginning to feel sad watching their faces, until Miss June touched my arm and offered me a large slice of fresh cream sponge; she had merely smiled and lifted my plate, then set the large helping in front of me.

The minister reminded me of something that had stepped out from amongst tomb stones in the dead of night in a horror film. I tore my gaze away from his red-rimmed eyes, lifted my fork and pushed it into the beautiful mixture on my plate. Just as it entered my open mouth the morsel of delicacy froze and the voice of the guest began:

"For what we are about to receive may the Lord make us truly thankful." His eyes were closed and directed at the ceiling.

I sat perfectly still with my mouth full and my eyes lowered until he had finished; but when I looked up his sad, dark eyes were looking disapprovingly at the fork I still held in my hand.

"*Parlez vous Francais, Mademoiselle?*" he said gravely.

I swallowed and answered,

"*Oui, Monsieur.*"

A delicate pink suffused the flower-like complexion of Miss June and she broke into the conversation,

"*Est-ce-que vous comprenez la Francais, Jaqueline?*"

"*Oui, Mademoiselle June. Je parle un peu!*"

Mother raised her eyes from the scone Mr William was coaxing her to have and said,

"William! What are they saying, tell me what they are saying!" Then voices rose as everyone spoke at once. "Where is my horn? Give it to me, William!" and Mother applied the listening horn to her ear.

"They were speaking in French, Mother," bellowed Mr William.

"Oh! how tiresome, why can't they speak in English," Mother complained.

She then proceeded to command the attention of the guest, and the discourse that followed was entirely devoted to her late husband. But the false sympathy had faded away with Mr William's desire to please his mother.

I delved into the feather-light jam and cream sponge, while Miss June, who was usually very quiet at the table, continued to speak in her soft voice,

"Miss Gillian and I attended boarding school in Edinburgh, we know the city well. I went from school to Athol Crescent to specialise in cooking. Miss Gillian has always preferred helping to run the farm, since father died, and is an excellent horsewoman."

Mother had become bored with the guest and her eyes were investigating her next indulgence on the tea-table. It was while she surveyed the scones and shortbread that I found myself being addressed by the minister again. He bowed his head slightly and fixed me with a red-rimmed eye.

"I haven't had the pleasure of being introduced to this young member of the family."

For a face that felt it was not its duty to smile, I could detect a softening in his features and his voice had become full of charm.

"Oh!" laughed Mr William, "Jaqueline is our land-girl!"

I felt the sudden change instantly; he withdrew his charm and while tea lasted he sniffed every time he looked at me as if I were a bad smell.

"More tea, Jaqueline?" Miss June smiled and filled my cup without waiting for an answer.

I had been aware of Miss Gillian, who sat on my left today, glaring down on me and the thought crossed my mind that she and the minister were strangely akin to one another. They were both in their forties, and neither radiated warmth nor pleasure.

For some unknown reason I felt delight bubbling up inside me and I had to repress the smile that must have been dancing in my eyes. When I glanced at Mr William his dark eyes twinkled and he turned his handsome, slightly plump face to Mother.

"Let me help you, Mother," he said, passing the honey pot.

"I can do it perfectly well myself," she answered, spooning the golden honey from the pot. "I do think crumpets are quite insipid without a good helping of honey poured over them. Do have a crumpet and honey, Reverend. I can recommend any of June's culinary accomplishments. And it is a blessing to have our own bees."

On the Thursday of that week, after a silent morning cleaning brooders with Sean, I had to stifle my amazement.

"My mother and sister would like you to come to supper tonight," he said.

The invitation had come like a bolt from the blue and I replied without even thinking,

"Thank you."

Miss June looked pleased when I told her, and answered,

"So we will be one less for supper this evening. Enjoy your night out, Jaqueline."

As the impact of the unexpected invitation began to wear off I found I was looking forward to meeting new faces, for up to the present the only villager I knew was Sean. He waited after we had finished work that evening until I had cleaned up and changed from my working clothes; then I gathered up the skirt of my dress, perched myself on the back step of his bicycle and we sped along to the far side of the village where he lived.

Sean was still unsure of me, and on entering his comfortable, well-furnished, scrupulously clean house I found myself being scrutinised by his equally suspicious mother and sister. At nine thirty, after what had become a very pleasant evening of supper and card games, I accepted their kind invitation to come again.

I waved to the mother and sister from the back step of Sean's bike as we wobbled along the narrow garden path towards the road. Then silently we moved through the darkening village along the winding road that led to Burnsyde.

"You didn't tell me your mother was a widow, Sean."

"No, why should I?"

We reached the short, steep hill he had raced down on the way in and I offered to get off and walk up.

"You'll stay right where you are," was his answer as he puffed and rose off the saddle to take the strain. We were wobbling dangerously and I smiled as we just made it to the top.

Once over the hill it was a winding run alongside the river and the dark fir plantation on the other side of the quiet, narrow road.

"Who owns those fir trees, Sean?"

"That's part of the Avonlea Estate. We passed the entrance gates about three quarters of a mile back. It's been commandeered by the government to house evacuees for the duration of the war. The grounds of Burnsyde end on this side of the road and on the other side it's Avonlea."

I was silenced by surprise at the interesting and lengthy piece of information that Sean had supplied, for up to the present I had known nothing about the area outside Burnsyde.

We turned in at the gates and I stepped down from his bike.

"Thank you, and goodnight, Sean," I said, "see you in the morning."

"I'll walk you up the drive, "he replied.

"You don't have to."

"I will though," he insisted.

We walked up to the house in complete silence, and he waited while I rang the door bell; then mounting his bike Sean shot off down the drive.

It could only have been a few seconds that I stood alone in the darkness, but suddenly I felt fear, and as the hair rose on the back of my neck I gripped the wrought-iron handle and tugged until the bell echoed through the house.

Then I was inside the hall and as I hurried up to my room Mr William slid along the bolts on the double, oak doors.

How foolish I was being over a few seconds alone in the darkness outside the closed doors of Burnsyde, but some sixth sense had warned me I had not been alone.

Chapter Twenty

"Oh! They're here, Jaqueline," Miss June called, pulling on her kid gloves as she entered the hall. She looked unusually attractive in her dark green, serge suit, the uniform of the Women's Voluntary Services, and the matching hat sat on her snow white, curly hair to perfection.

The car horn honked as we opened the main door and made our way down the steps.

"So this is Jaqueline," said the lady in the driving seat. "We really are delighted to have your help in the canteen." We smiled and shook hands through the open window before I stepped into her car.

I was introduced to a second lady as we moved off down the drive, and she chatted happily.

"It's so nice to have someone young and pretty, I just wish we could get a few more to help. The men will be with us for just a few weeks at the most. However, we'll manage! I don't suppose you can blame the people of the village for being so protective towards their daughters."

The canteen had been set up in an old church hall in the village centre; we walked in to find it furnished with card tables, chairs, a few settees and an ancient grand piano. Looking round the drab surroundings, I wished it could have been nicer, but I busied myself spreading bread for sandwiches and grilling bacon.

The officers began to arrive in groups of three or four, and soon they were crowding round the counter whisking away cups of steaming coffee as fast as it could be poured. They bowed and clicked their heels as we served them, and by nine o'clock the old village hall was alive with the sound of violins.

Our ancient, yellowed piano rang like a concert grand, and as soon as one officer left it another would take his place.

Groups of them lingered at the counter talking and answering us in perfect English. When we had a few minutes to breathe, Miss June passed me a cup of coffee.

"I love the atmosphere and the fairy tale manners," she said, "and there is no language barrier at all." Her face glowed with pleasure. "I thought we were going to have difficulty entertaining them, but we don't even have to try, it is they who are entertaining us."

"May I ask how you play this game, Madam?"

We stopped in the middle of coffee and conversation to help in any way we could, and the tall, young man who had addressed himself to Miss June clicked his heels and placed the ludo board on the counter. Miss June lifted the dice and dropped it into the cup.

"First, you must throw a six to start," she said, throwing a two. "Now I pass the dice to Jaqueline."

I threw a four and passed the dice to the smiling officer. Immediately, I had the feeling that he knew how to play. He shook the cup and turned out a six, while Miss June flushed with pleasure.

"Now you can start!" she said, placing one of the coloured counters, that had been set out on the board, in the first red box. He threw again and Miss June told him to move four places.

Several young officers had gathered round and we invited one to make up the four players. They laughed and shouted out the numbers against the background of music and the murmur of voices conversing in their own language.

Each time I looked up from the board I met a row of smiling eyes and I knew they were taking advantage of Miss June's eagerness to help. At the same time, I wondered why she had never married, because even at her age, she was a very beautiful woman.

The outside door opened and closed, and when the black-out curtain parted the men lounging by the counter came to attention, saluted, bowed and clicked their heels. Then they turned back to the ludo board as if nothing had happened.

But my eyes were on the man who had caused the interruption; he stood for a moment in the background, and then said,

"Beware of these ardent young men," he paused, "they seduce you with their eyes."

The foreign accent was thick, but the English perfect; he pushed his way to the counter. Miss June had already lifted the board and was directing them all to a table, while I poured a cup of coffee for the stranger.

"They live for today," he continued, as he looked into Miss June's startled, blue eyes, "because, for them, tomorrow may not come."

Miss June had gone quite pale as she listened and stood as though hypnotised, while the stranger continued,

"I am their commanding officer and must carry the responsibility for their behaviour while we are your guests."

He finished on a soft, low key; then he reached for Miss June's hand and lifted it to his lips as if it was the most natural thing in the world to do. She turned away and the roses burned in her cheeks; he released her hand slowly and at once she started to wash dishes. Miss June's acute shyness was distressing to watch.

I felt grateful for his dramatic warning, but I also felt we would be in more danger from him as he lifted his coffee mug and carried it to a table.

"It gets hot behind the counter, Miss June," I said, lifting a tea towel to dry the dishes, "I'm glad I put on a dress, I doubt if I could wear a uniform."

"I don't want you to wear your uniform, Jaqueline, a dress is much prettier!"

I had hardly been aware of time as the evening flew past.

"No, you stay behind the counter," insisted the ladies and they passed the dishes from the tables for me to wash.

At ten thirty I was bundled into my coat and almost pulled out of the canteen as Miss June made for the bus. It sat for a few minutes at the kerb before moving off and I turned in my seat to look at the doorway I had just come through, leaving so much music, laughter and conversation behind.

"We will be picked up every Tuesday at the same time, Jaqueline, but I'm afraid we have to make our own way home and the bus leaves at ten thirty. Time went by so quickly, I must apologise for almost dragging you out of the canteen."

"It was a bit sudden," I said, smiling, "I hardly knew what was happening until we were in the bus. I thought we would find it difficult to make ourselves understood, Miss June, but they all spoke English as well as we do."

"Yes," she replied, "and I doubt if our men could have entertained themselves and us with so much music."

We were still discussing the evening when Miss June turned the key in the door of Burnsyde, and I suddenly asked the question that had been at the back of my mind all evening.

"Why did you never marry, Miss June?"

We stepped inside and closed the door, and she answered simply,

"He was killed in the last war."

At the top of the staircase she turned right across the broad landing, moving past the two main bedrooms occupied by Mother and Mr William.

"Goodnight, Jaqueline," she said quietly.

"Goodnight, Miss June," I replied, turning left past the open bathroom door, to my little white room.

Chapter Twenty-One

I had dug the garden fork into a bale of peat-moss again and again to break it down, and half filling a sack trampled it until it was fine enough to please me, when Sean suddenly said,

"You were at the Polish officers' canteen last night, weren't you?"

"I was, just as I always am on Tuesdays."

"I've heard about their fancy manners!" he went on, and he snipped the metal bands from another bale of peat-moss.

"I suppose it's bred into them, because they even bow to each other," I replied. "Can I have the barrow for cleaning out the brooders?"

Sean emptied the barrow, then he lifted my tools into it.

"You won't need the moss, the brooders will be empty from now over the winter," he said, and the next moment he started pushing the barrow towards the brooders while I hurried after him.

"I'm working alone this morning," I reminded him, but he ignored me until we stopped at the first brooder.

Then I looked on in amazement as he clicked his heels together and bowed with his hand at his waist; he walked away quite calmly as if he had done nothing out of the ordinary.

We met again on our way to the kitchen for morning tea break and he gave a slight bow as he started to speak.

"This is the night the ghost of the tower comes into the house."

"What house?" I asked.

"Burnsyde!" said Sean, smiling down at me sympathetically. "Do you believe in ghosts?" he added casually.

"I don't think so, it's probably a vivid imagination that creates them. Anyway, I've never seen one."

"You'll see one in your room tonight, because the moon is full."

"Rubbish!" I replied, feeling slightly uneasy. "Why my room?"

"Because it's the first room at the top of the staircase, past the bathroom on the left, isn't it?"

"Yes," I answered, searching his face.

When we entered the back kitchen he became maddeningly polite, talking to Miss June instead of sitting like a block of wood as he usually did, if he came at all

"Do you think the canteen for Polish officers will be a success, Miss June?" he enquired politely.

"Why, yes, Sean, even more successful than I could have imagined possible."

Pity it's only for a few weeks," he answered.

I could hardly believe it was Sean speaking as I sipped my tea and listened; the thoughtful look on his face was utterly convincing. Hypocrite, I thought to myself.

"Yes, but I think their stay will make quite an impression on the village," Miss June replied, then she turned to look at Sean. "You are being talkative today!" she added, wiping her hands on a cloth. And his reply must have left me with my mouth hanging open.

"Only when there's something to talk about, Miss June."

I saw Miss June's eyebrows go up and she took the empty cup he handed her, then she concentrated thoughtfully on his back as he walked out into the yard.

At noon I had made up my mind to ask Mr William again about the tower. I still remembered Miss June's blood-thirsty story, and Mr William's romantic fantasy.

Slipping into my seat at the table, I found Mother had stayed in bed today and Miss Gillian was busy attending to her needs. Miss June had gone to the kitchen, so I began,

"Mr William, can you tell me more about the tower?"

"Yes, Father restored it, as you know, after the house was built on the sight of the castle that once stood here. You have been to where the boundary wall stood up by the reservoir, in fact, much of the wall was used to build the reservoir dyke."

"Is there really a ghost?" I asked.

His eyes twinkled as he answered:

"Come to think of it, she should appear this month when the moon is full and I think that is tonight, is it not?" Mockingly, I felt, he smiled across at me not realising that his words were ruining my appetite.

Miss Gillian had just taken her place at the table.

"Yes," she said, "this is the anniversary. There is a marvellous view to be seen from the top of the tower, but I shouldn't go up there, Jaqueline." Then she added, "If we found you lying at the bottom we might have acquired a second ghost."

She actually smiled when I blushed and Mr William laughed, then dabbing his mouth with his napkin, he said,

"Don't take it too seriously, Jaqueline! It's all history."

Most of my time that afternoon was spent collecting eggs, because it took ages to get round all the houses without Miss Gillian's help; she was too busy with Mother.

My mind kept dwelling on the tower and its ghost, and I had almost convinced myself it was all rubbish as I brought in the last of the eggs.

Then just as I was crossing the yard, Sean pushed out his bike from the garage and as he passed me, he said,

"The ghost walks at midnight when the moon is full!"

I felt utterly dismayed and could have beaten him with a big stick; but, instead, I just shrugged and replied,

"Rubbish!"

After supper I passed the evening darning my socks, and listening to Mr William trying all the stations he could find on the radio until Miss June begged him to stop. Miss Gillian was sprawled in the depths of an armchair puffing like an old chimney. I missed Mother's presence in the room; she had stayed in bed all day.

It was ten o'clock when I went upstairs and slipped into my pyjamas. The evening was unusually close with not a breath of air about, and the moon cast a silvery glow over Burnsyde. I pulled the top sash of my window right down.

It was only when I slipped in between the sheets that the tower and its ghost started to creep into my thoughts. I tried to sleep, and wished it were morning, but the minutes ticked slowly by.

The moon hung like a silver disc outside my window and I could see the hands of the clock move to 11.45 p.m. Drawing the covers over my head, I felt the perspiration starting to trickle cold and wet all over me. I lay rigid, waiting desperately for midnight to pass.

Stifled by the covers I peeped out to see a large, black shadow moving across the whiteness of my bedroom door. Petrified, I closed my eyes tight and heard a velvety swishing sound glide over me, as it circled the room. There was a slight scraping noise and the soft swishing sound stopped; the tension had become unbearable. What if I were to die? I wanted to see this ghost! Opening my eyes I turned my head cautiously to look at the window; the shadow was still moving on the door.

Silhouetted against the moon was the outline of a barn owl perched on the open sash of my window; as I watched, drained of strength, it spread its wings and silently glided off into the silvery night.

The hair clung stickily to the back of my neck, and my pyjamas stuck wetly to my skin. Exhausted, I felt my body suddenly relax and I knew no more until the morning dawned.

Chapter Twenty-Two

Sean had never asked if I had seen the ghost of Burnsyde. But after the awful night I had gone through, I was determined not to mention the terrifying experience with the owl and its enlarged ghost shadow on the door at midnight, making a dome-shaped head and long cloak.

I dug the darning needle into the top of my work basket, then folded the Land Army hose I was forever mending. From where I sat on the window seat the tower looked romantic in the dusk of evening.

Without even thinking about it, my hand selected an embroidery needle and I picked up my green poplin dress. If I finished it tonight I could wear it at the canteen tomorrow evening. Or should I select a book from Mr William's beautifully bound collection and sink into the depths of an easy chair? Before I had even given it a second thought, I started stitching into the rose placing each thread so that it was shaded to perfection.

"Sean's manners have improved of late, Mother," said Mr William, taking a seat by the fire, "he's becoming quite the gentleman."

"Is he, dear?" she replied.

"Yes, and he holds himself a lot better than he used to, no more slouching," he added opening up his paper.

"He is coming up to eighteen years of age and will soon be called into the forces," sighed Mother. "What a stupid waste of young lives, why will they never learn."

Miss June looked up at her brother and smilingly said,

"Yes, I agree, William, and Sean's becoming quite the conversationalist in the kitchen." Her needle delved in and out of the tapestry she had been working on for some time, then coming out of her own little world of thought again, she started,

"I must write out that notice advertising the coming Sale of Work for charity, and we can call in at the News Office on our way to the canteen tomorrow evening, Jaqueline."

"Mmm," said Mr William.

Putting aside her tapestry, she picked up pen and paper muttering to herself and constantly changing what she had written.

"The weeks seem to fly past since the canteen opened, and I have so much to attend to!" Miss June said anxiously.

"Mmm," replied Mr William from behind his paper, "can't say that I've noticed."

"It's your own fault, dear, you take too much upon yourself, June!" said Mother rather sharply.

"The village Gazette is expensive for advertising, I must get this down to as few words as possible." Miss June was speaking to herself, or anyone willing to listen.

The following evening we were dropped off at the News Office, while the other ladies drove on to the canteen further along the High Street.

"Evening, Miss June. I'll see it goes in to tomorrow's Gazette, never fear."

The man behind the News Office desk adjusted his spectacles, raced over the words of Miss June's advertisement and quoted the price.

"Oh!" she said in dismay. "I'll just see if I can shorten it a little." Then she looked at the man. "Is there not a special rate for charities?" she asked sweetly.

"Charities!" replied the man, "I can't run my paper for charities, no matter how noble the cause! Charity begins at home supporting my wife and family!"

The result of Miss June's thrift had made us late for the canteen; and as we at last hurried along the High Street the opening bars of the Warsaw Concerto reached our ears. Miss June spoke excitedly,

"We are fortunate indeed to be looking after these men; I wonder how much longer they will be in our village?"

We reached the doorway and heels clicked as Miss June and I entered the canteen. The other two ladies were standing spellbound as the concerto filled the air with its glorious sound. I never even noticed who had removed my coat, I was already caught up in the magic of the music and the nostalgic scene.

The music died away into quieter strains, and I could see tears in the eyes of the men who were far away from their homeland. We slipped in behind the counter busying ourselves serving coffee, and soon the sadness had gone.

The officer, who always said he played for me, reached for my hand and led me to a chair beside the piano; as he positioned himself on the stool he said,

"This piece I will play is from you to me!"

I thought he had made a mistake in his faultless English, but his fingers were already running over the keyboard effortlessly, so I waited to tell him.

The piece he played was music I had never heard before and I listened enraptured as the violins picked up the melody. When he finished, I rose amidst the clapping that followed to continue my duties; but as I moved he caught my hand and led me to a table.

Shyly I opened the conversation, while he positioned my chair:

"You made a mistake in your English when you said, 'you to me'," I began.

"No, I made no mistake, it was from you to me!" Then he dismissed the subject with a smile and took the chair opposite at the table. "I am twenty-seven years old," he said, looking straight into my eyes. "Before the invasion of my country I was a concert pianist," he paused, and his tawny eyes misted. "When we were invaded the members of my family were shot as I stood bound, unable to help them; I was sent to a prison camp. A Russian doctor saved my hands when I suffered frostbite; he was also a prisoner of war."

He sat silent for a moment and his thoughts were far away. Suddenly I realised I had been watching every movement of his face while I listened.

"How did you get out of the prison camp?" I asked.

"I escaped with the help of a German guard who was old enough to be my father." His eyes smiled. "He was sick of war!"

I became aware of Miss June's apologetic cough just behind me, but the officer continued,

"Without the help of these two good men I would not have been able to play this evening for one so beautiful." The mischievous sparkle had returned to his eyes and instantly my Scottish distrust of flowery speeches warned me to take his compliment lightly. "You must be Swedish to have such golden hair?"

"No, I'm Scottish," I replied, glad that Miss June hovered in the background.

"Your love of music is in your eyes." He reached for my hand across the table, "Are you married?"

His eloquence in speaking was having a shattering affect upon my peace of mind, and I answered,

"No, and I won't marry until I have travelled across Europe and seen something of the world."

"Would it not be better to marry and see the world together?" He waited, studying my face.

"Jaqueline, I need your assistance!" Miss June's voice had put an end to a conversation that was beginning to confuse me. I had been chatting to this dashing officer long enough. He bowed, took my hand, and clicked his heels before I left the table.

Safely tucked behind the coffee pots once more, I noticed how Miss June's complexion gradually toned down from red to pastel pink.

"Were you worried, Miss June?" I said.

She stammered as she answered and looked at her hands:

"Y-yes, you see, I am responsible for you, because I bring you here."

"I'm sorry for being so thoughtless, but you needn't have worried."

Again she stammered, and replied,

"W-we are all middle-aged and it is so nice to have someone young helping behind the counter."

An elderly officer had come forward with his violin clasped to his chest.

"When I fled from my country," he said, "I took only my violin; you must hold it!" He placed it in Miss June's small red hands and she blushed with pleasure. "It is a Stradivarius and is of great value!"

A fellow officer approached as he placed it in its velvet lined case, they greeted each other with a slight bow, and then they smiled and said to me,

"The piece that was played for you is known in English as 'The Maiden's Prayer'."

I smiled, and decided that my handsome, bronzed flatterer in the leather boots was in no doubt as to his accuracy when using our language.

He was by the door that evening when we left for Burnsyde, and clicking his heels he bowed, saying softly,

"You may kiss me."

Astonished at such a suggestion I looked into his sparkling, tawny eyes; the mischievous grin revealed perfect white teeth. Somehow, his twenty-seven years did not seem quite so old. After all, I was in my nineteenth year.

Feeling completely out of my depth and being unaccustomed to such polite bravado, I gripped Miss June's arm, tossed a disdainful smile and a hasty goodnight over my shoulder, then hurried towards the bus that waited at the edge of the pavement.

By this time all the officers had congregated by the doorway, and as the bus moved off they came to attention and saluted. We both waved shyly from the step, and having taken our seats we remained thoughtful and quiet all the way back to Burnsyde.

On Thursday evening Mr William walked into the dining-room wearing his Home Guard uniform.

"June," he said quietly, "the canteen is no longer needed."

"What are you trying to tell me, William?"

"Just that," he replied, "the men have been called to active duty, may God help them!"

Miss June looked up and a beautiful expression passed across her face touching me deeply; tears stung my eyes because I felt a sense of loss. But almost immediately, I was comforted by the feeling of having been in the right place at the right time.

"I was becoming weighed down by the responsibility of taking Jaqueline to the canteen, William. It's difficult to remain indifferent to the attractions of such dashing young men!" Miss June looked almost starry-eyed as she spoke.

Mr William stood with his head bowed in front of the large, open fireplace, and when Miss June had finished speaking he bent to lift two logs from the brass box that stood at the side, placing them on the glowing embers.

"Yes, I can see what you mean, June; you were once eighteen yourself, I remember Mother telling me all about it." And he walked out of the room.

"What was that, William?" Mother looked up from her book, but Mr William had gone.

"The canteen for officers has closed, Mother," said Miss June.

"Pity," replied Mother, "I know it gave you a lot of pleasure, June, but you will have a lot more time on your hands."

When I walked into the barn next morning Sean was already emptying meal sacks. I picked up a shovel with the intention of knocking over a sack and shovelling the contents into the bin.

"Leave it where it is, I can manage," said Sean. I felt rejected. Then there was a short silence and I wondered what to do. He looked at me. "I've seen that tall one with the leather riding boots in the village; he kissed your hand, didn't he?" Sean said, concentrating on the meal bin.

I suddenly felt very worldly, and answered,

"Yes, but it's just because they don't shake a lady's hand as you would do," I replied airily, "and they don't really kiss your hand."

There was another silence, then he turned to look at me as I stood there in drill cloth and boots.

"It's the uniform!" he said. "If they didn't wear a uniform they wouldn't be any different from the rest of us!"

"They've gone," I replied, pushing my hands into the pockets of my jacket and walking towards the door.

"I know," he answered.

"You seem to know everything!" I called back, and headed for the peat-moss shed.

Chapter Twenty-Three

The usual letter arrived from my mother and when I opened it, it read as follows:

Dear Jaqueline,

A special service is to be held in the Parish Church on Sunday. Please bring your uniform to wear at the service as it is to pay tribute to the men lost in the war from our area; many of them were your young friends.

There is another sad piece of news: two of Alex's friends lost their lives in the Firth of Forth. Their yacht capsized when a freak storm blow up, their bodies were washed up many hours later. It seems ironic, but the boys were in our house on that fateful day asking Alex to go with them. However, he had decided to work on his motorbike, or he would have been with them.

Please excuse the brevity of this letter, but I am just hurrying off to the factory to do my part-time war work. Housewives have all had to report to the factory if they have no children under eleven years of age in the house. Most children under eleven have been evacuated.

Love,
Mum xxx.

Time seemed to drag as I waited for the weekend; Sunday came and people were moving into our crowded church until it overflowed. We walked up the centre aisle to the family pew, my sister and brother on either side of me, my parents walking in front.

The doors of the crowded church were left open for those who had to stand outside. As the minister climbed the steps to the pulpit complete silence descended on the congregation.

Quietly he started to read out the names of the boys I had grown up with. I remembered the smiling faces of our cycling companions; they had been shot down in mid-air while on a paratroop mission over Scandinavia.

The minister talked on, describing how each one had given his life in the performance of his duty; and then he spoke of the boys who had lost their lives because of their love of sailing. It all seemed so unreal.

Then I noticed a change of tone in our minister's voice, it rose taking on a richness and he quoted the immortal words,

"They shall not grow old as we that are left grow old.

Age shall not—"

I barely heard his voice after that, only the weeping of the mourners as the words entered into their hearts; comforting and yet poignant, unlocking the sorrow of those who were left behind.

I looked up into the rainbow-coloured shafts of sunlight streaming from the stained-glass windows and filling the church with a flood of drifting colours. The music of the organ swelled in a glorious cascade of sound raising my thoughts above all the sadness; instead of sorrow, I had the strangest awareness of being left behind on some wonderful adventure.

When the service ended we went home, taking several relatives and friends. My mother produced the tin of best salmon she had been hoarding for just such an occasion as this, and not trusting my sister and I to use it sparingly enough, she made the sandwiches herself.

We filled the teacups using the best china, and passed them round the visitors. I had taken a seat at the table beside my sister, and at once we plunged into a discussion of why we still lived while so many of our school friends had died in the war.

"I'm convinced," my sister said, "that our mission in life has not yet been accomplished, Jaqueline."

"Pass the sponge cake, girls. And fill the teapot again, please."

We rose when my mother spoke, and I smiled when everyone praised the texture of the sponge made with dried eggs as being as good as when fresh eggs were used.

"They haven't tasted Miss June's sponge," I whispered to my sister.

"We don't all live in the land of plenty," she replied tartly, so I changed the conversation.

"What's that, What was that?" My ancient grandfather was suddenly bolt upright in his chair. "Stradivarius! Impossible! There can only be a few left in the world, they were made in the sixteen hundreds and are priceless!"

"It was, Grandad! I heard it play, and I touched it," I said earnestly.

"Couldn't have been!" he answered. "I've played many violins in my time, and repaired many more. But I've never touched an instrument made by Stradivari."

His blue eyes blazed, and the family were delighted with the scene as his long, white moustache and thatch of snowy white hair seemed to bristle all over. The stem of his pipe snapped and he threw it into the fireplace in disgust.

My father had missed nothing of the conversation between my sister and I.

"Did I hear you say canteen for Polish soldiers?" he asked coldly.

"No, Dad! Polish officers! I helped the W.V.S. ladies and Miss June."

"Your employers should have more sense than to allow a young girl in amongst foreigners!" he said angrily, and I knew it had been wrong not to tell my parents.

"But they are our allies, Dad," I insisted, in an attempt to vindicate myself.

"You say they have left the village now?" he asked, ignoring my plea.

"Yes! They were based in the village to await front line orders."

Both my father and grandfather cleared their throats for a few seconds, and I thought as I watched their discomfort, that the men of this world had neither trust in each other, nor love for one another. My father's annoyance made him start criticising my clothes,

"Go and put on a dress, between breeches and trousers we won't know if it is a man or a woman before long," he said sarcastically.

My mother's large dark eyes looked on patiently, then she intervened,

"Things are changing, Bill. It will never be quite the same again, trousers have become a way of life for women."

I missed my usual bus that Sunday and was late in arriving back at Burnsyde; we pulled in at the entrance and the entwined mass of branches hanging above seemed thicker than ever.

It was 10.45 p.m. when I stepped down from the bus in the darkness, carrying my uniform parcelled in brown paper and tied with thin string that bit into my fingers. The sky was cloudless and I could pick out the constellations of the stars easily.

Still going over the events of the weekend in my mind I walked in under the tall, overhanging trees towards the open gates of Burnsyde, and then I froze with fear.

Something tall and darker than the night was moving among the trunks of the trees. I tried to stay calm, but as it started towards me I was terrified.

I had dismissed the idea of ghosts after reaching the point of exhaustion over the owl that had flown into my room casting an ominous shadow; but there was no moonlight, only the stars and the blackness of the spectre taking on the shape of a man as it drew nearer. The greyness of a face was just visible beneath his black brimmed hat; he stopped a few yards from me, and I felt the blood drain from my limbs and I was rooted to the spot.

As I stood there, almost hypnotised by impending evil, the smell of camphor drifted towards me. I saw the grey-whiteness of hands appear at hip level, they fumbled at the front of his clothes. His body blocked the gates as he moved in. I tried to scream but the strangled gasp that came from my throat was scarcely audible.

There was nowhere I could run too, and fighting the beast that towered over me seemed impossible. He grasped my dress by the hem, pulling me towards him and started to fumble with my panties; somewhere in the night's silence I heard a dog bark.

Instantly my brain began to function. I swung my heavy parcel towards his head as he stooped and the force of the impact sent him staggering sideways. Sheer terror lent wings and I took to my heels racing up the drive with the faint smell of camphor clinging round me.

"Belle!" I gasped, "Belle!"

The large, golden labrador bounded towards me, prancing round in her enthusiasm and almost knocking me off my feet. Then Mr William came striding round from the direction of the barn.

"You're late tonight, Jaqueline!" he said, taking the three rounded steps in one stride and throwing open the door to the glowing hall.

Although I had raced up the drive, I could feel the goose-flesh standing up all over my skin and I shivered despite my fur jacket.

"It's not that cold, Jaqueline. But you had better have some hot cocoa before you turn in!"

I started to speak.

"There was some..." but my voice trailed off, because I was overcome by a feeling of deep shame.

"Yes?" said Mr William, and he waited.

"I was just going straight up to bed, thank you," I mumbled.

"Goodnight then, Jaqueline."

"Goodnight, Mr William."

He closed the door and pushed the bolts along, and I hurried upstairs glad to be in the safety of the house.

When I reached the landing my eyes were stinging and I hurried into my room and closed the door; I fell onto my bed and wept buckets of tears.

I could still feel the long, cold fingers on my flesh; shaking, horrified, I stripped off my clothes, pulled on my housecoat and ran to the bathroom to wash myself. I felt unclean.

When I crept into bed it was with the thought that no one must ever know about the degrading experience I had been through. It was something that didn't happen to well brought-up young girls; I had been led to believe it could only happen to a harlot.

I slept fitfully, waking up every now and then imagining the black apparition bending over me, but his hands had taken on gigantic proportions; sobbing my heart out I at last fell into a dreamless sleep.

Chapter Twenty-Four

"Well, Good morning, Jaqueline." He heaved a sigh and shrugged.

"Good morning, Mr William." My voice was so quiet and I only glanced at him and lowered my eyes. "Good morning, Miss June." My words were almost a whisper.

"What have I done?" said Mr William brightly, "I feel as if I had developed cloven hoofs and sprouted horns! Are you well enough, Jaqueline?"

I felt a dreadful numbness throughout my body and it was a great effort to smile at Mr William's pleasant face.

"Come, come!" he said jovially, "nothing can be that bad, you look as though the bottom has dropped out of your world!"

The sugar, as he sprinkled it, was making a watery film on his porridge, and without realising it I had been judging him alongside the evil man who would have ruined my life the previous night, in the few moments it would have taken to satisfy his lust. I could hardly bear the thought of the disgrace it would have brought to my family.

Mr William pushed away the sugar bowl, and then looked up,

"Ouch!" he said, as if I had struck him a blow, "I shouldn't pry into your private thoughts."

I almost smiled despite the despair I felt inside my chest.

"Your tea will be cold, Jaqueline," Miss June said, "shall I top it up?" Then she looked severely at Mr William. "You're being ridiculous, William!"

I was glad Miss Gillian had not yet appeared at the table. Shaking off the degrading feeling brought on by last night's foul experience was difficult enough. I felt I was being punished, and Miss Gillian's disapproving stares would not help matters.

What I had seen troubled me deeply; this was one of the gaps in my education, something I knew little about because it was an unmentionable subject and something I thought girls learned about after marriage.

Statues in the museum had their private parts covered by a fig leaf, and even then our class had lowered their eyes when passing male statues. But no fig leaf, however one stretched the imagination, could have covered what had been displayed to me at the entrance gates last night.

I excused myself from the table and wandered out by the side door, my romantic illusions about life shattered. Deep in thought, with my hands pushed into my pockets, I saw only the pebbles of the yard at my feet.

Casting my mind back to the last year of school, I remembered passing through a group of boys in the school grounds; one had caught my arm and started to undo the buttons of my blouse, and it was the first time in my life I had experienced fear of the male.

Several of the group had turned to watch, but one stepped forward and catching the shoulder of my would-be attacker, he said softly, "leave her alone". Freed from the brooding curiosity of the group, I had walked away knowing the intense relief of being rescued by the good knight in a fairy tale.

I felt my face relax into a smile, until I thought about the three girls who had to leave school because they were pregnant; if they had done it to defy their parents, or convention, then the price paid by one of them was death in labour.

The injustice of it all made me furious. Women could not walk freely in this men's world; and the contemptuous attitude towards the raped woman was a safeguard for the unprincipled male. If there were men with no scruples then they should lust after women from the same mould; I could feel the security of childhood in the family circle fast slipping away.

Deep in philosophising I was completely unaware of Sean's presence until he stepped in front of me.

"My sister would like you to come to her birthday party on Thursday," he said, and the sordid world I had been cast into suddenly seemed brighter.

"Oh! I'll have to speak to Mr William, but I can't come back to Burnsyde alone at night."

"Don't tell me you're afraid of the dark?" he said as he looked at me with a smile in his eyes.

"If it wasn't for the odd rotten egg among males I *could* come back by myself."

"Well! If you put it that way, I'll bring you back to Burnsyde."

Thursday could not come quickly enough to please me, but when, at last, the night of the party arrived, I dressed with extra care and took the seven o'clock bus to the village. Sean was waiting at the bus stop and, at first, I hardly recognised the very well-dressed young man who smiled when I stepped down from the bus.

"You look quite different when you're wearing a dress," he remarked on the way to his house, and I hugged my fur jacket to me.

"You look quite different yourself," I answered, and smiled up at him.

As the other guests arrived I noticed there was an acute shortage of young men, which limited the activities to a very bright, chatty, social evening and a marvellous supper; Sean was one of the few men below calling-up age left in the village.

I had to leave the party in time for the ten thirty bus, and as I slipped into my coat and said my goodbyes, Sean came in with some news:

"It's been snowing heavily; I think we'll have to walk back to Burnsyde. Quite likely the buses will have stopped running by now."

I was given a pair of waterproof overshoes, and the long hike began. The blanket of whiteness covering the whole countryside seemed to muffle the slightest noise, and we had walked the first mile in companionable silence before Sean spoke.

"It's going to be late before we got to Burnsyde at this rate. Can't you go any faster?"

"What! In high heels and overboots!" I answered indignantly. "Not unless I run! Has it occurred to you that I take two steps to your one, which means I'm making twice the effort!"

"I suppose you are," he replied, easing the pace a little.

When we reached the gates of Avonlea Estate I felt a stitch starting in my side, then suddenly Sean stopped.

"Look!" he said, "Fox tracks running along the river bank, keep an eye on them and see what direction they take."

The urgency to reach Burnsyde was forgotten, but while he examined the tracks it gave me time to catch my breath. The moon hung above like a slice of melon, casting an eerie glow over the white landscape. I shivered.

"I thought you were in a hurry, Sean?"

"Yes," he answered, stepping back on to the road. "This must be its regular route and it's heading up to Burnsyde."

He started off at a brisk pace and I ran along beside him.

"If I'm going to be late, then I'm going to be late!" I gasped, stopping to pant just as we reached the entrance. Sean stopped.

"I'll leave you here," he said, turning to walk away.

"No, you won't!" I grabbed his arm and hung on. "You'll take me to the door of the house and wait until I ring the bell."

He didn't argue, he just looked at my face and walked in under the trees holding my arm in his. When we reached the door of the house I could hear the hall clock striking midnight; I rang the bell, and when the door opened Miss Gillian's voice took me by surprise:

"How dare you come back at such an hour, go into the sitting-room!"

Sean was already heading down the drive without a word of explanation. When I walked into the sitting-room I found Mr William lacing up his Home Guard boots; he was still dressed in his officer's uniform.

"I was just going out to look for you," he said, his face flushed with anger.

Miss June stood twisting her fingers nervously and looked quite dismayed. I felt ashamed to have caused this family any discomfort.

"I'm very sorry," I said, pulling off my gloves, "but we didn't realise it had been snowing with the black-out curtains drawn, and we had to walk all the way back because the buses had stopped running."

I even found myself plunging into the account of the fox tracks we had seen leading up to Burnsyde. Then I became aware, as I looked at their faces, that no one believed me.

Relief showed clearly on the face of Miss June, but Miss Gillian and Mr William had been nursing their wrath, and I had arrived home glowing from the long walk in the crisp air, and the happiness of having spent an evening among people of my own age.

"Go to your room! Go to your room!" Miss Gillian said in disgust.

"I'm terribly sorry," I said again, and left the sitting-room.

Explanations would be a waste of time if no one believed me, and I had always been on the ten thirty bus on any other occasion. Perhaps in the morning things would be different?

At breakfast I was ignored, except for one tiny smile from Miss June. I felt despondent as I made my way to the peat-moss shed; I had done nothing wrong I argued with myself, it was the fall of snow that had kept me late and no one had expected snow.

The sound of Mr William's voice, raised in anger, drew me to the barn and I had just reached the door, when I heard him say,

"What do you intend doing about this disgraceful state of affairs?"

From where I stood I could see the furious farmer glaring up into Sean's serious face, and without waiting for an answer he raved on,

"There can be only one reason for keeping an eighteen year old girl out until midnight and you are just as aware of it as I am! Did you expect to walk away without facing up to your responsibilities?" He walked a few yards, and then turned to face Sean again with another flood of words:

"You will be called into the forces next year, and I am going to make sure anyone living under my roof will be protected. Jaqueline is my responsibility!" He glared at Sean's shocked face. "You are as much of a man as you will ever be and you will not sew your wild oats with someone in my charge!"

Completely overwhelmed by the situation he found himself in Sean remained silent. Laughter suddenly bubbled up inside me as I took in the ridiculous, unnecessary scene; why did no one believe us?

I turned and fled to the peat-moss shed, and it was only then that I thought of Mr William's words and what they implied, and I grew angry. How dare he think that I would do anything immoral! My parents would be deeply offended if they knew.

Exasperated, and not knowing what to do, I dug the pick into a bale of peat-moss and considered the situation as Mr William saw it. What if I had been a girl from the village who had lost her virtue? He was coming to the rescue of, what might have been, an unmarried mother. However, I was not, and I felt the full implication of his insulting words.

I was still wrestling with my anger when Sean appeared at the door of the shed, and said,

"Mr William thinks we misbehaved, because we were late last night." He looked at his feet as he spoke, "He thinks we should get married."

Sean's face was ashen, and I felt as near to laughter as I did to tears, then I calmed myself and replied,

"Didn't you tell him why we were late?"

"No, I tried to but he wouldn't listen." His voice had dropped to a hoarse whisper.

"He wouldn't listen to me either, but if we both took Mr William's advice we would be pleading guilty, and we are innocent."

We made up our minds to forget the whole unfortunate incident, but it kept churning over in my mind.

"I think Miss June believes me," I began, "she was the only one who smiled this morning. The others didn't. And Mother is never at the breakfast table, she probably knows nothing about all this fuss because she goes to bed at nine thirty."

Sean had become his usual relaxed self again while he listened.

"Would you really have married me, Sean?"

He coloured a little, and answered,

"Yes, if I had to!" His blue, Scandinavian eyes were full of resolution, but I was not flattered, and replied,

"I wouldn't marry just because I had to! I would have to love and respect the man I marry!"

He looked startled and took his time to answer.

"If someone made love to you and you were expecting a baby you would have no choice."

He had become the dominant male, and I bristled with indignation.

"Oh! yes I would," I said coldly, "I wouldn't marry a man who forced me into such a condition."

Sean's eyes were like slits and he spoke through tight lips.

"Who said you would be forced into such a condition?"

"I would have to be, because if I were not married it could never happen; and when you use the word love you abuse it; sex is just lust if there is no love."

I pushed the cutters under the metal band that held the peat-moss intact and squeezed, but nothing happened. I gathered my strength into my hands and tried again several times with the same negative result. Sean stepped forward, and taking the cutters from me he quickly snipped the four bands that held the bale intact. I felt deflated and weary after the silly confrontation, and had nothing more to say.

The day wore on and we worked together in complete silence, no longer able to communicate.

Chapter Twenty-Five

The day after the heavy snowfall, the weather changed from freezing to mild and wet; what had been a white landscape vanished overnight, which made me wonder if it had snowed at all.

Having heard the verdict and the sentence served on Sean and I, going to the dining-room at midday was an ordeal; how could I face three adults knowing what was in their minds? Saddened by the unfairness of it all, I walked into the back kitchen.

"Jaqueline, Mr William has taken to bed with the flu, and yet, Mother has managed to shake it off. Would you be good enough to take the trolley through to the table for me?"

"Yes, of course, Miss June," I replied.

"The doctor will be coming as soon as he can manage after surgery, so have your meal with Miss Gillian; I can eat after the doctor has been. I've convinced Mother she should stay in bed, there's so much to do."

I had just placed the dishes on the table when Miss Gillian hurried in.

"Could you possibly stay over the weekend, Jaqueline?" she asked. "We'll make it up to you later," she added, looking harassed.

I could hardly believe it was Miss Gillian speaking to me; her outraged moral sense, towards someone she judged to be a harlot, was forgotten in the face of calamity. The need to get through the labours of the weekend with a sick brother and an aged mother had changed her sense of values, at least for the time being.

"Why, of course I'll stay, Miss Gillian, I can phone my mother."

Miss June was already busy with trays for Mr William and Mother.

"It will be a great help to us all if you stay, Jaqueline," she said, hurrying out of the dining-room.

The weather changed each day with the direction of the wind, so that I wrapped a scarf round my face to keep off the biting cold one day, and sweated under a raincoat as it became wet and mild the next. The poultry stayed in their well-built, cosy, wooden houses, coming out into the wind and the rain only when I shovelled meal from the barrow into their feeding troughs.

Sunday was to be the only day I ever dined on roast chicken at Burnsyde; all other Sundays had been, and were to be, spent at home more or less fasting.

It was mid-week before Mr William made his first appearance in the dining-room, and from the window seat I watched as Miss June came fussing in with a blanket and draped it over a chair near to the fire. Mr William followed behind her looking slightly unsteady on his feet after so many days in bed.

"It's lovely to see you downstairs again, William," said Miss June, fussing with the blanket as he sank into the chair.

"How do you feel after walking downstairs, William?" enquired Mother, tucking away a stray strand of hair.

"Fine, Mother, just a bit shaky on the legs," he replied, and Miss June still fussed with the blanket around his shoulders. Then he noticed me sitting in the window seat.

"Good evening, Jaqueline."

"Good evening, Mr William," I smiled as I answered.

Then I stared in open admiration at the handsome face illness had revealed from beneath his podginess. The bone structure was clearly defined, and the fever had left deep shadows beneath his dark eyes setting off the long lashes. A lock of wavy hair hung over his forehead, and as our eyes met the pallor left his face and a light flush spread over it.

"I hear you stayed over the weekend, Jaqueline?"

"Yes, because you were ill," I replied.

Miss Gillian sat with her back to me and one jodhpured leg dangled over the arm of her chair as she started to speak.

"We will be glad to see you on the job again, William; the weather has been very unpredictable with freezing winds one day and rain coming down in torrents the next."

The years seemed to have dropped away from Mr William; he looked lean and handsome with the excess flesh gone, and I glued my eyes on my embroidery to stop me from staring. He only stayed for a short time, and I noticed when he rose to go back upstairs that his waist was visible. Gone was the slight bulge on his front. It was the third time that I wondered why he hadn't married.

By the weekend he was out and about again, and I went home on the Friday afternoon with four rashers of bacon and six large eggs. When I stepped aboard the bus I felt I had been away from home for a long time.

It was after the long weekend at home that I realised winter had set in; but in the comfort of my warm room with its polished oak furniture and rose carpet, returning to the cold, white room at Burnsyde was a hardship I didn't look forward to.

The skies opened up as I stepped down from the bus, and by the time I had reached the top of the drive the water was running from the rim of my Land Army hat. Lightning flashed in jagged forks above the hills, illuminating the scene with a ghostly greyness. I pulled on the door bell.

"Come in, Jaqueline." Miss June's hand almost pulled me into the hall, and she lifted off my hat and shook it outside the door while I unbuttoned my coat. "I'll take these through to the back kitchen to dry. I notice you're back early these days, would you like some tea?"

"Thank you, Miss June, I would. And can I leave my shoes to dry in the kitchen?"

"Yes, of course, just put them by the stove. Mother and Mr William have gone to bed early, and Miss Gillian is reading in her room. Do you miss your family?" she asked, pouring the ready-made tea into cups.

"Yes, but I'm getting accustomed to being away from home. How is Mr William?" I enquired.

"Oh! he's fine since he regained his appetite. Mother was worried because he looked so thin."

"I thought he looked very handsome having lost weight," I said, "and much younger!"

"Did you, Jaqueline?" Her eyes sparkled as she looked at me, and she tittered.

When we had finished tea we chatted until bedtime in the warmth of the kitchen with its cream-coloured, ever-burning, anthracite stove. Then we walked upstairs together, both carrying our lighted candles.

"Goodnight, Jaqueline." Miss June's eyes still sparkled as she turned right at the top of the stairs.

"Goodnight, Miss June," I replied, and opened the door of my room.

The cold, damp air of the room enveloped me when I stepped inside and closed the door. It had been cold in summer, but in winter my breath hung on the air like vapour. Quickly I changed into my pyjamas and slid in between the icy linen sheets thinking it would be impossible to push my feet down to the bottom of the bed; but when I did they touched the hard, warm bulk of a hot, stone water bottle. I thanked Miss June silently for her thoughtfulness.

Mr William was at the breakfast table next morning looking fit and well.

"Good morning, Jaqueline."

"Good morning, Mr William."

"It's some time ago since you accused me of not being a true Scot, and now you find me a handsome one!"

Miss June bustled in with a heavy tray as I blushed.

"Good morning, Jaqueline." She smiled and looked at Mr William liberally sprinkling sugar over his porridge.

"Good morning, Miss June, and thank you for the hot water bottle." We had almost finished breakfast before Miss Gillian arrived and grudgingly grunted a hello.

"Good morning, all."

Everyone acknowledged her, but her face remained like the weather, thundery. The blot on my character from less than two weeks ago had been forgotten and I was once more one of the family.

Chapter Twenty-Six

Now closed in by the long, dark nights of winter, the large dining-room with its blazing, log fire had become a haven from the bitter north winds that swept through Burnsyde.

I selected a book from Mr William's collection of the classics and became completely absorbed by Jane Austen's Lizzy; I found the beauty of her sister Jane insipid when compared to the interesting personality of Lizzy. Lizzy was full of life and she was pretty enough to please me, I preferred her and for me, as the reader, she dominated the story.

Suddenly I was aware of Mother speaking to me:

"Who taught you to darn, dear?" she enquired from the cosiness of her satin sofa.

"My mother; she was a dressmaker before she married my father; she always made all our clothes when we were children," I replied.

I noticed that she seldom used her ear horn when I answered; her eyes travelled to the socks lying on the arm of my chair.

"How do you manage to wear such large holes in your socks, dear?"

"My rubber boots are too large – they slip up and down on my heels."

"Then get a pair that fit you, dear!" she said in surprise.

"I just had to take the nearest they had to my size when they issued my working outfit at headquarters," I explained.

Picking up her ear horn she turned to Mr William who was sunk in the depths of his leather easy chair, almost hidden behind his newspaper,

"William, have we a size five rubber boot in the back kitchen she can wear in place of her own?"

"We haven't, Mother, the smallest is a size eight. Better to keep what she has and wear extra socks," he said loudly from behind his newspaper.

"You don't have to shout, William, I'm not deaf!"

"Where on earth are we going to put all these prisoners of war now that the Italians have surrendered?" Mr William was trying hard to concentrate on his paper as he talked, more or less, to himself.

His remark had gone unheard by Mother whose quick, little hands picked up the patience cards from a small table. She placed them in a circle at the hours of the clock, then flicked them over rapidly as she spoke.

"What is this course Sean has been sent on? Why isn't he back yet? It seems ridiculous to me they should take him when we need his help on the farm! Why do we have to put up with it, William?"

"He's gone on a training course with the air cadets for eight weeks, and if they decide to call him up in March or April we will just have to put up with it, Mother."

I smiled into the pages of my book. War had spread its tentacles over many parts of the world and all of Europe, but Mother brushed it aside. Italy's surrender had brought prisoners flowing into Britain, and how we were managing to feed and guard them all was Mr William's main concern as he pored over the evening paper. But he could never discuss the war and its progress until Mother was tucked up in bed with her hot water bottle.

Miss June had heard his remark on prisoners, and coming out of her own private little world she spoke from where she was seated at the dining-room table.

"There are standards we must maintain for all prisoners, William, whether friend or foe; they are human beings like the rest of us and will be treated as such!"

"What was that, June?" Mother looked up from her cards.

"People must be cared for, Mother, regardless of who they may be!"

"Yes! True! And I am sure you will see to that, June."

At that moment Miss Gillian strode into the room. She walked over to the side of the large, open fireplace, lent an elbow on the mantelshelf and looked across at her brother.

"Well, and how did the meeting go?" he enquired. "What are the plans for next year, Gillian? Any promising young riders?"

"They're discussing the possibility of something different in the jumping section. It's the same lot that pick up the prizes every year," she said crossly. "It gets boring!"

"Oh! come, Gillian, the younger ones will soon be experienced enough to compete. Just as the older ones have to step down." I could see the gleam glistening in his eyes as he waited for her reaction. She glared at her brother as she swished past him on her way to the door. "Comes to us all, Gillie!" he said lightheartedly. She left the room flicking her riding crop on the side of her polished leather boot. "Might even consider borrowing a horse and trying my luck!" he called after her.

"Can't see it happening," she called back from the hall, "not while your Jaguar and that old relic you call a car are housed in the stables!"

"Father's car will be worth a fortune, one day, Gillie! Mark my words!"

Chapter Twenty-Seven

It had been discussed among the family that I should be given a week's holiday over the Christmas and New Year period. When the time came I left Burnsyde on the Christmas Eve with the gift of a large cockerel. In my small suitcase I packed my clothes and a week's rations, plus four ounces in sweet coupons.

My mother had done well with the chicks Miss June had given me, but they were more like pets than birds raised for human consumption. My father was as proud of the hen house he had built as my mother was of her well-looked after poultry.

"Why haven't you used a cockerel for a meal?" I asked my parents.

"Oh! they're too young," replied my mother.

"They're not, Mother, see the size of them, they're huge!"

"Oh! there's plenty of time, no hurry, Jaqueline."

At two a.m. on Christmas morning my sister and I were crowed into wakefulness by a lusty cockerel, then at four a.m. the loud cock-a-doodle-doos shattered our slumbers again. Just as I was dozing off at six a.m. the air was filled with a chorus of crowing cockerels asserting their right to supremacy over the hen-run.

The neighbours had complained bitterly over the unexpected outbursts of crowing during the dark, winter mornings. But freshly laid, rich brown eggs straight from the nesting box had made their disturbed sleep well worth while.

I slipped into my housecoat and went through to the kitchen to put the kettle on; it was another hour before the sun rose.

Cosseting had brought about early maturity and at the first sign of light the hen-run was alive with activity.

From the twelve chickens Miss June had given me six hens and four cockerels had survived. The bully of the four males was the largest one I had ever seen. He strutted behind the heavy net fence enclosing the hen-run, his long red wattles dangling fiercely from his face. *He* was the one who reigned supreme over the six plump hens scratching around in the loamy soil, all of them completely unaware of the uproar they caused in suburbia every morning.

After breakfast I watched with interest as my mother crept up to the gate, opened it and dashed to the food trough to empty her bucket as fast as she could; as she turned towards the gate the large cockerel lowered its head, stretched its wings and rushed after her.

I laughed out loud when she just managed to slip out of the gate and slam it shut. Her pet cockerel was stopped in his tracks by the heavy rope netting that formed a barrier to the rest of the garden.

We dined well on Christmas Day and shared the Burnsyde cockerel with the friends and relatives who called.

My mother's noisy, strutting cockerels and her plump, contented, bright-eyed hens had fired the enthusiasm of the neighbourhood. Having become an expert on poultry and their diseases, through books borrowed from the local library, her help and advice was in great demand by any neighbour rearing day-old-chicks under their kitchen boiler.

My father, with a pencil stuck behind his ear, could be seen taking measurements and supervising the building of hen houses in several back gardens during the Christmas week.

While I was at home the house bustled with friends and relatives. It was then that I realised how isolated I had become at Burnsyde, and how I longed for the activity of the city.

"How is life in that little Eden you live in? We haven't had time for a heart to heart talk in ages," my sister said, starting on the mound of presents that had piled up for both of us.

"It's quiet," I replied.

"Don't you have any friends?" she asked.

"Only Sean, and it's hard work trying to get a word out of him unless he's in the mood to talk."

"Don't you have barn dances to go to?" she said in surprise.

Lifting a large square of multicoloured silk from its wrappings, she held it up to her neck, and glanced at the effect in the mirror of the dressing table while I watched her reflection.

"Have you nothing to talk about, Jaqueline?"

"As a matter of fact, Sean's away on a course with the air cadets and I didn't know anything about it until Mr William mentioned it to Mother. Can you imagine having a life partner like that, Margaret?"

"Sounds like a bad case of the superior male, unless it's hush, hush, war stuff!" she replied.

Picking up my parcels I walked over to the small sofa by the window. I did miss the company of young people at Burnsyde, and the thought of going out alone at night to the village cinema frightened me. Getting the news of Sean's training course second hand through Mr William was depressing, and I felt slighted.

Sean was my only means of relief from life with the family at Burnsyde. Miss Gillian always made me feel like an intruder and I resolved, as I watched my light-hearted sister, to do something about it. I felt envious of my sister with all her friends and the three pounds, fifteen shillings she had in her Christmas pay packet this week. I felt poor with my unvarying weekly nineteen and sixpence.

It was not until New Year's Eve that tragedy struck and my mother was thrown into a fit of gloom. She had crept cautiously into the hen-run with her bucket of meal thinking the bullying cockerel was safely in the hen house; but as she stooped over the trough to empty her bucket he stepped out from behind the hen house, where he had been concealed, crowing loudly.

She turned to dash for the gate as he lowered his head, stretched his wings and hurled himself at her. I watched helplessly as my mother slipped on a muddy patch and fell skidding sideways still clinging to her bucket. The huge, heavy, young cockerel was unable to stop and as he hit the rope net, enclosing the hen-run, his head went through it; there was a flurry and a flap, and then he hung there still and silent.

My mother picked herself up and still he remained motionless. While she slipped cautiously out of the gate my father appeared.

"He's caught in the net, Bill, and can't get out, help him!" she said, scraping the mud from her clothes.

"What happened?" he asked drolly, his eyes taking in my mother's mud-covered appearance.

"Help him, Bill!" she said again.

He leaned over the net, lifted the heavy bird and announced in his matter-of-fact way,

"He's dead – he's broken his neck. We might get some sleep now."

My mother looked up, stared at the dead cockerel, and then her eyes filled with tears.

"But, Mother, you can get into the hen-run without any trouble now," I tried to reason with her, but she was inconsolable.

"I know," she wept, "but I reared him from a wee bundle of fluff!" The house seemed quiet on New Year's Eve with the cockerel plucked and hanging ready for roasting. At half past eleven my father made his usual remark:

"It's going to be a quiet New Year. Don't think you'll get many out on a night like this?"

The bottles of whisky for men and sherry for ladies, were on the sideboard ready and waiting for anyone who called after midnight. We had cut up currant loaf and shortbread and arranged them on doily-covered plates; the third traditional item, saved from the week's ration, was thin fingers of cheese.

There was a sudden hush while waiting for Big Ben to chime midnight over the radio; the house glowed with cleanliness and smelled of furniture polish. Then we raised our glasses and toasted the New Year as the chimes rang out.

Although the black-out blinds had been lowered and the heavy curtains drawn, I knew that every pane of glass in the eight windows of the house sparkled like crystal.

The last stroke of midnight had barely died away when the door knocker clanged loudly through the hall.

"Well, somebody's braved the rain and the wind to first foot us!"

With pleasure spreading all over his face my father put down his glass and moved with alacrity through the hall; who would be the first foot to cross our threshold in the New Year?

"The one with the darkest hair among you, who is it?"

"It's me, Uncle Bill!"

I could hear my cousin's voice and my father answering,

"I hope you're right! Be the first to enter and bring us luck! Now! Come in the lot of you!"

They swarmed into the hall, shaking hands, hanging up their coats and shyly kissing the ladies, everyone wishing each other a Happy New Year. The bottles gurgled their contents into glasses and again the toast to the New Year rang out. Slanjivar! Slanjivar!

My father's eyes glowed with fun as he held his glass up to the light, then he said to my cousin,

"Where did you get this rubbish you call whisky, John?"

"It's good whisky, Uncle Bill," my two young cousins and their friends blushed and protested. "It's just the name that's not well known!" they insisted.

"Put it on the table and have some decent whisky out of my bottle," my father replied, generously pouring out his good whisky. "And what will the lassies have?"

The girls in the group modestly asked for cherry cordial, just as I would have done at sixteen. But now I was standing there with a glass of sherry in my hand, feeling a warm glow creeping up the back of my neck and with each sip the room was becoming slightly hazy.

The sherry tasted strong to my unaccustomed palate, and I would much rather have joined the girls with the rich, red, cherry cordial glowing in their glasses; my head felt light and fuzzy, so I put my glass down on the sideboard and left it there. It was the first time my father had ever offered me sherry and happily I had taken it.

The sound of the door knocker continued to echo through the hall as uncles and aunts arrived bringing gifts of fruit, and small pieces of coal to throw on the fire for luck.

"It'll be over this year, Bill!" an uncle was saying, "and then we can get away from all this rationing and settle down to a decent way of life." He took a sip of the whisky his son had poured into his glass and spluttered, "What terrible stuff! The sooner the war's over the better."

"Yes, Sandy, it can't last much longer!"

I had heard the same words repeated year after year ever since the invasion of Poland.

With a toast from each male that arrived and refilled his glass my father was becoming less coherent, and the effect on his speech was noticeable as he sat in his armchair nodding and agreeing with the political views of one of my uncles.

"It's true enough, Bill! We are only pawns in the hands of the people at the top, and the irony of it is, we put them into power." Turning his attention to me, he remarked, "You're looking a bit wan, lass."

"Well, Uncle Sandy, you can't put it down to lack of fresh air this time, because I'm seldom indoors."

"True, true," he said with an almost irritating softness, while his shrewd, blue eyes regarded me keenly, "but taking too much out of yourself won't help to end the war! It's in the hands of the people at the top." His last sentence was uttered almost absentmindedly, and he swirled the whisky at the bottom of his glass.

"Would you like some water in it, Uncle Bill?"

Instantly my eyes went to my father's face and I waited.

"Water! What nonsense is this? Wasting good whisky! I'll take a nip just as it comes from the bottle."

"But, Uncle Bill, we all take it with water now, just like the American forces do!"

"Piffle!" he replied, "coming across here with their new-fangled ideas!"

Again the door knocker banged loudly; I ran through the hall and opened the door to the extrovert of my father's six brothers. This gentle giant breezed in and waltzed me across the hall into the sitting-room.

"I've walked all the way from the other side of the city to first foot you, but I see I'm too late. Never mind!" he said, producing a bottle from inside his overcoat. Picking up a glass from the sideboard he poured some whisky; his smiling eyes sought out my mother and he offered it to her.

"You know I don't touch whisky, Frank, and I still have some sherry here."

He put his arm round her shoulders and started to sing, while my mother blushed and smiled, and his ruggedly handsome face was close to hers as he crooned with the perfect French accent:

"Can it be true, someone like you could love me, love me?"

Given the cue, my cousin Katrina turned on the piano stool and ran her fingers over the keyboard. Lightly, my favourite uncle danced his big muscular body into the centre of the room and went through a remarkable impersonation of Maurice Chevalier.

Amid cheers for more we quickly cleared one end of the large room while my cousin's nimble fingers played on.

We were a close family, because these six brothers and one sister had been the offspring of a grandfather, whom I had never known, born in the United States of America. He had been sent to Scotland to be educated at a famous Edinburgh school.

The romantic story went something like this: grandfather had fallen in love with a Scots girl who had a mass of red, curly hair and they had married very young. But when the time came for grandfather to return to America with his bride, she had been terrified of crossing the Atlantic and so they lived their lives out in Edinburgh. Except for a slight drawl in their speech and the narrowing of some vowel sounds by my uncles, I would never have noticed their American connection. My grandparents, on my father's side, had never been more than a faded, sepia picture in the family album.

No New Year gathering would have been complete without a few reels and as the men took off their jackets we selected a record. For the next hour we danced until the exhausted dropped out, and then the kettle was filled and the cups and saucers set out on the table.

I had seen my father's foot tapping and he and my mother joined in as we danced round the floor. Then I saw him walk unsteadily to a chair and sit there tapping his foot; I knew he was singing, but it was only when the music stopped that I heard the words"

"It ain't gonna rain no more, no more. It ain't gonna rain no more!"

We served tea and passed around the New Year fare while the talking grew louder, and all the time my father sat tapping his foot and repeating the same words like a broken record,

"How in the hell can the old folks tell if it ain't gonna rain no more!"

I had never heard him sing before; he was a quiet man. Eventually, when all attempts to switch him off had failed, they carried him into the hall where he sat on the floor still singing and tapping his foot.

The last visitor left at seven in the morning and we all went off to bed to catch up on a few hours of sleep. Come midday, the large cockerel, having been stuffed by my sister and I, was put into the oven.

My mother had managed to spend all her time in other parts of the house, never once coming to the kitchen. At two thirty the succulent bird, roasted to perfection, was carried to the table.

"Everything's ready, Mother!" I called from the hall window.

"I won't be a minute, just start without me!" and she busied herself with the hens.

"Have you told your mother the meal's ready?" my father asked.

"Yes, Dad, I called her from the back window, she's in the hen-run."

"Would anyone like more chicken?" he asked, slicing into the bird that had weighed seven pounds before it was stuffed.

"Yes, Dad, I'll have more! It's a whopper, isn't it?" my brother said, passing his plate as he continued to speak, "Mum treats them all like members of the family."

"Go and give your mother another call, Alex!" said my father shaking his head, and my brother hurried through to the hall window.

"Hey, Mum! If you don't come soon everything will be cold!"

A few minutes later she walked into the room, took one look at what remained of her favourite cockerel, and fled to her bedroom in a flood of tears.

The holiday over Christmas and New Year had come to an end, and the following day I was back at Burnsyde working alone in the ever-changing weather, too busy to notice the weeks passing and determined not to think about Sean. I was always glad to run to the kitchen and Miss June to escape my loneliness over a cup of tea.

Chapter Twenty-Eight

Sometimes Mr William's brother came to visit Burnsyde with his wife, their two teenage boys, and the baby daughter who was now five months old. The house echoed with voices. The large mahogany dining-room table, fully extended, was packed to capacity with food, and completely surrounded by chairs and people on these occasions.

Just before they arrived for the midday meal, which was now half an hour behind the usual time, Mother was calling out instructions to the family from where she sat on her sofa, resplendent in a mauve silk dress with a frill of lavender lace at the neck.

"There's a piece of Dresden on the small table, you had better take it upstairs or the children will break it," she called.

Her quick little hands expertly fastened the tiny covered buttons on the sleeves of her dress using a small, metal hook, and when the last button had been closed she smoothed back the lavender lace cuffs at her wrists.

"Would you bring out the serving spoons, Jaqueline, before you tidy up?" Miss June cast an eye over the table as she spoke, "Yes, I think that will be everything." Then she hurried away.

"William! Do you hear me? William! Bring the other fire guard – this one is not big enough for the dining-room fire, it will do in the sitting-room!" called Mother.

The family, having moved all her precious ornaments to a place of safety upstairs, switched the fire guards from one room to the other. Only then did Mother feel happy about the safety of her ornaments and her grandchildren.

The guests arrived crowding into the hall, and bringing with them home-made preserves and a sample of celery for comparison with Mr William's renowned celery. As he examined it a smile crossed his face.

"No, Bob! The pit's the best! Mine is much whiter and much more crisp than this. We'll have a look round the garden after we've eaten."

I dashed upstairs to tidy myself and put on a fresh shirt and clean dungarees in honour of the guests. Everyone was seated at the table when I slipped into my place amidst the chatter and serving of vegetable broth.

Miss June's voice managed to penetrate the happy prattle as she served the soup and watched it pass from one pair of hands to the next on its way up the table.

"Have you been introduced to Jaqueline?" she asked.

All eyes turned towards me and they realised there was a stranger in their midst.

"This is my brother, Robert, and his wife, Gwen." Miss June smiled at her sister-in-law, then turned to the two boys and said, "Andrew is sixteen and James almost fourteen."

Heads nodded in my direction, but the boys gave me a very thorough look, blushed and went back to their soup as their mother addressed me.

"We have a baby daughter, Jaqueline, but she's asleep just at the moment."

Smiling, she then resumed her interrupted conversation with Miss Gillian who glared at me from across the table. I stacked the empty plates on the trolley at my side and I doubt if anyone noticed that I didn't take soup, they were so full of news and conversation.

Home-made preserves were under discussion and Miss Gillian said,

"Yes, it was very wet when we picked the fruit this year, but what can you do if it rains every day?"

"Then I doubt if it will keep?" replied the sister-in-law, "I find there is a tendency to mildew in preserves if the fruit has been damp when picked. Seems a pity after hoarding sugar for so long to make them."

Mother had been fully engrossed with her grandsons, and the younger of the two was deliberately whispering into her ear horn, until the older boy nudged him in the ribs.

"I don't think the boys should be allowed to ski, Robert, I think it is much too dangerous," said Mother.

"We can't wrap them up in cotton wool when all the other boys at school are having lessons, Mother," Mr Robert replied. "They would be laughed at!"

The sister-in-law's mind was still on fruit:

"It's such a waste of lovely fruit when we can't get the sugar to preserve it, and the children need jam for energy."

From the expression on the face of Miss June and her lack of comment on the subject, I had the feeling that she had no regrets where the endless preparation of fruit was concerned. Her puffy red hands, especially today, had experienced enough of vegetable peeling and water.

The meat course was carried into the dining-room on a metal platter by the older boy Andrew.

"Easy does it!" said Mr William good-naturedly, lifting the carvers and running them up and down against each other as soon as the crisp-topped roast lamb had been placed in front of him.

Everyone seemed to be moving about carrying dishes except myself and Mother.

"Where will I put it, Aunt June?" asked James.

"There's a space beside Jaqueline, put it there."

He placed the large tureen groaning with potatoes baked in their jackets between me and his mother, and glanced at her for approval.

"That's fine, James," she said.

At the other end of the table Mother's eyes glowed as she looked across at her son Robert.

"That's what I love to see, a good platter of lamb! I can't abide the humiliation of meat pies from the village baker on Thursdays."

Dignified disgust was written across her face as she straightened her back, and her hand went up to her hair lifting a small tendril that had escaped her top-knot and tucked it in.

"Everyone seems to be producing boys these days, but I have managed to produce a girl; it must be the natural balance of nature. Men have been slaughtering each other for so many years."

I listened thoughtfully to the conversation between this tall, angular woman and Miss Gillian. Perhaps she was right? It seemed to be a reasonable assumption that more boys should be born.

"I will bring the sweet when you're ready, June," she said, looking at the flushed face of her sister-in-law, "just finish what's on your plate, there are plenty of helpers today!"

Miss Gillian was still demolishing her seconds, and her eyes were fixed on my empty plate as she chewed steadily. I was hoping she wouldn't raise her eyes to my face, when her sister-in-law spoke to me.

"More empties for you, Jaqueline!"

"Thank you." Relieved to be occupied I took the dirty plates and cutlery and stacked them neatly on the trolley.

"I hear you are a career girl, Jaqueline?" I turned to the gentle, intelligent mother beside me. "You will have to do well in business school if you hope to trespass in a male stronghold," she said, smilingly waiting for an answer.

"I was top girl in a class of seventeen, but I gave it up to become a land-girl."

"Do you think that was wise?" she replied.

"I think we are all ready for sweet now, Gwen!" Miss June had broken into our conversation, and I was left to wonder whether or not I had been foolhardy.

Mr Robert's wife rose from the table to bring the sweet, and I noticed how well she carried the large floppy sweater and her slim tweed skirt.

Only a scraping of white sauce was left on the large oval serving dish; it had been carried in piled high with cauliflower and white sauce covering it with a satiny sheen. The two large dishes of peas tossed in butter were empty, a thin oily film was all that remained inside them.

"There's not enough room on the trolley, Jaqueline, I'll just carry these large dishes straight to the kitchen," said Miss June, taking them from me.

"Don't forget the carvers, Andrew." And Mr William placed them on the metal platter as the boy lifted it, empty but for the well-scraped bones. "Pass the mint sauce and the gravy boat to Jaqueline, James." I was putting them on the trolley when Mr William returned to his conversation with his brother, "The Keir's Pinks are fine, but I like a drier potato, Bob."

The brother, who was as like to his father's picture as a son could be, answered,

"Yes, you have a point there, but I've decided to try the Arran Pilot which is highly recommended for its keeping qualities. It's also a nice floury potato, I believe."

I looked down at my hands, still aware of the frown on Miss Gillian's face when James had passed the gravy boat and the mint sauce.

Mother, whose head was nodding, sat up as the sweet was carried in. It was one of Miss June's specialities, pancakes with sugar and lemon. Apart from Home Guard duties and the humiliation of meat pies from the village baker on Thursdays, as Mother had put it, the war hadn't touched this cosy haven.

Having stuffed themselves with two helpings of the delicious sweet the boys were eager to leave the table.

"You may," said Mother, "but remove your shoes before stepping onto the Tientsin, I don't want it marked! June! Make the boys take off their shoes in the sitting-room."

"Yes, Mother."

Miss June's sweet face looked perplexed by her mother's insistence. But the boys had not come to sit on chintz-covered chairs.

"Can we take the skis, Sir?"

"Yes, but remember, the hill is much steeper than anything we have at home," their father answered.

Quietly I excused myself from the table, while Miss Gillian reached into the serving dish for another pancake.

"Mother?" she glanced along the almost empty side of the table.

"I don't think I can manage another, Gillian dear. Oh! well! Just a morsel!" and she passed her plate.

Just as I reached the door the baby started to cry and I looked back at their sister-in-law, but she had already heard her daughter and we both smiled.

Keen to see how well the boys could ski, I went out through the back kitchen dressed for Arctic conditions and the job of scraping the floors of snow-bound hen houses. When I caught sight of them they were toiling up the hill against a white blanket of crisp snow.

The air was cold and calm, and just as the boys started on their way down, the family were gathered to watch at the back door. Quickly the boys gained speed as they headed towards the wide gap alongside the stream, and then the younger boy lost control and careered towards the water.

With the urgency of a mother contemplating danger the sister-in-law started to run towards her son.

"Don't panic, Gwen! He'll be all right!" called Mr Robert from where he stood at the door.

But just as she drew level with me the crash came; James skidded towards the stream and came to a sudden halt. He sat in the water clutching an ankle, unable to rise.

"Here, take the baby, Jaqueline!" she said, hurrying to where I stood with the barrow.

By the time the others reached the stream his mother had removed the skis and was helping James to his feet. Miss Gillian strode across the snow and snatched the baby from me; startled by her lack of gentleness it began to cry.

"The car, William, bring it round to the door!" Mr Robert said urgently, lifting his son from the shallow, icy water. "We had better run him down to the doctor's house just in case anything's broken. Sorry, Gwen!" he added, as they made their way to the car.

Before half an hour had passed I saw the car return; but it was not until teatime that I saw the patient. His foot was bound up like a bad case of gout and he was enjoying every minute of the fuss. As they helped him to the tea-table even Mother was trying to assist.

Tea was a fantasy of sugared shortbread, fresh cream sponge, scones with butter and rolled crumpets oozing honey, each item a credit to Miss June's cooking skill. I slipped into the back kitchen as the affectionate family rose from the table, already making their farewells.

The house was unusually quiet that evening when we gathered in the dining-room to enjoy the blazing log fire; except for Mother who was lamenting over how far away the family lived, the others were silent.

"I do wish I could see them more often!" she said. "But that is the trouble with farming, it demands all your time and there is little chance of leaving livestock for more than a few hours. My grandchildren are growing so quickly. I rarely had the pleasure of seeing them as babies."

Her elder son's farm was some thirty miles from Burnsyde, but to this old lady, the distance was far too great for her to travel.

When the ornaments had been replaced and the fire guards put away, Mother said,

"I love to see the family, but I am so glad when they have all gone home," she sighed, sitting quite still for, at least, a few minutes. The room was peaceful and everyone felt her melancholy mood, then her back straightened, and when she spoke her tone of voice had changed,

"Have you closed the sitting-room door, Gillian? Are there any marks on the carpet? I don't want my Tientsin ruined! Be sure to take up all the crumbs!"

The dining-room had become charged with energy, and we all scuttled about as there was no peace until she was satisfied.

"The piano sounds much better when we have had the sitting-room fire burning, we must make a point of lighting it during the cold weather, June!" Mother was, once more, in command.

I enjoyed the changeable moods and demands of this octogenarian; she had more fire and enthusiasm than all her children put together, but they were the ones who laboured. The lives of her family were here, under her command; nothing was done without consulting Mother. And what would they be like when she was no longer with them?

Suddenly I felt exhilarated by the realisation that I was free to go in search of my own destiny.

"We are tired after such a busy day, an early night would do us good," Mother said, yawning daintily behind her fingers. And I wondered if she had used the royal "We" in this case, or was Mother speaking for all of us?

Picking up the little hook, with its mother of pearl handle, Mother busily flicked open the tiny covered buttons on the sleeves of her dress; Miss Gillian was already waiting to offer her arm.

Mr William had gone through the nightly routine of carrying the lamp to the table, heating it with methylated spirit, then pumping it up until it hissed and glowed.

The nights were long; and the white world, which had kept the snow plough busy on the narrow, main road for the past two days, reflected the last of the light in the evening sky. I felt restless, and after Miss Gillian's show of hatred, when she had snatched the baby from me, I could barely wait to escape her company and was glad when she left the room.

"Wouldn't it be better to install electricity, Mr William?" I said impulsively, knowing I was taking a liberty and expecting a rebuff.

"We are too far from the road and it would cost several thousand pounds to bring it from the nearest pylon, which is just over the hill."

"But surely the benefits would be enormous," I replied. "Being able to flick a switch in any part of the house instead of using paraffin lamps and candles." I was beginning to feel hot under the collar at my own insistence, but Mr William went on,

"There's something wrong with the system when the pigman can have it installed free of charge because he lives on one side of the road, and the one who has to pay an outrageous sum is the owner of an isolated house," he said, and stared broodily into the fire.

Miss Gillian had come into the room, and lighting a cigarette she lounged across a chair puffing clouds of blue smoke towards the ceiling. I felt more at ease when Miss June entered and quietly picking up her mending, she said,

"I do wish you would show a little consideration for others, Gillian, the air is quite thick with smoke!"

The sudden rebuke from Miss June made the smoker rise and stride out of the room. With her gone, it was peaceful in the glow of the log fire and Mr William spent his time examining the new paraffin lamp and pumping it up until we were blinded by its brightness.

I finished sewing, and without even thinking about time I took my candleholder from the sideboard.

"Goodnight, Miss June, Mr William."

"William, you have the matches, would you light the candle for Jaqueline?" Miss June's voice sounded unusually loud and she continued, "I sometimes think it would be money well spent to install electricity! I could have an electric iron, and an electric food mixer", her face had become quite flushed as she rushed on, "and there would be no need to lift the carpets and beat them outdoors as we do if I had a vacuum cleaner."

I suddenly realised just how much work the uncomplaining Miss June had to do in this large house. Mr William and Miss Gillian spent a lot of time walking round the farm with their hands in the pockets of their jodhpurs.

Miss June's hands began to shake and she dropped her mending, then she blurted out,

"It's all right for you and Gillian, but I have to spend most of my time in the kitchen; and you seem to think that this house cleans itself!"

I turned in utter dismay to look at Mr William who still stood beside me with a burnt out match in his hand. Then Miss June ran past us with tears streaming down her face. My eyes were wet as I went upstairs with the flickering candle and turned left past the bathroom to my icy little room.

Chapter Twenty-Nine

When I became conscious of water dripping steadily from the roof outside my window, I opened my eyes to the morning light; the thaw had set in and spring was in the air.

I felt reluctant to go downstairs after Miss June's tears last night. But when I did she was seated at the end of the table smiling.

"Tea, Jaqueline?" she asked.

It was such a relief to see her happy again and even Miss Gillian's presence couldn't dampen my spirits. But I had made up my mind during that long, cold, almost sleepless night – I would leave Burnsyde.

Everyone was quiet at the breakfast table, with Miss Gillian munching steadily, and Miss June sipping her third cup of tea.

"Aren't you having any breakfast, Miss June?" I asked, breaking the silence.

"No, Jaqueline, I don't feel hungry."

Behind her sweet smile I knew she was still upset and I could do nothing to help.

"Sean is long overdue, he should have been back by now," said Mr William, frowning at no one in particular. "I'll fill the meal bin for you, Jaqueline."

We left the table at the same time and I ran upstairs for a handkerchief. It was on my way down when I reached the half open dining-room door, still wearing my slippers, that I heard the sisters speaking.

"Harlot, sitting there looking all wide-eyed and innocent!" the hoarse voice was saying.

"You have no proof, Gillian!" Miss June answered sharply.

Turning quietly into the narrow corridor leading to the back kitchen I knew I had made the right decision during the night. The sun was bright when I stepped out to the yard, and I could hear the thud of a meal sack hitting the bin as it was emptied.

On the slope leading down to the stream the green spikes of daffodils were piercing their way up through the melting snow; I would be gone before they bloomed and I would never see them, just as I had never seen inside the walled garden.

I felt resolute; it would be difficult to explain my reasons for leaving, because the family had never openly accused me of anything. The unfairness of it all drained me of emotion, I stood looking at the slope picturing the hundreds of daffodils that would bloom there, and walked into the barn.

The figure shaking the meal sack over the bin was tall, and a little broader than when I had last seen him. I felt a surge of pleasure.

"Good morning, Sean, nice to see you back!" I said.

Before answering, he turned to look at me.

"Good morning," was all he said, but he was smiling. So I answered,

"I've been carrying the peat for the floors in sacks, and I've bagged the droppings for collection later when the snow clears."

"We can take the barrow today, because it's thawing fast," he replied.

Sean trundled the barrow back and forth taking the bagged droppings to the tip behind the walled garden; and all the while I busied myself feeding and watering the poultry. The crunchy snow was breaking up under my rubber boots and turning to water as I plodded across the field.

On the stroke of ten I made my way to the kitchen, looking around me as I walked. With the last fall of snow my character had been ruined by suspicion, and had forced me into the decision to leave Burnsyde, but I felt light-hearted now that I had definitely made up my mind. There was a lot to learn about people outside my own family circle and friends, it was time to move on and learn more.

I could hear Sean's boots crunching behind me across the yard, but I didn't turn round, until he said,

"Hi, there! I'm coming with you, I haven't seen any of the family this morning, except Mr William."

I smiled in answer feeling even more determined to go my own way, and walked into the back kitchen with Sean following.

"Sean!" exclaimed Miss June in delight, "How nice to see you again!"

"Good morning, Miss June," he said, grinning down at her from his lofty height.

"You're looking very fit, Sean, sit down and tell me all about the course?"

At the end of the table, feeling almost remote from the pleasantries in the kitchen, I sipped my tea; in another week I would be cut off from all this, but I had no regrets. I would give them my notice on Saturday in the proper way.

Whatever guided me through life had helped my decision, because for many nights before going to sleep, I had asked in my mind to be guided regardless of where it may lead. Through my busy thoughts I listened to the conversation.

"It was mainly physical training, Miss June."

"Yes, it has been to your advantage, Sean, you look more adult. I think we can say goodbye to the boy who left here before Christmas!"

"We did have highly technical tests on paper," he added.

"You enjoyed these, no doubt!" Miss June picked up her cup and smiled.

"Yes, I did," he replied.

"I've just realised that you'll be eighteen in March, Sean. Then it will be the air force where you can fulfil your ambition to become a pilot. We shall miss you," she added thoughtfully.

I heard footsteps in the narrow corridor and when I looked towards the door Miss Gillian entered the back kitchen.

"Hello, Sean!" she said heartily, striding to the table and shaking his hand.

He rose politely to his feet and murmured,

"Hello, Miss Gillian."

She only stayed for a moment before striding out to the yard, and again I felt slighted. If I was a harlot, then what was Sean? And yet she gushed over him, and brushed past me, glaring spitefully.

"Can I have one of your rubber bands, Miss June?" I asked.

"Why, of course, Jaqueline."

I swept my hair back from my shoulders and pulled it through the band.

"I must get my mother to cut my hair at the weekend!" I said, surprising even myself, but it had diverted my thoughts for long enough to hold back the tears that threatened, another weakness that made me detest myself.

During the late afternoon while we were clearing rubbish away from the side door, Sean mentioned being called-up into the forces.

"I expect to be called-up next month at the latest! When I go, will you write to me?"

"Yes," I answered, "but I won't be at Burnsyde after next week, because I'm handing in my notice tomorrow!"

He turned quickly.

"Tomorrow! Why?" he asked, looking at me keenly.

"I'm an intruder in the family, and I just found out this morning from Miss Gillian's own words that she looks upon me as a whore."

The tears started and I hurried into the avenue where I could escape observation from the house. Then I heard Sean drop the metal bin he was lifting and hurry after me.

"Jaqueline!" he called, "Wait a minute, where will you go if you leave here?"

"Wherever they send me!"

"If you go they will just have to get someone else!"

"Perhaps they will, a change might be a good thing for all of us!"

Up to that moment, the future and where I would go had not really entered my head; but the sudden thought of it turned off my tears, and as I tried to picture what it might be an impish thought crossed my mind.

"That's the first time you've used my name, Sean, in all the months I've known you; it was your sister who introduced me at the party."

He flushed as he strolled beside me trying to look into my face, but I hurried on.

"They need a land-girl at Avonlea Estate, that's the large house the government has commandeered to use as an evacuee hostel for boys. Why don't you apply there?"

"Who told you they need a land-girl? Are you just making fun of me?"

When I glanced sideways he was looking down at his feet, and after a slight hesitation, he replied,

"I just know, because I'm friends with the older evacuees."

"All right!" I said decisively. "Take me down to Avonlea on your bike, right now, it's after finishing time, so my time's my own!"

I turned instantly and started back along the avenue. The aspens formed a grey canopy above and as I looked up into them I was hoping my courage would not fail me. It had turned colder, and walking with Sean to where his bike stood, I shivered.

There was no one about as we crossed the gravel area past the back door and on down the steep drive. I could feel my heart pounding with excitement, there would be no turning back now.

Once we had reached the road, it was only seconds before we were speeding towards Avonlea. I felt exhilarated as we rushed between the white banks built up by the snow plough.

I only left Burnsyde at weekends, because I was afraid to come back after dark. It seemed ridiculous! But I was a prisoner of my own fear, completely dependent on Sean to take me anywhere.

We slowed down at the neat little lodge standing in its own garden by the roadside, then turned in at the large, ornamental, stone pillars of the main entrance to Avonlea.

I knew I had been impulsive and should have visited the area supervisor first, but we were now on our way along the wide drive and the ancient, turreted, stately home looked magnificent. Sean pulled up at the main entrance of the house and before I had time to think we were in the hall.

"Wait here till I get Matron!" He hurried across the hall and in through a door, then he was back in seconds. "Matron's in her sitting-room," he said, knocking on the door just a few yards from where I stood.

When the door opened a slim, middle-aged lady, dressed in tweeds, and of about my own height, smiled at Sean.

"Good evening, Sean," she said, as if she knew him well.

"You wanted a land-girl, Matron?"

"Yes, I do!"

"I've brought you one!" he answered, stepping aside.

She looked at me, taking in my breeches, rubber boots and heavy jacket.

"You certainly have!" she said, "And all ready to start work by the look of her. Shouldn't you have gone through the proper channels, young lady?"

"Yes, but if I had waited until next week it might have been too late. That's when I leave Burnsyde."

"I will accept you on Sean's recommendation," she answered, frowning, "after you have seen your area supervisor!"

It was growing dark when we made our way back to Burnsyde; but in a month's time, when the hours changed for British Summer Time, the light nights would come rushing in. But right now I would have to face the family.

There was still no one about when I entered the back kitchen and I wondered how I would tell Mr William about leaving. I felt agitated at the thought of it, but it had to be done. I pulled off my boots.

"Jaqueline, will you just empty this for me in the dustbin?" Miss June's voice called from the kitchen.

I rose at once and took the rubbish to the bin.

"Thank goodness the snow will soon be gone!" Miss June came bustling through with a mop and ran it across the marks on the tiled floor. "Mr William is so careless!" she muttered.

"Miss June," I began, "I ran upstairs this morning to get a handkerchief, and on my way down I overheard the conversation from the dining-room. I can't stay now, knowing what's in Miss Gillian's mind. Nothing ever happened between Sean and I. Will you tell Mr William for me? I find it difficult to give him my notice."

She listened quietly and when I had finished, she said,

"I'm sorry, Jaqueline, I'm going to miss you very much!"

At the supper table Miss Gillian kept glancing at me furtively, but not once did she stare in her offensive way. Mr William and Mother were as pleasant as they had always been.

After breakfast, on the Saturday morning, I went about my work feeling happier than I had felt during these first two bitter months of the year. From where I worked in the high field I could see the turrets of Avonlea reaching above the tall, dark, pine trees; the stately home stood on the bank of a river, at about the distance of a mile, and was well screened by a fir plantation.

Sean was working in the walled garden that morning, and but for a smile in passing there had been no chance to speak. It would be time for the morning tea break in a few minutes, so I dropped my tools into the barrow and started down the avenue; high above I could see catkins forming on the aspens; long, delicate and silky-grey.

I was thinking, as I walked, that no one had mentioned my leaving at supper last night; surely Miss June had told them? Then my thoughts drifted to the daffodils on the bank; long after they had bloomed and faded, the leaves of the aspens would be whispering and spinning in the still air.

Mr William had not said a word at breakfast about my leaving and I was deeply puzzled when I entered the back kitchen. Miss June said,

"Sit down, Jaqueline, I'll be with you in a moment!" The back kitchen was chilly, so I kept my jacket on until she came through with the tea. "I spoke to Miss Gillian last night and told her you had heard her malicious remark, but she is unrepentant. Because I thought it would be wiser, I waited until after breakfast this morning before telling Mr William you were leaving. And he has said that you may leave today without working the week's notice. Will you have a biscuit, Jaqueline?"

I took the biscuit and nibbled it, glad to be free of Miss Gillian's insulting stares. But I would miss the others, especially Miss June. Relieved, I smiled at her as she chatted away as she had always done:

"Sean has told me you may work at Avonlea; I hope you will be happier surrounded by young people; and may I say, my apologies for the distress you may have suffered through my misguided family."

The rest of the morning flew past, and when I entered the dining-room at midday there was no one but myself at the long, mahogany table. I sat looking round the room, the fireplace had been cleaned and was ready with fresh kindling and logs.

On my side plate was the small, manilla envelope containing my weekly wage, Mr William usually presented it to me just before I left for the weekend. I read the deductions on the front of the envelope and found, to my surprise, that I only had sixpence for my week's work.

The cold meat and salad, generously piled on my plate, had lost its appeal; rising from the table I walked over to the window clutching the manilla envelope. Thank goodness I had a return ticket in my purse to take me home to Edinburgh.

Outside, the tower wore a crown of snow and the hills beyond the valley were white.

With one last look round the familiar dining-room, I made my way upstairs. It took only minutes to freshen up and change. The few belongings in the drawers were quickly emptied into my suitcase. Before closing my bedroom door for the last time, I glanced at the black and white striped pillow and mattress already naked of covers, they seemed to add the finishing touch to this cold, austere room.

The house felt empty when I walked across the polished hall to the main door with my suitcase, then Miss June came hurrying through from the kitchen.

"Jaqueline, you wouldn't go without saying goodbye to me?"

"Why, of course not, Miss June, it's just that the house seems so empty!" I replied, putting my hands on her shoulders and lightly kissing her cheek. "Thank you for everything, Miss June, I shall miss you, and your cooking, very much."

There was a crunching of feet on the gravel just as we opened the main door, and there was Mr William helping Mother out of the car. I stood aside, while she climbed laboriously up the three steps.

"Oh! good morning, dear!" she exclaimed, "I've just been down to the village shoe shop and I feel quite tired."

"Let me help with your coat, Mother," said Miss June, full of concern. "After all, it is your first outing this year."

Mr William got back into his car, so I hurried down the steps.

"Excuse me, Mr William, may I ask why I have only sixpence for my wage this week?"

He looked at me coldly and answered,

"Nineteen shillings have been deducted for tax, and sixpence for National Health Insurance, as you can read on the envelope, and so you are left with sixpence!"

I smiled into his brown eyes, but there was no answering glow. It would be a waste of time to argue when he was in a spiteful mood, and I had a bus to catch. Before turning away, I said politely,

"Thank you, Mr William, and goodbye."

From the open door I could hear Mother saying to Miss June,

"Why is she taking her suitcase? Is she not coming back, June?"

It would be three hours before the next bus if I missed this one, so I hurried towards the steep drive. My persecutor and judge was not to be seen anywhere, but as I looked for the last time at the beautiful, white house, I saw a hand move the net curtains at Miss Gillian's bedroom window.

The sun was sparkling among the branches of the overhanging sycamores when I stepped through the ever-open gates of Burnsyde, but as I passed that evil spot which made my insides lurch sickeningly, I glanced furtively towards the trunks of the trees.

The seedlings from last year were pushing their way up through the soft, loamy soil in the shaded light, and I wondered how many would survive to reach the canopy above. It would not be long before new leaves transformed this place into a fresh, green grotto, hiding Burnsyde even more from the outside world.

I heard the bus approaching and ran out across the road to wave it down.

"Give me your suitcase, Miss!" the conductor said. "You came out of there as if the devil himself was chasing you!"

I smiled at him, feeling a great sense of relief steal over me as I sank into a seat.

Part Three

Avonlea Estate, 1944

Chapter Thirty

"Is it coffee with cream, Madam?" the neat waitress asked.

"Yes, please," I answered, and she hurried to the counter where the coffee percolated fresh and fragrant.

'Fullers' had not changed, although it seemed like ages since I had last been there. It was still the same luxurious, sprawling coffee lounge on the first floor. The castle stood high and noble in the gardens opposite, and a few patches of snow still lay in the crevices of its dark, brooding rock.

It was Monday morning, and my friends only gathered once a week on a Friday at lunch-time, so I sat alone. But I had come up to Princes Street to look at the familiar surroundings on my way to the tax office.

Although money was short and had to be carefully used, I had been unable to resist the coffee shop, and now, seated in my favourite place by one of the large, quaint windows where every pane of glass was bevelled at its edges and set into a framework of delicate, white painted wood, Burnsyde seemed far away.

The dark, impenetrable fir plantation opposite Burnsyde's entrance came into my mind; would I be accepted for the post at Avonlea Estate?

I smiled at the neat waitress in her black dress with its tiny, white organza apron. The matching wisp of a frilled cap was perched precariously on her hair as she placed the coffee in front of me. Quickly she wrote on a pad, tore off the bill and left it face down on the table. I would have to leave a tip, and yet, I earned less than she would earn in tips alone during the course of a week.

Men were busily cleaning the fountain in the gardens, while the traffic moved along Princes Street, and the bandstand was being made ready for the approach of summer. Hundreds of people would crowd into the seats to watch and listen, while music played and kilted groups danced.

It was warm today, one of those days that fooled you into casting off clothes too early in the year, 'ner cast a clout till May be out' the old folks would be saying. But I was young and healthy and I felt comfortable wearing a blue velvet dress with matching hat and court shoes; it was ridiculous to wear a coat on a lovely day like this, but I would never have gone out walking in Princes Street without gloves and a hat.

As I watched the activity across the way, a sudden spout of water gushed up from the fountain and the droplets fell like rain, sparkling in the morning sun. I suddenly realised I was seeing my city through the eyes of a stranger.

How clean and fresh it looked; soon the blossom trees would add their delicacy to the gardens. For a whole week I was home again to the comforts of gas and electricity, the entertainment of the ice-rink, theatre and ballroom dancing. My father disapproved of dance halls when so many men from the services were in Edinburgh, and that included Englishmen and Americans on his list of dislikes.

His attitude puzzled me, knowing as I did that his own father had come from the USA

Switching my thoughts to the purpose of my visit to the West End, I glanced at my watch. The tax office staff would be in the middle of their tea break, and probably in a better frame of mind to listen to my complaints by the time I saw them.

I put aside my latest disappointment in human nature, still wondering about Mr William's pettiness in leaving me with only sixpence. Had I not had some money of my own I would have been left without the tram fares from the bus station to my home.

Lingering in the coffee shop for a moment longer I gazed through the window, and placing the price of my coffee plus a tip on the table, I made my way across the thick carpet to the wrought-iron staircase leading down to Princess Street.

Walking along through the West End, I found it difficult to believe my nineteen and sixpence take-home-pay was subject to tax. At His Majesty's Tax Office they took a detailed statement of my earnings. I explained how the farmer deducted food and room from my wage then gave me the remainder after sixpence had been deducted for National Health Insurance. Leaving me with nineteen shillings and sixpence.

"You are quite sure you received only sixpence for your take-home-pay on Saturday?" said the frowning civil servant, who looked at me as if I was trying to defraud His Majesty's government. In answer, I produced the small manilla envelope with the detailed deductions clearly written on the front by Mr William, the sixpence still inside.

He offered me a chair, and while I waited a fifteen minute debate by three of His Majesty's tax officers progressed in my favour. They seemed oblivious of my presence and each one expressed his personal opinion on my weekly earnings. Then, grinning widely, the wittiest of the trio spoke to me with more than a hint of humour in his voice,

"As it would take longer if we paid the sum into your bank account, we, of the tax office, have decided to pay you the nineteen shillings in cash!"

Their repartee was amusing and they wished me well in my new post, and although I kept my thoughts to myself, there was nothing really amusing about having no money. I left the tax office with my nineteen shillings, thinking how fortunate I was to have parents and a good home to come back to.

My strict father had mellowed like a good wine since my sister, brother and I had become responsible teenagers. Some day I would marry, as I was expected to do, but I wanted a career and independence first.

Official acceptance of my request for the post at Avonlea came two days later. I was to report to the kitchen on Sunday evening before supper and, as I had expected, the weekly wage was to be the same as I had earned at Burnsyde.

The rest of the week had flown by, my mother fussing over the spotless, well-ironed contents of my suitcase. My boots gleamed with black boot polish, and the webbed leggings that had started out an olive green shade had been scrubbed until they looked faded grey.

At last I was ready, my work clothes immaculate enough to pass my mother's exacting standards. Tomorrow would be a new beginning, with new people; but this time I felt no excitement, only calm expectancy as to what lay ahead.

There was none of the glow I had felt on setting out for my first post at Earlson; or the apprehension I had experienced on leaving home for the first time to live and work at Burnsyde. This time I was the experienced worker, with confidence in my ability to endure hard work and long hours in all weathers.

Although unaware of it at the time, it was an attitude that was to carry me through the hard year that lay ahead.

Chapter Thirty-One

"One to Burnsyde, Miss?" the conductor asked, and I looked up at his familiar, pleasant face.

"No, Avonlea, please," I replied, smiling.

"Mmm!" he said, and winked his eye knowingly.

The journey had passed quickly, because my mind was full of what lay ahead. What kind of people I would work with? What would my room be like? Would it be cold as it had been at Burnsyde?

Before I realised it we had stopped at the massive, ornate, stone pillars that framed the entrance to Avonlea Estate.

"Best o' luck, Miss," said the conductor, passing down my suitcase.

"Thank you," I called, and gave him a wave as the bus moved off.

The ancient stately home stood by the bend of a river at the end of a long, broad drive, and scattered in clumps over the wide lawns daffodils were bursting forth in shades of yellow gold.

I took a deep breath and walked on past the impressive main entrance of the house, with its four stone columns, right down to the silently flowing river. Crocuses clustered in thousands along its banks, and under the still bare pendulous branches of weeping willows snowdrops drooped their shy, white heads.

Retracing my steps past the main entrance I turned left round to the side of this turreted mansion. Towards the back of the house I passed a utility building, which could have been a garage. Then just behind that was an entrance door, the bins and brushes standing to one side telling me it was the kitchen.

I knocked, and was looking at the brushes when the door opened.

"Come in!" said the thin, wiry woman who held the door open, and I smiled into the bright blue eyes that twinkled behind her thick glasses. Then she added, "I'm Bridget, the cook," and gripping my hand she shook it vigorously as I stepped inside.

"Pleased to meet you, Bridget, I'm Jaqueline, the new land-girl. Matron told me to report to the kitchen on arrival."

While I looked round the large, clean kitchen the cook chatted on,

"Oh! and did she now! Then I'll introduce you to the staff. Bridget turned to a smiling, dark-haired girl seated at the kitchen table, "This is, Mary, the kitchen maid." We shook hands and murmured a greeting as Bridget spoke again, "Karen is the table maid!"

The tall, shapely Karen rose from the bench that ran the full length of the table, gave me a brief nod and busied herself with a silver tray.

"Matron's sugar bowl is empty!" she said, her primness a complete contrast to the kitchen maid who lingered happily over her food.

"Hang Jaqueline's coat in the hall, Karen, and she'll join us for a bit of supper," said Bridget, placing some freshly cooked ham on a plate.

With a toss of her head, Karen took my coat and flounced out of the kitchen, her high heels tapping on the stone floor.

"She'll just about speak to the kitchen maid," remarked Bridget, "but I doubt if she'll have anything to do with the land-girl." Then she placed the plate of ham on the table and nodded, "Sit yourself down there and help yourself to salad."

I had walked into the kitchen of Avonlea a stranger and already I felt part of it. I realised, within the first few minutes of my arrival, that being a member of the staff in a stately home would have its ups and downs, and, unfortunately, I had joined them as the lowliest member of the staff as far as Karen was concerned.

"Is this what's known as class distinction in the kitchen, Bridget?" I asked the busy cook.

"Now, don't be letting it bother you, Jaqueline, it takes all kinds to make a world!"

"Yes, Bridget," I answered, amused at the situation I found myself in.

She turned from her task of stirring oatmeal into a huge, black, cauldron of a pot and looked at me sharply.

"Then you'll be taking my advice with a pinch of salt, will you not?"

Mary, who had been listening while she finished her leisurely meal, made no attempt to join in the conversation.

The freshly cooked ham was slightly salty and the thick slices cut down into chunky mouthfuls; there was nothing I enjoyed more than the fresh vegetable salad served with it.

Karen had flounced back into the kitchen to collect Matron's tray and while she stood waiting with her nose in the air, Bridget filled a silver coffee pot.

"You'll take your orders from Tam, the gardener," Bridget said briskly, turning to me as Karen left with the silver tray. "Be down here at 7.45 a.m. for breakfast. Tam will be waiting in the furnace room at eight, looking at his pocket watch."

Each statement had been delivered with a slap of her hand on the kitchen table, so I answered,

"Yes, Bridget."

Putting her hands on her bony hips, she said,

"You'd better be taking me seriously, because it's serious I mean to be!" But the twinkle was still there behind her glasses.

There was a scuffling noise behind the half-open door leading to the hall, which drew my attention, and a little face peeped round then vanished.

"Off to bed with you!" shouted Bridget, "you'll see the new land-girl tomorrow!"

The small face had not appeared again, but a whispered discussion could clearly be heard behind the kitchen door. Bridget, who had gone back to stirring the oatmeal in the outsized black pot, placed her wooden spoon on a plate and tiptoed across the floor, and quickly pulled open the door. Four little pyjama-clad boys fell onto the kitchen floor.

As they scrambled to their feet, Bridget's hand gave a sharp pat on the nearest bottom and they scattered across the polished floor of the hall towards a wide, sweeping staircase.

"These are four of the little ones from the nursery, they just couldn't wait to see what you looked like," she said, turning to pour coffee from a tall, brown, enamel pot into white mugs. "Pass one to Jaqueline, Mary. Do you take sugar?"

Before I could answer, her next statement rang out, "Because it's only one spoonful you'll be gettin', and we don't keep it on the table because the boys would be off with it every day!"

Having dropped a spoonful into my mug she placed the bowl back in the larder, locked the door and dropped the jangling bunch of keys into the pocket of her starched, white apron.

"Have to keep everything under lock and key, or there would be nothing left to cook with," Bridget remarked calmly, and sat her lean frame down in the brown wooden chair at the head of the table. She sipped her sugarless black coffee. "You'll be expected to lend a hand with the patching and darning in the staff sitting-room, and as we are short of staff, the girls could do with an extra pair of hands when the small boys are in the bath at six o'clock.

I was about to remind her that I was the land-girl, but the cook's bright eyes silenced me, as did her constant flow of conversation that seldom required any answer. There was a murmur of voices from the hall, and with a glance in my direction Bridget rose, just as Matron walked into the kitchen.

"The new land-girl arrived while we were having supper, Matron, so I asked her to join us." Bridget's remark drew a cold look of disapproval from Matron, and, as if the cook had not spoken at all, she turned to me and said frigidly,

"Good evening, Jaqueline, why did you not report to me on arrival?"

Bridget gave me a sharp look, so I decided not to mention the letter I had left at home, telling me to report to the kitchen. I felt myself blush in confusion, and replied,

"Sorry, Matron, I would have disturbed your supper."

When Matron had gone back to her sitting-room, pleased with my explanation, Karen, who had felt the awkwardness of the situation, blurted out,

"She asked if you had arrived when I was serving coffee."

"Is Matron difficult to get on with?" I asked.

"Now, now! I won't have you discussing Matron," said Bridget.

There was silence after Bridget had reproached us and I turned to Karen:

"Where in England do you come from, Karen?"

"The south," she replied briefly in her refined voice, and walked out into the hall.

While Bridget swung the large pot of porridge away from the heat and covered it with a lid, Mary cleared the coffee mugs from the table.

"Take Jaqueline up to her room, Mary. And don't forget to take your suitcase with you," Bridget smiled as she spoke, "it's a long hike upstairs!"

We made our way out of the kitchen into the large hall, where Mary pointed to a corridor on the left, saying,

"The staff sitting-room is at the end of that corridor, Bridget's room is on the left of the sitting-room and mine is on the right." Moving towards the grand staircase we started up, and Mary pointed, "That's Karen's room at the top of the stairs and all the dormitories, and the nursery, are on her floor."

Turning left, to the far end of the spacious first floor landing, we came to an archway and Mary hurried through. Then I followed her up carpeted steps that spiralled round a stone pillar.

"Is it much further?" I asked.

"You're in one of the turret bedrooms, it has a good view of the main drive and you'll be able to see Tam's lodge from your window."

Mary produced a key and opened the door of my bedroom.

"I hope you'll be comfortable," she said, "if you need anything, just ask."

"Thank you very much, Mary," I replied gratefully. And as she turned towards the stairs, she called,

"The bathroom's next door."

I stepped into my room, closed the door and looked round. The whole place seemed to glow with pinks, lavender and soft greens; I couldn't have been more delighted with my new surroundings.

A large wardrobe shone golden-grey with the skilful blending of satinwood, and my clothes looked lost in the ample space it provided. Chintz frills draped themselves round a kidney-shaped dressing table, co-ordinating with the cushions on a comfortable basket chair. In the triple mirrors of the dressing table I could easily see the sides and back of my hair.

When I lifted the fringed, white bedspread, the legs of the unusually high bed were set into rounded blocks of wood about eight inches tall. At the head of the bed rods radiated into a half circle of highly polished brass.

The whole room was quaint and cosy and I could stretch myself out flat, with room to spare, on the well worn, pale pink carpet that completely covered the floor. I had thought it was a seat round the

wall in the turret window, but when I investigated it was a shaft
bringing warm air into the room.

I settled down for the night feeling well pleased with the move I
had made from just over a mile along the road, and cast out all
thoughts of the little, cold, white room; perhaps I would meet Miss
June one day in the village?

While I lay there in my high, luxurious bed gazing across the room
at the turret window, I tried to think of Burnsyde, but it was already
receding into the past with the last of the fading light.

Chapter Thirty-Two

I had just finished breakfast and was still seated at the table on my first morning at Avonlea, when the back door to the kitchen opened.

"Mornin', Bridget!" I turned to look at the owner of the gruff voice, but his eyes were on the silver pocket watch he held in his hand.

"Mornin', Tam!" replied Bridget. "Well, I've no doubt you'll be pleased to see the new land-girl. This is, Jaqueline." While she spoke, she pointed towards me with her rolling pin, then opening the oven door in the large, black range passed her hand over the top shelf to test the heat.

The newcomer gave me a baleful glare.

"Punctuality is what we want!" he said, and his black, walrus moustache barely moved. "Are you ready to start?"

"Yes," I replied, thinking that this revoltingly rude man would be hard to please.

He turned and walked outside and Bridget gave me a smile as I followed. Just a few yards from the kitchen door, on a low extension, he put the toe of his boot to a narrow door and pushed it open.

"This is the furnace room!" he barked, starting down the eight narrow steel steps and beckoning me to follow.

On the floor of the furnace room there was just enough width for us to pass each other; a coal bunker was set into the full length of the wall on one side, and on the other side stood three iron furnaces.

"Take that poker, unlatch the top door and give it a good rake up." He pointed to the middle furnace as he spoke, and I followed his orders. "Now, open the bottom door, set that hook in here and pull it back and forward. Look as though you mean it!" he added.

The grey ash fell through into the container below as I pulled and pushed, then a sudden shower of sparks appeared.

"Stop! That's enough!" he said gruffly. "Now take the ash can up the steps and empty it into the bin outside the kitchen door."

I climbed the steep steps with the can of hot ashes in my gloved hands, wishing I could grip the hand rail. But it took both hands to support the can and I flinched as the heat started to penetrate my gloves. When I stepped out through the narrow door the breeze licked the top of the ash can setting it ablaze, and I quickly held it away from me.

"Put it on the ground!" a voice called, and some boys who were kicking a ball came running across. Between them they tipped it into the bin, slammed the lid on, then ran off kicking their ball.

Flustered by the flames leaping up at me, I hurried back down the steel steps with the empty ash can to where the gardener waited.

"Stoke up the furnaces, and break down these big lumps of coal with the sledge hammer. We use only two of the furnaces," he added, and pointing to the heavy sledge hammer he left me to my work.

When I tried to lift the long-handled sledge hammer I felt sure it must be stuck to the floor; so I slid my hands halfway down the shaft and tried again; it moved!

I managed, after much pulling and heaving, to get the heavy hammer onto my shoulder, and from that position I could drop it onto the large lumps of shiny, black coal he had lined up down the centre of the floor; they shattered easily under the solid lump of metal.

With the two furnaces stoked and the shattered coal shovelled into the bunker, I straightened my trembling legs and climbed up into the sunlight, leaving it to the wind to blow the ash and coal dust from my hair and clothes.

Bridget's brisk, friendly voice called me from the kitchen door:

"Come and wash the dust out of your throat with a cup of tea!"

Thankful for the chance to sit down until my legs regained their strength, I sat on the doorstep emptying the dross from my boots, and swallowed down the stewed remains of the tea we had had for breakfast: it tasted like nectar!

In the meantime, the gardener had returned and was checking up on my work in the furnace room.

"Sweep up the dross and throw it into the bunker, you'll find a brush behind the third furnace." He stood there scowling while I hurriedly tied my boot laces. "You stoke up at noon, before cook serves lunch, and then at five before tea. At night, about ten o'clock, you stoke up again then close down the dampers on both furnaces, or they'll be out before morning!"

The dislike or loathing on his face brought me quickly to my feet, and I vowed as I looked at his hard eyes that I would never let the furnaces go out.   I felt guilty about the few minutes I had spent drinking Bridget's tea and emptying my boots.   As if he had read my thoughts, he came at me nastily,

"Fetch the baskets and put them in the barrow!"

"What baskets?" I asked politely, looking straight into his angry, black eyes.   He spluttered, and before he could answer Bridget was passing the two baskets from the kitchen doorway.

"Put them on the barrow and we'll go down to the kitchen garden," he grunted.

Thrusting my hands deep into the pockets of my jacket I followed him along the paths, past the lawns.   Skirting the fir plantation he turned the barrow sharply to the right.   We had gone about a third of a mile together, when he almost ran down a steep, narrow path between banks of azalea bushes.

I gasped, enraptured by what lay before me. If I had missed anything of beauty by not being able to see through the solid wooden doors of Mr William's walled garden, I now saw before me a panorama of colour and order to delight the eye.

While the gardener fumbled with the lock, I could see through the delicate pattern of the tall, wrought-iron gates a pink and white world of blossom trees.   The petals drifted lazily down to the paths giving the garden an ethereal appearance.   The flowers of spring bloomed in profusion across the dark soil of well-raked borders like patchwork.

There were three main paths running the full length of the garden; these were intersected by smaller paths running across the way creating beds for flowers, roses and fruit bushes that would bloom in summer.   At each point where the paths crossed stood perfect specimens of apple, ornamental cherry, and almond trees.   He pushed open the tall, black gates and we stepped into a lightly perfumed, calm atmosphere where the petals drifted down like confetti.

Abruptly he turned and closed the gates which were the only entrance I could see in the sandstone walls.   My admiring gaze was on the fruit trees skilfully trained along the walls and looking like very old, gnarled vines.   From my history books I knew that the Romans had cultivated vines in Britain, but this was very far north, it would be impossible.

It was too early in the year for growth, and because of his surly nature I would never ask the gardener what kind of fruit trees they were, then he spoke:

"You touch nothing unless I tell you to!"

He sounded ominous, and his eyes held no light of pleasure in the surroundings that delighted me. We walked down the centre path and turning right approached an opening in the wall I had not noticed from the gate, and as we passed through it he said,

"This here is quarter of an acre used for growing the basic kitchen vegetables. In that shed by the greenhouse you'll find onions and sacks of potatoes. Put one of the sacks in the barrow with a string of onions, then pick up the baskets of flowers as you leave."

My hand went to my pocket for working gloves, but I had left them in the furnace room. Without gloves my grip on the sack of potatoes was puny. As I struggled to lift it, he stepped forward, picked up the sack and dumped it on the barrow; his uncomplimentary abuse stung my ears as he strode away.

I had started through the opening in the wall, and had picked up the flower baskets on the way, when he called out,

"Leave the baskets in Matron's sitting-room! Take the rest to the kitchen!"

While I listened, my eyes were on the assortment of narcissi in the baskets. Some were paper white, others had vermilion edges on their short trumpets. Long trailing branches of forsythia draped themselves over the wheel of the barrow, and when I moved forward with the load some onions dangling over the side pulled the whole string with them. The gardener hurried over and picked them up.

"They won't be fit to eat if you throw them about like that" he said, placing them back on the barrow. Without a word I headed for the gate. "And close the gate behind you to keep them buggers out!" he roared.

On the steep, short slope running between the azalea bushes I toiled upwards, eventually pulling instead of pushing the one wheeled barrow with its heavy load. I stopped on reaching the main path to regain my breath and gaze at the forsythia's yellow blossom.

The quarter acre, which lay outside the sandstone wall of the garden, was edged on the remaining three sides by a twelve foot hedge of holly. As I looked down on the arrangement of the low-lying garden, the only visible entrance was through the tall, black, wrought-iron gates; the boys would have to scale the high stone wall to get in.

Lunch was almost ready when I tipped the potatoes into the bin in the kitchen.

"Time to stoke up the furnaces," said Bridget, "then clean up for lunch. Oh! and you had better put Matron's flowers into her sitting-room!"

"Which room will that be, Bridget?"

She came to the door and pointed across the hall:

"The last door on the left, it's the best room in the house. And you'll soon know the place like the back of your hand!"

The large hall was panelled up to a high picture rail, in polished oak, and as I approached the door of Matron's sitting-room I stepped onto a faded Persian carpet; it seemed lost in the large hall. Behind double glass doors the vestibule displayed another Persian carpet.

To one side of the sitting-room door stood a white marble bust on a pedestal, its blank eyes were almost level with my own; I knocked.

"Come in!" a rich, deep voice called out instantly. I opened the door and stepped into the room.

It had church-like windows along one wall and the sun streamed through on a multitude of ornaments and period furniture. Aged paintings in heavy, gold frames covered the far wall where the sun could not reach. From where I stood I could see the top of a head, a hand holding a crystal glass filled with port, and a foot in a carpet slipper resting on a stool.

"Excuse me," I said, feeling as if I had stepped into a bygone age, "where shall I put the flower baskets?"

"Put them on my wife's desk by the window."

Then the hand rose to indicate the position of the desk.

Quickly and quietly I crossed the room to where the desk stood with its matching chair; both were inlaid with ivory and smelled of mustiness.

"So you are the new land-girl!" the rich voice said. I put down the baskets and turned to face the man in the chair, and answered,

"Yes, I'm Jaqueline."

He studied me from head to toe and I became acutely aware of my boots, drill cloth coat and dungarees; the light fawn material was grubby with coal, and with mud from the potato sack.

"Just put another log on the fire before you go!" he said.

His large body flowed into every part of the red leather easy chair, and a roll of fat rested on the silk scarf softly knotted where his neck should have been.

The carpet slipper had been cut to accommodate a bandage around his foot, and as his plump hand picked up the decanter to refill his glass, the effort turned his complexion to the same colour as the burgundy velvet jacket he wore. I quietly left the overheated room after adding another log to the already blazing fire.

"How did the Warden injure his foot, Bridget?" I asked on entering the kitchen. The cook put her hands on her bony hips and laughed.

"It's injured by way of his mouth," she said, "he's troubled with the gout!"

The gardener was already standing outside the back door when I finished lunch. I had not hurried, freshening up for lunch, but had flattened myself out on the pink carpet in my pretty, homely room on the second floor to rest, and had felt pleased with the floral paper covering the rounded walls of my turret bedroom. The other walls were covered in regency stripe and blended perfectly with the pink and lavender of the floral paper.

Through the white haze of net framing my turret window I had a wide view of the estate grounds, and I had stood there for several minutes before going down to lunch. I had felt the need to rest and relax more than the pangs of hunger.

Determined to take the full hour I was entitled to have I ignored the crunching of Tam's impatient feet outside the back door. Bridget gave me a nod as the kitchen clock struck the hour, and I had just risen from the table when he pushed the door open; we then walked silently down to the garden. The main sections of the lawns had been cut, filling the air with the smell of newly mown grass and leaving the large areas of daffodils nodding in the breeze right down to the river bank. Burnsyde's daffodils would be still in bud.

It was a very mild spring and the air was humid; I had never felt humidity so early in the year on the east coast. Perhaps the West Country *was* milder in spring, as the Land Army supervisor had mentioned at headquarters.

When we reached the garden gates the gardener again went through the fumbling action of opening the lock.

"The hedge needs trimming on the outside; can you use a hand scythe?" he asked, stomping towards the quarter acre entrance.

We had entered the creasoted hut where all the tools were kept neatly hanging on the walls, and I glanced round the collection and answered,

"I don't know what a hand scythe is!"

He spluttered and snatched a small sickle from the wall.

"I've never used one of these," I said, "but I can use those hedge shears!"

"You'll need the small saw for the thick wood and take it well in, I don't want it done by half," he grunted.

Carrying a stepladder, the hedge shears and a saw, we made our way through a stout, wooden door, hidden behind a large clump of rhododendron bushes, in the back wall of the garden. The hedge was like wildly overgrown trees; then he cut into a section with the shears, sawed off some two foot lengths, and tossed the shears and saw into the long grass at my feet.

"That's how I want it done!" he said, stomping off towards the door we had come through in an ape-like manner.

When I looked up and along the hedge seemed endless, and it was over twice my height. I walked to the corner to look at the front.

"You won't get it done standing looking at it!" he shouted, his words coming back to me muffled by the hedge. I started with the feeling that I would never make it.

I had been working steadily for two hours and my arms had gone through the aching stage to a dull rubbery numbness, when I heard his voice hail me from inside the garden,

"Go to the kitchen for a cup of tea and be back here in fifteen minutes!"

It was very warm working in this low-lying area; I rubbed the sleeve of my jacket across my brow and climbed down from the ladder feeling dazed. The walk back to the house cleared my head and eased my aching arms.

"What's he got you doing now?" was Bridget's smiling remark when I entered the kitchen.

"I'm cutting the outside of the holly hedge round the quarter acre."

"For the love of holy Mary!" she said under her breath, and the strong tea poured from the spout of her brown, enamel teapot into a white mug. "He means to break you in the hard way."

It was difficult not to smile when she crossed herself with one hand and placed the never-empty teapot on the hob with the other. While I was drinking my tea at the well-scrubbed, pinewood table Matron walked in.

"Jaqueline, I want some daffodils moved this afternoon before they fade beyond recognition. It's a small clump of pale pink daffodils I have come across," she said thoughtfully. "I want them planted in front of the sitting-room windows. I'll show you where they are," she added in her high-handed way.

I made to rise, but she stopped me with a wave of her hand.

"Finish your tea, I will see you on the side lawn in ten minutes!"

"Tam's not going to like that!" remarked Bridget, as soon as Matron had left the kitchen.

"He told me to be back in fifteen minutes."

"That's what I mean," she replied, "he'll be up here looking for you."

"Can I have some more tea, Bridget?" I had swallowed it down and absorbed it like blotting paper and my mug was empty.

"Indeed to goodness you can, you're going to need it when you meet up with Tam!"

Down by the river Matron pointed to a patch of daffodils.

"None of my friends have anything so unusual in their grounds. I wonder why I have never noticed them before?" she said, puzzled.

"They could be young bulbs that are flowering for the first time," I suggested.

"Yes," she said, "that could be the answer." Then her voice took on a sharp edge as she continued, "Be careful, Jaqueline! Dig only round the edge of the clump!"

Lifting the bulbs in a cluster from the leafy mould in which they had developed, I placed them lengthwise in the flower basket to prevent the peachy-pink blooms breaking away from their food source.

Matron picked up the hand trowel I had used and dropped it into a canvas bag she carried, and we walked up to where the bulbs were to be planted beside the white narcissi outside the sitting-room windows. Delving into her canvas bag Matron handed me an implement that could only be described as a large apple corer.

"Push it into the ground and leave the plug of soil you have removed at the side of the hole."

"Yes, Matron."

Then she knelt on a pad of rubber and watched, while I pushed into the loamy ground and drew out a plug of soil.

"Now carefully pull the bulbs apart so as not to damage them, and insert one in each hole you make."

Following me on her knees, engrossed in the task of crumbling each plug and pressing it in with her fingers to support the stems as I planted the bulbs, she chatted away.

"They will show up nicely beside the white narcissi. They looked quite insipid beside the yellow daffodils."

"Yes, Matron," I agreed, becoming aware of the gardener's feet crunching on the path as he drew near.

It was not until he stopped and spoke that Matron looked up. He glared at me ignoring her completely.

"You should have been back in the garden fifteen minutes ago!" he said, closing the lid of his silver watch and pushing it back into the pocket of his waistcoat.

My eyes were fixed on the silver chain that dangled from the watch, clipped on somewhere beneath the heavy leather belt about his waist. This rude man had still not addressed Matron, and the seconds ticked by in the charged silence as I waited determined not to speak, knowing it was my employer's place to answer.

"She's here to work!" he said suddenly, "not to play!"

"Yes!" replied Matron, "gardening *is* playing!"

I saw the side of his mouth twitch, and his eyes blazed, and he turned his powerful body and strode up the drive towards the lodge.

Chapter Thirty-Three

I had been at the beck and call of Matron for about two weeks, and the cutting of the hedge round the quarter acre had come to a standstill. We were busily digging up the largest clumps of daffodils as they began to fade, and transplanting them to bare patches along the river bank when, without warning, the sky went dark, and the rain suddenly poured down in sheets.

Matron rose in a panic from the little rubber mat she knelt on, stumbling in her anxiety to run for the house. In a flash I had pulled off my drill cloth coat and placed it over her head and shoulders, she fled on up the path while I hurried along behind. When we reached the shelter of the colonnaded entrance she handed me the sodden jacket.

"Enough bulbs have been transplanted, Jaqueline. Now come to my sitting-room and collect the bottles and jars the boys have given me with their offerings of daffodils," she smiled, "they are quite dead now so I can dispose of them; just throw them all into the dustbin!" As I lifted the tray of smelly jars and dead flowers, she added, "I have told the man to be here in the morning; I want the grass cut before the azaleas bloom. And, I wonder, should I let him cut down the daffodils? It could be all done at once."

Working hours meant nothing to Matron, she would knock on my door late in the evening and in her overbearing manner, say,

"Jaqueline, your help is required in the staff sitting-room, there is mending to be done!" The assumption that I was a mere lackey to do her bidding was due to her upbringing as one of the privileged classes.

However, as always, I went downstairs dutifully and started on the mound of torn shirts and trousers, socks where the whole heel had to be darned, and the tin box overflowing with buttons for cuffs and shirt fronts. While I stitched I felt satisfied that the more I did the sooner the war would end.

I had been so deep in thought it was only when Matron spoke that I realised she had been watching me from the doorway.

"You know we are short staffed, Jaqueline, and I expect you to stay over the weekend to help out. It is not right that you should be allowed home every weekend while the others have only one weekend in the month."

Matron's overbearing manner had the same effect on me as did Bridget's bullying assertiveness; and because I treated all this as a phase in my life that would pass with the war, I found it amusing. It satisfied my desire to help in any way I could when my country was deep in war, and I answered,

"Yes, Matron. Just as you say!"

She had not asked me politely, and there was to be no thanks for my time or effort. My pleasure came from Mary, the kitchen maid, being given her weekend off.

The hedge had been forgotten, and the daffodils spread across the lawns defying Matron's urgency to mow them down. They continued to multiply in all their golden glory, and even the ones we had transplanted along the river bank stood tall and delicately golden against the background of the river.

Primroses clustered beneath the still bare trees, their poses fragile and dainty against the dark, loamy soil.

As we moved slowly into April the March winds had not blown as Matron had insisted they would; and the April showers came down in torrential sheets, passing as if they had never been, leaving the grounds refreshed and the air humid.

Matron had her way with the fading daffodils; the man arrived one morning with his mowing machine and chugged across the lawns churning everything in his path into a shower of green.

The noise of the mower had brought me out early, and I stood in the morning sun with freshly shampooed hair, clean shirt, jacket and dungarees spotlessly laundered, and my boots as black and shiny as Bridget's kitchen range.

The chopped grass, and what was left of the daffodils, was showering out behind the mower as Tam, the gardener, approached. He had told me the day before not to stoke the furnaces at ten that night, but to open the dampers and let them burn out. When I had asked why, he had merely grunted.

On his shoulder Tam carried a bundle and as he drew nearer I could see it was a set of brushes, the kind that chimney sweeps used. Having put the bundle on the ground he unwound it and tossed a sooty length of sacking at my feet.

"See that the furnaces are out, and hang that over the first one, leaving the top door open." His face was full of arrogance as he spoke, and I went below.

My clean fawn working outfit was already smutty with soot, when he followed me down the steel steps. Selecting a brush he lifted the edge of the sacking cover, and with a muttered oath rammed it through the open door of the furnace. As the brush and its handle went up the chimney he screwed on an extension piece and pushed again.

"I'm going up top, keep adding another length until I give you a shout," he said, "then start pulling the brush down again."

I groaned inwardly, why had he not told me last night? I kept adding extension pieces and with each push a shower of soot flew out from under the sacking. I was almost in tears as it billowed into my face and settled all over my clean overalls. Hopefully I buttoned up the neck of my beige airtex shirt.

A smothered, owl-like hoot sounded in the chimney and I started pulling down the brush, removing each section as it appeared. When the brush came into view it was followed by a load of soot that landed with a soft plop, filling the furnace room with a black cloud and engulfing me from head to foot. I stood there breathing into my handkerchief with my eyes closed.

"Fill that sack with the soot and hand it up," rasped Tam's voice.

He stood in the doorway looking down on my feeble attempt to lift the sack I had just filled. Eventually I tipped half of it out, realising that soot was very heavy stuff; and as he took the offering he remarked, with his pipe clenched between his teeth,

"Soot's grand for the garden; cover the other furnace with the sacking and get busy with the brush!"

I felt angry as I started on the second furnace, black and bewildered I tried to console myself by muttering that a Girl Guide smiles and sings under all difficulties, but my philosophy turned sour when I thought of the waste of hot water and precious shampoo.

Tam gave me a withering look as he placed the bags of soot from the second chimney in his barrow.

"Clean up the mess and rekindle the furnaces! I'll see you after lunch!" he said.

I breathed a sigh of relief at his parting remark. At least I would have time to have a bath and change.

Bridget doubled up with laughter when I walked into the kitchen, and Mary stopped in mid-trill on her rendering of Ave Maria, covering her face with her apron she shook all over with suppressed mirth. I felt more like crying, until Bridget composed herself and said,

"Look here, Jaqueline, in the mirror!"

My hair and face were completely black, with just the red-rimmed, greenish-blue eyes startlingly clear in the reflection.

"He could have told me last night, I've wasted my shampoo!" I said angrily; but all of a sudden I was laughing at the soot-covered reflection looking back at me from the mirror.

"Tam likes everyone to learn the hard way," said Bridget. "He never gives any warning, but there's enough hot water for a bath and you can use my shampoo!"

A momentary shadow clouded her bright eyes, and then she ran through to her room and brought back a bottle of golden-coloured liquid. I was beginning to feel better already.

The rationed amount of bath water, as advised over the radio, was six inches. Even the King stuck to this regulation to conserve fuel. However, on that day I wallowed with the bath almost overflowing. If I had used six inches it would have been the consistency of mud. Then I rinsed with fresh water until an overpowering sense of guilt made me turn the tap off – I felt sure the King would have been horrified.

With hair shining, and wearing a complete change of clothing I made my way happily down the wide staircase to the kitchen. Karen, Mary and Bridget were discussing Tam when I took my place at the table, and the sixteen year old Karen turned to me as she rose.

"He's a nasty old man and I wouldn't work for him, Jaqueline!"

"Well, I don't really work for him, do I, Karen? I'm doing my bit to help win the war as a land girl; but I must admit I didn't expect to be sweeping chimneys!"

"There's no use offering advice to a person who thinks as you do, you'll just have to learn the hard way!" Karen replied.

She wore her light brown hair piled on top of her head, and a freshly starched cap sat on the nest of curls to match her dainty white apron. I envied her trim, black dress as she left the kitchen with Matron's tray. Karen turned at the door and said,

"He's wicked, it's his fault Heather's so ill!"

"Karen!" Bridget looked fierce, and she almost shouted, "Take Matron her tray!"

Still seated at the table, while Bridget prepared lunch, I silently pondered the heated remarks. The cleaning woman, busily working her way across the floor on her hands and knees with a scrubbing brush, lifted the large, greyish-white cloth from her bucket, wrung it out, and muttered,

"By God, it's true!"

"Hold your tongue, Jenny!" snapped Bridget. "Matron doesn't tolerate gossip!"

Bridget had put an end to the discussion leaving me completely in the dark as to who Heather might be.

Chapter Thirty-Four

The very first thing that caught my eye when I wandered into the sitting-room that evening, was a paperback lying on a small table by the window.

Since coming to Avonlea I had been so busy patching and darning after supper, that it seemed the whole day was taken up and then it was time to stoke the furnaces before going to bed.

Not realising how weary I felt I picked up the paperback and sank into the comfort of a brown, plush, easy chair, completely ignoring the mound of sewing.

Tam had started me on the holly hedge as soon as I entered the garden after lunch, and after the chimney sweeping episode of the morning, holding a needle in puffy, rubbery hands that trembled after an afternoon's sawing and cutting was almost impossible.

I opened the paperback and was soon carried away by the ingenious mind of Agatha Christie, the fatigue of my body forgotten.

"Jaqueline, Jaqueline!" Matron said my name twice before I realised she was standing in the doorway. "You should be upstairs helping with the younger boys at bath time if you are not mending. You know we are short staffed because the other maid has not yet returned from her holidays!" She sounded furious as she tutted over the absent maid, who in fact never did return from her holidays.

Putting down the book I followed her meekly upstairs to the nursery bathroom where Mary and Karen were busily drying a group of little boys, and dressing them in their pyjamas

"Right, out you come, Chip!" And Mary lifted the little boy out of the bath water as she turned to me, "Thanks for coming to the rescue, Jaqueline. Just make sure the backs of Martin's legs are clean, it's usually the dirtiest area."

Martin's wide, blue eyes were already fixed on my face, and he piped up,

"I can wash myself because I'm nearly four!"

Mary gave a nod and quietly said,

"Always encourage them to do for themselves."

I found it awkward to know where to start, or what to say, but Mary bundled Chip on to my back and I carried him through to bed.

The bathroom floor was littered with clothes when I took Martin out of the soapy bath water, and Mary had gone down to the kitchen to help Bridget, leaving Karen and I to finish off in the nursery.

With all the little boys sitting up in bed looking as though they had never been dirty in their lives, Karen clapped her hands.

"Prayers, boys!" she said briskly.

All at once, eyes closed and hands came together beneath each little chin; then they repeated the lines after Karen:

"Thank you for the world so sweet,
Thank you for the food we eat,
Thank you for the birds that sing,
Thank you God for everything!
Amen."

The chorus of tiny voices had copied Karen's perfectly spoken English as they repeated her words clearly. I felt glad Matron had taken me away from my book, and then Karen said,

"If Chip wants to say his prayer tonight we will all listen."

The cherubic faces were still bent over, and the little hands pressed together beneath their baby chins. I controlled a wide grin as only their eyes turned to look in the direction of Chip. We waited, and I wondered which three had had their bottoms smacked only yesterday, when Matron had found them in her front garden skinning live frogs.

In the angelic silence I turned to look at Chip as he said in his baby voice,

"Help us to be good, and always in the perfect mood.
Help us every day, to grow up in the proper way.
Amen."

At the first word all eyes had closed. The still damp, golden curls tumbled over his forehead, and when his eyes popped open they caught me smiling at him. Chip, suddenly overcome with shyness, slid under the bed covers.

Karen switched off the main light leaving the night-light glowing comfortingly at the end of the nursery; then we kissed the cheek of each child and quietly said goodnight, leaving the simple comfort of the nursery with its polished wood floors.

On our way to the sitting-room we picked up the bundle of shirts minus buttons, socks with holes, and the inevitable pair of trousers with no seat. A build-up of patching and darning kept us busy in the sitting-room until nine thirty, when I excused myself in order to stoke up the central heating and hot water furnaces for the night.

Much of this large, castle-like mansion house had been closed up since the beginning of the war, and only the part we lived in was kept heated. The unused furnace stood in the corner red with rust, and it set me to wondering what state the closed up part of the house would be in.

I stoked-up and closed down the dampers. And all the while I pondered on the sheer strength of character that motivated a tiny, middle-aged lady to rule Avonlea the way she did. Matron could expect little or no help from her husband, whose appetite for food and wine had bound him to the red leather chair in which he spent most of his time.

Having finished in the furnace room I climbed the steel steps and walked out into the cool, moonlit night. It had been a long, hard day; and on reaching the cosiness of my room I walked over to the turret window and looked up the broad drive to where Tam's lodge stood. In the silvery light of the moon, which no black-out could extinguish, the lodge was the perfect miniature of the large mansion house; Tam's own little castle, complete with turrets.

Chapter Thirty-Five

When raising my eyes from the smooth lawns, on my way down to the garden, I noticed that the willow trees down by the river wore a haze of pastel green. It would not be long before the leaf buds swelled and opened.

I felt refreshed this morning after a sound sleep; it amazed me to find myself none the worse after the previous day's introduction to sweeping chimneys. And the utter fatigue I had felt after spending the whole afternoon sawing and cutting the holly hedge was gone.

For some unknown reason Sean slipped into my thoughts. He would be in the air force now. But where, I had no idea. He had not written to tell me anything, so I shrugged him to the back of my mind as I stopped in front of the tall wrought-iron gates.

Many of the blossom trees were past their springtime glory, but a graceful Japanese cherry stretched its straight branches into the morning air, almost hidden under the dense show of pink double blossoms; it must surely have been the most beautiful of all blossom trees.

Through the black lacework of metal I could see a sheltered corner where a magnolia balanced large, white, waxen flowers along its branches; I sighed with pleasure at its silent beauty.

Pushing to open the gate, then glancing down at the padlock, I was surprised to find it still locked. Yesterday, in the afternoon, I had worked on my own without being hounded by Tam, but I couldn't imagine why he was not in the garden this morning.

Turning about I headed back towards the house. In the grounds a huge gnarled oak stood as though dead, not a sign of life among its twisted branches. And yet the other giant trees, carefully positioned in the well-kept grounds, wore a faint aura of the fresh green that was to come.

Beyond the walled garden stood a long row of tall poplar trees, I assumed their reason for being there was to create shelter from the bitterly cold north winds I had endured at Burnsyde. In their uppermost spidery branches crows nests were scattered like black growths and there was no sign of spring buds. I passed the three chestnut trees, easily recognisable by their well-manicured shape; would their candles when they blossomed be white, or rose pink?

The house came into view and I started to think of the tasks that lay in store for me today. Cutting and sawing along the holly hedge, moving the stepladder yard by yard, was something I dreaded; but the job had to be done so I hurried to the house.

Matron suddenly appeared in the main doorway as if she had been looking out for me, then she waved and hurried along the path with her hands clasped in front of her; it was a mannerism which gave the impression that she was cold, or worried.

"Jaqueline," she said decisively, falling into step beside me, "can you manage for a week on your own to let the gardener have a holiday?"

"Why, yes," I answered, "I think so."

Tam was just opening the doors of the garage-sized building at the side of the house near to the kitchen entrance, and my curiosity was roused as I hurried behind Matron. I had never seen inside these doors, he was either unlocking them as I left for the garden, or just closing them when I was on the way back.

"I want a word with you," Matron's head and neck were stiff as she addressed Tam, "you had better show Jaqueline the power house! I want you to take a week's holiday!"

It was a command, and Tam glared at her, but before he could answer, Matron said,

"I will not take no for an answer! And I have already discussed it with your wife. Jaqueline will manage for a week."

He swung the doors open, and I looked round neat shelves lined with heavy, glass batteries. At last I was seeing the inside of the mysterious building, and the object of Tam's possessiveness. In the centre of the concrete floor, anchored with large bolts, sat a sturdy, petrol-driven engine. Finger and thumb slipped into a small slit pocket at the waist of Tam's thick trousers, and he drew out a key, rubbed it between his fingers, then gently inserted it in the ignition; with one turn the engine for generating Avonlea's electricity leapt into life.

"The batteries are kept topped-up to this level with distilled water, not above and not below," he said quietly and coldly.

I could feel the tension as Matron braced herself to face this arrogant man; there was no gratitude towards the woman who had given him a home and a livelihood, but there was also no respect for the man who had devoted his life to her service.

The light of battle was in Tam's eyes, but I saw only the cool calm of superiority in Matron's, her frail body rigid, and white showing round the knuckles of her clasped hands.

Matron walked away as Tam coldly explained the workings of the power house, but as soon as she was out of sight he glared fiercely, and spat out,

"You'll get the key to the engine when I leave on Friday, not before! Now get about your business, I want that hedge finished!"

"The garden gate's locked," I said, watching his cold, black eyes; and if looks could have killed I would have dropped dead where I stood, when he answered,

"The door in the back wall is open, or didn't you think about that?"

There was no point in answering this illogical man, so I turned and headed for the garden.

With no Tam to harass me I stood back and surveyed the work I had done up to the present; the sight of the neatly trimmed hedge with its straight sides and flat top pleased me. The end section of the holly hedge was half the length of the front. Although almost naked of leaves it was now very neat from where I stood looking down its length. Until now I had not realised I was more than two thirds of the way along the front, which meant I would be on the third and last side when I reached the corner,

Spurred on by the thought that the last side would be the shortest, because the quarter acre tapered slightly towards that end, I set up the steps, moving them about until they were steady on the uneven ground, then with saw and shears clasped in one hand I climbed to the top.

The face of the section that I was working on had been very overgrown, and nothing but the chopped ends of bare branches faced me until I reached the swaying, overgrown shoots sprouting wildly on top of the hedge.

With professional confidence, I turned the shears upside down and cut along to form a straight edge as far as I could stretch without toppling from the steps. Then, turning the shears upwards, I leant across and cut in, and as the shoots toppled in front of me the garden came into view.

Down again to ground level clipping and sawing for another yard or so, I worked my way along with the stepladder, when suddenly I realised I was at the end of the hedge and should have been turning the corner.

This last side of the hedge looked as if it had never been cut at any time, and the only way to judge where to start turning the corner was by cutting across the wildly sprouting top until the well-trimmed inside was exposed. In desperation I sawed in at the top, dropping long branches to the ground; then slowly I descended the stepladder, hacking and sawing in as straight a line as possible to make a corner out of the overgrown jungle that stretched in front of me.

Looking up at the hedge which stood at more than twice my height I was never nearer to swearing in my life, but my upbringing forbade swear words, so I cried instead. Deep in the misery of my labours, I heard a call from inside the garden,

"Off you go, its teatime!"

Using the inside of my jacket I wiped it all over my face until the tears stopped. Then Tam shouted again:

"I'll finish what's left of the hedge! You can make a start on the paths tomorrow! I want them hoed and raked until there's not a weed to be seen! And finished before I get back from my week's holiday!"

I shrugged; what a horrible, inconsiderate man this was. I was becoming as rude as him, because I refused to answer. I would do as much as I could while he was away, but I certainly wasn't going to lose any sleep over it. On the other hand, losing sleep was an impossibility; since coming to Avonlea I had been sleeping like a log as soon as my head touched the pillow.

My escape from the hedge sent me hurrying along the path singing to myself, tears and fatigue more or less forgotten as I headed for the kitchen.

Bridget smiled at me over her mug of hot, sugarless tea.

"It'll be a bit of a break to have Tam out of the way for a week. You'll be able to catch your breath," she said.

"Yes! And he's going to finish the hedge round the quarter acre."

"High time he did!" Bridget muttered. "You'll not have to look for work while he's away. To be sure, it'll find you!"

I laughed at Bridget's manner of speaking; her expressions were a source of entertainment even when she was being serious.

"I'm starting on the paths today to clear the weeds."

"Well don't you be rushing at it! Rome wasn't built in a day!" she lectured, wagging her forefinger. "Take it nice and easy, just as Tam does. He must think you're capable of managing on your own to be taking a holiday like this, he hasn't had one in years!"

"Matron didn't give him any choice, she spoke to his wife first," I answered, rising from the table to rinse my cup at the sink. "See you at lunch-time, Bridget, and thanks for the advice!"

"Be off with you!" she replied, pushing me through the doorway.

On the way down to the garden I felt quite happy about the prospect of being left on my own for a week. Tam would be finishing up tomorrow afternoon and, no doubt, leaving me with a list of jobs that would take more than a month to get through

As soon as I stepped into the garden, he started,

"This is how it's used," he said, pushing a hoe into the pebble path and sliding it back and forward as he moved along. "Then give it a good rake and put all the weeds into the barrow as you go, or they'll just take root again, and I don't want any left lying about!"

I had left the steps and tools outside the quarter acre before going up to the kitchen, and knowing the unpredictable mind of the man in front of me, I said,

"I had better put the steps and tools in the shed before I begin the paths."

"Humph!" he answered irritably. "Get started on the paths, I want to make sure they'll be done properly! I don't want you wasting your time while I'm away!"

"I won't," I answered, giving him a smile as he glared nastily. It was galling for Tam to leave me in charge and his irritation showed in his movements.

For the rest of the day I concentrated on hoeing and raking the pebble path which ran right up the centre of the garden, while Tam swore, sawed and hacked on the outside of the quarter acre hedge. He had certainly chosen the worst part to do, I had to admit.

Parrot tulips stood tall and green in the borders, easily recognisable by their frilly petals, but there was no hint of the colour to come. Canes set into the soil, to support peony roses, were almost lost among the lusty growth of leaves and buds as they spread up through the crossed twin; as one show of colour faded there would be another to take its place.

Tam was still using blasphemous language outside the quarter acre, and I hummed happily to myself as I listened and worked. After lunch he was waiting for me at the kitchen door grunting as he looked at his watch.

"Your watch must be wrong," I said airily. "The hour hasn't struck yet!"

Tam almost choked with disbelief at my remark, and strode over to the power house. I was being rude to an older person and I despised myself for it. That was the second time I had answered back that morning, but the words seemed to flow out before I was aware of them.

While he demonstrated attaching and disconnecting leads I watched and listened.

"You run the generator for as long as it takes to charge the batteries, they're fully charged when the needle on the dial reaches this point," he said, moving about wiping bits and pieces with the rag in his hand, while a slight hissing sound came from between his lips; it could have been whistling.

Without thinking I touched the belt on the generator and he immediately drew a rag across the spot. I stepped back as he turned the key and the engine spluttered into life; within a few moments he had forgotten I was there, and I watched and absorbed his pleasure still hearing the half hissing, half whistling sound coming from between his slightly parted lips.

I was convinced that Tam would rather have stayed in his own little kingdom, but his wife and Matron had other ideas.

Chapter Thirty-Six

It was Friday morning at long last, and Tam had been on the job since before I left the kitchen. By lunch-time he had put away the steps, and the shears and saw hung neatly on their respective nails, but the hedge was still unfinished.

Before going to the kitchen for lunch I climbed the stairs to my room with just the slightest feeling of doubt in the pit of my empty stomach.

Had I taken on too much? Would I be capable of running the generator to supply the large mansion with electricity? I stretched out flat on the pale pink carpet to contemplate the week ahead, and wondered if the grumbling in my tummy was hunger or nerves? I almost wished Tam would not go, but if he had become ill I would have to have done it. So why should I worry?

Rising to my feet I walked over to the turret window and gazed up the long drive. Outside the main entrance gates stood a taxi, framed on either side by the tall ornamental columns. As I watched, Tam, dressed in a navy blue suit, was helping his wife into the taxi, and then he climbed in, closed the door, and it moved off.

Well, it was too late now for misgivings, I was on my own, able to do it or not, and it was only Friday midday.

Mary was busy at the deep sink when I walked into the kitchen, and turning off the running water she went to the range, spooned some stew, vegetable and a potato onto a plate and set it down at my place on the table.

"Bridget's with Matron, Jaqueline, planning the week's menus, but she wants you to bring a sack of potatoes from the garden shed this afternoon; and Matron said to remind you to feed and clean her hens."

When I was about to leave for the garden I heard Bridget and Matron crossing the hall, and before they had finished their discussion Matron looked into the kitchen.

"We need plenty of logs in the sitting-room for the weekend, Jaqueline, and don't disturb the Warden with any unnecessary noise when you take them in. Do it now!" Then she continued her conversation with Bridget.

Bridget had been right, I certainly would have no trouble finding work, it would find me!

At the back of the house stood the woodshed screened by a semicircle of bushes and trees. I went at once and loaded the barrow then trundled it round to the main entrance. There was no answer when I knocked on the sitting-room door, but a door on the opposite side of the hall opened and Matron called:

"Just go in, Jaqueline, but don't disturb the Warden!"

"Thank you, Matron," and I smiled as her door closed.

Turning the handle in front of me I pushed open the door and went in with the basket of logs. I quietly crossed the faded carpet. While piling the logs into the alcove at the side of the white marble fireplace, I noticed the cherub carved in the centre aimed its arrow at the ceiling.

Without making a sound I turned to bring in the next load of logs; then I almost jumped out of my skin as a loud, strangled grunt erupted from the sleeper in the red leather chair. While I stood there rooted to the spot for fear of disturbing him, his eyes flickered, he half choked, snuffled, then lightly grunted his obese body back into silent slumber. I tiptoed out of the room.

When I crept back to stack the last of the logs in the alcove, I looked up at the ceiling to where the cherub's arrow pointed. I should have been entranced by the heavy, crystal chandelier that hung from a centre piece of deeply sculptured plaster leaves; but it was so dirty that nothing could have reflected on the beautifully cut crystals.

Finished with my task I tiptoed out of the room, and just as I pulled the door gently to close it another loud choking grunt and a few garbled words burst from the sleeper in the leather chair. I closed the door and hurried away to bring Bridget her potatoes.

It was a lovely, sunny day and the whole weekend would be the same, but I would not have the chance to go home, and the thought occurred to me that even the next weekend would be forfeited. However, if Tam had not taken a holiday in years, I felt pleased to be standing in for him now that he had been forced to take one. As for

Matron's half dozen hens; I had never given them a thought! Tam must have looked after them for her.

The distance to the garden was no distance at all when my mind was occupied. I went straight to the shed and put the barrow into position at the door, then heaved a sack of potatoes across to it. It was while I was struggling to lift the sack on to the barrow that a shadow fell across me and I looked up to see Sean; he stood on the path smiling, dressed in his usual working clothes and wearing his leather jacket.

Without saying a word he walked over, picked up the sack of potatoes and dumped it into the barrow. I was completely unprepared for the surge of pleasure I felt, just seeing him there. He made no attempt to speak, so I asked,

"Are you on leave?"

"No," he answered, studying his boots, "I've never been away." He sounded disappointed.

"But I thought you would be called-up by now?"

"Not yet," he replied, "when they're ready, they'll send for me!"

Having got over the surprise of seeing Sean standing there, it struck me as odd that he should appear on the very afternoon of Tam's departure.

"How did you know I was on my own this afternoon?" I asked.

"Because Tam's my uncle." His reply startled me.

"If Tam's your uncle then I can tell you he's a real slave driver!"

Sean shrugged his shoulders, ignoring my heated retort, and said,

"I'm setting the traps because Burnsyde was raided again; this time it was seventeen dead birds. Causes quite a drop in egg production." He watched me steadily, telling the story with the minimum of words. "I really came to ask if you would like to go salmon poaching, two of the older evacuees are coming with me."

"Poaching! Is it allowed?" I asked.

"Of course it's not! But that doesn't stop us from doing it!"

He had never taken his eyes off mine all the time he was speaking and a feeling of recklessness made me answer,

"All right, I'll come!"

"See you in the furnace room at half past seven tonight," he said without waiting for an answer. Then he walked through the opening into the main garden leaving me with a conscience that felt uneasy.

This was ridiculous, like something from my childhood. I was thinking of the terrible feeling in my chest when I stole an apple from the minister's garden; it had been hanging just within reach over the wall and I had stood on tiptoe and plucked it from the branch. But it had been hard and horrible, and not worth the pain it had caused in my chest. If it was wrong to do something, then why do it?

I spent most of the day arguing with myself; but at half past seven I opened the kitchen door, and as I did so Sean and two boys stepped from the furnace room. Sean beckoned me to follow with a nod of his head, and silently we made our way round to the back of the house past the wood shed and down on to the path by the river.

Up to this point not a word had been spoken; then the younger of the two boys fell into step beside me.

"Do you know anything about fishing?" he asked, looking at me suspiciously.

"No, not really!" I answered, hoping it sounded casual.

"Well, there's fishing when you use worms, and fishing when you use torches," he explained.

In the silence that followed I looked at the carrot-headed evacuee, he scuffed his feet as he walked, hands thrust deep into his blazer pockets.

"Oh! I see," I replied; it was the best answer I could think of at that moment. Carrots' grey eyes were almost level with my own and he looked at me in disgust.

"Does she have to come along?"

"I asked her," said Sean, "so why not!"

The fourth member of the poaching party was quite pleased with the arrangements Sean had made, and offered me his hand as he introduced himself,

"I'm Robert, call me Rob! I'm the oldest evacuee at Avonlea, and I work weekends in the mill upstream."

We had been walking along the river bank for about five minutes, when in the fading light I saw a small, Roman-type bridge. It straddled the narrowing part of the river in two sections and looked as if nature had grown it there.

The boys stopped, took off their shoes, and, rolling up their trouser legs, slipped silently into the water; their voices were down to a whisper. I decided against getting wet up to the knees, because the water was icy.

"That's what I thought she would do!" hissed Carrots in disgust.

Boys knew nothing about girls having periods, or about them having to keep their feet warm and dry at that time of the month, and I wanted to avoid having dragging pains low down in my body; so I treated his remark with the silent contempt it deserved.

Rob gave me a dazzling smile, and eased my supposed cowardliness by saying,

"She can keep watch for the Gillie!"

They stood knee deep in the peaty water with hand torches shining on a spot in front of their legs, and I tightened my jacket belt resentfully. It had been the same situation in the last few years at school.

"You girls who have periods!" the gym teacher would say, collecting us all together like lepers, "will not enter the life-saving tests being held this week in the swimming pool. Now, wait in the cloakroom while the rest of the girls are in the gymnasium!"

It had made me feel old and left out, and as I sat in the cloakroom silent, forbidden to participate, a voice inside me had screamed – is this going to be the story of my life! I shook off the memory from the past, and glanced up as the moon drifted from behind the clouds. Splosh!! A large, silver salmon hit my leg and dropped to the path.

"What do I do with it?" I called as quietly as I could while the powerful body writhed in the soft dust on the path.

"Make sure it doesn't get back into the water!" came the answer.

Quickly I pushed it over into the grass as another silver streak flew past me and dropped beside it. The boys climbed up the bank and clubbed the two salmon with a heavy stone, while Carrots gasped excitedly and tried to lift the largest one.

"That's a whopper!" he said in absolute awe.

"Put them in this bag and keep quiet!" Sean's commands were law, and we stood silent while he asked, "Did you see anyone passing over the bridge while you were standing here?"

"No, I haven't seen a soul," I answered.

"Let's move then; the Gillie walks the bridge at nine o'clock and I make it 8.50 p.m." Sean's words killed the excitement we were experiencing, and we hurried away like hunted fugitives afraid of being caught.

I felt Sean had timed it a little too neatly, and asked,

"Does the Gillie ever come early?"

215

"The Gillie come early. Never! It would give him a heart attack to change his routine after thirty-three years."

"I suppose he's your uncle?" I said cheekily.

Sean's eyes twinkled, and he replied,

"No, he's my mother's uncle!"

We took the small path that ran beneath the bridge at the river's edge, and tense excitement returned as we stole away with our loot. Carrots' eyes were glued on the large silver tail sticking out of the bag shining as the moonlight caught it.

"It must weigh twenty-five pounds at least!" he said in a loud whisper, and as he pushed past me I slithered off the path and slid into river.

The intense cold shooting up to my waist took my breath away; and they walked on not noticing my predicament until Sean looked back from a distance of about ten yards.

"What the blazes!" I heard him say, and then he was hurrying back along the path while the other two stood gaping.

I found it impossible to get a hold on the slippery bank, because my boots were squelching into mud on the river bed. Sean took a firm hold on a sturdy bush, then stretched out his hand; within seconds I was standing on the path in a growing puddle as the water ran from my clothes.

"Empty your boots, and hurry!" he whispered urgently, tugging at my laces.

He gripped my hand as I tied the last sodden lace, jerked me to my feet and hurried me along the path. We climbed the stile and moved into the trees, safe once more in the vicinity of the house.

When we reached the kitchen Bridget was hovering by the door, and she hissed,

"You're late! Into the deep sink with it!"

I was surprised to find we were expected; our spoil was dumped into the sink and we were shooed out of the door.

"Now off with you down below and I'll bring you a hot drink!"

Relieved of the two salmon we beat a hasty retreat down into the furnace room. After a few minutes had elapsed Bridget appeared, she passed down a tray of hot cocoa in white mugs and a plateful of sandwiches.

Carrots could no longer contain his enthusiasm, and blurted out,

"The big one must weigh twenty pounds!" No one agreed with him. "Well, eighteen pounds," he insisted.

Rob said,

"I would say fifteen pounds!"

Sean let them argue on, then interrupted:

"Right! Each will say the weight he," and he glanced at me, "or she thinks the largest salmon is, and when Bridget weighs it we will find out who is nearest."

My own knowledge of fish was what came out of the wrappings from the fishmonger's shop, so I made no comment; but I decided to take the average weight from the betting males once they reached their final decisions.

Having thrashed it out amongst themselves, they turned to me.

"Do you bet?" asked the thirteen year old Carrots.

"Yes, I would say it weighs sixteen and a quarter pounds!" I answered knowledgeably.

The warmth of my furnaces and the pleasure of satisfied tummies made the boys helpful, and while they stoked-up for me, I gathered the mugs and carried them to the kitchen with the feeling that I was an interloper in their male world.

Sean set off for home on his bike taking the smaller of the two salmon, and Carrots, Rob and I went indoors.

"Goodnight, Jaqueline." His dimples deepened as Rob smiled.

Carrots grunted, and his rusty head was level with Rob's shoulder as they climbed the stairs to the older boys' dormitory, deeply engrossed in conversation.

Chapter Thirty-Seven

"And you will just have to put up with it!" my mother had said, the first time it happened. "If you wake up feeling queasy, don't jump out of bed, get up slowly; and you only have yourself to blame if you don't keep your feet dry and warm at that time of the month!"

The slight bilious taste was there at the back of my tongue, but I felt fine lying under the covers. However, I had to get up, so I pushed back the covers, slid my legs slowly over the bed and sat up. It was instantaneous; the blood raced away from my face and I put up my arms as I toppled forward, the pink carpet seemed to rush up to meet me.

The room was hazy in the morning light and as long as it kept spinning round I had to lie there on the carpet. The pains were already twisting in the lower part of my body as if my insides were going through a mincer. I groaned; some aspirin and a hot cup of tea would help if I could only get up and into my clothes. Perhaps I should have gone without a hot bath last night; but what else could I have done soaked to the waist in peaty river water?

The warm kitchen was like a haven when I at last sat down on the bench, and without saying a word Bridget filled my mug with strong tea and placed the aspirin bottle beside it.

"There's no one but yourself to blame!" I swallowed two aspirins and sipped the hot tea. "You should have had more sense than get wet up to the waist last night!" she raved on, just as my mother would have done. "You knew you had started a period!"

"But Bridget! I was pushed into the river – it was an accident. We were on the way back when it happened; and anyway, how did you know it was that time of the month for me?"

She dropped a mound of chopped vegetables into the cauldron of a pot, then dragged it from the hob until it stood directly over the fire with flames leaping under it.

"It's written on your face in the form of dark shading round the eyes." She turned and looked at me, her hands resting on her bony hips. "Just as if you had painted it on, and if it's possible for you to look paler. Then you are! Now just sit right there and have another mug of tea. Tam's well out of the way and the furnaces can wait another fifteen minutes!"

Picking up a thick, lead pencil she scribbled a few notes on a scrap of paper and handed it to me.

"I'll need a few things from the garden before lunch." Bridget glanced up as I put down my mug. "Sit where you are! There's no rush!"

True enough, this was not the city where everything went by the clock. There was no train waiting at the station ready to leave dead on time, unless the guard had seen one of his regulars hurrying towards the platform; then the whistle stayed away from his lips just a little while longer.

I missed the daily train up to the West End of Princes Street, whether it was lovely weather like this, or when it rained and I hurried out of the station under my red umbrella, thin rubber boots pulled on over my court shoes with the little cuff neat above the ankles.

I would be a real oddity dressed as I was now; young ladies never wore trousers. Looking across the kitchen to where my boots waited I almost laughed out loud. Could I ever again become a young business lady? At least the snooty Karen had accepted me and it made me feel pleased, and amused.

Bridget had poured tea for herself and was now seated in her chair at the head of the pinewood table, she patted her apron pocket and said,

"'Tis a letter from my good mother and I haven't had the chance to read it yet." A quietness descended on the kitchen while we both thought of home. Then Bridget spoke, "You're looking fine now, Jaqueline, but remember it's only the necessities you'll be doing today. No need to hoe the paths at the weekend! You can pick up a few things in the village for me if you decide to go in this afternoon."

The tall, church-like windows filled the well-scrubbed kitchen with light, and the brusque kindness of Bridget had soothed my pains. I leisurely pulled on my black leather boots. The heavy metal studs on the soles, and the half ring of metal on the heels clinked noisily in the quiet, airy warmth. I slipped out of the kitchen door and left Bridget absorbing the contents of her mother's letter.

The morning flew past, and as it neared lunch-time I hurried round to the wood shed to chop up kindling for the kitchen. The supply of logs and kindling was going down, and the furnaces were eating the coal in the bunker since the chimneys had been swept. I had raked down the coal from the back of the long bunker, trying to judge how long it would last before summer arrived,

Eventually, logs would only be burned in the open fireplaces late in the evening, and then there would be time to build up stocks during the long summer days to come.

Although Bridget had said only the necessities were to be done at the weekend, it was after the little ones' bath time before I could say I had got through the daily necessities. Carrots popped his head round the bathroom door as I lifted the scattered clothing and wet towels from the floor.

"Psst!" he hissed, "furnace room at seven o'clock!"

The mop of red hair had vanished as quickly as it appeared, and I glanced round the bathroom to make sure he had been speaking to me. Karen was still bent over the bath busily washing away the tide mark round it, her high heels neatly placed to one side.

"I'll leave the clothes piled up here, Karen, and I'll collect them on the way down."

"You're not going back to hold his hand, Jaqueline, surely?"

"Yes, I am."

"He's only playing up to you. Don't you know how children's minds work? If you do it this once, he'll be at you for ever after!" She slipped into her high-heeled shoes and flounced past me. "Don't say I didn't warn you!"

I hesitated, watching a curl that had escaped from the top of her hair bouncing at the back of her neck as she left the bathroom. The little boy had said he was frightened, even with all his little friends in their beds around him; I had to go back just to make sure.

Creeping silently into the nursery I sat on the chair by his bed and took the tiny hand in mine. Neither of us spoke, but the tears trickling down his face gradually stopped and within five minutes he was asleep.

I rose from the chair feeling as Florence Nightingale must have done, and tiptoed quietly from the nursery. My hand was still on the handle as I turned to close the door silently, when several tiny giggles escaped from under the blankets. Stifling the laughter bubbling up inside me, I closed the door and hurrying into the bathroom picked up the inevitable mound of grubby clothing. I had been fooled by a mischievous four year old; perhaps I would take Karen's advice next time.

I went downstairs quickly and at a few minutes after seven, after dumping my bundle beside a thoughtful-looking Bridget in the staff sitting-room, I opened the door to the furnace room and three solemn faces looked up.

"Come on, you're late!" grumbled Carrots, but Rob was smiling, and Sean looked more aloof than ever.

I climbed down and sat on a step; the same feeling of being an intruder in their male world was seeping into me.

"Put your hand out!" said Sean, and when I instantly obeyed he dropped some coppers into it. "You won! You guessed correctly!"

He studied me with his keen, blue eyes, so I hid my astonishment and listened to their congratulations on my ability to assess the weight of the largest salmon.

"There's more to the female than I thought," Sean was saying, and I felt myself blush as I thought of the method I had used; the average weight had never occurred to them.

"They have such cissy names," remarked Carrots.

"My brother calls me Jackie," I volunteered, feeling like an awkward schoolgirl in my attempt to win Carrots' respect.

"That's better!" said Carrots, brightening up.

I started up the steel steps glad to get away from such frankness, and called over my shoulder,

"Goodnight, boys!"

"Goodnight, Jackie!" replied Carrots; at last we were friends, my abbreviated name was much more suited to their masculine world.

"Goodnight, Jaqueline." At the sound of Rob's voice I turned to smile, still clutching my winnings, and thought how different this town boy was to his country cousin who still sat aloof and slightly pensive.

"Goodnight," said Sean quietly, and I closed the door of the furnace room leaving them to ponder the mysteries of the female mind.

Bridget was still sitting quietly in the staff sitting-room when I started on the mending, and after reading over her mother's letter for the third time she excused herself and went to her room.

"It can't be bad news, or she would have told us by now. I looked at Mary's calm, little face aware of the concern darkening her eyes. "Would you like to hear my latest record, Jaqueline?"

"Why yes! A little music would help to kill the monotony," I answered, pushing my finger through another hole.

Setting aside her mending Mary hurried out of the room to return in a short time with her precious record.

"I've got quite a selection, but this is Deanna Durbin's latest!"

She put the record carefully on the turntable, after blowing on it a couple of times, then wound the handle of the gramophone. Lifting the arm she placed it on the edge of the record.

"It's a Russian song," she said shyly.

With no radio at Avonlea, except for the one in Matron's sitting-room, music and how the war was progressing had to wait until I was at home. I was now two weekends overdue and my mother kept asking in her letters when I would take some time off.

The needle continued to scrape along the edge of the record until Mary touched the arm lightly with her finger, and then the hauntingly beautiful music drifted through the room. The sweet soprano voice, sounding crystal clear, flowed effortlessly up and down as it formed strange words in Russian.

A night at the cinema was something I hadn't indulged in since coming to the West Country. There had been no one to go with at Burnsyde, and the furnaces at Avonlea had first priority on my time.

I sat quite still, listening to the language so perfectly pronounced and made more beautiful by the pathos in the young, fresh voice. When it ended Mary placed the record in its cardboard cover.

"I'm only allowed to play one," she said, "and it's time I was in bed anyway; goodnight, Jaqueline."

"Goodnight, Mary."

I wandered slowly upstairs, after Mary had gone, lingering on the spiral section leading to my turret room, the light and shade of the music filling my mind. Why did people who created such beautiful music fight wars? But the question answered itself. They were only protecting themselves from the ruthless madman who had risen to power over his own people, as had happened before and was now history.

I stopped at the bathroom door; if I missed my bath I would be physically tired all day Sunday, so I ran the hot water, singing the strange words and music still fresh in my mind. The water splashed into the whiteness of the bath, and the steam rose to mingle with my song. It was amazing how well you could sing in the bath. Even the discouraging remarks of my grandmother coming into my mind were having no effect: 'Sing up,' she would say, 'or we won't be able to hear you behind a newspaper.' But then, she had never heard me singing in the bath.

I settled down in bed that night planning to travel afar and mingle with these people and their strange words. Drifting on the verge of sleep I wondered if people in foreign lands were motivated by the same longings as I had, regardless of language or skin colour.

Chapter Thirty-Eight

The whole house just buzzed with activity on Sunday morning and eventually the boys were lined up in the hall, scrubbed clean, clothes immaculate, and Matron stiffly examining behind ears, or fastening the odd shirt button left open behind the knot of a tie.

"But it's too tight, Matron!" one boy complained.

"Nonsense!" was her reply. "If it can be fastened it's not too tight!"

He was a thin boy but his shoulders and neck were broadening, and his trousers hung two inches above his shoes. I wondered, as I watched, if Matron would take notice before teenage growth left his trousers just below his knees.

The door of the sitting-room opened and, by the time she had finished scrutinising the boys, the Warden was standing supporting himself with one hand pressed against the door post.

"Hup! Two, three, four, right turn!" the Warden's fine voice rose to echo round the high vaulted roof of the hall.

The boys had been put on their honour to go to church on Sundays without any of the staff accompanying them; it would be lunch-time before they returned. They marched through the main entrance, and while their feet crunched up the pebbled drive I rolled the Persian carpet back across the vestibule floor, and Matron closed the double oak doors.

Red in the face with the effort it had cost him the Warden gingerly turned round awkwardly carrying his obese body, too exhausted by his exertions to even close the sitting-room door. 'Eat to live,' my mother had instilled into me, and never 'Live to eat.' How right she had been!

Matron looked at me haughtily, and I felt she had read my thoughts. Had the expression of pity registered on my face, I wondered? Then she snapped at me,

"The flower beds outside my sitting-room need watering, Jaqueline, it would be best done this morning since you have nothing else to do! Did you feed the hens?"

"Yes, Matron, I did."

"And are there enough logs for this evening?"

"Yes, there are."

"Then see that you bring them into my sitting-room!"

"I already have, Matron!"

She swept across the hall towards her room, full of indignation. What was I to do with such people? I shrugged, I would put it all down to experience gained during this unusual period in my life.

There had been very little rain in the past week, and the effect of the warm weather was beginning to show on the drooping leaves of the elephant ears plants, and the heads of the primulas were shrivelling.

"Jaqueline!" Matron had turned at the door of her room. "I expect you to help with the spring cleaning. The chandelier in my sitting-room will require the tall steps from the garden if it is to be cleaned comfortably. You had better bring them now."

"Yes, Matron, I will."

Her door closed, and I walked into the kitchen heaving a sigh.

"You'll be going down to the garden then, Jaqueline?"

"Yes, Bridget, to get the steps and put on the sprinkler. Tam will never forgive me if his wallflowers suffer from drought."

"Then I'll be walking down with you for a breath of fresh air while the boys are at church."

Bridget seldom left the house; the only fresh air she got was at the dustbin putting out rubbish. We left by the side door and walked slowly round by the back of the house; when I looked across the river, I gasped.

"Why, look, Bridget, the leaves on the willows are out!"

"Oh! so they are," she replied dryly. "You're a great one for the outdoors, but me, I like my kitchen!"

I smiled at her answer, and spoke my thoughts aloud because I had a companion,

"The pines are always green, and you never realise they shed their needles until you walk under them where it's all bouncy and dry."

"Yes," she agreed. "Jaqueline, that letter I got from my mother." Bridget looked down at her feet. "She's pregnant again." She crossed herself absentmindedly, and I waited for her to go on, sensing her agitation. "No woman should be carrying a child and helping to look after her own grandchildren. She's done enough and suffered enough," she said bitterly.

Again I waited, wanting her to talk to ease her agitation; I had been aware of her sadness ever since she had opened her mother's letter. Her voice became low and dismal.

"I was only six years old when my mother collapsed on the kitchen floor doubled up with pain; I brought my second brother into the world." I let her talk on without interrupting, and all the time I saw the pain registering on her face; she bit her bottom lip but the tears had started.

Her face mirrored the agony she had witnessed so many years ago, and as she removed her spectacles to wipe her eyes with the back of her hand, I could hear myself saying,

"But, Bridget, you're still suffering for your mother; you shouldn't, because she forgot her pain as soon as your brother was born."

I felt puzzled by my own words; how could I know such a thing? But the effect on Bridget was miraculous and she opened her eyes wide, then answered:

"That's probably true, Jaqueline! I always feel her pain when I think back to that day." She wiped her eyes again with the back of her hand, and replaced the glasses on her ridiculously small nose.

"But that's not the life I'm going to lead!" she burst out, lifting her chin defiantly. "My life's my own! And I don't have to answer to any man, or spend my life being pregnant!"

"Will you be good enough, then, Bridget, to help me with the stepladder? That is, if you can climb down from your soap box for long enough."

Her mood had changed so rapidly, from deep despair to defiance, and I was quite unprepared for her playful push, which caught my shoulder, sending me rushing down the slope to stop at the garden gates. There was nothing delicate about the weight behind Bridget's hand.

I turned on the sprinkler at the top end of the garden and watched it slowly start to spin, showering everything within its range. If Matron had not mentioned watering her flower beds I might never have thought of it.

Then Bridget and I walked back to the house each taking an end of the long stepladder. Matron hurried across as we reached the drive, calling,

"Bring it straight into the sitting-room, please, I want you to start cleaning the chandelier now, Jaqueline!"

Bridget looked at me wryly, and answered,

"She will, when we've had our cup of tea, Matron."

For a moment Matron eyed Bridget rather vaguely, before answering hesitantly,

"Oh! Yes! Why, of course!"

It was nice to have Bridget's support, because I would have done as Matron asked instantly, Sunday or not. I felt relieved as we went into the kitchen where the brown enamel teapot sat singing on the hob. Bridget lifted the lid and poured in a little water from a hissing black iron kettle before filling two white mugs.

"She doesn't trust just anyone touching the chandelier; it's usually Tam in his stocking foot that climbs up to clean it. Karen has no head for heights."

I was always aware of the banter in these confidences, and answered with a smile,

"It wouldn't matter if I was trembling like a leaf, Bridget, Matron would send me up the steps to clean it, don't you agree?"

"Indeed I do!" Bridget replied, setting down a washing-up bowl with soap and a cloth. "I can't remember when it was last cleaned. But take your time, it is the Sabbath."

"Yes, 'six days shalt thou labour and do all thy work'," I quoted. "But Matron doesn't seem to be aware of the ten commandments, and neither does the Warden know about the seven deadly sins. However, his gluttony only brings pain to himself "

"My, my!" exclaimed Bridget. "We are being very profound this morning, now off you go before the water gets cold!"

Why I never retaliated during the long, thankless, working hours mystified me. I knocked on the sitting-room door, but there was no answer, so I turned the handle and went in. The large body of the Warden lay sprawled in its red, leather chair, and, not wishing to disturb him, I quietly brought in the stepladder, setting it up in the centre of the room.

With the bowl of water in one hand I climbed up and started to clean, wiping each crystal with the soapy cloth and rinsing it in the water. Then placing each one back on its tiny gilt hook, I leaned back to admire the light that seemed to glow from inside through their many facets.

The ceiling was in shadow but the clean, wet crystals caught and reflected light, magnifying colour and sending it flickering round the room to mock the silent discoloured faces of the ancient paintings. The more the chandelier sparkled the more interested I became in cleaning it, until the sludge of spider's webs and sooty water sent me back to the kitchen for the fifth time in my soft indoor shoes.

With fresh soapy water I started again, moving the steps round until only the crystals hanging beneath the chandelier wore the coating of dust and smoke from the open fire. Hanging right in the centre, just an inch or two below the others, was a round, heavy crystal; I lifted it down, wiped it with the cloth, then dipped it into the water on its beaded crystal chain. Suddenly the silence in the room was broken as the Warden said,

"You can wish on a crystal, Jaqueline, just like the one you hold in your hand, but you must always hold its image in your mind if the wish is to come true."

I held up the wet, crystal ball sparkling as it slowly turned on its beaded crystal chain, and silently counted the triangular facets round it. All the while I wondered how long the Warden had been awake.

"If you had a wish, Jaqueline, what would it be?" he asked, his rich voice full of inquiry. I listened to the voice, still fascinated by the crystal, then answered,

"Happiness!"

"Not money?" he asked with a hint of bewilderment.

"If money is happiness then that is what I wish."

Hanging the ball of crystal in its place of honour at the centre of the chandelier, I stopped its spin and climbed down. The Warden's eyes had closed, but there was no occasional snort or grunt so I knew he was not asleep. Overindulged from the day of his birth I envied him nothing that money, or his privileged position in life had bestowed upon him.

Quietly I removed the stepladder. Then I went to the alcove and lifting a log threw it into the fire; the flames leapt and danced, reflecting on the shimmering chandelier.

The Warden had not stirred, so I stood bent beneath the arrow of the white marble cherub in the centre of the fireplace, the heat scorching the seat of my dungarees, and judged where his arrow would fly if it were released from the bow he held. Before the heat became unbearable, I judged it would fly straight towards the crystal I had chosen to wish upon; the whole mysterious idea made me sparkle inside.

Leaving the collection of dusty, worldly goods from many centuries ago, I closed the door of the overheated room as the Warden erupted into a series of snorts, grunts and splutters.

Chapter Thirty-Nine

There was plenty of quiet time to think while I hoed the paths and moved the sprinkler until it had refreshed every part of the garden. I could not agree with Bridget's vow never to marry; home was a wonderful place to me with my parents, brother and sister. The longer I stayed away working at Avonlea the more vivid it had become.

Perhaps it was difficult to see Bridget's point of view when I was only one of three children. I might feel quite differently if I were one of sixteen with a seventeenth expected, as was the case in Bridget's family.

The thought of producing a child almost every year like a cow owned by a farmer shattered me. I had a reasoning mind that rebelled against it; Jim, the foreman at Earlson, had said cows were only fit for sausage meat when they came to the end of their calf producing lives. If I had no say in how many children I would have, then I was not at all interested in becoming a household drudge between bouts of pregnancy sickness and giving birth to numerous children. Bridget had said her mother was in her early forties; how many more would she give birth to?

Shaken by the thought of such an existence I decided one of each sex would be my lot, if I decided to marry. To remain an unattached virgin with a good career seemed much more attractive I thought, when a familiar voice said,

"Hello, why don't you ease off when Tam's away?"

"Sean! How did you get in here? You didn't come in by the gate or I would have seen you."

He was leaning against a tree in his usual casual manner.

"I can come in any time whether the gates are open or locked!" And taking the hoe from my hands he started scraping at the path.

"What were you thinking about just now?" he asked.

"Bridget. She's religious and yet—" I paused thoughtfully.

He looked up as if waiting for me to continue, then said,
"You shouldn't try to fathom out religion, it's impossible."
"I'm not trying to fathom it out, but if a pair of shoes hurt me I don't wear them!"
He changed the subject abruptly:
"I was at a party last night, and I kissed a girl. Do you kiss boys?" He looked down and scuffed his feet on the gravel.
The answer to his question was something he should have known, so I answered,
"Girls don't go around kissing boys, it wouldn't be considered nice. And it's the same with dancing, the girl has to wait until she's asked. It's not really fair!"
But he ignored what I said, and asked,
"Are you going to marry some day?"
"Yes, when the war ends, and I'm going to have two children. That is, when I've done all the things I want to do!"
Sean had been away from Burnsyde long enough to have checked the traps twice over; he left abruptly, leaving me with my thoughts and the questions I had just been asked.
It was Thursday before he turned up again, and when I mentioned going home at the weekend he startled me by saying,
"Not this weekend, you won't!"
"What do you mean, Sean?"
"Tam's in hospital for a check-up. He has a metal plate as part of his skull from the Fourteen-Eighteen War, it's more likely to be three or four weeks before you have a weekend off."
I turned away bitterly disappointed, the tears stinging my eyes. Was I never to have time off from my labours? I felt trapped and a little desperate. Sean said,
"Will you come with me to see a film at the village cinema tonight? The furnaces will keep till we get back."
Angry with Matron for not telling me all this before Tam left, I walked with my tools to the shed and locked up.
"Jackie, will you come tonight?"
"Yes, thank you, I will."
This would be an evening away from mending in the staff sitting-room, with the privilege of listening to one of Mary's records; and

Matron could try to browbeat me as much as she liked, I would go to the cinema with Sean.

The rich, lavender-coloured lilac bloomed and its sweet fragrance hung on the air. Nearby, the pale lemon lanterns of the laburnum tree draped themselves gracefully among fresh green leaves. As I walked through the garden beside Sean I made up my mind to take a stand against Matron's tyranny. I would not ask permission to go out tonight.

Summer had come at last, and I felt my whole dedicated attitude towards working hard to help win the war was weakening; I was being taken for a willing fool. It would be the end of May before Tam returned to Avonlea, if what Sean had told me was true. Had I been consulted like an intelligent human being, instead of treated like an underling, perhaps my attitude would have been different. In Matron's eyes, my willingness to help was a sign of inferiority.

I was cocooned in my own indignation as we walked along the path, but I was very aware of Sean moving silently at my side. My eyes roamed over every familiar tree now haloed in new leaves. It seemed like ages since Tam had taken off.

"Jackie, I'll see you at the entrance gates in time for the seven thirty bus to the village."

"Right, Sean. Seven thirty."

Resolutely I made for the house and went straight up to my room. Food seemed unimportant; I ran the bath to wash off the sweat and dirt after the day's work. I had my off-white trenchcoat in the wardrobe, and the halter-necked dress with blue flowers on a white background; both were perfect for an evening show in an overheated cinema.

With the dirt and tiredness steeped away in the bath, I slipped on my precious silk stockings and stepped into my dress; it seemed like months since I had felt so feminine. A dab of perfume and a touch of lipstick before leaving my room made me walk on air, and Sean was beginning to use my name.

The feel of the silk-lined dress moving away from my legs as I made my way downstairs was a luxury I missed in the working world of dungarees and cord breeches. Off-white trenchcoat draped over one arm, I walked into the kitchen.

"Phew!" said Bridget, while Mary and Karen stared. "You've had little chance to get out of working clothes since coming to Avonlea, but you're powerful stuff in a dress and high heels."

I laughed with the excitement I felt, and answered,

"Sean's taking me to the cinema."

"Have you known Sean long, Jaqueline?" Karen asked.

"Yes, I worked with him at Burnsyde for six months."

"Oh!" they answered on a note of approval and fell silent.

I had finished a tasty, light meal of omelette and mushrooms, and Bridget was pouring the coffee, when Matron entered the kitchen.

"Where were you when the little ones were in the bath, Jaqueline? You know we are short staffed! And why are you dressed up like this?"

Matron's superior manner had the effect of silencing everyone in the kitchen, but I was ready for her.

"I'm going to the cinema, Matron."

"With whom?" she demanded.

"My friend, Sean."

"Did you ask my permission?"

"It wasn't necessary, Matron, regulations state my evenings are my own and it seems that Tam will be gone for longer than you intimated."

Her eyes moved from my face and she coughed into her hand.

"In future you will ask my permission," she replied, and moved to the door.

I stayed silent, but my excitement had changed to restlessness. I was overwhelmed by the desire to get up and run before she found some excuse to detain me.

"I shall report this to your area supervisor," she flung at me before entering the hall.

I felt no triumph in having to answer someone older, in a situation like this, but I was glad of my early training on how to handle an often inconsiderate public. Pushing my arms into my coat I rose and hurried to the back door of the kitchen.

"Enjoy yourself, Jaqueline!" Bridget said quietly, and she closed the door behind me as I slipped out past the dustbins.

Hurrying along the path at the side of the house I wished I was already on the bus. It was beginning to look thundery and dull, I turned into the main drive and hurried towards the entrance gates.

How ridiculous this all was, like playing a part in some Victorian novel; Matron's disapproval hung over me just like the thundery weather.

I felt the fear of being out alone in the descending darkness. What if Sean had forgotten? I wanted to turn and run back to the security of the kitchen and the staff. But I tightened the belt of my coat and hurried on. Suddenly realising I had no handbag, nothing to defend me from the unexpected, I felt the goose flesh rise all over me, and then I saw him step from behind one of the ornamental columns.

Sean walked towards me, took my hand and hurried me through the main entrance just as the bus came round the bend in the road. All my apprehension had vanished by the time we took our seats, and when the dimly-lit, blacked-out bus moved off he was holding my hand.

"Why were you so scared-looking coming up the drive?" Sean asked.

"Oh, I wasn't scared!" I answered, blocking out the memory of the tall, dark spectre looming over me at the entrance to Burnsyde. But an involuntary shudder ran through me.

"See! You were!" he replied.

"No! I just felt chilly!" I insisted.

The short trip to the village ended and the bus pulled into the square; it was then that I remembered.

"Oh! I forgot to stoke-up the furnaces before supper," I said in dismay. "That's because *you* were there, Sean, distracting me."

He looked down at me and smiled.

"Forget the furnaces, I'll rekindle them if I have to!"

Inside the cinema we groped in the darkness as the usherette shone her torch directing us to seats, then we excused ourselves all along the row while everyone rose to let us move into the last two empty seats against the wall.

The film had started and arrows flew from Indian bows across the silver screen. While the noise of guns roared through the cinema, men fell writhing in agony with arrows sticking out of their bodies. One Indian crawled through the shadows, blood oozing from his many bullet wounds, then he shuddered and lay still.

Sean put his hand over mine as it rested on the arm between our two seats, and we stared at the carnage flashing across the screen. What had been a blazing building inside an army fort, was miraculously brought back to its original, unburned shape with a few buckets of water passed in chain fashion from a well.

When the Indians had been driven off in a hail of rifle bullets the wounded were attended to. I watched arrows being pulled out of the strong, silent soldiers who gritted their teeth to hide their agony. Then the decent thing was done, with Indian braves being given a Christian burial alongside their dead enemies.

I kept wondering if the audience had been as unmoved as I was; especially when ladies in long crinoline dresses appeared from the previously burning building with not a hair out of place, or a soot smudge. Dutifully they stood by the open graves and wept buckets of tears into wisps of lace that never got wet. The soldiers, having found the strength to dig graves after their arrows had been removed, stood nobly to attention.

The jaws of the man seated on my right had been chewing in time with the high-powered action; but now they were still with respect as many a handsome Hollywood hero was lowered to his last resting place. The strains of a lone bugle died away, and the lights in the crowded cinema went up. Sean discreetly removed his hand, and when I turned my head to look around me, the male of the chewing jaws started winking furiously as if sand had got in one eye.

Quickly I turned to Sean, and asked,

"Was that the main film we were watching?"

"No," he answered, "it's a Chicago gangster film."

Visibly wilting, I settled down to an hour or so of cops, gangsters, bleeding bodies and machine guns. The film had barely come to an end when there was a desperate exodus before *God Save the King* had time to follow the familiar roll of drums. Safe against the wall from the stampeding audience, Sean and I stood respectfully silent until the last strains of the National Anthem died away, and then we made our way out into the warm night air.

The stars winked from a dark, velvet sky, and we walked to join a line of people moving steadily towards the bus. Then the conductor called out,

"Sorry! That's all I can take and this is the last bus!"

"We'll have to walk," Sean said, "can you walk a mile in these shoes?"

"Why, of course I can, but you'll have to shorten your stride so I can keep up with you."

The cinema had been stifling and I walked with my coat on my arm, feeling the warm air moving over my bare shoulders. Sean was wearing a fine tweed sports jacket; he looked so different. I felt happy and refreshed just being in his company in spite of the appalling films we had been watching; both of them based on manly revenge and helpless women. Glancing down at Sean's neatly fitting flannels, I said,

"Do you always go to see such bloodthirsty films, Sean?"

"Usually!" he replied, catching hold of my free hand. "What kind of films do you like?"

"Oh, musicals and operettas, or classical stories like the novels of the Brontë sisters."

"Oh, Heathcliffe!" he said innocently enough.

But when I glanced up at him his smiling eyes held a gleam that made me try to withdraw my hand from his. I tugged, but he was too quick for me and I was swept off my feet. He had become aware of his masculine strength, and I realised as I was carried along by this tall, laughing male that he was no longer the immature boy I had known at Burnsyde. I would have to keep him at arm's length, if he would only put me down.

"Sean!" I said, as primly as I could, "I don't want to be blamed for encouraging you, so put me down!"

He stopped and grinned knowing I was powerless, and then slowly lowered me to my feet, his arms moved round my waist to hold me against him. My head felt light, and I was alarmed by the emotions he had stirred in me. This was where I would have to keep a cool head, but it was difficult with his face so close to mine.

"Jaqueline," he murmured into my hair, "I want to kiss you."

"No, Sean!" I said, deliberately hiding my face against his chest, while I noted the use of my full name.

"Jaqueline, I can stand here all night if I have to."

I thought about it for a moment, well aware that he was enjoying himself rubbing his face lightly against my hair and moving his hands further up my waist. When I thought his grip had slackened I pushed against him, but his arms instantly locked round me.

"All right!" I said bluntly, lifting my face. "You forced me into this, and Matron will be furious if I'm any later!"

But he was already brushing his lips across my neck, and my objections died away with the headiness I felt. A mild electric shock ran through me when our lips met, shattering the stars above as if we stood in a shower of gentle, silver rain. I wanted to stay in his embrace forever and lost all sense of urgency.

Then suddenly he held me away from him.

"Jackie," he said, taking my hand, "it's time I took you back to Avonlea."

The night was enchanting and I walked along very much aware of the new Sean. When he pulled me close to him at the gates of Avonlea I melted into his embrace as if it was the most natural thing in the world to do. Time had ceased to trouble me, and it was only when he took my hand and started to hurry down the main drive that I remembered the furnaces.

"The furnaces will be out, Sean," I wailed, "and it's so late!"

"Go straight up to your room and I'll see to them," he said quietly, almost pushing me into the kitchen and closing the door.

I turned the key in the lock and crept through the darkened house carrying my shoes, then climbed the stairs to my room. No matter how late it was I brushed my teeth and splashed my face with warm water in the bathroom. I became aware of a great difference in me and locked the door of my room and dropped my dress to the floor; carefully removing my silk stockings I draped them over a chair and slipped into bed.

Sean had become aware of the female, and he would never be satisfied now until he had unravelled the mystery. Tonight he had been trying out this new awareness within him, and it had awakened in me dormant emotions I had never experienced until a few hours ago.

Instinct warned me to beware, or I would join the band of foolish girls, as they were called, who had fatherless children. This was the growing up process I had been warned against without ever knowing what it was, until now. Nature did everything in her own time, and I was glad this awareness had not come when I was too young to understand its implications.

My eyes were closing, and as I drifted into sleep I could still feel his arms around me and his lips caressing mine. Vaguely I wondered what tomorrow would bring.

Chapter Forty

"No, you're not with us this morning, Jaqueline," said Bridget, looking at me with concern in her eyes, "you're overworking yourself. I warned you! I'll be glad when Tam gets back to take the load off your shoulders."

I yawned sleepily behind my hand.

"Sorry, Bridget, I was a bit late last night."

"Did you enjoy the film then?" she asked, dropping pieces of meat into the frying pan and turning them over to brown.

"Yes, but we had to walk back because the bus was full."

I left the kitchen repeating in my mind: don't forget the furnaces, remember to feed the hens, check the batteries in the power house, logs in the wood shed almost finished. Where will I get more when they are all gone?

It was nearly lunch-time before I got down to the garden, and I had to push my way past the sprouting azaleas glowing in corals, lemons, pale pinks and flame; they had narrowed the steep path down to the gates and I was loath to cut them to make it wider for the barrow.

When I walked into the quarter acre the soil between the vegetables had been hoed and there was not a weed in sight. I knew Sean had been there that morning doing my work.

I started to think about last night and knew that nothing would ever be the same again. Some boys had kissed me before; but with one it had been like a sink plunger closing over my mouth, rubbery and sloppy. And there had been the one with his tongue shooting into my mouth so that I wanted to vomit. I had decided then that life with the male was not for me.

The tulips stood tall and colourful, and the scent of wallflower rose from the borders as I wandered through the garden not quite sure of what work I should do. I felt myself blush at the memory of Sean brushing his lips gently across mine, causing vibrations to run through me so that I was caught up in the magic he wove. A tear ran down my cheek; I was lonely, and I almost wished Tam were here to bully me into action.

It had been the warm night air and the velvety, dark sky with its shimmering stars. And, of course, the fact that I had not been out at night for such a long time. I had been like putty in his hands and I had been powerless to do anything about it. Another tear rolled down my cheek and I didn't even bother to wipe it away.

It had taken a long time to get started on the paths, but by five o'clock I felt I had done enough and gathered up my tools singing softly to myself. I reached up to hang the tools on the wall of the shed, and, although I had not heard a sound, his arms slipped round me. I tried to turn and face him but his arms tightened.

"Stop it, Sean," I said, turning my head to look up at his face, but his lips stopped my words. I was trapped by him, and he was much too confident. "Stop it, Sean!" I managed to gasp, struggling round to push him off.

"What's all the panic!" he said, smiling down at me and holding me tight against him. "I'll let you go when I'm ready."

To struggle was a waste of time, so I looked up at him and drifted into the world of sensations he could create, knowing it had not been the warm night, or the stars. It had been the man he had become. He suddenly released me and stepped back, leaning on the door post.

Calmly I slipped on my jacket and flipped out my hair from the collar. It was only a matter of time before he went further, so I faced him.

"You should be tied up beside the farmer's bull across the way, with a ring through your nose! You can't just go around grabbing girls and dragging them off to your cave; this is not the stone age!"

He just stood there smiling, the soft glow in his eyes deepening.

What could I do? I wanted to cry or run away, there seemed to be no escape. The girl at the party had not impressed him, and now he was concentrating on me. I walked up to him, put my hands on his neck and looked up into his smiling eyes.

"All right then, go ahead, ruin my life!" I said softly.

The glow in his eyes faded and he lifted my hands down.

"Sorry, Jaqueline, I didn't mean to upset you, but I can't help it."

"Neither can I," I answered, stepping on to the path, "but I must!"

I ran only six inches of water into the bath that night forcing myself to regain a firm grip on myself. I would have to pull myself together and keep Sean in his place. It was only then that words from my school days came to mind.

"You shouldn't go around kissing boys, Anna!" had been my innocent remark. "It takes more than a kiss, Jaqueline," she had answered, and I was puzzled, because she seemed like an adult instead of my school friend. "So avoid getting boys stirred up," she went on, "and stay with the crowd. Don't be left alone with any particular boy! I was forced into this," she ended quietly, touching her swollen body. Anna's baby would be three years old by now. Did it know who its father was?

Anna had left in disgrace before the end of term in our last year at school, and the teacher had said, "Let that serve as a lesson to all of you girls!"

Ignorance had been my protection, and now I had been stripped of it by Sean. He learned fast and excelled in everything he attempted to do. I went to bed full of resolve. It was only now as another piece of the puzzle slipped into place that my mind fully accepted what had happened to Anna. I was unsettled and unsure; a good night's sleep would be the answer, but my dreams were to be full of him.

Sean rode into my dreams on a white charger and swept me up onto his saddle, my pink chiffon nightie drifting around us like a soft cloud. His eyes had that glow, and I nestled against him as he guided his steed to a plain halfway between heaven and earth. Snowy white, kitchen sinks floated past filled with golden dishes, and we rode on towards the stars.

In the morning I crawled out of bed knowing I was badly smitten for the first time in my life. I had come a long way from being dumped into the rubbish tip at Burnsyde. He was becoming a thing of beauty to my eyes, and the more he courted me the more I saw my freedom slipping away.

I was beginning to think of Tam as my protector, if only he would come back. Halfway down to the garden, after breakfast, I turned and raced back to the furnaces; I had forgotten them again. Vaguely knowing the meaning of the forbidden words "sexual intercourse", before my horrific experience at the gates of Burnsyde, they were now quite clear in my mind. I would have to avoid Sean, or that would be his next demand. I slowed down to think clearly; if he came I would be ready for him.

Several days passed and I was beginning to walk around with an easy mind. Tam would be back soon. The tools hung neatly round the walls of the shed, and I had pushed my arms into my jacket easing it up round my shoulders, when Sean appeared. He stepped forward, gripped my jacket and pinned my arms neatly behind me.

"No Sean!" I said, desperately trying to free myself from the jacket he held with only one hand. I felt like a rabbit waiting for the chop at the back of the neck. Then he was crushing me to him.

"I love you, Jaqueline," he murmured.

"You're not talking of love, it's sexual intercourse you have in mind! Brute!" I tried to say, but his lips blocked the words and I gave up struggling.

How easy it was for him, but I had to be firm or all my dreams of travelling across the world and having a career would be ruined, as Anna's had been. I heard myself whimper like a trapped animal and suddenly he stood back, pulled my jacket up over my shoulders and lifted my hair free of the collar.

"Sorry, Jaqueline, I just couldn't help it."

How long would it be before he closed in capturing me with the magic he had learned so well? And I burst out,

"I wish Tam would come back before you rape me and say you just couldn't help it! Don't you think I have the right to say what I want to do with my own body, or do I have to become a nun?"

"You don't understand, Jaqueline. I love you!"

He had most of the qualities I admired in a man, so I stuck my hands in my pockets and faced him. I had to get through to this developing male who thought I was there for him to practice on.

"I could love you very much, Sean," I said seriously, "but you've come into my life too soon!"

He smiled, and there was a shyness about him that made me worship him even more than I did. He moved towards me, but I stepped back.

"All right! If you don't want me to, I won't," he said casually.

We walked together up the path, then he moved into the break in the fir plantation, and picking up his traps he hung them over his shoulder and gave me a wave. I stood there watching until he was gone out of sight.

Chapter Forty-One

The time had passed, and Tam would be back the following day. In a way I was relieved; there would be no more wondering if my virtue was in danger. It had been a lovely day with just an occasional light shower. The peonies had grown up through their supports of canes and string and here and there in the border the large blooms blazed deep red.

Buds on the rhododendrons, that concealed the back door to the garden, were opening out to lavender-pink. I walked down to check the back door, it would be more than my life was worth if Tam were to find it had been left open all night. Gripping the metal ring, I tugged, all was secure; that would be one less item for Tam to complain about.

Resigned to what tomorrow would bring I turned and touched the largest bloom at face level on the rhododendrons, it had patches of deep purple on the lavender-pink and smelled of clean, fresh air after the light rain. Then I sensed Sean's presence and turned to face him feeling almost sad. Tam would be back tomorrow, but that would be time enough for Sean. He picked me up in a bear hug, rocking me gently from side to side, and I was lost in his magic. When he at last spoke, he murmured in my ear,

"Jaqueline, couldn't we just—?"

I didn't let him finish, because I knew what he was going to suggest.

"No, Sean! Just a few minutes of satisfying your curiosity about girls could mean a lifetime of misery for me!"

"We could get married," he whispered.

"No," I whispered back, "you haven't even started a career yet, and you've come into my life too soon."

I reached up and lifted back the lank strand of fair hair from his forehead, knowing how disappointed he was.

"Will you go out with me now that Tam's due back?"

"No!" I answered, looking straight into his smiling, Scandinavian eyes.

"Why?" he demanded.

"Because I don't trust you, Sean!" He grinned and his eyes glowed. "I know you're working on me, but it just isn't going to happen!"

How tempting it was to remain in this garden of Eden and take a bite from the forbidden fruit. The furnaces were waiting, and the little ones had to be bathed. I pushed against him.

"Let me go, Sean!"

But he held me trapped determined to keep me in his enchanted world and I was enraptured by his nearness. Then suddenly he released me, stepped back, and for a moment we stood looking at each other. Without a word he knelt and picked up the traps lying on the grass where he had silently placed them. We walked through the garden, and while I locked the gate he had gone. A silent tear trickled down my cheek.

I walked through the estate alone feeling the light rain refreshing my face, and then all the tension of the past few weeks left me. It would soon be June, the month of roses; and I was free to live my own life. There was work to be done! And a war to be won! I started running towards the ancient house, but the thought of Tam made me slow my steps. He'll be back tomorrow, I must make a point of being down in the kitchen early, I thought.

The morning dawned bright and warm and I sat at the kitchen table watching the clock; in another thirty seconds Tam would push open the door and look at his watch. I waited, but nothing happened. Bridget raised her eyebrows and her forehead wrinkled.

"Mmm!" she said.

Opening the back door I made straight for the furnace room. He had either changed his tactics, or was not back yet. I shovelled thoughtfully. Then with gloves and Bridget's vegetable list in my pocket I collected Matron's flower baskets and headed for the garden.

If he was back it would be slavery from now on. If he was not, I would have to keep Sean at bay. Which, I wondered, was the lesser of the two evils? I shrugged and walked on. I was ready for whatever lay in store for me; at least I thought I was.

I could see Tam in the garden as I opened the gate. It was his place to say good morning, which he never did, so I made for the shed in the quarter acre to collect the secateurs. With half an eye on Tam I snipped and placed the flowers in the baskets. He strolled round examining everything critically, and then just as he reached me he stopped.

"I want these gates painted before they're red with rust!" he stared at me as he spoke, and I looked back into his cold, black eyes. There was not a word of praise for my efforts in the garden, especially when Sean had worked wonders. The fact that I had held the fort for three weeks was never mentioned, it was back to the grindstone at once. "Be quick with Matron's flowers, and I'll get the vegetables, I don't want them trampled into the ground!"

My mouth must have gaped in surprise as he stomped away, because the vegetables were hoed perfectly, just as Sean had left them. I stayed in the kitchen for a cup of tea before returning to the garden and Bridget was already noticing my gloom.

"I've never painted gates. The man's mad!" I complained.

"No," she replied, "he's got his head screwed on the right way, you need have no fear of that!"

When I got back to the garden he set me to the task of scraping rust off the gates with a wire brush; the following day I started with the paint. Specially formulated for wrought-iron work, the thin, black paint ran up into the bristles of the brush when I reached up from my perch on the stepladder. It trickled up my arm and dripped from my elbow, gradually finding its way into the short sleeve of my beige shirt.

I was angry, but determined, and I wondered if saying Tam's swear words to myself was as wicked as saying them out loud. The brush started to slither in my coated fingers and I wiped the handle with a saturated cloth.

Three days later I was finished, having dabbed the black paint into the centre of all the whirls of metal that made up the intricate design. I had kept my lengthening hair securely held back in a pony tail with one of Bridget's thick rubber bands.

The tall, delicate looking gates were more decorative than ever. I felt the effort had been worth a ruined shirt, and I stood outside the garden, hands dripping with paint, admiring the effect. Suddenly Tam grunted behind me,

244

"Clean yourself up with the white spirit and come up to the firebreak in the plantation. I'll see you there!"

During his three week holiday I had resolved not to be such a willing horse when he came back, because the more I did, the more he harassed me to do, barely letting me draw breath between jobs. He was exactly like Matron in that respect. He had not mentioned the tea break, but before going to the plantation I went to the kitchen and chatted to Bridget, drinking her strong tea and liking it more each day.

"You'll be going home this weekend, Jaqueline?"

"Yes, Bridget, and I just can't wait to see my family! I felt the same way when we were snowed-in at Burnsyde."

"It's about time I had a break, myself," she half muttered.

"When were you last at home?" I asked, curious because she had not been away for a weekend since I had come to Avonlea.

"It'll be every bit of three months and more; I mean to speak to Matron about it. I'm entitled to one weekend in the month, not to mention a full day off during the week!" Bristling with indignation at each word she uttered, Bridget banged the ladle down on the table, "They don't take a blind bit of notice, knowing you'll work on for the sake of the boys when we're short staffed!"

"Then I'm not the only willing horse at Avonlea?" I remarked, and Bridget's answer came quickly and abruptly.

"Indeed to goodness you're not! You have more time off than any of us!" Her Irish accent came through thickly, and I smiled feeling sure that Bridget would be able to handle Matron when she was ready.

Tam was waiting in the plantation firebreak, and two trestles stood there bolted and ready for use. He glared at me, and said,

"Right, take the other end!"

I walked to the end of the tree trunk he had pointed at and stooped. Putting my hands under it I tried to raise it from the ground, but I noticed something and stood up.

"I'll take the top end of the tree!" I said, walking down its length. "It's narrower!"

He marched to the bottom of the tree, and I waited. Then we both stooped and heaved.

"Get your back into it!" he bawled, almost purple in the face with the effort, and we lifted the tree and dropped it onto the trestles. "Humph!" he grunted, taking his double-handled saw and pushing one end over the tree trunk towards me. "Don't just stand there! Grab the handle and get started!"

I gripped the handle in my gloved hands and he tugged the saw across the trunk almost pulling me off my feet. His holiday had done nothing for his manners, or his consideration for the uninitiated. But he goaded me on, and I held the saw lightly letting my arms go loose when he pushed. In that way I kept my feet firmly on the spot, only putting effort into pushing and cutting into the tree.

Back and forward we pulled and pushed in the cool airiness of the firebreak, and the ten inch lengths of log dropped from the end of the trestle.

I felt invigorated by the exercise until weariness crept in, but I had caught the rhythm in his movements and the strain diminished. The tree trunk was down to a third of its original length and now rested on only one trestle. I waited for the order to lift and move it along for the next cut. However, the strain of lifting and sawing was beginning to tell on both of us and my prayer that he would stop was answered.

"Pile them into the barrow and take them down to the woodshed! And you can split them into kindling for the cook when you have nothing else to do!"

I was tempted to ask when that would be, but thought better of it. I started to pick up the ten inch lengths, piling them into the barrow while he lit up his pipe.

"When you get back," he called after me, as I trudged off with the laden barrow, "we'll cut some longer lengths for the sitting-room fire!"

I turned onto the path and he stood there puffing clouds of smoke into the clean, fresh air. His working day finished at five o'clock, and after a second tree had been sawn into lengths for the sitting-room, he walked off towards the lodge at the appointed hour leaving me still piling logs into the barrow.

He had gone without a word, so I dropped the lot in the firebreak and hurried along to the furnace room to stoke-up. Things were definitely going to change. It was no good moaning to Bridget about the unfairness of it all, or weeping to myself from sheer exhaustion.

Chapter Forty-Two

Having to settle down to the daily routine with Tam once more, I was much more independent now, going for my much-needed tea break or lunch without waiting to be told.

Jenny moved across the kitchen floor on her knees as I started on my lunch, and the greyish-white, soapy cloth slopped round the leg of the pinewood table.

"She can't be married in white!" she was saying to Bridget, "It would be blasphemous for the minister to marry them at the kind of wedding she wants, when she's pregnant."

I sliced into the new potatoes from the garden, thinking I could make a meal of potatoes alone if they were as good as this. Tam could, without a doubt, grow tasty potatoes. They couldn't compare in size with the Burnsyde giants, but they were delicious!

"Can I have another potato, Bridget?"

"Why, of course! Of course! There's plenty of them. Help yourself!" Then turning back to Jenny, she answered her, "'Tis a terrible thing to get herself into that condition. He could just as easily walk away with his hands in his pockets. And 'tis a disgrace to be marrying in white! I don't know what to think of the younger ones these days."

I had listened while they titted and tutted between each other over some unfortunate girl in the village.

"Can I put a word in here, Bridget?" I asked.

"To be sure you can, to be sure! But what would you have to say about a brazen hussy? 'Tis a wonder God does not strike her dead at the alter!"

"Would God not see her as something more sacred than a virgin when she carries a new life in her womb?" I said quietly.

There was a prolonged silence during which Matron entered the kitchen. They should be defending their own sex I thought.

"Jaqueline, the windows in my sitting-room are to be cleaned, Mary will do the insides; everyone is helping with the cleaning and I expect you to do the outsides as Karen has no head for heights!"

"Yes, Matron," I answered, still harbouring rebellious thoughts against Bridget's and Jenny's stupidity.

"When you have finished lunch," Matron continued, "you will find the tall stepladder, a bucket, and two chamois leathers outside the sitting-room windows. The gardener would prefer you to stay out of the garden this afternoon to allow him to catch up on the neglect of the past few weeks."

I swallowed hard on the food in my mouth, knowing that the garden had never looked better.

"Yes, Matron!" I answered, fighting the urge to commit murder where Tam was concerned. "And I'll be going home for the weekend tomorrow at noon," I added.

Matron turned without saying a word in reply and walked haughtily out of the kitchen. Bridget gave me a thoughtful look and went back to her cooking.

I had spent the morning pushing barrow-loads of logs from the plantation to the woodshed and splitting kindling for Bridget. Tam had not appeared, so he must have gone straight down to the garden from the lodge. He had plainly changed his tactics.

There was something calming about washing the dirt of months from the tall sitting-room windows. They curved into a point at the top like a church window, and the glass sparkled like the chandelier had done each time I wrung out the chamois to wash and wipe.

How foolish Bridget and Jenny had been to run down their own sex. They should have been defending a girl with spirit, instead of condemning her. Women were their own worst enemies when it came to the most important thing in their lives, or the most important thing in the world, if one thought about it.

I worked on not caring what task Matron gave me to do, I would stick to my own standards and not allow myself to become agitated over Tam's pettiness, or Bridget and Jenny's ignorance. I knew Tam hated me, because he had come back to a paradise instead of a weed patch he could have complained about. The house had not run out of electricity or hot water during his absence. The only problem that had threatened was kindling for the kitchen and logs, but he had come back just in time.

My thoughts raced on while my hands were occupied. I would never confess to the work Sean had done, that was something I would keep secret. The next second I almost fell from the stepladder with shock at the sound of the Warden's voice below me,

"Hello there, Jaqueline! Beautiful day!"

"Hello, Warden!"

He hobbled on with a walking stick in each hand, it must have been his first venture out of doors with the coming of summer. When I had started on the first window he had lain spread-eagled in his red leather chair.

The weather was indeed beautiful, but it had been pleasant ever since I had come to Avonlea in March; and there had been the three weeks with Sean. I stared dreamily through the freshly cleaned glass and the chandelier sparkled back at me.

Sean would never come to Avonlea now that Tam was back, and although I had been glad of Tam's return something wonderful had gone out of my life. I felt the stepladder wobble and grabbed it.

"Careful, careful! Jaqueline!" The Warden was on his way back along the path, and he dropped his stick and put out a hand to steady the stepladder as it wobbled. "Why are you up on that stepladder without anyone to steady it below? Where is Tam?"

"He's in the garden, Warden."

"Then I insist you come down at once! You may do the bottom half of the windows, but never let me see you at the top of this stepladder again, risking life and limb!"

I climbed down feeling touched by the Warden's concern, and he walked on towards the main entrance doors with only one stick; the other lay on the ground where he had dropped it.

Chapter Forty-Three

It was noon the next day before I finished the chores Matron had found for me, and when I sat down at the kitchen table it was a very thoughtful Bridget who served me lunch before I left for a weekend at home.

"You're sensible, Jaqueline, to be taking a break. The mind becomes fogged when you're tired and you don't realise it. I'll be speaking to Matron myself, soon; because there's good reason to be seeing my mother."

"I'm glad, Bridget. I've learned the hard way that it doesn't pay to become a willing slave at Avonlea." Bridget was quiet when I rose from the table to leave by the back door, so I called cheerily, "Goodbye, Bridget, see you Sunday evening, keep the kettle on the boil!"

It was as if I had left one world and walked into another when I stepped off the bus in Edinburgh. The city breathed with activity, and I ran to catch my connection for home. My mother was in the garden when I arrived and looked as though she were promoting sun tan oil; her short, dark hair was bobbed at the tips of her ears.

"I was hoping you would come this weekend, Jaqueline. Do you want me to cut your hair?"

"Just let me get here, Mother, before you start shearing me! And anyway, I'm leaving my hair long, it's easy to tie back, or wear in a pony tail."

"Saves shampoo if you keep it short!" she insisted, and then ran on, "I can't say you're looking tanned, Jaqueline, but there is a goldenness about your skin. Put the kettle on and I'll be in, in just a minute." My mother felt pity for people who didn't go brown with the sun.

I had just filled the kettle when the tall, blue-eyed, golden-haired man who was my father, appeared at the back door.

"It's a relief to see you home this weekend, Jaqueline." His eyes looked troubled, "Heavy work is not for women! You need time off at the weekend to rest, Tam or no Tam; it's lack of organisation that's the trouble."

"But, Dad, there's a shortage of staff!"

"What's wrong with these teenage boys you help to feed, there's no shortage of them around!"

"Some have tried to help me, but Matron says it's my work and not theirs, their homework is more important because they are the rising generation of men."

"Piffle!" my father answered, "rising generation of weaklings!"

My mother bustled into the kitchen to stack the cups and saucers on a tray.

"Bring the teapot!" she called. "There's something quite different about you, Jaqueline, and I just can't put a finger on it. You've lost the plumpness you put on at Burnsyde. Give Alex a call, Bill, the tea's ready!" And she swept into the sitting-room with the tray.

"I know I've lost a bit, Mother, because I went to the cinema with a friend, wearing my halter necked dress. I couldn't get into it at Burnsyde. My waist must be back to twenty-three inches."

My father and brother walked into the room while my mother busily poured tea.

"Hello, Jaqueline, long time no see!" said my brother.

"Hello, Alex, how many motorbikes have you got now?"

He grinned, but before he could answer my mother said,

"What friend, Jaqueline?"

"Oh, just Sean, the boy I worked with at Burnsyde. Will I fill up the pot?"

"Yes, but go easy on the tea, we don't have an ever-flowing pot like Bridget. It's rationed, just in case you've forgotten!"

I went through to the kitchen and my brother followed.

"What's Sean like?" he asked, and I turned towards the kettle before answering him:

"Oh, he's just a boy I know, Alex!"

Opening the kitchen door to let me through with the teapot I passed him and he grinned again knowingly.

"Sean's the difference in you, Jaqueline. Isn't he?"

"He could be!" I answered, unable to keep the glow from my eyes.

"He is, Jackie!" he said, following me through to the sitting-room.

Anxious to cut short the interrogation by my brother, I turned to my mother who listened to every news bulletin on the radio, and had done so since the war started.

"Fill me in on the war situation, Mother. It's like another world at Avonlea, we have a gramophone in the staff sitting-room and that's it! Matron has a radio in her room but it's never on above a whisper. Tell me what's happening!"

My mother glanced at my brother, and it was as if they had come to a silent decision. I felt a reluctance to tell me anything.

"Alex can tell you more than I can, but it's all hush-hush stuff."

Again I was aware of their hesitancy to tell me what was happening, but while my father sat engrossed in his newspaper, my brother started to speak with a precision that made me listen to every word.

"I've been on a lot of trials in the Forth, and there's a huge, combined military-naval operation underway. The yards are working night and day on large structures. I'm earning an awful lot of money for an under-eighteen year old, because we're going flat out, as is everyone else in engineering. The beginning of June is the deadline; and I'm afraid that's all I can tell you, Jackie."

"But June's not far away, Alex. Will whatever is being built be ready on time?"

He grinned, and his eyes showed a glint of satisfaction when he answered,

"We can make it! Show me an engineer that can't!" Then his expression changed as he continued, "I want to get into the air force to learn about aero-engines, but they keep fobbing me off with this reserved occupation excuse."

I knew it irritated him to be held back from his ambitions, he had always been that way. Then I asked him,

"I thought you were studying to be a chief engineer on a liner?"

"I am!" he replied. "But that doesn't stop me from wanting to learn about all kinds of engines!"

"Have patience, Alex, it will all happen when the time is ripe and not before. And don't look so annoyed about it!"

Sunday dawned on another lovely day and I could smell the salt in the air on the breeze drifting up from the Forth. At the breakfast table

Alex was at me again asking about Sean, but I had managed to dodge his questions.

"Put on your shorts, Jackie, and I'll take you for a spin on the big-twin!"

While my brother revved-up his latest motor bike, I changed.

"I can beat the police cars on this one," he said. "It's eleven hundred and forty-two c.c.!"

He started off gently enough, but I put my arms tightly round his waist as he moved into the roundabout.

"Don't exceed the speed limit, Alex," I said, as his speed increased.

"Throw yourself over, Jackie!" he answered. "Just move with me, or I'll have to keep slowing down on every bend!"

We travelled out along the coast road and he let it "cruise", so he said. I could feel my eyelids being forced against my eyes, so I pressed my face into his shirt and held on tight as we raced along the empty road.

"Stop at the tearoom!" I shouted against the wind.

"Okay, okay! No need to panic, I was only trying it out!" he answered, slowing down to turn back.

"You've got goggles and trousers on, I haven't!" I said, refusing to admit to fear.

He turned left down a steep slope and Crammond Island lay in front of us. The tide was out and we could have waded out to the island, but Alex wanted to sit on the sea wall and talk.

"He must be taller than me and quite dashing?" he began. "Not necessarily very handsome, but definitely athletic I would say. But I don't think he'll make it with you unless he has a brain like Einstein to go with all the other virtues."

"You mean Sean?" I said, laughing out loud.

"Who else?" he replied. "I hope he hasn't tried anything on with you, Jackie, or I'll flatten him!"

I listened and smiled watching his tawny eyes, which were more flecked with green than usual, flashing. His sandy fair hair was cut in what he called the D.A. and its crinkly waves gave it lift at the front, they also held it in the V shape at the back.

"I'm just concerned about you, Jackie, because I know what most boys are like!"

"Yes, Alex, I never got the chance to know any boys well with you protecting me. Or were you keeping me on the job as assistant while you took your motorbikes apart?"

"Not assistant, Jackie. Apprentice! But you learned a lot about engines. Didn't you?" he grinned widely.

"However, Alex, I have to look out for myself now. Strange, I suppose it must come to us naturally, and yet, everything remains vague until you come face to face with reality. It's a protection in a way, this innocence before we mature, or are ready to accept life as it really is."

We walked along the foreshore, and the waves rolled on to the reinforcements built to protect the half-finished new road.

"Alex, Mum wept her heart out after finding something in your suit pocket." He looked startled, and answered,

"What are you talking about, Jackie?"

"You know what I'm talking about, she does press your suits!"

"Oh, gee! Poor Mum! But I am growing up and it's perfectly natural."

"Yes," I agreed, "but last night she took me through to your wardrobe to show me the rubber sheath you keep in a handkerchief in your top pocket. I didn't know what it was, until she burst into tears and told me. Poor Mum! She doesn't want us to grow up at all."

"The girls I go around with are not like you, Jackie, they really know how to live!"

"Do they?" I replied. "Mum told me about her wealthy friend who has two, beautiful, golden-haired children; they're sightless because she had a venereal disease when they were born. So it all comes back to what you call living. You're creating the world you have to live in, so don't come crying when it goes wrong," I said quietly, but he didn't answer, he just sat there looking at the sun dancing over the waves. "Will you marry one of these girls you go around with, Alex?"

"No, there's plenty time when my career is fixed and then I'll look for a nice little girl." He turned to look at me and the grin was back on his face.

"You mean a virgin, Alex? A girl like me who refuses sexual intercourse outside marriage."

"Of course!" he replied.

On the way home I hung on to my brother a little less terrified of leaning over when he took the sharp bends.

"That's right, Jackie!" he called against the wind, "throw the bike over and we go round without losing speed!" The road was too near my bare leg for comfort, so I gritted my teeth until the house came into view and he slowed down. "Mum doesn't like me to drive too fast," he said, and I heaved a sigh of relief.

My sister had arrived home by the time we got back.

"How did you enjoy the ball at the Assembly Rooms, Margaret?" I asked.

"Two of us spent the night at Trudy's house. There were ten in our party and my dancing shoes must be worn out!"

"Better than a barn dance?" I asked.

"More glamorous, but not necessarily better. Is Tam back?"

"Yes, I wouldn't have come home if he hadn't been."

"I'll be going up north on the tractor to help at harvest time, Jaqueline. I can't wait to see the other estate, it lies on the far side of the Firth of Tay in the Angus region, and we're paid overtime."

She started unpacking her overnight case, and I had hardly anything to say because my social life was almost nil.

"I was out for a run on the new motor bike. I can't even hold it up it's so heavy."

"They don't come any bigger, thank goodness! That's three Alex has now, Jaqueline. Which reminds me! He's quite the man about town these days; I can see seven brothers from the Crescent taking him by the scruff of the neck and making him do the decent thing by their only sister. And Mum still calls him the baby of the family. It gives me a pain in the neck!" she finished, looking disgusted.

"What a thing to say about your only brother, Margaret!"

"I wouldn't say it, if I hadn't heard it last night."

"Then you better tell him before he's in trouble."

"Men make the rules, and if they break them they should suffer the consequences. Women have to!" she said.

"Takes two, Margaret," I replied, feeling very grown up, because all the perplexing, obscure part of my education on sex in humans was clearly in focus at last.

My sister glanced at me with a thoughtful look in her eyes.

"What about yourself, Jaqueline? Nothing much happens in your life these days, except work and more work. But you look happy enough on it!"

"I've painted the garden gates, since Tam got back. And learned a bit about lumbering. And, of course, I helped with the spring cleaning because of the staff shortage."

My sister almost exploded as she turned on me,

"Staff shortage! If you were dead tomorrow they would find staff! But if you keep on slaving right over weekends and up to bedtime, of course they won't bother to find staff; and all those big, lazy boys around. How can you stand it, Jaqueline? I couldn't!"

By the time she had finished I wanted to forget all about work at Avonlea, but I wondered what Tam could possibly find for me to do that I had not already done. So I changed the subject to the thing that occupied my mind most.

"Alex was saying we would soon be coming to a turning point in the war, what do you think, Margaret?"

"I don't think anymore! It will either end, or go on for the next hundred years. Anything I can do wouldn't make the slightest bit of difference. I used to think Uncle Sandy was a bore with his politics, Jaqueline, but he's always been right! There's nothing we can do, we are only pawns in a game of chess played by the ones who rule. And that's not our royal family, they're only figureheads."

I started to tidy some drawers and we were quiet for a while. She began again,

"If they had shot the madman who started it all in the first place, it would never have gone this far. And I can only think of one other thing; the biggest moneyspinner is armaments, and as long as the wealthy feel safe they will allow war to happen." There was a pause in her flow of words, and she walked over to the window and stood looking out towards the Forth; then she turned. "I don't think they will ever let a woman become Prime Minister, but if they did, would she be any different from the men?"

"Woman Prime Minister! I very much doubt it, Margaret. However, it's something to contemplate." Enough had been said about work and politics, and I wanted to talk about Sean. "I went to the village cinema with Sean," I began, aware of the glow coming into my eyes at the thought of him.

"That's the boy who was going into the air force, Jaqueline. Isn't he away yet?"

"No, not yet, and he doesn't say why."

"Well, I'm glad, little sister. It's time you had a bit of entertainment; you should have been at the ball last night!"

I smiled at the thought. A ball! And the only thing I could see in the room that would have made a ball-gown was the blue, silk bedspread I was sitting on; I would keep it in mind because my clothing coupons were just enough for the necessities. Borrowing a gown, as my sister had done, didn't appeal to me.

"It shouldn't be difficult to keep him in his place, if he's still the moron who dumped you in the rubbish tip at Burnsyde."

The gown taking shape in my mind as I gazed at the blue of the bedspread was princess line, with a billowing, centre-back panel coming into a tiny train, but the picture faded when I answered my sister,

"Oh, he's much nicer now! More grown up." Then I stopped talking, suddenly preferring to keep the wonderful thing that had happened between Sean and I to myself.

"I could do with some help in the kitchen, girls," my mother called, and the chance for sisterly conversation had gone. The rest of Sunday had flown by in the company of the family before we again went our separate ways.

Chapter Forty-Four

I felt Avonlea was beginning to dominate my life; but a weekend at home had brought back the feeling of something temporary, something I would just have to put up with until the war was over. Hundred years! What rubbish! I had been surprised at my sister's lack of optimism and held on to the hope that my brother had inspired.

We moved into the month of June, and I wondered if the engineers had managed to complete the huge undertaking Alex had told me about on time. It would never be mentioned in letters, so I would have to wait until I was at home again for news of the outcome.

The roses in the garden began to bloom in all their glory and the air was filled with their scent. When I went to bed that night the wind had risen. The garden was a very sheltered place, and I hoped the roses would not be blown and bruised when they were so fresh and new.

Sean was in my thoughts often, but the turn in the tide of war hinted at by my brother seemed more important. After all these years of war a ray of hope shone on the horizon. I had developed from an immature girl to a woman against the background of war, sirens and rationing, and now I laboured like a man.

I would be expected to stay at Avonlea this weekend, and as the days passed I settled down to the routine. It was Friday morning when Tam appeared at the back door, his voice as he spoke impatient as ever.

"The coal supply's here!" he began, looking at his watch. "I want you to shovel it into the bunker when the men empty the bags, so flatten yourself against the far wall of the furnace room."

The clock struck the hour and I rose from the table to follow him outside. Making no attempt to answer I started down the steel steps, then he grunted,

"Put the shovel in front of your legs when the men empty the bags."

With my back against the wall I watched the first two bags of coal pour down bouncing on the steps and clanging against the shovel.

"Don't just stand there! Start shovelling!" he bawled. I began to shovel the coal from the floor into the bunker on my right. "Back against the wall!" he roared from the top of the steps, and another two bags poured down.

Large lumps shattered on the steel steps as they fell, splattering pieces at the furnaces and clanging against my shovel. I closed my eyes, but after a few sharp pings on the cheek I put my gloved hands over my face leaving the shovel to protect my legs.

When the noise of falling coal had stopped, I gasped in the cloud of coal dust filling the furnace room and started shovelling. Only when the tenth bag had been dropped did the men stop for a smoke. Tam looked down on the mound of coal blocking the steps; there was no way out until it was cleared.

"Shovel it all into the coal bunker and clean up the dross with the brush," he said, turning away to light his pipe.

I had just straightened up from heaving some large lumps into the bunker, when the men started again. Finally, they dropped the last two bags and were gone. Gradually the dust began to settle and looking round me I thought, this is what hell must be like.

The furnaces would have to wait until I had cleared some of the mound before I could stoke them, and until the steps were cleared there would be no cup of tea. When I, at last, climbed up the steel steps I was taken by surprise, because the effort of lifting one foot past the other exhausted me. I had not cleared even half of the coal into the bunker, and had lost all sense of time.

Before entering the kitchen I shook out as much coal dust from my dungarees and jacket as was possible, removed my boots and stepped through the doorway. Bridget placed some newspapers on the table and bench, and I sat down.

"It's long past the tea break, Jaqueline, so I'm giving you an early lunch," she said seriously, looking into my face.

"Can I please have a cup of tea first, Bridget?"

"Of course, Jaqueline, but you shouldn't work on for hours like that, it's nearly midday!"

"I had to clear the steps to get out, Bridget, and stoke the furnaces, or you would run out of hot water!"

I knew I had been sitting in the kitchen for more than an hour, picking at my lunch and drinking another large mug of tea; I was absorbing the tea like blotting paper. I felt too tired to get up, and hated the thought of going down into the furnace room again.

Black from head to foot I sat there, and Bridget said nothing. But the job had to be done. Then I reminded myself that men were dying for their country, not just shovelling coal. I left the kitchen and made my way down into the furnace room. Tam was keeping well out of the way.

It was pointless messing up Bridget's spotless kitchen, so I worked on determined to finish the task. After what seemed like eternity, I brushed up the dross and threw it into the bunker. The heat from the two furnaces had become unbearable, and opening the doors to stoke them I felt my face scorch. With the task completed I staggered up the steel steps on legs barely able to support me.

My hands felt like rubber inside my working gloves and seemed to have swelled to twice their normal size. What hell it was to be one of the weaker sex, how I wished for the strength of a man. The air outside was refreshing, and after removing my boots I walked unsteadily into the kitchen and sank down onto the newspapers still lying where Bridget had carefully placed them.

I would rather have Mary laugh into her apron, as she had done when I was the chimney sweep, but she was silent and Bridget crossed herself before taking her scones out of the oven. The butter melted into the scone Bridget had opened, and then she poured tea.

"It's after four, Jaqueline, take this before you have a bath." And she put the buttered scone and mug of tea in front of me, my hands trembled as I lifted the mug.

Some time later I made my way stiffly upstairs to run the bath, and the tears poured down through the coal dust on my cheeks. I thought how ridiculous it was for me to use only six inches of water, so I let the tap run until the bath was full, and soaked until all the stiffness had gone. I washed the coal dust out of my hair with hands that had little feeling in them.

The clothes I had taken off lay on the tiled floor, and when I stepped out of the bath after rinsing down with clean water I dropped in the bundle and left them to steep.

Tam stayed well out of the way after the coal delivery, and it was Monday morning before I saw him again.

After dumping my filthy clothes into the bath, I had made my way down to the staff sitting-room to start on the mending. If Tam wanted me, he could come and find me! My hands still felt useless and I sat trying to push wool through the eye of a darning needle; it was how Matron found me when she came raging through with Bridget close behind her,

"How dare you leave your filthy clothing in the bath, I demand an explanation!"

I looked at her furious face from my seat by the window, her hands on her narrow hips. She seethed with rage.

"It seemed like a good idea to steep them in the bath water when they were so dirty, Matron."

Bridget stood behind her silently watching the scene.

"You will remove them at once and clean the bath!"

There was no point in mentioning the benefit of steeping clothes to someone who had never washed clothes, so I climbed the stairs with a packet of soap powder, wondering how my mother ever got through the mound of sheets, towels and clothing she washed every Monday morning. All I had ever done was drop the soiled clothing into the linen basket, and the next time I saw it, it was washed, ironed and neatly placed in one of my drawers.

I crawled into bed that night thankful for the blessing of sleep and its ability to restore energy.

It was Matron's voice and her insistent pounding on my bedroom door that woke me the next morning.

"Jaqueline, it's eight o'clock and you should be downstairs!"

"Yes, Matron!"

I scrambled into my housecoat and hurried to the bathroom. Why had I overslept? I scrubbed at my teeth and splashed my face. It was the last thing I wanted to do! Then I stopped panicking; it was Saturday morning, and I recalled the coal delivery of the previous day. How did I get myself into such situations? I should have refused to shovel the coal, and the fuss over my clothes steeping in the bath had been unnecessary.

Matron was walking up and down the kitchen floor when I made my appearance.

"Have your breakfast, Jaqueline!" she snapped, then she started to lecture. "I will not tolerate laziness in the morning! Have you not the shining example of the cook and the kitchen maid who rise much earlier than you do?"

I looked at her, but I could think of nothing to say.

"Have you not a tongue in your head, insolent girl!" And turning towards the door leading to the hall she muttered something about rudeness, it was then that I found words,

"I have never in my life shovelled a ton of coal, until yesterday, and if I overslept it was understandable; I just didn't hear my alarm, Matron."

She stood in the doorway listening without turning to look at me, then walked off to her room across the hall. Bridget waited, and when Matron's door closed she brought me a sandwich tin from the cupboard.

"Stand your alarm on that," she said, hitting it with a wooden spoon. "And by the holy mother of Jesus it should wake up the dead!"

I suddenly found myself laughing, then Bridget continued in a more subdued voice,

"I shouldn't be taking the name of Our Lady in vain, but it's not me, it's something that drives me to it."

I finished breakfast still smiling at the explanation of this dear, honest soul. Something had prevented me from apologising to Matron, and if I were to define it I would have called it indignation. The injustice of her holier-than-thou lecture, when I was driving myself to the limit for King and country, had made apologies impossible.

Instead of going down to the garden I spent my time weeding the flower beds outside the sitting-room windows. The stalks of the parrot tulips stood bare, and their colourful petals blown by the breeze lay scattered on the rich, dark soil like cast off frilly skirts.

Plucking a leaf from the sweet bay I crushed it between my fingers to release its sweet fragrance. I wondered how long I could go on doing the kind of tasks Tam found for me to do. I had slept right through the alarm, and my legs had been like jelly on the way to the bathroom this morning.

If Tam had come then and asked me to shovel another ton of coal, I knew in my heart that my strength would have failed me. I was only fit that morning to kneel on the little rubber mat and pull up weeds. The basket was already overflowing, because Tam avoided working on Matron's flower beds, so I tipped the weeds into the sack I had left on the path. Just then I saw a large, black car turn into the main entrance gates and make its way slowly down the drive.

I had started again on the weeding, and by the time the car had passed me and come to a stop at the house entrance Matron was hurrying down the steps to greet the newcomer as he opened the car door. I concentrated on pulling up weeds, while Matron walked up the steps arm-in-arm with her guest.

"We didn't expect you until tomorrow, Adrian," I heard her say as they entered the vestibule. "The gardener will bring your luggage. Oh, just a minute, I can get Jaqueline to bring it!" She came hurrying out and called from the top of the steps, "Jaqueline, bring the luggage from the car!"

I stood up and brushed down the legs of my dungarees, while answering,

"Yes, Matron!" Walking over to the open door of the car I reached inside and lifted a gun; for shooting game, I imagined.

"Here, let me take that! It could be rather dangerous." The guest hurried down the steps as I reached in for a briefcase, then I gave him the two items. "Thank you, m'dear," he said, his bright eyes twinkling from beneath bushy eyebrows. Putting his arm inside the car he released the lock on the back door. "Hup, boy! We're here!"

What looked like a mound of shaggy sheep skins lying on the back seat of the car began to move. It rose and lumbered out of the car; I could see no eyes, because long white and black hair hung from all over its head and body. It stood on the drive for a moment, then started to shake itself. While the long, shaggy coat swished round about it I caught sight of four large paws placed firmly on the ground.

"I'll get the luggage, m'dear, it's far too heavy for you! Just take Shep round to the kitchen door and ask cook to fill his water dish."

"Yes, sir," I answered, and slipping my hand under the heavy studded collar I tugged, but he just stood there as if he had taken root.

"Bridget, go round to Bridget, Shep!" and at the sound of the tweedy guest's voice the shaggy mound began to make its way along the path to the side door of the kitchen. I looked at the guest and smiled, and he raised his hand and touched the edge of his deer stalker hat. His eyes shone with amusement as mine did. I started to follow the plodding animal, and the guest called out,

"It's an English sheep dog, m'dear!" At the sound of his voice I turned to smile, and the straight-backed man with the twinkling eyes nodded.

I followed behind the large, slow creature until it stopped right in front of the kitchen door. It put its front paws on the step and let out a "woof". The door opened almost immediately, and Bridget shouted,

"Keep that big, ugly, lumbering animal out of my kitchen!"

"It needs water, Bridget," I said apologetically.

"Then hold on to it and don't let it in here!" And she promptly closed the door.

While Shep and I waited for the water he turned his head and looked at me, although it was difficult to tell, because I still couldn't see any eyes. The tail gave a single wag, so I said,

"Hello, Shep!" and patted his head until the water was passed out.

The news of Shep's arrival had gone round like wildfire, and studies were abandoned as the boys poured out on to the lawns. Just before I went into the kitchen for the morning tea break I saw the little ones throwing themselves on to the big, shaggy creature, then rolling off on to the grass in sheer delight.

In the kitchen the light of battle was in Bridget's eyes and she started to say slowly,

"You put enough down in front of it to feed a family of five and before you can straighten up the bowl's licked clean. Then it stands there like the great, muckle lump that it is and wags its stupid stump of a tail for more." Bridget was almost out of breath, so she turned to the cupboard collecting more items for her recipe and began to rave again. "It gets in here and parks itself in front of the range, and I can neither get into the pots or the oven until it decides to move." She put her hands on her hips and looked me straight in the eyes. "So the doors stay closed while Matron has her brother visiting! And that's my final word!"

"Yes, Bridget! But don't you think he's cute?" I was just leaving the kitchen as I spoke and she almost threw the rolling pin after me.

"Be off with you!" she said, her face suddenly wreathed in smiles, and I closed the door.

The flower beds in front of the sitting-room windows looked neat and tidy after weeding, and I decided to leave the petals of the parrot tulips where they had fallen, because the beautiful colours and the picot edges looked pretty lying on the dark, loamy soil.

I picked up the trowel and the rubber mat, pleased with my work, when Matron drew my attention by tapping on the sitting-room window. In a few moments she was standing beside me, frowning and saying irritably,

"Jaqueline, Bridget will need Mary's help in the kitchen today, because my guest has come a day early. I want you to assist with the boys when they go to the matinée at the village cinema after lunch. Karen will be in charge." She was about to turn away when she saw the petals. "Pick up these petals, Jaqueline, they look most untidy!"

After stoking the furnaces I cleaned up and changed into a dress and sandals, and I was sitting at the kitchen table after lunch when Karen came tripping in ready for the cinema.

"Have you ever been on cinema duty before, Jaqueline?" she asked.

"No, but I'm looking forward to it."

"It's quite a responsibility," said Karen loftily, helping herself to coffee, "and the boys must walk in pairs on the footpath. It's not quite a mile, but they must be kept firmly under control in case of traffic. The older boys won't come to see Snow White."

I listened to the perfect diction and the slightly overbearing intonation in the voice of this girl from the south. It came from her lips as naturally as Bridget's Irish accent.

We could hear the boys beginning to assemble in the hall, and when Karen opened the kitchen door they were standing to attention. The Warden stood in the sitting-room doorway, and behind him Matron's brother watched the proceedings. He looked even more straight and military without his hat. The older boys had opted out to study.

"Hup, two, three, four! Right turn!"

Matron's brother suppressed a large grin, and his eyes sparkled as the boys wheeled at the sound of the Warden's deep voice. From the tallest to the tiniest they all turned as one, shoulders erect and chins pulled in like guardsmen.

Karen tripped across the hall in her high heels and stood there looking perfectly in command of her charges; then the Warden shouted,

"Quick march!"

The boys filtered through the front entrance of the house and out on to the drive, while the Warden, who was supporting himself on the side of the sitting-room door with one hand, made to turn. By habit he had intended returning to his red, leather chair, but his path was blocked.

"I have your sticks, Cedric. Let's watch the boys march up the drive!"

The Warden looked startled, but he answered instantly,

"Oh, just as you say, Adrian, a bit of air will do me good!"

From the day of his arrival Matron's brother was to hound the Warden from his red, leather chair, the decanter of port, and the depressing stuffiness of the sitting-room with its blazing log fire.

I followed the column out onto the drive, where the sun shone down from a cloudless sky and a light wind caressed the face. The bigger boys had already lengthened their stride and the little ones were running to keep up with them.

"Hey there! Slow down!" I called.

Had the Warden managed through the house entrance yet? I turned to glance back and there he was, steadying himself on two sticks. The military man stood easily at his side with his hands in his trouser pockets, just a little taller than the obese Warden.

Shep came lumbering across the lawn and he almost broke into a run to catch up on the boys.

"No, Shep!" I called, but he came on as if I had never uttered a word.

"Send him back, Jaqueline, he mustn't leave the grounds!" called Karen from the front of the column. I ran across and grabbed the heavily studded collar.

"Stay, Shep, stay!" I commanded, and again it was just as if I didn't exist. He broke into a trot pulling me along with him until he was pushing in amongst the boys.

"You might as well let go of him, Jackie," one of the boys said.

I released Shep and he pushed his way into the column, knocking over the little ones as he tried to hide in amongst their legs.

"Halt!" Karen cried, when we reached the main entrance. "Go back, Shep! At once!" Shep stood there with his tail wagging halfheartedly and his head drooping. "At once!" repeated Karen in her most dictatorial voice.

The great, shaggy creature flattened itself out on the drive and lay there with its face between its front paws. I tried to suppress a giggle, but Shep had heard it and rose to his feet wagging his tail.

"You must be firm, Jaqueline, or we will never get started! He only needs the slightest bit of encouragement," said Karen sounding exasperated.

Calling for the help of two boys she closed the main gates leaving a small gap in the middle, through which the boys squeezed in single file out on to the pavement.

Shep stood patiently waiting until all but myself had squeezed through, and then he pushed his head in front of my legs until I was forced to close the gate. I waited for him to turn away, but Shep was biding his time knowing that I would have to open the gate to let myself out.

A loud guffaw sounded from the bottom of the drive, and when I looked up Matron's brother was gathering speed as he sprinted towards me.

"Right, m'dear, I'll hold him till you get through the gates!"

I hurried along to make up on the boys and we made good time on our march to the village, but I felt sure our numbers had swelled when we stopped at the cinema. My attention was rivetted on the little ones as I had been made responsible for six of them. With all the village children milling about, I stood there with three on each side of me clinging to my hands.

"As you haven't been on cinema duty before, Jaqueline, I'll go inside to make sure we are all seated together," and as she spoke Karen walked authoritatively past the doorman and into the dimly lit cinema.

I waited while the doorman allowed our column to enter.

"Right!" he said, holding up his hand, "That's twenty!"

"But what about the little ones?" I asked in dismay.

"Twenty have gone through that entrance and that's the lot as far as I'm concerned!" he replied, his solid body blocking the way.

My charges clung to my hands and sucked their thumbs while I argued.

"What nonsense is this?" Karen's face had appeared looking over his shoulder. "Let the children through, or I will report you to Matron, it isn't our fault you can't count!"

Completely humbled by the intolerant voice she had used the man stepped aside to let me through with my six charges. Inside the cinema Karen had seated the boys in two neat rows and as she pointed to the seats for the little ones the doorman marched in.

"Where is the Avonlea bunch?" he demanded.

"This row and the one behind!" called Karen above the din of every child in the village.

Our boys sat quietly in their seats as he counted them, while the rest of the cinema audience shouted, banged their seats up and down, and scrambled on hands and knees to catch crawling toddlers. The doorman was completely oblivious of the commotion around him, and he picked up a baby from between his legs passing it to a school girl who was in charge of about six brothers and sisters.

When he had counted twenty he turned to Karen with a sneer:

"Where are the rest of them?" he asked scornfully.

"These are our boys!" she replied, "and I see you can count after all!"

I was amazed at her impertinence, and the man turned away defeated. The village gate-crashers who had joined our column had sensibly taken seats elsewhere.

The lights slowly dimmed and a great cheer went up, then the film started; as the cheering died away we could hear the opening music. Our boys were completely absorbed by the fairy tale unfolding on the screen. There was the odd thump of a seat springing up, and a yell when some brother or sister was slapped for not sitting still, but the rest of the audience, including Karen and I, had become lost in the enchanted world of Disney.

When the queen gazed at her reflection in the mirror and asked who was the fairest in the land, the magic mirror told her it was the princess Snow White. We watched her fly into a terrible rage, because Snow White was fairer than she.

Gasps of horror rose from the audience when she turned herself into an old hag, and filled an apple with poison before going in search of the dwarfs' cottage.

Deep in the forest Snow White sang happily while she cleaned the dwarfs' cottage; she did not recognise the queen in her disguise and accepted the beautiful red poisoned apple from what she thought was a poor old woman.

Snow White lifted the apple to her lips, and a chorus of children's voices rang out,

"No! No! Snow White! It's poisoned!"

Unfortunately, Snow White had fallen to the floor the moment she bit the apple, and lay quite still. Unaware of the terrible thing that had happened the dwarfs marched from the mine where they worked singing happily, while the audience sobbed.

On finding Snow White lying as though she were dead, the grief of the dwarfs brought a tear to the eye. Karen and I dabbed with our handkerchiefs; and as we sniffed a murmur ran through our boys who had not made a sound or shed a tear. Then a small voice at my side whispered,

"Don't cry! It's only a fairy tale, and she marries a prince at the end."

Outside in the bright sunshine, away from the dimly lit interior of the cinema, the boys lined up in pairs; and the song of the birds was drowned by the song of the dwarfs on the march back to Avonlea.

Chapter Forty-Five

How the week had flown by since the arrival of Matron's brother. The Warden abandoned his comfortable, red leather easy chair, and walked through the estate grounds with the lean, tweedy man who needed no one to urge him into action.

"I've asked for a weekend off before the school holidays begin," said Bridget, and she looked quite determined when she turned from the kitchen range to face me.

"And has it been granted?" I enquired.

"Not yet, but I won't take no for an answer!" and from her determined reply I could see Bridget was not going to be put off again. She had been quiet over the two days that had passed since making her request.

Matron had talked me out of going home this weekend with one of her stand-by speeches,

"It is your duty," she had said, "to stay and help when we are short staffed; need I remind you that the country is at war!"

My gaze had been steady on her face while she lectured me on duty, and I had seen her for the first time as she really was: middle-aged, infuriated by a war that had invaded her book-worm world with its servants. She had been robbed of the leisure that was her birthright; her mansion house had been commandeered by the government; it was considered a luxury in wartime when children had to be evacuated from the cities to safer areas.

Deep in thought I sipped my tea, unaware that the kitchen door had opened until Matron's voice spoke almost into my ear,

"Jaqueline, I will be going through the names, dates of birth, and parents or next of kin with the boys at roll call tomorrow mid-morning." She placed a clip-board, with the boys' names listed in alphabetical order on a long sheet of paper, in front of my mug. "I will call each boy's surname and they will answer giving their

Christian names, date of birth, then parents' names, or next of kin in that order."

"Yes, Matron," I answered, and without saying another word she walked out of the kitchen.

The broody hen was not in her nesting box when I returned to scrape the floor of the hen house, and I noticed that one of her six eggs was slightly green in colour; on closer examination I realised it was a duck egg.

Who had put a duck egg among the hen's eggs I wondered? It could only be Tam, or perhaps Matron? At first I was tempted to remove it. Would a little duckling be accepted by a hen when it hatched? It seemed like a thoughtless thing to do, because a duckling's habitat was water, and the hens loathed even the rain that fell. If I removed it I would have to face the wrath of someone, so I left it where it was, but I worried.

At lunch-time Bridget had still not heard from Matron, and it was afternoon when I walked into the kitchen, remembering to close the door for the dog, that the transformation was obvious.

"You've been given permission to take the weekend off, Bridget."

"Yes," she said quietly. "It's all arranged for a week tomorrow; a woman from the village is coming in to take over the kitchen. Once the school holidays start there will be no peace for anyone."

"You see, it can be done if you push the issue, Bridget."

I was still sitting at the table, with my mug of tea, when I felt Bridget's eyes on me and I looked up as she started to speak:

"Jaqueline," she said thoughtfully, "will you come home with me on my weekend off? I would like my mother to meet you."

It occurred to me instantly that she had not included her father, but I smiled with the pleasure I felt and answered,

"Why, of course, Bridget! I'd love to come."

It would be the end of June before I saw my family again, but it seemed unimportant with Bridget's invitation to look forward to, and I began to wonder what size of house Bridget's parents would have with so many children.

The boys lined up in the hall next morning for Saturday roll-call, and Matron handed me the clip-board with the list of all their names. In the short time I had been at Avonlea new boys had arrived and older boys had gone back to the city.

"When I call your name," Matron began, "I want you to say your full Christian names, then date of birth, and last of all the names of your parents!"

The under five year olds had not been included, and Matron droned on through the list as the boys stood to attention. I listened and ticked off the details making any adjustments that arose.

"Mmm! Father unknown!" Matron looked the boy up and down with disapproval registering on her face; the boy hung his head in shame.

"Stephens!" I read from the list, and Matron repeated it while her eyes sought out Carrots. "Stephens!" she called again, and Carrots mumbled. "Speak up, Benjamin! I can't hear you!" Carrots' face had gone bright red beneath his thatch of rusty hair, he mumbled again, but no one heard. "Benjamin Elijah!" said Matron loudly, and turned to me irritably.

While I ticked his name, Carrots looked as if he wanted to slip down between the floorboards. He stood there sullen and red because of the names he hated until the list was complete and the boys dismissed. The hall was empty in seconds and Matron took the clipboard.

"Give me the pencil, Jaqueline," she said. "This nonsense of using two words when one will suffice!" And running a line through 'father unknown' she replaced it with 'illegitimate'.

Later, I piled kindling wood into the barrow for the kitchen and my mind ticked over. Illegitimate children would never be part of my life, but it could so easily have happened. I knew from Rob that Sean was still at Burnsyde and only Tam's presence was keeping him away.

If I allowed him to take me out in the evenings Sean would never be satisfied until he had seduced me. He could be called-up at any moment, and once out of sight, or mind, would he even remember me after he had had his way?

It was no longer a casual boy and girl friendship, I had learned what lay in the mind of the maturing male; the consequences of sexual intercourse before marriage had come fully into focus as I came face to face with reality along the way. It had all suddenly clicked into place in my mind.

How I wished that the reproduction of the human species had been put to us in a straightforward way at school, and not treated like some dark, evil, unmentionable subject; I still could not admit to myself that it happened, at home, between my parents.   And yet, the proof was there in myself, my brother and my sister.

Chapter Forty-Six

A whole week passed in a flurry of activity, while Bridget fussed and prepared food that could be kept in the larder for the weekend. It was almost as though she was going away for a week instead of Saturday afternoon and Sunday.

At noon on the Saturday she was satisfied, and handed over her kitchen to the plump lady from the village. The long overdue weekend had come at last, and we both walked up the drive to catch the bus going west.

"You know there's sixteen of us!" said Bridget in her brisk way. The excitement of a visit to her family brought a glow to her pale skin as we settled into our seats on the bus. "Five have married, but not my eldest brother. He's still at home with the others. It's a small village we live in, and there's a prisoner of war camp just up the road."

"Does it worry your family to have a prisoner of war camp so near them?" I asked.

"No! Not at all!" Bridget replied brightly, and continued to chatter on like a school girl.

The bus swung into the terminus where we were to wait for our connection before continuing the journey to Bridget's home.

"We have, let me see, twenty minutes to wait," said Bridget, glancing at her watch. "I think I'll pay a visit to the church across the road."

"Can I come with you, Bridget?"

"Gracious, yes! Anyone can go into our churches," she replied in amazement, then she gripped my hand and hurried me across the road.

I had the feeling of trespassing as we entered the cathedral-like building, and just inside the doorway Bridget dipped her fingers into a silver bowl of shimmering water, and crossed herself murmuring something in Latin. I followed her to the altar.

She paused for a few seconds, and lifted a candle, placing it in a holder and lighting it with a long taper. Crossing herself again she watched it splutter into a steady flame and stand glowing softly beside the others. I could feel the peace of the place seeping into me, while Bridget knelt and murmured a few more lines in Latin, crossing herself several times.

Then she motioned me towards a pew where we sat watching the rows of glowing candles burning steadily on the altar, and after a few moments had passed Bridget knelt again and prayed. My thoughts turned to my own church that had no glowing candles and was kept locked except for set services. I usually attended the Sunday morning service and there was no peace because of the ranting and raving of the minister.

When he paused for breath during his hour long lecture on the blackness of our souls, paper bags rustled and pan drops clicked against teeth. Then he would thump his hand on the pulpit to bring the aged from their slumbers, and warn us of the cloven hoof in our midst while his face changed from red to purple.

Leaving my own church after a service was the time for parading fur coats that smelled strongly of mothballs. The looks of disdain on the faces of the wearers had filled me with disgust as I grew into my teens. Even as a child, when I dropped my penny into the box for the black babies, it had been all smiles for those who were well dressed and looks of disapproval for those who were not and had no penny.

The candles on the altar merged into a softly glowing wall of brightness and Bridget still knelt in prayer. Thinking back, I could feel the tenderness of my scalp from the hard fingers of my father who usually washed our hair. It would have been a sin to go to Sunday school without having been scrubbed all over, and shampooed until it was painful to put a comb near your head for at least two days.

A smiling priest passed silently down the centre aisle, and a moment later Bridget raised her head and glanced at her watch;

"We've got three minutes to catch our connection," she whispered.

I felt completely refreshed as we moved quickly towards the door of the church. Once outside, we dashed across the road to the bus that stood with its engine running and started on the second half of the journey to Bridget's home.

Bridget was much more relaxed after her visit to the church and hardly spoke at all until we turned into a little hamlet of houses edging a park. The bus draw up outside the gate of a neat detached villa where I was to meet the woman who had borne sixteen children and was carrying yet another tiny soul to be brought into the world.

Inserting her key in the lock Bridget turned it gently, and when we had entered the house she tiptoed across the hall and stood looking into the sitting-room at her mother. The mother's face, framed in a halo of dark hair, had the same slightly transparent skin that Bridget had inherited. She sat in a comfortable, straight-backed, armchair knitting a delicate shawl that flowed on to a white cloth spread out on the carpet.

Bridget walked into the room and hugged her mother, then she introduced me,

"I'm pleased you've come," her mother said, putting aside her knitting, "for Bridget would not be bringing home anyone I disapproved of. She's a good daughter to myself, but it's sad I am that she never has a kind word for her good father." I found myself listening for the soft lilt that was even more pleasing than Bridget's. "It's not that I want to complain, if the Good Lord wills it, but I hope it will be my last." Her voice dropped to a far-away whisper.

She rose from her chair, and taking a hand-crocheted cloth from a drawer she spread it on a round, polished table. I gazed into a face that contained a beauty I was unable to describe. The best china was taken from a glass-fronted cabinet and set out on the table while she chatted away.

"We will be havin' our special visitors this evening from the prisoner of war camp, I always invite four!"

"Are prisoners of war allowed out of camp?" I asked in amazement.

"Oh, indeed! And fine boys they are! We are of the same religion so there can be no harm in them," replied the mother.

Astounded by her logic I could make no answer.

From time to time the smiling face of a brother or sister would look shyly from the doorway as we enjoyed our tea.

"Don't be going upstairs with dirt on your shoes!" the mother called, "I want the place kept clean for your good father when he comes in. When you have washed your hands, come and be introduced to Bridget's friend Jaqueline."

We washed up the china after tea, carefully returning it to the cabinet, after which Bridget took me upstairs to a pink and white bedroom.

"The girls will share their bed with us tonight," she said, "so put your things in here, Jaqueline, and freshen-up."

In the kitchen the evening meal had been prepared, and as Bridget's mother put the finishing touches to some trifles there was a knock on the back door.

"'Tis me, and will you be ready for church?" said a soft, urgent voice.

The mother answered her neighbour without opening the door:

"'Twill be yourself then, I'll be with you in a minute and I'll be bringin' our Bridget and her friend."

For the second time that day I found myself being hurried into church, this one was smaller but the procedure was the same. The bowl of water just inside the doorway, rows of glowing candles on the altar, and the perfect peace that refreshed me physically and mentally. Bridget, her mother and the neighbour moved into a pew and knelt to pray, but I could not bring myself to kneel as they did, because it was too humble an attitude to adopt. Instead, I closed my eyes and bowed my head knowing that I trespassed.

When we arrived back at the house the front door stood open, and the voices of several men could be heard coming from the sitting-room. On entering the room, chairs were pushed back as five men rose to their feet. Four of them were in uniform, and the other, who was Bridget's father, wore a sports jacket and grey flannel trousers.

The quiet spoken father shook my hand before introducing me to the others, and as they each took my hand, bowed over it, and greeted me, I was once more aware that foreigners could speak very good English, and their manners made me feel like a princess.

When we moved into the long, narrow dining-room for dinner the seating was arranged so that every adult had an empty chair on either side of them. After we had taken our places, the chattering, lively children filed in to fill the empty chairs and immediately became silent as they looked at the adults.

Bridget and her parents engaged the commanding officer in conversation at the top end of the table, and during the meal the children on either side of me passed the vegetable dishes and the condiments.

"They're not allowed to speak at the table when we have guests," Bridget's eldest brother said from across the table as if he had read my thoughts.

Then a young Italian officer, who was seated on my left just past a small sister, answered,

"It is an excellent arrangement when there are so many children, they have a duty to perform attending to the adults and they feel the importance of it." I turned towards the speaker, who smiled and continued, "I cannot picture you as a worker on the land, but Bridget tells me you are the land-girl at Avonlea where she is cook?"

"Yes," I replied, suddenly feeling that shovelling coal, sweeping chimneys and the dozens of other jobs I did at Avonlea seemed ridiculous.

Dressed as I was in rose pink linen with my hair hanging loosely over the narrow straps on my shoulders, and wearing dainty sandals on my feet, I felt isolated from the work at Avonlea and was unwilling to discuss it, so I satisfied my curiosity by asking,

"Is your commanding officer also Italian? He is very blonde!"

"Yes," said the handsome, dark-eyed lieutenant, "he comes from Florence, where the people can be very fair." My eyes wandered to the dark hair against his deeply tanned skin, while he continued to speak. "They say, in Florence, the only true blonde has brown eyes."

"Then you will be telling us," interrupted Bridget's eldest brother, "that Jaqueline and I are not true blondes, because our eyes are not brown. Is that not so, Reno?"

We all laughed merrily and the children who had been listening joined in. Then the commanding officer raised his head and spoke from the top of the table where he had been deep in conversation,

"You see!" he said, "who among the ordinary people would wish to be at war with one another?" I looked down at my plate feeling uncomfortable, because the knowledge that we were on opposite sides in a war had been put into words, but he continued, "Do not be embarrassed, Senorina! We were forced into war by our leader. But we surrendered at the first opportunity, because we did not wish to fight the British whom we have always admired. Their blood will not be on our hands!" he said with conviction, and after a slight pause added, "Some day we will punish the leader who has brought disgrace upon our heads." His eyes hardened with whatever thoughts had come into his mind, and I knew there would be no mercy for their leader.

The children looked up, having listened to all that had been said, then they quietly turned to passing the dishes of delicious trifle while their mother served.

A thoughtful silence had descended on the adults, but the children were growing restless; having devoured the trifle they looked towards their father, all of them anxious to escape from the table. He nodded, and they rose carrying their plates to the kitchen, the chatter and laughter drifting back from the hall as their exuberance returned.

"You, Jaqueline, are from the capital city where the castle looks down over the Street of Princes."

I turned to Reno and smiled; he had made Princes Street sound so romantic.

"Yes, do you know Edinburgh?" I asked.

"No, I learned about it in school," he replied, laughing. "But I wanted to impress you with my knowledge."

Bridget had moved quickly up the table clearing empty dishes, then placing a coffee pot in front of her brother, she said,

"Pour the coffee, please, Fian."

The eldest brother filled my cup, and turning to Reno, he said,

"Glasgow is the capital city!"

I turned at once to meet his broad grin, and answered,

"Oh, no – Edinburgh is the capital city! I was born there so I should know," I challenged him.

Fian's only answer was another broad grin, and he moved on up the table pouring coffee.

"He is only teasing you," said Reno, passing the cream and sugar. "I was born in the capital city of Rome," he added proudly.

"So you are descended from the Romans who invaded and plundered most of the world, according to my history lessons in school," I replied, my interest rising.

"Yes," he answered, and his dark eyes glowed with fun. "We still have the ruins of the Colosseum to remind us of the gladiators, and the Christians who were thrown to the lions."

My history lessons came flowing back to me, and I answered daringly,

"But you never did manage to subdue the wild tribes of Scotland, did you?"

I waited eagerly for his answer, but he moved into the chair next to mine and in a quieter voice replied,

"No, but it is something I can rectify; it is my duty as an officer of Rome," he said, smiling, and looked straight into my startled eyes. I felt myself blush.

Only then did I realise we were the only ones left at the table. We rose together, and taking my arm he walked me across the small hall to join the others in the sitting-room.

"Come and sit by me!" said Bridget's mother, and I hurriedly took the seat beside her and Bridget.

Reno joined the men in conversation, and they continued to discuss the futility of war and the helplessness of the ordinary people who had no say in the matter.

Bridget's mother demonstrated the lacy stitch that had created the snowy-white shawl she worked on. Then she placed it in my hands and I worked a few stitches to please her; but I knew that I blushed, or turned pale when my eyes were drawn to where Reno stood, because the smiling, dark eyes of the young lieutenant were constantly studying me.

Their allotted time away from the prisoner of war camp was soon over and an army car pulled in at the garden gate. The guests, their faces showing happiness and gratitude, thanked their host and bid us all goodnight.

I woke up on Sunday morning to the peal of church bells and found myself hanging on the edge of the large bed that had slept four of us. The two younger sisters were still asleep, and from the opposite side of the bed Bridget's voice enquired,

"And did you sleep well then?"

"Yes, I did, but I thought one of us would end up sleeping on the floor!"

"When there are so many children you soon become an expert at sleeping on the edge of a bed," Bridget answered wryly. "Now, let us get up quietly and go to the second service, because we have missed the first."

Within fifteen minutes we were hurrying across the park on our way to the small church.

"Do you always go to church like this, Bridget?" I asked, almost out of breath.

"Yes, it's good for the soul and I've been starved of it at Avonlea. We will have breakfast when we get back."

This time it was the Sunday morning service and the priest led the prayers in Latin with the congregation. In the middle of prayers some boys slipped in at the back of the church hoping they would not be noticed. However, the priest had seen them and called them to where he stood at the altar.

He listened patiently to their excuses for being late, and I watched with growing interest. Then suddenly the boys were holding their hands over their heads, ducking to ward off the blows while the priest boxed their ears. I smiled at the comic scene in front of the altar, but no one else did. After lecturing them in a loud voice the priest pushed the boys into an empty pew still cuffing them as they sat down, then he continued with the service in Latin.

On leaving the church we walked slowly back across the park and I could see Bridget's father standing at the door of the house.

"There's someone waiting to see you, Jaqueline," he said, when we reached him. He put his hand across my shoulder and led me through the hall.

When I entered the sitting-room, wondering who on earth would come to see me at this hour of the morning before I had had breakfast, the door closed softly behind me. Then I saw silhouetted against the window the broad, uniformed shoulders of the blonde commanding officer. He turned, smiling as he spoke:

"Be seated, Senorina." Then he walked the length of the room before speaking again, and I waited in wonder. "I have come on behalf of my young lieutenant who wishes to ask for your hand in marriage." I was completely dumbfounded by what he had said, but he continued, and his words sent a warm glow of happiness through me. I sat quite still listening. "He is from a wealthy family and you would have all that you could wish for."

Amazed by the unexpected offer of marriage, I was recalling last night and the confusion I had felt at finding myself alone in the dining-room with the dashing lieutenant. His words had meant more than just happy conversation between two young people, and they ran clearly through my mind, "No, but it is something I can rectify, it is my duty as an officer of Rome". No matter what path I chose, I would never forget his words – they were sacred to me now.

Then I became sensible of the commanding officer waiting. He stood there by the window. And suddenly I knew, with a sharp pang of unhappiness, that I would have to refuse. I had purposely not mentioned religion when I wrote to my parents to say I would be spending the weekend at the cook's house, because I had wanted so much to come.

"My parents would never accept your religion," I said quietly. I had learned young, that I was expected to marry one of my own kind and that it meant someone from our side of the border. Disappointment welled up inside me, I felt the tears pricking my eyes as I talked on, "My family are of a different religion and they would never give consent," I said unhappily.

"You do not have to give your answer now, Senorina! Think about it, until you come again with Bridget."

"It's no use, they would never agree!" I answered, and hurried from the room before the tears overflowed.

Bridget and I left, that day, in the afternoon and for a long time we were quiet on the swiftly moving bus, then she said,

"Would you not take our religion, Jaqueline?"

"Yes, I think I would, because we all believe in the same god, but think of my parents and grandparents, they would never allow it! We have always been of the Scottish Church and we don't even read the prayer book as they do in the Church of England." To talk about my family and their attitude towards religions other than their own, brought some sort of relief to the misery I was feeling. "Would you give up your religion, Bridget?" I asked.

"Putting her hand over mine she answered quietly,

"No, that I would not, that I would not."

Chapter Forty-Seven

Bridget had looked really different at the weekend dressed in her tailored navy suit with the pale blue bow of her blouse tied at the neck; and now she looked quite funny swamped by the large, white, stiffly starched cooks' apron that was her uniform.

She had been making conversation to draw me out of the thoughtful mood I had been in since visiting her home. Even my sense of humour had deserted me, and until I had spent a weekend at home with my family everything seemed vague. The roses from the garden which I had cut for Matron's silver bowl only made me sad. And I looked into the nesting box at the pale green egg, feeling even more sad for the little unhatched duckling.

Reno had been so alive, so real. I could still remember the glow in his dark eyes as he studied me from across the room. But I was duty bound; duty towards my parents and our religion, duty towards my work and my country, as Matron constantly reminded me. I lay in bed at night still astounded by the fairy tale happening at Bridget's house. I wanted to discuss it with my mother and was glad when the weekend came to escape my bewildered thoughts.

To be asked for my hand in marriage, after spending only a few hours in Reno's company, made me glow with happiness. And then, because of the impossible problem of religion, I lay restless until sleep carried me away from all the unlikely situations I had had to face since coming to the West Country.

My life had changed dramatically after joining the Land Army. I had met people from all walks of life and done work that I had thought impossible. Sexual awareness had been thrust upon me by a rapist. And now, a foreigner, a complete stranger wanted to carry me off to his own country as his wife. I was no longer the fashion-conscious, naive, city girl who had volunteered to work on the land.

My mother was waiting to fuss when I arrived home, but she was quite unprepared for the surprising events of the weekend at Bridget's home. As I spoke the facts became clearer in my mind, and I realised that marrying someone from another country would make me part of that country: the warm climate, the vineyards that grew on sunny slopes, the melodious language, the acceptance of a different religion and what it would mean to my life.

"Ever since I can remember, Mother, I've wanted to have two children," she listened quietly, letting me talk on without interruption, "but if I had accepted this offer of marriage I would be bound to pregnancy until nature decided to release me from the bondage of womanhood. Is there such a word as womanhood, Mother?"

"The dictionary will tell you, but it sounds good enough to me," she answered, and a smile played across her face. "You take life so seriously, Jaqueline, everything has to fit into a pattern. Don't you see anything romantic in all this?"

"Yes, I do! But there's nothing romantic about Bridget's mother carrying her seventeenth child and praying to God it will be her last!"

"You're your father's daughter, Jaqueline, and I have every respect for his ideas on how life should be lived, even what we should be guided by. But isn't there to be any romance?"

She seemed to be questioning my refusal to marry Reno, so I remained silent, then she continued:

"However, Dad is very sensible when he says: people should only reproduce themselves, or the world would be overpopulated with too many children as cannon fodder for the next war."

Suddenly turning to the materials and patterns spread out on the table she changed the subject.

"I'll tack these seams together if you would like to help by running them up on the sewing machine, Jaqueline. I'm making trousers for the church sale of work. There's plenty of good material left in these old coats to make trousers for the five to six year olds, and with no coupons needed, they sell well! Put every scrap of left-over material into this bag, the ladies work party will be glad of it for rug making."

"What about the buttons, Mother?"

"Oh, yes! Drop them into this jar."

While we chatted on about the church fête I felt a new sense of release coming into my mind, release from a very sheltered, obedient childhood.

"I'll be interested to see Dad's reaction when he hears of the decision you had to make." The delighted smile that filled her eyes began to play across her face. "You know, Jaqueline, dedication and hard work are important in life, but there is also an ingredient called adventure, or taking a chance on things that dreams are made of!"

"But we have to face facts, Mother! Or reality, as Dad always calls it."

"It can't be our doing that makes you what you are, Jaqueline." It was as if she had ignored what I said, and she went on almost absentmindedly, "Because your sister and brother are entirely different from you. But just occasionally, try to be guided by your heart."

I had been the only one at home with my parents that weekend, and it had been interesting to watch their reactions to my news. The fields looked lush and green with sprouting crops as the bus travelled back to Avonlea on Sunday evening. What had been a very puzzled, unhappy mind, was now untroubled; soothed by the balm of fulfilling my obligations to my parents. Only an occasional pang of remorse troubled me when I thought of the noble-minded foreigner who had sought my hand in marriage.

I had seen my parents in a different light for the first time.

"She made the right decision!" my father had said almost grumpily when he heard about Reno.

"Did she?" My mother's aloof reply had surprised me, and the amused smile was no longer dancing in her eyes. I had the feeling, then, that my father was in some doubt over his set ideas on religion and foreigners.

The bus stopped at the entrance to Avonlea and I stepped down from it wearing a dress and high-heeled shoes. My uniform had become obnoxious to me, at least for the present. Several of the boys came running across when I entered the grounds of Avonlea.

"Our holidays start tomorrow, Jaqueline, because we have more students than teachers teaching us now!"

"Do you like being taught by students?" I asked.

"It's okay!" came the reply, "but we know more than the students; so school's closing early for the summer holidays." They were as happy as spring lambs about their holidays, but I was thinking of the overworked staff while I laughed with them, enjoying their company.

Because Matron insisted on the boys keeping up their daily studies during the holidays, the ones who didn't like hard work hid behind pen and paper and took their exercise in games.

Tam had gone to a large horticultural show in Glasgow, and, so far, I had been on my own all day. During this time I kept the garden gates locked, but still the strawberries vanished from under their nets and there was nothing I could do about it.

There was sawing to be done in the firebreak, removing branches from a tree Tam had felled to stock up for winter. I put the saw in the barrow, then tossed in a length of rope that would be handy for pulling unwieldy branches to the trestle, and started towards the plantation.

How remote I seemed to be from the creature who had lingered over coffee chatting easily to the young, dark-eyed lieutenant of Rome. I smiled at the memory; that had been the *real* me. At ease with someone of the same intellect, and just two or three years in age giving him superiority. Why did religion and all its unbending laws have to interfere between us? Even my parents had been weakening. My mother had said things possibly unspoken in her mind for years, because she had never been faced with this situation affecting one of her own children until my weekend at Bridget's.

As I walked along pushing the barrow, it was now only words whispered on the wind: marriage, perhaps the beginning of a wonderful adventure. But I had been too well programmed by my family to break the unwritten rules of prejudice.

"Hi there!"

I came out of my musings to see Rob standing by the felled tree.

"Hi!" I replied.

"Come on, let me give you a hand with those large branches. You're certainly not cut out for this kind of work," he said, and I was fascinated by his dimples when he smiled.

"Oh! I thought I was doing fine!"

"You are," he admitted, "but it's tough on you; even Sean says so!" He grinned when I tugged at another long branch, then walked over to help just as Sean would have done. Together we pulled it to the trestle.

"What are you going to do when you leave the academy, Rob?" I asked, feeling the intense relief of having a helpmate.

"I like navigation so my career will be at sea."

"My brother studies at nautical college, because he wants to be a chief engineer on a liner," I answered, glancing up at him and seeing his dimples deepen.

"I'll be up on the top deck with the captain, but your brother will be down below," he replied, looking at me cheekily.

"Huh! Class distinction on board as well as in the kitchen," I answered, "if that's what you're getting at, Rob?"

"What did you do before joining the Land Army, Jaqueline?" he asked, changing the subject that had made me retaliate, because class distinction was stuffy and out of date like the ancient, dusty paintings in their gilded frames.

"I was a manageress trainee and went to day-release classes at college," I answered primly.

"When I'm settled in my career," he said boyishly, "I'm going to marry a girl like you! Are you going to marry Sean?"

"I don't want to think about such things, Rob, because there's so much I want to do, and I won't be pushed into marriage." He looked steadily at my face while I spoke and his eyes smiled, but I had the feeling that I was never being taken seriously by him or Sean, so I added, "Girls are just as ambitious as boys, you know!"

"Tea break!" he replied, brushing his hands together. Then giving me a light push in the direction of the house, he said loftily, "Sean said I was to keep an eye on you during the summer holidays!" His brown eyes glowed with the importance of Sean's assignment, and I hurried to keep up with him.

What an immature being I felt myself to be among these budding males with their physical strength and high ideals. But I would force myself to keep up with them physically and mentally if it was the last thing I did!

Chapter Forty-Eight

School holidays were now in full swing, and the big boys went fishing along the bank of the river, while the little ones played on the lawns in sight of the house. Always there was Mary or Karen to keep an eye on them, or Matron would sit on the garden seat with her book for an hour if the staff were busy.

I had just climbed up from the furnace room when Bridget called from the kitchen door,

"Don't forget the baskets, Matron wants some flowers today, Jaqueline!"

Picking up the baskets from the doorstep I put them into the barrow and started on my way towards the garden. It was glorious weather, and as I headed for another day of digging in the quarter acre the children playing on the lawn caught my interest.

I stopped with the barrow to watch our two three year old boys in their white sun hats and romper suits; they were filling a bucket at the river's edge, then staggering across the grass with water pouring from a dozen holes. Just as they reached their objective, the cow, the bucket was empty. The two little boys looked at each other, looked in the bucket, then turned towards the river to fill it up again.

As I stood there Matron called from the main entrance of the house,

"I want only the best flowers, Jaqueline! Tall ones, preferably, but not too many!"

"Yes, Matron!" I replied, gripping the handles of the barrow and starting along the path.

The brilliant colours of the azalea blossoms had passed, and I guided the barrow down the steep, short slope between the new growth of fresh green leaves. They had not been pruned back to allow the barrow through when it was loaded with vegetables and flowers.

I wondered whether I should mention it to Tam, very meekly, to prevent his hackles from rising, or should I take the secateurs and cut myself a wider path through the sprouting azaleas to ease my labours? In these first few days of the holidays Tam's temper had frayed, and I was keeping well out of his way to avoid a confrontation, whenever possible.

Once through the gate I closed it behind me, but as I did so I heard a noise from the top of the garden. Leaving the barrow where it stood I hurried along the centre path to investigate, and then I saw Tam's familiar boots showing just above some shrubs, thrashing the air wildly. I was gripped with concern as I hurried towards him.

He lay beneath the apple tree, where he had fallen from the stepladder, his face and hands torn by the sharp gravel on the path. The spasmodic jerking of his legs made it difficult for me to get near him as he slowly rotated on his back.

I waited until his boots were away from me and kicking at the apple tree, then I lifted the stepladder lying across his body and knelt behind his head. My handkerchief was already folded into a hard pad, and I knew from my Girl Guide days that I must get it between his teeth to protect his tongue.

White foam edged his dark moustache, and thick blood oozed from the side of his mouth. Slowly I pressed my fingers into his jaws to open the grinding teeth, but they were clamped together as though held in a vice.

Epilepsy had been only a word in my vocabulary, not quite understood; but here I was facing the harsh reality and in desperation I tried to pull down his chin. The blood streaked his white shirt; and I hoped that his tight waistcoat was protecting his back from the sharp gravel on the path.

"I'll do it, you go and tell Matron!" I turned and I could have wept with relief. He stood there quietly watching with a trap slung over his shoulder. "Go on! Tell Matron!" said Sean, "I'll take him back to the lodge when he comes out of it."

I hurried away from the garden relieved at Sean's timely arrival, then I set to wondering just how often he was around when I was completely unaware of him.

The little ones, when I passed them, were seated on the grass examining the holes in their bucket. The cow's long, pink tongue was slopping round their ears, but they brushed it aside as if it were a troublesome fly and continued to study the holes in the bucket.

The next morning my antagonist was in the garden, his whole face purple and swollen, his hands encased in bandages. What could I say to this man who never answered my good mornings? I knew he would scorn pity.

I glanced at him, and defiantly went to the garden shed, and taking the secateurs from their nail on the wall I walked past him on my way to the garden gate. It was the first time I had seen the flicker of a smile in the black eyes almost hidden in his, now, unrecognisable face.

While I hacked down the azaleas on each side of the narrow, sloping path I was aware of him watching; but he made no move to stop me, he just stood there, watching. The events of the last two days poured into my mind when I retired to bed that night. Was Tam's affliction the price he had paid as a soldier in the Fourteen-Eighteen War?

Would there be medals tucked away in a box somewhere to remind him of some act of bravery, now forgotten. But the metal plate that was part of his skull would always be there. And there would be a pension for war wounds, reduced to a pittance by inflation as the years passed. I had heard it all discussed between my father and his brothers many times.

Great events had taken place, in this, the Second World War, since the beginning of June. It was now 1944, and without breaking his oath of secrecy my brother had told me as much as he could of what was happening in the world of engineering. But at Avonlea we were detached from the news of progress, and were much too busy with our work to have time to think of it.

Having defied Tam for the first time by cutting into his azaleas, I felt restless; progress in the war would have to wait until I was at home again. Perhaps no news was better than bad news?

Chapter Forty-Nine

While the hours of darkness were few in the height of summer, I woke early to a sun-filled room. This weekend would be spent at Avonlea, but Saturday was usually an easy working day and I rose from my bed eager to be out in the fresh air.

In the hen house there were throaty noises coming from the broody hen. And her warning, when I went to collect the freshly laid eggs, made me stay well back from her. Would the duckling hatch, I wondered? And what would be her reaction to one odd little chick?

On entering the kitchen I took the eggs from the basket and placed them in the bowl reserved for Matron and the Warden.

"Can we swim in the river pool after lunch, Bridget?" Carrots was asking.

"Did you ask Matron?" came Bridget's brisk reply.

"Yes, but she's gone visiting without giving us permission. She said she would let us know later."

After lunch I changed into my swimsuit to sunbathe for an hour since it was very hot. But as I made for the side door Bridget caught my eye, while the boys clustered round her pleading to swim in the pool.

"Jaqueline, would you warn the boys about fifteen minutes before the three o'clock bus arrives? They want to go swimming in the river pool." Looking up at the kitchen clock, she added, "Make sure they get out of the water in plenty of time, or Matron will be furious!" Then turning back to her oven, she followed up with, "I know nothing about your swimming boys, you're on your own!"

"Thanks, Bridget!" they called, and charged out of the side door.

I followed with a large towel and stretched out on the lawn to keep an eye on the little ones. In their white summer clothes they clambered all over Shep while he sat panting in the heat. He was the biggest, shaggiest, English sheep dog I had ever seen, and he took no notice of the children tugging at his long, thick coat.

With fifteen minutes to go before the bus arrived, Shep rose to his feet and shook off the children. Then he plodded slowly up the drive; it was my signal to warn the boys in the pool. I hurried down to the river, and because the water looked so inviting I decided to have a quick dip; then I climbed out and sat on the bank refreshed and dripping.

"Hurry, boys, Shep's at the main gate waiting for Matron's bus!" I called for the third time.

Then I noticed that my skin was quite red. The boys, who were reluctantly leaving the water, were also red. We all fled to the kitchen and tried scrubbing with soap on our legs.

"It's not budging at all!" said Bridget, wrinkling her brow. Then just as the boys and I were dashing upstairs to the bathrooms the Warden opened the sitting-room door.

"Kindly walk on the stairs, boys, accidents will happen if you run; and not so much noise, please!" Then he stared. "Just one moment, come here and let me have a look at you all!" I felt embarrassed standing with a towel draped over me, but he was still examining our skin when Matron arrived. Her face froze.

"You went swimming without my permission! You know I do not allow you to swim unless I am in the house! You have forfeited your sweet ration for one month! As for you, Jaqueline, I will see you in my sitting-room when you are dressed!"

Matron lectured long and hard on rules that had to be adhered to while I was employed at Avonlea. I listened to a list of rules never mentioned before, she was pouring the blame on to me and I felt I should object.

"I didn't tell the boys to go swimming, Matron," I interrupted.

"Then who gave them permission, I want to know?"

I was trapped. If I mentioned Bridget I would feel like a traitor, and to say the boys had made the decision by themselves would be even worse. I looked at my feet without answering.

"Foolish, silly girl, encouraging the boys to break rules! I shall speak to your area supervisor about this!"

The police were called in to investigate the red dye that had settled in the bottom of the river pool. It was traced to the mill upstream and a charge of illegal dumping of chemicals was to be made.

"By disobeying the rules," said Matron's brother to the boys assembled in the common room, "you have come across a practice that would have become worse if it had gone unnoticed. It could have endangered the fine salmon so plentiful in the river, and would have been harmful to the wild life along its banks. However, let there be no more flaunting of the rules!"

The Warden was grateful to the boys, as his main interest in life was fishing with his friends in the river that ran through his estate. He would have given them back their sweet ration for the month, but Matron was unyielding and the sweets were withheld.

After a good steep in a hot, soapy bath I washed down to a healthy pink, and, because I had only slipped into the pool my face and hair were free of dye. The boys, who had been diving, suffered peculiar reddish hair for quite a long time after the dye had faded from their faces.

"'Tis deaf I am in both ears!" said Bridget, when the boys complained about their sweet rations. "There would be no living with you at all, if we didn't have rules!" And while they stood in a thoughtful group by the kitchen door she shouted, "Now, be off with you, there are those of us that have work to do!"

The first few weeks of the holidays had passed in a hive of activity, and there would be no weekends off for the staff unless a relief was brought in. Matron's brother had organised outings for the boys on most days, and their studies took up several hours of their time each morning.

With the start of the second week in July I saw a change come over Bridget.

"If it's servants you want," she bawled, "I've got more than enough to do without becoming a handmaiden to the lot of you." Her Irish accent had thickened as she ranted and raved.

I had only come into the kitchen as always for breakfast, but this was a side of Bridget I had never seen before; I felt sure she was overworked .

"Why don't you ask for a woman to help in the kitchen, while Mary's so busy in the house, Bridget?"

"Keep your nose out of what doesn't concern you!" came the loud reply.

I stayed quiet after Bridget's rebuke, waiting and hoping for a miracle. On the way down to the garden I began to realise how much I relied on the happiness and good manners of others to create my own happiness.

Tam was in conversation with a friend when I picked up the fork, dug it into the ground and stood on it to wriggle it down through the hard soil.

"It's a fine way of breaking up the ground when it's been lying dormant for a year or so," I could hear Tam saying, "just drop them in using the dibber, there's nothing like a crop of potatoes to break it up. Other than that, it would mean running a plough through it."

I heard myself gasp in disbelief, it was me that was opening up the ground, and not the potatoes! Then Tam's friend walked across to where I was digging, and started to speak to me:

"Let me see the fork, Miss! Just dig it halfway in to start with, remove the grass, and then the shaw as you lift the potatoes." And he demonstrated. "Now, do it again in the same spot going deeper, and you'll get the rest of the potatoes with a lot less effort. There's always an easier way if you give it a little thought; take it a little slower, you can't rush manual labour."

I felt relaxed when he gave me back the fork and smiled until I looked at Tam; the smoke was belching from his pipe as he almost chewed the stem of it in silent rage.

It seemed to me, at lunch-time, that everyone was avoiding the kitchen; so I went upstairs and collapsed flat out on my bedroom carpet. The moment I had stepped into my room the lovely, soft, lavender-pink glow made me feel better.

After a morning of digging up potatoes and beating them out of their cocoon of hard earth, I could have screamed with the weariness I felt. The light shone through the newly washed, filmy white, net curtains that draped my turret window. Thank God, I thought, for Jenny, who had to clean until everything sparkled and glowed like my room did.

After ten minutes rest the colours around me looked even brighter, and I rose from the pink carpet not noticing how worn it was. I would have to face the quarrelsome atmosphere that had filled the kitchen during this second week in July, if I wanted to eat. Reluctantly I started on my way downstairs.

"So her ladyship has decided to come for lunch, has she?" said Bridget, when I walked into the kitchen. "It's obvious we don't all have slaves to wait on us!" she added, banging my plate down on the table at my usual place.

I suddenly felt too weary to eat, and again realised how important a smiling, happy mother had been in my life. I was managing to struggle through the hard work driven on by noble feelings of helping my country in war time. But Bridget's nastiness was harder to take.

Slowly and silently I ate the food, leaving Bridget and Mary to revel in the caustic remarks they threw at each other. Even Jenny was quiet, working her way across the kitchen floor on hands and knees.

When I got back to the garden Tam's friend had gone, and I picked up the fork and dug it halfway into the ground.

"Get your back into it!" Tam roared, walking across and snatching the fork from me. "Right into the ground like this!" And he stamped his heavy boot on the fork until the prongs were well below the surface. "There's half as many again still under the ground!" And he dug at the shaw I had been working on.

After such an outburst I jumped on the fork with both feet and wriggled it back and forward. I had been throwing aside the tufts of grass and digging into the stale ground for two hours, hot, sticky and exhausted, when Tam appeared.

"Off you go for tea!" he said in disgust, as his friend came through the opening to the quarter acre.

"Afternoon, Miss." The friend smiled and touched his cap when we passed each other.

I felt my whole body ease, and smiled back. At least there were still pleasant people around, but, with the exception of Tam's visitor, there were none at Avonlea!

Bridget was still raving at no one in particular when I reached the kitchen, so I took a mug from the sideboard and filled it with tea, then I poured in milk from the jug. But there was no sugar bowl.

"Have some of Matron's sugar," whispered Karen.

"Thanks," I whispered back, then I asked, "What's upsetting Bridget and Mary?"

Karen looked up through her mascara-coated lashes, shrugged her shoulders, and left the kitchen with Matron's tray.

"You're not singing these days, Mary," I said pleasantly, during a pause in the scalding remarks that charged the air, but there was no answer.

The next morning I went down to breakfast resolved to accept whatever came. And determined to spend as much time as possible cleaning out the hen-run, because I was now anticipating the arrival of the broody hen's chicks. I threw the scrapers, brush and shovel into the barrow, then filled a bucket with balancer meal and some grit from where it was stored in the woodshed.

The clamour of boys' voices grew as I neared the hen-run, and then they were all pulling me towards the wire netting fence.

"We've got chickens, Jaqueline, six chickens and they're all yellow and fluffy!"

The broody hen had hatched the lot and they ran after her as she pecked her way across the hen-run. I noticed, while the boys gasped with excitement and the little ones pressed their noses against the wire, thumbs stuck in their mouths, that one chicken was slightly different from the others. The odd one had a tiny flat bill, a long body, and rather big feet. But the hen saw no difference, they were all her chicks.

I spent ages scraping the floor and perches, then renewing all the straw in the nesting boxes. When Tam came looking for me I was industriously raking over the hen-run and sprinkling fresh sand here and there.

"Humph!" he said, catching sight of the hen and her chicks. "Does Matron know they're hatched?"

"I couldn't say!" I replied, raking hard at the lumpy ground to smooth it, and he stomped off.

When I went down to the garden later the whole grassy section had been dug over and the potatoes lifted. Heaving a sigh of real relief, I collected the vegetables for the kitchen. I couldn't imagine Tam finishing off such a task to ease my labours, but I had seen his friend picking up the fork when I left the garden the day before for my afternoon tea break, and Matron had kept me busy for what was left of that day.

The delicious smell of hot roast filled the kitchen at midday, and I sat down to small new potatoes, fresh peas, and sliced venison soaked in gravy. Everything melted sweetly in my mouth, and my first taste of venison delighted me. Matron's brother had gone shooting with a large party of sportsmen on a neighbouring estate just after his arrival.

All I needed to complete the meal was coffee from Bridget's brown enamel pot. Lifting a mug I made for the pot, but Bridget swung round.

"Stay where you are and don't get in my way!" she shouted, and snatched up the pot so that the coffee poured dangerously from the swaying spout, it splashed into my mug and spluttered onto the table.

Suddenly I felt quite unconcerned and smiled at the pantomime that had been going on, for about a week, at Avonlea. Just as I reached the kitchen door, after rinsing my cup at the sink, Mary's voice rang out,

"Hooray for Good King Billie! And up the battle of the Boyne!" Then she rushed from the kitchen and fled to her room as the curses rolled off Bridget's tongue.

My father would have given me a good, long, hard lecture if I had carried on in such a way over history. And yet, here were two good friends quarrelling over something that had happened several centuries ago, in the year 1690. It was incredible, but then, we were now in the throes of the Second World War, and had it not all started through old hatred being stirred up by a fanatic?

As I walked down to the garden I thought about life in the city; there had been little time to ponder over the ways of the world. It had been all learning and business, then a visit to the theatre, or an evening of dancing had filled what was left of the six working days. I began to realise just how little I had seen of the sun, or daylight, during my working life in the city.

I was closing the garden gate behind me when the sound of aircraft engines caused me to look up, and I saw two black dots approaching in the clear blue sky. They dipped and darted like swallows in flight. On the impulse, I dashed into the centre of the garden for a better view; I should have taken cover, but I felt no sense of urgency and was only interested in the manoeuvres of the aircraft as they dived and climbed.

Without warning a sharp rat-tat-tat filled the air, and I ducked; my hands went up to my face as a thin line of fire sped towards the plane with the crooked cross on its tail. Then I watched a stream of black smoke erupt from the square lines of its body and it started to fall into the distant trees.

The smaller plane climbed upwards, its red, white and blue circles clearly distinguishable as it headed towards the east. A rainbow arched its way across the garden, and the droplets from a passing shower pattered heavily on the broad, green leaves of the vividly coloured hydrangeas. I should have been happy in such surroundings, but an infinite sadness seeped into me.

My thoughts turned from a desperate man in a burning plane, to the teenage girls raised under the dictatorship of the madman who had started this war in Europe. Helpless to do anything about it, or have any say in the matter; the girls were sent to baby factories to produce a child for the Führer.

Their fanatical leader had stated that only fair-haired girls with light eyes were to produce his master race. I shuddered at the thought of what would happen to all the teenage girls in Britain, including myself, if we should be defeated by the enemy.

They had said over the radio, that Britain would pour barrels of oil on the waters around her shores to be set alight if the enemy tried to invade our island.

The sheer hopelessness of what the situation could become made me furious. I stabbed at the ground with the hoe and made a vow to kill myself rather than be raped in a baby factory. But the sun shone and the garden glowed with the colours of summer. Then I decided to forget all my gloomy thoughts, because good men would always triumph over evil.

I felt tired the next morning, and all the sad thoughts from the previous day rushed into my mind: the pilot burning to death as his plane went down in flames, the teenage girls on both the enemy side and our own who were helpless to defend themselves. Yes, I would definitely kill myself if we lost the war. No one was going to force me into bringing a child into a world so full of hate.

Resigned to a depressing destiny I walked slowly down the narrow steps from my turret bedroom towards the main staircase, and then I heard Mary's silver-toned notes flowing effortlessly up and down in a glorious cascade of song,

"This means I offer my love to you, to be your own," she paused sadly, "if you should leave me I will be blue and waiting all alone."

Bridget was stirring the large pot on the range and breakfast lay on the table when I entered the kitchen.

"You're late this morning, Jaqueline," Bridget said pleasantly. "Eat your breakfast before it gets cold!" She was back to her busy, brisk self.

I sighed with relief and started on the scrambled eggs on toast that looked so inviting. Bridget certainly knew how to get the best out of dried eggs.

Mary had reached the hall with her duster and the 'Indian Love Call' poured forth. The older boys were on the move and I could hear them mimicking the answering call from above, it sounded as if it was coming through mouths full of toothpaste.

"Jaqueline?"

"Yes, Bridget?"

"Would you not come home with me on my next weekend off?"

Reno had been in my thoughts from time to time, and there had been doubts about whether or not I had made the right decision.

"Thank you, Bridget, but I don't want to start anything I can't finish. The answer must be no!"

Deep in thought I made my way along to the garden. Had I been influenced by family prejudice? Or a religion that condemned me to life-long pregnancy? Or was the price of freedom, to do all the things I had dreamed of, more important? I was still unsure, but I was learning to think deeply on everything and not just to accept.

Chapter Fifty

Lush fresh strawberry and raspberry sweets were plentiful on Bridget's menus while the fruits continued to grow and ripen. Matron waited impatiently for the berries on the blackcurrant bushes to change from green to black in anticipation of the new season's jam.

In Tam's greenhouse unripe peaches clung to a well-trained, fan-shaped tree. He unlocked the door to enter and tie down the new shoots away from the swelling fruits. Bunches of small, green grapes hung from a gnarled vine trained along the greenhouse roof; the vine had been planted outside the greenhouse, then led in through a ventilator to produce fruit in the warmth created by the sun. This was Tam's domain and I was not allowed to trespass. I watched the growth from the outside only.

Under the thick foliage of the outdoor vine on the garden wall, there were tiny bunches of lentil-sized grapes, they never grew to maturity. Tam spent a lot of his time nipping out the smallest, or the diseased apples as they began to swell on the many trees in the garden.

Between the beds of strawberries, and fruit bushes, four foot frames stood covered in sweet peas. I took bunches of these pastel-coloured, delicate flowers to Matron every day.

In the kitchen Bridget had excelled herself after a party of the Warden's friends returned from a long trek down the river, their baskets heavy with fish and small game.

With so many visitors calling the plump woman from the village became a thrice weekly addition to the staff, and each time there was a gathering of the local gentry she brought along her daughter to assist Karen and Mary.

The boys remained unimpressed by fresh salmon, and they would say,

"Haven't you got any tinned salmon, Bridget?"

"You don't know what's good for you!" she would answer in exasperation, when they ate the vegetables and left the freshly cooked salmon on their plates.

There was no time to think about weekends off, they flew by while Matron entertained guests in her sitting-room. The guests came in cars, on horses, or on foot in tweedy clothing and brogues; and never once did I see a familiar face from Burnsyde. Mr William and his sisters must have been classed on a lower social stratum. Where, then, did that place me on the social scale, if I was already graded as the lowest level in the kitchen? I laughed at my predicament.

Titles sat in front of every name on the guest lists Karen kept. They were the kind of people who looked down on the staff who made possible their comfortable lives free from toil. Pretty, elegant Karen, with her beautiful speaking voice, was referred to as 'that girl with the drinks tray, or the coffee'.

I, in my boots and dungarees, was something they turned their backs on, if I had the misfortune to pass them in the grounds while pushing the harvest of the garden to the back door of the kitchen in the one-wheeled barrow.

"Outside, outside with you!" Bridget shouted, dashing for the brush and shooing the duckling out of the kitchen. The yellow down faded as his feathers grew in, and he followed me everywhere I went, peering down into the furnace room, or sitting contentedly watching while I chopped kindling wood for evening fires and the kitchen range.

The rest of the brood stayed close to the mother hen, wallowing in the dust to clean their feathers as the hen did, and running to the shelter of the hen house when it rained. But the little duckling revelled in the rain, throwing himself into puddles and running after me as if inviting me to join him.

"Yuk!" the boys said, when the aroma of duck cooked with orange drifted into the hall each time the kitchen door opened.

"It's roast with vegetables for you lot, so don't fret, the duck's for the guests!" And they would laugh and jostle their way back to the common room when Bridget added, "With apple pie for sweet!"

I was carrying in the vegetables from the barrow outside the kitchen door, when I noticed how Bridget sagged if no one was around.

"It's nice having the guests in summer, Jaqueline, but it's a lot of hard work, even with the help from the village," she sighed, and we both sat down with our mugs of tea while Bridget talked on, "I sometimes feel I want to run away from all the jaded palates to cater for among Matron's friends. The boys are easy to please. But I won't be sorry when the holidays are over and they're having their midday meal at school."

The clock ticked loudly on the wall, and delicious smells rose from the cooking pots on the range. Bridget stood up refreshed, and emptying the oven she quickly refilled it with another tray of apple pie. Thoughtfully I rinsed my mug at the kitchen sink, and because it was unusual for Bridget to complain, I found myself stuck for an answer.

The door leading to the hall swung open suddenly and Matron walked in with two friends in riding breaches.

"There will be another two guests for lunch, cook!" She sounded more patronising than usual, and her guests looked at Bridget and simpered.

Bridget squared up to them with a frozen look on her usually pleasant face.

"Yes, Matron," she answered, and turning back to her pots she ignored them all.

Their eyes swept over me and they turned away disdainfully as if the sight had hurt. There was an awkward pause, then the three of them tripped out of the kitchen chattering gaily and the door closed behind them.

The dedicated Bridget was showing signs of stress, and I wondered how long it would be before anyone of us would have a weekend at home. My brain was dulled by hard work, and the boys bouncing all over the estate so full of life and mischief left Tam's temper worse than it had ever been.

Bath time was later in the evening, because of the long, light nights of summer. When I had carried the last of the little ones to bed, and listened with Karen to their prayers, I stumbled up to my room, glad to sit down and write to my uncles fighting in the Burmese jungle. Letters must be light-hearted and entertaining to keep up their morale, my parents had said.

Letter writing was restful, and Matron encouraged it. It kept me away from an evening of mending in the sitting-room, but the mending had doubled by the following night. There was no escape from chores for the staff at Avonlea unless they were in bed fast asleep. How I wished I could have dumped the mending into the empty, idle fingers in Matron's sitting-room, where she and her friends chatted and were waited upon.

As I wrote about life at Avonlea to my uncles, I began to wonder about all the noble-minded stuff I was fed by Matron, "duty to your country" she would remind me, when I asked for a long overdue weekend at home. The question popped into my mind while I wrote; were her leisured classes excluded from duty?

No one had mentioned the enemy plane that fell into the far trees a mass of flames. And Tam only spoke to issue orders, or curse, because I was "a bloody land-girl from the city" as he called me, instead of a strong country lad.

Feeling abused by Matron and Tam, and weary of the long, hard working hours I endured because of my strong sense of duty, I made up my mind to go home when the weekend came.

On Friday Bridget served steak pie with mashed potatoes and tender, fresh, green peas. The boys had hung about the hall waiting for the midday meal, and it was just after they had finished lunch that I told Matron I would be going home for the weekend.

"It's out of the question, Jaqueline, when the boys are on holiday!" she replied.

"I need the rest, Matron," I answered, "if I become ill you will have to do without me."

"Nonsense, you don't work any harder, or longer than the rest of the staff!"

"I do a man's work, Matron!" I insisted.

She turned away to join her friends having ignored my request, and they wandered down to walk along the river bank for exercise. I pushed my laden barrow round to the kitchen door firmly resolved to go home at noon tomorrow.

The next morning seemed long, because I felt uneasy and drained of vitality, but I was still determined to go home at midday. I finished my work, then I dressed and headed up the drive. I missed lunch, and the haughty reminder of duty Matron would deliver if I stayed for that meal.

The fact that I was doing nothing wrong gave me confidence while I waited by the lodge for the bus; and then I was speeding away from chores that the boys, who were bigger and stronger than myself, could easily do if they sacrificed their games and church over the weekend.

The boys would be no more heathen than I for missing church on Sunday. Work made it impossible for Bridget, or myself to be good church-going Christians. 'Six days shalt thou labour and do all thy work', I thought as I sat at the back of the bus, but only if it pleased Matron. God would have to wait in line with his commandments, like the rest of us, if they interfered with Matron's plans.

I was beginning to have my doubts about the commandments: thou shalt not kill; and yet, if governments gave their permission men could go out in uniform and kill as many human beings as they wished. And there was Tam: he would hunt out every bird in his garden, tear their nests apart and stamp on the contents. I had hurried away from such scenes sickened, as I had been when the enemy plane plunged into the far trees a mass of flames.

Edinburgh was alive with people, and the expectancy in their faces stirred my tired mind. I stepped from the bus and joined the throng. What had been happening while I slaved at Avonlea for the nineteen and sixpence jingling in my pocket? Matron had handed it to me sealed in the little brown packet, as she always did, on Friday night.

On the bus-run down to my home, I could smell the sea air drifting in from the Firth of Forth. As soon as she opened the door my mother was aware of the dullness in the eyes of one of her brood.

"I must cut your hair, Jaqueline, it's nearly down to your waist!"

"Give me time to get in the door, Mother," I answered, hanging my coat in the hall.

"It's sapping your strength! As it always did! Let me cut it!" she insisted.

"No, Mother, I like it long."

She hurried into the kitchen to put the kettle on, and I glanced into all the familiar rooms glad to be at home.

"Hair needs to be fed like any other part of your body, and you look as if you need all the strength you can get, Jaqueline."

"What's happening in the war, Mother, we hear nothing at all at Avonlea! And it's difficult to get a weekend off with the boys on holiday, but they go back to school next week at the beginning of September."

"Why! Paris has been liberated by the French partisans and the Allies, Jaqueline! The news has been so exciting in the past few days. The tide of war has been turning since the Allied landings began; I just hope they can put a stop to these dreadful V-1 bombs falling on England before the cities are in ruins; Scotland must be out of their range," she added thoughtfully, carrying the tea tray into the sitting-room.

I listened, stunned by the wonderful news of the partisans playing havoc among the enemy while the Allies advanced.

"Do you still have the white French beret with the black motif on it, Mother?" She nodded, and I felt the excitement rising inside me, because Paris had been liberated. "You can cut my hair, I'm going to wear the French beret!" I cried. "It will look nicer with short hair!"

Taking advantage of my excitement she started to cut at shoulder level while I sat on the bedroom stool, and I could feel my head go forward as the weight of hair was snipped away. Gold tresses fell onto the carpet, and through the mirror of the dressing table I could see them lying there; I almost wept. But by the time my hair was shampooed and dried it had bounced up into soft, shining waves, the weight of it gone.

"Alex and Margaret are staying with friends this weekend, because there's been quite a bit of celebration going on with all the good news. But the house is so quiet when no one's here. Don't know what I'll do when Alex goes into the RAF. And I'll be down to two ration books with only Dad and I."

"Are you lonely, Mother?" I asked.

"Yes. I'm glad to see you home for the weekend, Jaqueline. But you should take more time off, you know how Dad worries about the work you do. He's gone fishing today," she went on, while I relaxed and listened. "I'm still doing my part-time war work at the electronics factory, it's not what I thought a factory would be like. It's so modern and clean; and dust proof, they say!"

It had been an interesting afternoon, chatting and listening to the latest news reports. How I missed the news at Avonlea. That night, when I settled down in bed in my own familiar room, I was recalling how it had been four years ago when I was still at school. Deep despair had hung over Britain as the enemy goose-stepped its way across Denmark, Norway, Holland, Belgium and Luxembourg; I had watched the hopelessness in the eyes of adults through the eyes of a child.

Then the terrifying evacuation of Dunkirk came. Followed by the fall of France, which almost took the heart from us. All the grown-ups had been quiet and sad; and to me it had been like the end of the world. I had changed from girl to woman during these years, and now, as I lay in bed, I could feel a warm glow growing inside my chest. This weekend was like a new beginning with the liberation of Paris.

But the news had not been all good: thousands of soldiers had died on the beaches, and until the enemy was defeated there would be thousands more.

My two uncles were now presumed dead in some swampy jungle on the other side of the world. There was no longer the need to write; but I would not give up hope.

I fell asleep dreading the next delivery of coal at Avonlea, and all thoughts of war had gone from my mind; when I had stoked the furnaces at midday the long bunker in the furnace room had been almost empty.

Chapter Fifty-One

When journeying back to Avonlea on Sunday evening, I saw from the bus the harvest and the golden grain falling beneath the blades of the reaper. In the hedgerows the rowan berries glowed brilliant red. I was no longer tired, but ready for the work that lay ahead. There was a slight coolness in the air, but the sun shone warm and every cottage garden was a riot of colourful roses.

When I stepped from the bus at Avonlea with my case and started down the drive, long shoots were spreading themselves halfway across my path from the overgrown ramblers, straddling the wall of white stone running down one side of the drive from Tam's lodge. I had reached the spot where the wall ended and the path to the garden branched off on my left, when a voice hailed me,

"Good evening, m'dear!" called Matron's brother.

"Good evening, Mr Adrian," I answered politely.

"I hardly recognised you, m'dear! Here, let me take your case!"

I let him take my case because it pleased him, and he walked with me towards the house. I was smiling, happy to be back at Avonlea. The short, wavy hair and the little French beret looked well with my military raincoat, and black calf court shoes added the perfect feminine touch to my appearance.

"It's hard to realise we have such an elegant young lady hidden inside these dungarees and boots you always wear," said Mr Adrian, his eyes twinkling with good nature.

We had reached the path leading to the side door of the kitchen, and thanking him I put my hand out to take the case as I turned right.

"No, no, m'dear! I'll leave this in the hall where you can pick it up later." And he continued on to the main entrance.

I had just entered the kitchen, ready to greet a smiling Bridget, when the door to the hall opened and Matron walked in.

"Mr Adrian is not here to act as porter to you," she said, "and remove your suitcase from the hall, now!" There had been no greeting, so I answered with a polite,

"Yes, Matron." And she left the kitchen without saying another word.

"That's better, Jaqueline!" said Bridget brightly, as soon as the door to the hall had closed. "Let me try your beret, it would be just perfect with my tailored suit. You must be glad to be rid of all that hair. Just think of the saving in shampoo alone!"

"Yes, it does make a difference," I replied, handing her the beret. "Can you tell me what day the coal supply is due, Bridget?"

"Oh!" she answered, moving the beret from one side of her head to the other while she peered in the small kitchen mirror. "It arrived Saturday afternoon just after lunch and there was pandemonium! Tam refused to shovel it into the bunker, because, he said, it was the weekend. But he counted the bags as they were tipped into the furnace room, while four of the big boys took it in turn to shovel it into the bunker."

My legs went weak, and I sat down at the table feeling a great load lifting from my shoulders. Then Bridget turned from the mirror with my beret in her hand.

"Good thing you left before lunch yesterday, Jaqueline, or you would have been at it through till this morning. A double load was delivered. This beret's French, did you say? Can I borrow it on my next weekend off?"

"Of course you can, Bridget! The label inside tells you it's from Paris."

My guardian angel must have been on duty this weekend, guiding me away from Avonlea just before the coal supply arrived, and taking me home to all the good news.

"Is there any tea in the pot, Bridget?"

"There's always tea in the pot!" she answered, pouring out a brew that had been stewed to dark brown.

"Have you heard the news, Bridget?" I asked, sipping the tea that had become the staff of life to me.

"What news?"

"Paris has been liberated by the partisans and the Allies, and the war has turned in our favour!"

Bridget stared into space for a moment, then her hand rose and she crossed herself.

"It's about time!" she said. "Never would have gone on this long if they had done the right thing at the beginning and shot the upstart!" Then she put the beret on her head and turned to face me. "Does it suit me?" she asked earnestly.

"Push it further back on your head." I smiled and waited.

"That's it! You look great, Bridget!"

In the morning a fine mist hung over the estate, which slowly started to rise as the sun broke through and I saw the garden again in all its glory.

The gladiolas stood tall and beautiful on their stems, and asters, dahlias and chrysanthemums blooming against the green of their leaves. Behind this array of golds, pinks and mauves stood a stately clump of marguerites, their large, yellow eyes staring from a fringe of white petals. I reached across to the soft grey of the lavender bushes and picked a purple top from a tall stem; I inhaled its fragrance and dropped it into my jacket pocket. Then I heard a cough and turned.

"I want these ramblers on the stone wall of the main drive cut back," said Tam. "You'll need the secateurs, a tarpaulin, and a small saw to cut out the dead wood. The boys will be back at school by mid-week, start the job then! Right now, you can bag these potatoes, and tie up the onions to the rafters of the shed."

I followed him to the shed where he plaited a string of onions and hung it from a hook in the roof. In complete silence I stood watching this man; would he have left me to shovel two tons of coal without any help? In my mind I despised him.

"Don't take all day!" he grumbled. "I want that section of ground turned over ready for the first frosts!" He glared in his usual unfriendly way, then marched off as I settled down to plaiting the tops of the onions.

The apples were swelling on the trees and some were already blushing. I stole over to the greenhouse where the grapes hung green and swollen from the gnarled vine. Just as with the peaches, the grapes would vanish and I would never know what they had tasted like; none of them would come to the kitchen.

Climbing roses clambered over sections of the garden walls heavy with scent and blooms. Tam was nowhere around, so I filled

Matron's baskets with the best of the flowers and a generous bunch of roses for the silver bowl in her sitting-room. Then I made my way to the kitchen with the baskets balancing on top of Bridget's vegetable supply.

Filling my mug from her singing teapot, Bridget thoughtfully dropped in a spoonful of sugar and turned back to her pots. With the barrow now empty I sat down at the table.

What a wonderful feeling of relief it had been going down into the furnace room and seeing the coal bunker overflowing with shiny black coal. I felt jubilant thinking of Matron's four precious boys black and sweating as they took it in turns to shovel the coal into the long bunker; probably choking with the coal dust, as I had been. I wanted to laugh out loud having missed the hell of shovelling alone.

Suddenly, Bridget's voice broke into my vengeful thoughts.

"You mentioned the war situation yesterday, Jaqueline, are things really improving?" She looked at me anxiously, "We're kept in the dark here, we know nothing of what's going on. And there's never time to read a paper."

"Well, Bridget, the Allies are advancing on all sides, heading straight for the city where it all began. If you can close your eyes to the cost in lives, then the war situation has never been better; my mother thinks it will soon be over."

Bridget poured her tea with the one hand and crossed herself with the other, and we sat silently sipping our tea.

On Thursday the boys went back to school, and as I worked down in the garden, alone, the estate seemed strangely quiet. It would be afternoon before I could start cutting the ramblers, because everything was heavy with mist and dew. Bridget's work load would be lighter, thank goodness, with the boys taking lunch at school.

The dark nights were already creeping in so bath time for the little ones was earlier, giving us all a longer evening to catch up on the mending. There might even be a free evening for the cinema; my mind was full of thoughts of leisure, but was it possible at Avonlea? The daily paper lit the range before we had time to read it.

Bringing my thoughts back to the work of the moment, I found a tarpaulin in a corner of the shed and was just gathering up the tools to start work on the ramblers sprawling halfway across the main drive, when Tam approached.

"Leave that and help me with the herbaceous borders." He snatched the secateurs from my hand. "Cart the cuttings to the dump outside the back door and burn them as I clean up the borders."

I lifted the heavy tarpaulin sheet from the barrow and set it back in the corner I had taken it from, while Tam watched, and pushed the barrow past him without saying a word, heading for the herbaceous section he was working on.

He set about the task of hacking down the clumps of flowers that had bloomed and faded, throwing great bundles of withered stems and leaves on to the path. Stoically I filled the barrow, walking with each load to the wooden door behind the evergreen rhododendrons, which had bloomed so beautifully in early summer when Sean came visiting.

My mind had been empty of thought, and suddenly it was filled with memories of Sean. Was he in the forces yet? Would I ever see him again? Probably not, because I had refused to be his partner in what would have been, I felt sure, his first attempt at sexual intercourse. I had too much respect for the unborn, their start in life would have to be equal to my own, or even better.

The path was piled with cuttings and uprooted annuals; Tam was like Matron who could hardly wait for the daffodils to fade before she ordered the man to mow them down. Plants in full bloom with unopened buds littered the path.

I set a match to the tinder dry mound I had piled outside the back wall of the garden, and the flames leapt up, crackling and sparking as they consumed the waste. While I stood there feeding the flames I thought about the black babies I had given my pennies to every week in Sunday school. They had parents who bore children regardless of what their future would be. The pictures brought back by missionaries only made me realise that ignorance caused most of their hunger. All the pennies gleaned from hard-working, thrifty parents like my own would never solve the problem; the world's hungry would need to be educated on the basic principles my parents had taught me, "if you can't support yourself, then you can't support children!"

The flames had died away, so I threw another bundle onto the ashes that glowed red and it ignited immediately. When the right man came along, I thought as I gazed into the leaping flames, I would know, and accept.

Tam and I worked together for the rest of the day and my clothes and hair reeked of smoke from the fire. But it had pleased me to see the rubbish gone and the herbaceous borders tidy. In his enthusiasm to clean up the garden and prepare it for the coming frosts Tam had forgotten the ramblers on the main drive, and a week of carting withered plants, and burning them, had passed.

It had been easier to concentrate on jobs to be done with the boys back at school. I spread a paper on the kitchen bench to keep it clean before sitting down to a well-earned lunch.

"Mr Adrian will be going home at the weekend," remarked Bridget, "and I won't be sorry to see the last of his great, hulking, beast of a dog!"

"I like Shep, Bridget! But I might think differently if I were the cook."

I smiled at the thought of the huge, loveable, shaggy creature while I spoke; the boys would miss Shep, and so would I. His eyes would remain a mystery to me, because they were always completely hidden by long, white, shaggy hair.

I could hear Tam stomping about outside the kitchen door, and rising quickly from the table I opened the door as he put out his hand to turn the handle while still looking at his watch.

"Come along, I can't wait all day!" he grumped, "I'll show you how to prune back the climbers and ramblers and they'll be done before the winter sets in."

The ramblers and climbers were in the same state as the hedge round the quarter acre had been before I cut it; and now, faced with a hundred yards of roses stretching along the main drive, I considered myself fortunate. Tam's end of the holly hedge lay still unfinished.

"Cut all the stems that have flowered, right from the bottom, like this!" Tam said. Then he cut in mercilessly, pulling long, thorny stems out of the tangled mass that hung from the six foot wall. "Tie up the new shoots that will flower next year, and cut them back to about four feet in length. When the whole section of ramblers is pruned, make a start on the pink climber and all I want you to do is remove the dead wood."

He knelt to cut into a hard thick stem demonstrating how he wanted it done; then he was grunting and cursing as the heavy climber toppled over him catching in his hair and clothing. As he would have done with me, I stood back and watched while he tore himself free of the roses he cursed. It was, I thought, a taste of his own medicine, but I was disturbed by this hardness which was new to my nature. Although I was a novice at gardening, it was plain to see that these roses had been left to run wild for more than a year.

"Lay the stems lengthwise across the tarpaulin and we'll get rid of the lot when you've finished!" Then he marched away, rolling up his sleeves as he went.

The secateurs were sharp and easy to handle, and dragging the long stems of the ramblers across the drive I piled them onto the tarpaulin. I had been working for some time when Shep came plodding up the drive. He stopped when I said hello, and his stump of a tail flicked once in reply; then he wandered on towards the main gate to wait for the school bus.

I was tugging and struggling to cut off a long stem that had swung out from the ramblers attaching itself to the seat of my dungarees, when a loud screeching of brakes sounded outside the main gates. I looked up to see a lorry grinding to a halt, but I kept on with my task of cutting the long, thorny stems hanging out over the drive.

Then a tall, broad-shouldered man was coming towards me carrying a large shaggy bundle. He laid it gently at my feet, and as the tears stung my eyes, he said,

"I'm sorry. I can't tell you how sorry I am. But it stepped into the road just as I came around the curve; I could never have stopped in time!"

I gazed unhappily at the still body of Shep, while the man wrote down his name and address and handed it to me. Suddenly, while I took the scrap of paper from his hand, I thought of the school bus and all the boys aboard it; as the man turned to go I grasped his arm.

"Would you please put him in the lodge garden, I don't want the boys to see him! Not yet!" I said, near to panic.

The lorry driver lifted the limp body of Shep from the drive, his shoulder muscles bulging under his checked shirt, and put him behind the hedge in the lodge garden. I ran to tell Bridget; she would know what to do! Sadly I went back to my toils with a heavy heart.

As soon as the school bus arrived the boys noticed Shep's absence and made straight for the kitchen to find out where he was. I put my tools aside and followed, as Bridget had asked me to do.

"Shep wasn't at the bus stop, Bridget! Has Matron taken him to the vet?" they asked, eyes wide with expectation.

They chattered, and scurried in and out of the kitchen, pulling off their shoes and placing them below where they hung their coats in the hall. In slippered feet they ran back to the kitchen still breathlessly waiting for an answer.

"Sit yourselves down on the floor, boys!" she said, and Bridget's hands lifted the flour from the bowl as she rubbed in the fat, then she began, "Shep's gone to heaven. We all go to heaven, some day, and he'll be waitin' to play with you when you get there! He's to be buried behind the lodge, and you will have to make a cross and paint his name on it to mark his grave."

It was not Bridget's brisk, business-like voice that spoke; but a more lilting, soft voice. It flowed into the minds of the boys filling them with what had to be done, easing their anguish. As I listened I felt the tightness leave my throat. The row of little faces crumpled, and they wiped the tears on their sleeves; then they started asking questions.

"It was like this," Bridget replied, "he was waitin' for you by the gate, when a lorry came round the bend and hit him. The driver said he ran out on to the road, so I can only think that he saw a rat or a mole and went after it."

Bridget let the words sink in before continuing, and she lifted the flour from the bowl letting it run through her fingers. The trusting eyes of the boys watched her face, while their young minds absorbed every word.

"He was twelve," she began again, "and that's quite old for a dog. Now, Matron and Mr Adrian have gone for a walk along the river bank," her voice had become brisker, but it was still as soft and persuasive as her gentle smile. "So go and wash your faces, or they will know you have been crying when they get back!"

The boys rose quickly, discussing whether it was a mole or a rat Shep had gone after, and what size of cross would they make? Then they moved out into the hall still discussing what had to be done. I walked away from the window where I had been standing, and as I reached the side door we both smiled. It was just a faint smile that lingered in Bridget's eyes, but it was full of deep understanding and relief, because the boys had taken it so well, but how had Mr Adrian taken the sad news?

Chapter Fifty-Two

It was very hot and dry in the furnace room and fine ash floated up on the warm air as I raked out the coals. I could hear the boys racing noisily up the drive to board the school bus; and this would be the day Matron's brother left for home, after they had breakfasted.

By the time I went down to the garden for Bridget's vegetables the estate would have become deserted. All the hustle and bustle of school holidays and summer guests was passing, and we were preparing for the approach of winter.

I bent to scoop up a shovel of coal and throw it into the furnace, when a shadow fell across me from the open door at the top of the steel steps.

"Goodbye, m'dear, I'm just leaving." I looked up at Mr Adrian and smiled. "You shouldn't try so hard, m'dear, they're not worth it!"

Just as he finished speaking I heard Matron calling from the end of the path,

"What are you doing, Adrian? We're waiting!"

"Goodbye, m'dear!" he repeated, and touched the edge of his deerstalker hat in polite salute.

"Goodbye, Mr Adrian!"

When he turned away I could see his shoulders were straight again; they had slumped at the news of Shep's death. He would lock his hurt away inside himself as I had done with the loss of my two young uncles.

I dug my shovel into the opening where the coal trickled through and more rattled down behind the boards; work gave me little time to dwell on sadness. With the furnaces stoked and closed down I climbed up into the misty air. It was mild, and a watery sun was pushing its way through to lift the moisture that hung over Avonlea. I would miss Mr Adrian and Shep.

The weekend would be full of extra chores with Mary having a well-earned stay at home; then it would be Karen's turn and next, of course, Bridget's. My turn would eventually come; I had settled down to the realisation that each member of the staff could only have a weekend at home if I stayed, but perhaps it was Matron who made it seem that way.

For some unknown reason I felt lonely, and I looked forward to the boys rambling all over the estate tomorrow and Sunday; it brought life to Avonlea, even if it did mean more work. Their innocent dependency tied me to my duties as nothing else could.

The day had seemed long, and when I at last made my way down into the furnace room at nine thirty to stoke up and close down the dampers for the night, I could hear Mr Adrian's voice saying, 'don't try so hard, m'dear, they're not worth it!' I looked up to the open door at the top of the steel steps, but there was only a patch of the night sky with its sprinkling of stars.

Who had Mr Adrian been referring to? Was it the staff, who could only have a weekend off if I stayed and worked? Or was it the big boys who hid behind pen and paper with their studies unless they were forced to work, like shovelling up the coal supply into the bunker; just thinking of it made me smile.

I felt puzzled when I climbed up into the night air. I made my way through the deserted kitchen and wandered upstairs to my cosy room. I could pick up a book and read, seated in the chintz-covered chair surrounded by the warmth drifting from the vents round my turret window. There were no more letters to write to my uncles, and I was too weary to sew for myself; what mending I had done in the staff sitting-room had made little impression on the growing mound.

The weekend passed in a hive of activity, with the boys chasing after the first of the falling leaves as they were whisked by the wind over the paths and lawns. The weather was mild, but in the early morning and at night I could feel the changing of the seasons.

Monday morning dawned bright and I rose early; Tam would be at the annual Autumn Horticultural Show in the village town hall, standing guard over his prize onions and chrysanthemums for most of the next two days. He had spent ages fussing with tweezers to arrange the petals on his bronze chrysanthemums. Then folded handkerchiefs were placed on top of the giant-sized blooms to prevent the petals from rising and spoiling their perfect round shape.

Now all was ready for the autumn show and I had been briefed on jobs to be done during his absence. It was the kind of day when the mild, light air made breathing easy; in my pocket my hand touched the letter that had arrived from home. I walked quickly down to the garden and closed the wrought-iron gates behind me, then I took the letter from my pocket and started to read.

Dear Jaqueline,

Please read and return the enclosed air mail letter that has come for you from Uncle George. Isn't it wonderful to know that they are still alive when we had given up all hope of ever seeing them again. I had no other choice but to open your letter before sending it to you.

The mail is very erratic, and you are the only one to have received a letter. The government has not yet contacted your aunts. According to what Unole George writes, your letters must be more interesting than the others he receives from the family. As you will be working this weekend, please send the air letter home as soon as possible.

Love,
Mother xxx.

I glowed with inward happiness at the good news, and with the relief of knowing my uncles were still alive; I read over the air letter already opened by my mother.

"Which boyfriend is it from?" I was startled by Sean's voice, but I didn't turn round; I knew he would be leaning on the tree just behind where I stood on the centre path. I continued to read my letter, and he walked over to where I stood. "He must be very special to be worth a few tears," he said quietly.

"Yes," I replied, and handed him the letter to read.

Then I made my way into the quarter acre going over the letter in my mind.

Dear Jaqueline,

I can only hope that my letters get through from this hell. I am writing from the base hospital where fourteen of us are recovering from our ordeal in the jungle.

Uncle John is in the next bed suffering from a bad attack of malaria. All of us have dysentery. Some are very ill from wounds that had to go unattended for weeks.

We had been fighting in the jungle for months, when a group of us were cut off from the main body of men and surrounded. After what seemed like eternity, with no supplies coming through, the heavy tropical rains started. Our attackers moved out, and in came the neat, smooth-skinned natives with their deceptively fragile-looking women; they guided us back to the base camp carrying our sick and wounded.

During the weeks of siege I read your letters over and over again, I always carry them with me; I passed them amongst the men to keep up their spirits. There are those among us who never receive any letters when the mail is handed out.

We could almost feel the cool breeze and see the spring blossom through the wrought-iron of the garden gates as we read. All the while we waited in the unbearable humid heat that comes before the tropical rains for whatever lay in store for us.

The men adore Bridget! They would have given anything to be seated at her kitchen table drinking a mug of stewed tea and listening to her apologies to the saints. Look after the evacuees! For they are the men of the future. And no matter how weary you feel, pick up your pen and write! Your vivid glimpses of home gave us the courage to endure the torment we have been through.

Fondest Love,
Uncle George.

"Sorry if I sounded nasty a few minutes ago," said Sean, making up on me. "It's just the way I am! Will you write to me when I go into the air force?" he asked.

"Yes, if you want me to."

Sean stayed for only a short time, but before leaving, he said,

"I'll drop in tomorrow morning!"

"Tam might be here," I replied.

"While his precious chrysanthemums are in the show? Not him, he would have to be ill to miss the chance of taking a silver cup."

After he had gone I waded into the work, and then set out for the hen-run with the barrow and tools. The yellow chicks were now fast-growing Rhode Island Reds, hens and cockerels, and waddling in amongst them was the duckling on webbed feet. He made harsh, quacking noises from his flat bill, which caused his sisters and brothers to look up disdainfully from their pecking.

When I had finished in the hen-run, I pushed the barrow along to the woodshed and the duckling waddled after me.

"Your friend's growing up."

I turned, then smiled.

"Don't you have a job to do, Sean?"

"It can wait! Why don't you take the duck down to the river, it's his natural habitat."

"I hadn't thought of it," I replied.

"It's cruelty to keep him on dry land, so let's take him down now!"

I felt a slight twinge of remorse as I looked at the duckling; he had to be closed in the hen-run so I could get down to the garden without being followed.

"All right," I agreed, lifting the water bucket.

We went round the long shrubbery that hid the river from view, and the duckling ran after us without any coaxing. The sight of a whole river flowing past was too much for him to resist and he threw himself in floundering as the current carried him slowly downstream.

"I'll catch him at the bend!" called Sean, hurrying along the river bank.

I stood there dismayed at the sight of the floundering duckling. Puddles always stayed where they were; but even as I watched he was fighting back against the current. Then Sean came back with him cradled in his hands.

"He's too small to be left on his own," I said, half filling my bucket with water and sitting the duckling in it to carry him up the path.

"You can't keep him forever," called Sean, heading up the river. "And happy nineteenth birthday! It is this week, Isn't it?"

I had forgotten my birthday, so I looked up with a smile and waved. Birthdays came and went with hardly a mention as you grew into your teens. While I climbed the path with the duckling swaying in the bucket, I felt nostalgic for my childhood; when a cake had been made with tiny lighted candles glowing on top. Then with one puff their flames vanished and you were already thinking about the extra candle that would be added in a year's time.

It had taken a long time for a year to pass when I was a child, but as you grew up the years passed more quickly.

"I'll be nineteen tomorrow, Bridget!" I announced, walking into her warm kitchen.

"Congratulations!" she replied, turning from her pots to smile.

"Do I look any older?" I asked teasingly.

"Age is only a number," she said, "You're as young as you feel!"

The news of my birthday spread through the boys like wildfire, and while I stoked the furnaces early next morning, a bunch of them tossed down a ball of string.

"Keep this in your turret window, Jaqueline, then at seven o'clock tonight lower the end down to us. We'll be waiting!"

I put the ball of string in my pocket, laughing at their antics when they dashed off to catch the school bus.

At bath time I was presented with a long necklace of shiny horse chestnuts.

"Happy birthday, Jaqueline!" the little ones said, and they stood shyly looking at Mary tying a knot in the hairy string at the back of my neck.

"Thank you, boys. It's beautiful!" It was impossible to do anything else but smile, because the necklace of chestnuts reached down to my knees. Laughing delightedly they raced through to the nursery and climbed into bed.

"You'll have to wear it every bath time until you're left with only the string," said Mary, and she shook out the towels, tossing the clothing to me. Wondering at her droll expression, I asked why, but she only grinned and replied, "Wait and see!"

At seven o'clock I was standing by my window with the ball of string, fingering the rich brown chestnuts that hung round my neck. Then I heard a whistle from below, and when I looked over they told me to lower the end of the string. Slowly unwinding it I watched it creep down the wall. When it had reached the boys standing below they tied something on and signalled me to pull it up. Full of curiosity I pulled it up quickly, and when it reached my window Rob, Carrots and some other boys shot off round the front of the house.

I sat down in my basket chair to unravel the knots that held the string round a tiny wooden box, and when I opened it, inside was a folded piece of paper taken from a homework book. While laughing at the mysterious presentation from the boys I unfolded the note and read:

"At Avonlea there lives a lady fair,
And she has the most lovely golden hair.
She's carefree, doesn't care a jot,
As she works with old Tam in his plot.
We've never tried to kiss her yet,
But— —? ? ?"

I looked over the turret window but the poets had vanished completely. Carefully I folded the paper torn from the exercise book and closed it in the little wooden box. Never again would I be sure of what went on in the minds of school boys, especially in the case of Carrots.

Over the weekend the little ones were constantly bouncing around the hall just outside the kitchen door, and as the days passed I gave each of them that asked me one or two chestnuts from my necklace.

"Just to borrow, Jaqueline!" they assured me. And I untied the hairy string to remove another chestnut. Then Martin looked up with round innocent eyes, "You can have them back again! But we can't take that conker," he said, "it's Rob's best crusher!"

Martin knew every chestnut and who it had belonged to. Gradually the necklace grew shorter until it was reduced to a hairy piece of string and one chestnut; fondly I placed Rob's best crusher beside the little wooden box in the corner of my drawer.

Chapter Fifty-Three

Ever since Sean had spoken about the cruelty of keeping him away from his natural habitat, there was no getting down to the river for water, now, without the duckling.

Conscience-smitten, I let him follow me each morning and he hurried along at my side making throaty noises. His excitement at the sight of the river was comical to watch, but he had learned to be careful about entering the water and stuck to a hollow in the bank away from the slow-moving current.

We had been going down to the river together for about a week, when, one morning, I saw the duckling standing absolutely still by the water's edge, his attention rivetted on the opposite bank. I looked across to where the willow trees trailed their drooping branches over the quiet water and saw a family of ducks. They dived and preened themselves, darting across the surface of the water, but always staying close to the mother duck.

The duckling, who had been standing perfectly still, suddenly threw himself into the water and shot across the surface to the opposite bank at amazing speed. Never having been backward about approaching anyone or anything he joined the family, diving and preening, and copying everything they did in their play.

Sean had been wise, and I watched in sheer delight wishing he could see for himself as the duckling mingled with his own kind. Then I felt a sense of loss when I stooped to fill the bucket, my little web-footed friend would no longer need the company of hens or humans.

I started back up the path with the bucket reluctant to take my eyes from the scene, but there was work to be done and time would not stand still; Matron would be hovering around the kitchen to see how many fresh eggs the hens had produced this morning.

Then I saw the little duckling stop in the middle of his play, and make straight for the mother duck, looking up into her face and wagging his whole body. She touched him gently with her bill and tucked him into her side as if he were one of her own. He was just the same greyish-brown colour as the rest of the ducklings, but a little smaller.

I watched while the family followed the mother onto the bank, and then she stretched her wings, rising up on the water and fluttering round in a circle while the water sprayed over her. When she had settled down, the ducklings, and there were five, darted out from the bank and swam around her.

Slowly I turned away with the bucket of water feeling happy for the little duckling; but I also felt sad as I made my way up the path alone.

Before I had reached the shrubbery I heard the throaty little voice calling me. He was stumbling over stones almost twice his size in his struggle up the steep path. I lifted the duckling and floated him in the bucket of water, with a sigh of relief escaping from my lips. I knew that one day he would go, but he was not ready yet!

There would be no more opportunities for Sean to call now that the Horticultural Show was over, in the village. Closing the gate of the hen-run behind me, I lifted the bowl of eggs and made for the kitchen.

Tam's presence had certainly put a stop to Sean's amorous advances. The air force could claim him any day, and he had asked me to write, but he would have to write first to give me his address. I could accept his invitation to go out with him for an evening. But at what cost? I would not be blamed for encouraging Sean, nor would I put myself in the position of having to fight for my virtue. The female's lot in life was most unfair.

The delicious smell of spices wafted across the kitchen when I opened the door.

"What is it you're making, Bridget?"

"Christmas pudding. Can't start too early, you know!" she said, measuring the flour and dropping in the spices, while I listened to her chatter.

"Mary and Karen plan to see 'Bitter Sweet' at the cinema tonight, and they want to know if you would like to go along."

"Yes, Bridget, I would, but what about you?"

"I'd rather get on with making my Christmas cake; can't stand all that hysterical singing, or watching these sopranos walking about with enough material hanging from their waists to curtain the whole house.

Then they have the effrontery to almost cover their bosoms with a wisp of lace. Disgusting, I call it! A good, hard day's work would kill them!"

I sat smiling into my mug, while Bridget rubbed a thick chunk of bread through the grater and dropped the crumbs into the bowl of flour and spices. A night at the cinema was just what I needed, and it was a musical, Hollywood style!

Hurrying through the work, always finding more to do, the time passed quickly, and with a last glance at the furnaces from the top of the steel steps I closed the door on them and dashed upstairs to help with the little ones.

Matron had already given her permission, and Mary, Karen and I arrived in the kitchen breathless, but clean and dressed for a night at the cinema.

"There's plenty of time for a meal before you leave!" said Bridget, and restlessly we sat down to supper.

We were on our way up the drive, jubilant at finding ourselves free for the evening, and having missed the bus we started off along the road chatting and laughing. When we reached the cinema people were pouring out of it after the early show, and I noticed quite a few of them had red, weepy eyes. We walked into the queue for the best seats in the circle at one shilling and ninepence, and filed slowly into the warm cinema.

Mary was fine during the first half of the programme, but when 'Bitter Sweet' started she went silent, and gradually as the film progressed she slumped further down into her seat between Karen and I. Her handkerchief came up to dab at her eyes in the darkened cinema, then she sniffed. I swallowed a few times as the story unfolded, then I went for my handkerchief, and all three of us were dabbing our eyes.

Mary's hand was now clamped tightly over her mouth, and every now and then she would give a strangled snort and shudder violently. As she slumped further down, I looked across at Karen with concern, while we both wiped our tears. Then Mary heaved, and sobs wracked her body as she pushed her handkerchief into her mouth. As if she had expected it, Karen calmly passed a fresh handkerchief to the agonised Mary, while another burst of sobbing shook her further down into her seat.

Worried by the flood of emotion from a now helpless Mary, I leaned across and whispered to Karen:

"Should we leave before the end of the film? Mary's in a dreadful state."

"Oh, no!" came back Karen's answer, "she's enjoying every minute of it."

I settled down to weep silently over the destiny of the two lovers. And then in a final flourish of haunting theme music it ended; the lights went up to reveal hardly a dry-eyed female in the cinema. Mary, who had to be guided from her seat, was still sobbing bitterly into Karen's head-scarf, the only absorbent item left to mop up the tears.

On the walk back to Avonlea in the darkness the odd, shuddering sound still escaped Mary's lips, but Karen and I supported her on each side with an arm linked through hers. Bridget was waiting for us, and the mugs were set out on the table while the kettle sang on the hob. The delicious smell of Christmas pudding rose from the lid of a large fish kettle steaming merrily on the spotless kitchen range.

Bridget looked shrewdly at Mary, before remarking,

"I can see you enjoyed the film, then, by your swollen eyes."

"Oh, yes!" shuddered Mary, "it was beautiful!"

Chapter Fifty-Four

Autumn was advancing on Avonlea and through the haze of morning mist the trees, heavy with dew, glowed gold and red; the fallen leaves lay like a russet carpet on the rich green of the lawns.

In the kitchen Mary was still singing the songs from 'Bitter Sweet', but she was now managing without drowning the vegetables in her tears.

October was yielding a rich harvest of apples from the well-tended trees in the garden. The diseased and distorted had been nipped out in their infancy, leaving perfection to mature for storing over the long winter months ahead.

The weather grew cold with the wind changing to the north, and it dried the falling leaves, blowing them across the lawns until they stood piled as high as my waist in drifts.

Under Tam's instructions, I walked with the dustbin-sized incinerator balanced on the barrow, moving from drift to drift around the ancient house. Setting the metal bin, which was punctured with holes, on its three metal legs, I lifted the leaves between two pieces of board and piled them in. Crisp and dry they flared up at the touch of a lighted match, and what had been mounds of leaves piled up to my waist vanished in the flames until only white ash remained.

The grapes on the gnarled vine that clung to the garden wall were still the size of lentils, but inside the greenhouse the last of the ripe, luscious grapes had been picked. I was disappointed; I would never know what they tasted like, or how sweet they had been. "*C'est la vie,*" I murmured, shrugging my shoulders as I turned away from the locked greenhouse.

As Hallowe'en drew near, the inside of the hedge round the quarter acre glowed bright with rich, red berries against its dark green, prickly leaves, the outside a wall of chopped branches. I took the key from my pocket to open the garden gate, it was now kept locked to keep the boys away from the ripe apples; they would have their fill of them at the Hallowe'en party.

The open fires burned the logs hungrily while the north wind blew, drawing the heat up the chimneys, and stocks were getting low; I thought perhaps I should tell Tam, but he would probably bristle with indignation if I reminded him of his responsibilities and stride off arrogantly as he had done before. I decided to hold my tongue on the matter.

He would not allow me to pick the apples from the trees, so I wiped them with a cloth and arranged them on trays for storing. It was late that afternoon when I carried in a basket of logs to the common room to stack in the alcove at the side of the fireplace.

"We'll help you, Jaqueline!" said several of the boys, and they left their homework to relieve me of my burden. "We can stack them, you don't have to do it!"

I let them take the basket of logs and stood waiting, because they insisted on emptying it for me.

"You're getting smaller, Jaqueline!" said one tall boy, grinning cheekily.

"No, I'm just as I've always been, it's you that is shooting up like a mushroom," I replied, smiling.

"Jaqueline! Have you brought these logs?" Matron's sharp voice cut in from across the hall.

"Yes, Matron, they're here in the common room," I answered, as she entered.

"What on earth are you boys doing?" Her annoyance was obvious and she glared at the boys lifting the logs from the basket. "Jaqueline is quite capable of doing her own work, you have your studies!" She turned to me with disapproval written all over her face, and said, "I won't have you encouraging the boys to do your work for you, put some of these logs in my sitting-room, I'm waiting for them!"

Her eyes roamed over me from the tip of my polished, black boots up over my leggings, fawn dungarees and belted jacket; finally, they came to rest on my face, and I returned her insolent look with a smile, saying,

"I have more in the barrow outside the kitchen door."

I could not have said why, but all I felt for this woman with the discontented face was pity. A blanket of hot, stuffy air wafted from the sitting-room door when I opened it, making me cough as I carried the logs in, and the Warden remarked:

"Cold coming on, Jaqueline?"

"No, it's just that I'm always in the cooler air outside, and the heat in the room makes me cough."

"It's time you were wearing some extra clothing; the weather is becoming quite cold!" he replied, his face expressing concern as he sat bloated with the heat inside his immaculately dressed mountain of flesh.

With the departure of Matron's energetic brother the Warden had returned to sloth, no longer taking an interest in venturing outdoors. I could feel the sharpness in the air on my way to the woodshed for another load of logs, and when I returned to the common room the boys were studiously bent over their books. The little ones sat among them with their thumbs stuck comfortingly in their mouths, watching and absorbing.

Tam called to me from the top of the steel steps on the following morning.

"We'll be sawing up the felled trees in the fir plantation, so bring the barrow. I'll see you up there when you're finished with the furnaces!" And he walked off with the large, two-handled saw slung across his back.

The open fireplaces would need an awful lot of logs to take us through the winter, I realised, as I pushed the barrow into the clearing where the trestles stood; Tam stepped out from amongst the trees.

"Right, take an end and lift it on to the trestle!" he ordered.

The usual gleam was in Tam's eyes, and the dismay that I never could hide must surely have been in mine. By bracing my back and legs I managed to lift my end of the slim tree trunk and drop it across the trestles at the same time as Tam. Then I realised I had left my gloves in the furnace room, but he was placing the saw across the trunk and I knew he would be furious if I asked to go for them.

"Right! Slowly until it bites!" His words came through tight lips and his eyes looked like black pebbles.

I gripped the handle of the saw and was pulled towards the trestle, then I held it lightly down on the trunk, remembering from the last time, letting it bite in as Tam pulled. My feet were firmly planted on the ground when I pushed and I was ready for his sudden tug.

"Get your back into it!" he growled meanly, because I had been prepared for him.

We pushed and pulled and I gripped the handle lightly. I had caught the feel of the saw and could keep up with this man who took a strange delight in goading me whenever there was something difficult to be done.

The logs piled up as we worked relentlessly, and when it came to the morning tea break I eased my numb hands from the handle of the saw. My palms were bright red and hot, and on my way to the house I looked in disbelief as blisters swelled up until I was unable to close my hands. On reaching the kitchen, I had a fat blister cushion covering each palm completely and small blisters had popped up on the pads of my fingers. I held my hands out palms up.

"I forgot my gloves, Bridget," I said, and Mary gasped while Bridget said,

"Holy mother of God!" She hurried for the first aid box. "When you get blisters, you certainly make a job of it, to be sure! I'll pour your tea first, then we'll attend to your hands. You must be in agony!"

"No, Bridget, I don't feel a thing, my hands are just hot and numb."

I held my mug awkwardly and sipped the hot tea; my fingers felt stiff as the blisters reached their limit, but there was still no pain.

"A needle won't be much good on that lot!" said Bridget, "I'll use the small scissors." Then she dropped the scissors into a dish and poured on boiling water, while Mary slipped out of the kitchen in tears. "Let's see your hands!" Bridget settled down beside me, and continued to say, "I'll have to cut down the centre of the blisters."

While Bridget snipped the lymph ran out, and she gently pressed the skin back onto the palms of my hands; then she punctured the blisters along my fingers. Placing a pad of white lint over each hand, she cut it down between each finger.

"There, now! The doctor couldn't have made a better job!" she said proudly, as she bound each finger with a thin bandage.

My hands had started to sting a bit, but by the time she had finished they felt fine, comfortingly encased.

"Thanks, Bridget, you've done a fine job, I feel like the beginnings of an Egyptian mummy."

While we both laughed, she said,

"Make a point of telling Tam what your hands are like. And don't forget your gloves again!"

"Yes, Bridget! And thanks again, but we've finished sawing for today."

When I left the kitchen I eased on my working gloves and no one would have known what lay inside. If I had wanted to mention blisters to Tam I had little chance, because his voice called me as I walked along the path.

"Pile the logs into the barrow and take them along to the woodshed!" he shouted, and strode off to the garden.

With my well-padded hands the trips to the woodshed were easier than I had anticipated, but Tam was an impatient man and before I was finished he stood at the door of the woodshed.

"Why didn't you tell me earlier that the logs were running out?" But before I could answer he turned away with a snort. "Be ready to get down to it next week!"

My hands were beginning to trouble me badly by mid-afternoon, so I lifted them to my shoulders to ease the gnawing ache and headed for the kitchen. When I entered, Mary and Karen had just gone upstairs to bring down the laundry. Bridget filled my mug with tea and sat down opposite me, then she began to say softly,

"Will you not come home with me on my next weekend off? My family would be pleased to see you, Jaqueline." Clumsily I tried to lift a spoon, not wanting to remove my gloves. "Here, let me do it for you!" As she added sugar and stirred, Bridget looked at me keenly. Then she hesitated and looked down at her tea. "I've told you before that Reno is anxious to see you."

Her words made me feel indecisive and agitated, and I answered,

"I'm a coward, Bridget, and I've made up my mind just as you did. I'm not ready to think about marriage and children, there's so much I want to do before I become 'just a housewife' with no rights and no salary, and never-ending pregnancies like your mother."

Tam was stamping outside the kitchen door making me aware of his presence. I rose from the table with my mind racing over the possibility of a new religion and the endless pregnancies it would bring.

"Thank you, Bridget, for asking me to visit your family, but I haven't got the courage to face what might happen."

The rain clouds hung dark in the sky, and I took the apples from Tam and placed them carefully in the basket. He would not allow me to pick his apples, or even touch his trees, and he spluttered as an apple dropped from my gloved hands,

"Don't throw them in," he roared, "lay them in the basket!"

Silently I worked on, and I wondered why I reacted to the things that happened in the way I did. I would have to learn to trust my own judgement, or become unhappy thinking of what I might have lost. For instance, with Reno. And then, no matter what I decided with Tam he would always get at me; I could never please him.

A few spots of rain fell from the heavy skies, but Tam paid no heed. I lifted the basket of apples and carried it to the garden shed. It was already past time for stoking the furnaces and on the spur of the moment I decided to head for the garden gate. If Tam refused to tell me to go, then I would go without his permission.

The house was in sight when the skies opened up, and I raced from the deluge that poured down to the shelter of the furnace room. That night, luxuriating in a hot bath with my bandages still on, I thought about the little duckling's delight in the cold waters of the river; but I felt glad that he was safe in the cosiness of the hen house.

The following morning Matron went to collect the eggs from the hens herself. She insisted Bridget use only fresh eggs for the Christmas cake, which was to be baked and stored to mature in plenty of time for Christmas.

"I don't want any last minute catastrophes!" said Matron irritably, looking hard at Bridget before closing the kitchen door behind her.

"Will this mean the loss of your weekend, Bridget?" I asked.

"The eggs will keep in the larder till I get back!" replied Bridget, with a toss of her head. "I won't be slyly done out of my weekend, or it might be the last I see 'till Christmas has come and gone."

The hard-working Bridget rose at five thirty every morning to light the fire in the range and prepare her programme of cooking for the day.

"No, that I will not," she murmured quietly to herself.

When I went along to the hen-run I found the door open and the duckling gone. Hastily I grabbed the bucket and hurried past the long shrubbery on down to the river, but there was no sign of him. The water looked dark and heavy, and the brooding sky and everything I looked at seemed threatening.

I stood there waiting, wishing I knew where he was. Perhaps he had joined the duck family and would learn to fend for himself before the harshness of winter. There was no time to waste searching. I turned with a leaden heart wondering what had become of him. If only Matron had closed the gate of the hen-run. All day I went about my tasks worrying about the duckling.

The weather became stormy during the night and leaves and broken branches littered the estate grounds. Bridget left for her weekend, and Matron was forced to bring in the woman from the village. The kitchen was not the same welcoming place it had been; it lacked Bridget's efficiency and sparkle.

She was a placid woman, who came from the village, with no conversation, and she stood tasting everything she cooked so that her jaws were constantly munching. She would smile when Matron gave her an order, then go on doing exactly as she had been doing. I noticed Matron frowning in disgust.

Bridget did not return on Sunday evening, as expected by all of us, and the boys who had been peeping round the kitchen door went soberly to bed, as I myself did.

Come morning, she arrived with the first bus before any of the household had stirred. I saw her from my turret window walking swiftly down the drive, and I hurried down to the kitchen. Bridget sparkled with vitality after the weekend with her family, and I looked forward to a cup of tea that had been stewed. The woman from the village made tea exactly as my mother did.

The week began well, full of preparations for Hallowe'en, and Bridget sang in her off-key voice as she started on the recipe for Christmas cake. There was no shortage of fresh eggs.

I was busy working in the garden, when the boys chorused through the wrought-iron gates,

"Matron sent us down to select the turnips for the Hallowe'en lanterns, Jaqueline!"

Stepping from the herbaceous border, I threw the cuttings from the withered plants into the barrow.

"All right, I'll open the gate!" I called.

Tam shot out of the quarter acre, and he seemed to quiver all over at the sight of six boys walking down the centre path.

"Gerrout!" he bawled. "Who told you buggers you could come in here?"

I looked at the boys to reassure them, but they had stopped in their tracks at the sight of the enraged man, so I turned calmly and said,

"Matron has sent them to collect large turnips to make lanterns for the Hallowe'en Party."

"Stay on the paths!" Tam roared, and the boys followed him to the shed to collect their swede turnips.

When they left, carrying their turnips, the alarm caused by Tam's outburst had been forgotten and they walked undismayed through the garden gates laughing and talking. In the afternoon I was sent to find the four wooden tubs for the party, stored somewhere in the woodshed. Having found them under a pile of sacking, I carried them one at a time to the common room. Matron was waiting impatiently for the tubs and I never seemed to be quick enough to please her. I sighed, and hurried back to the woodshed for the last of the four tubs, which were getting heavier with each trip to the common room.

It was then that I saw Sean standing by the door of the woodshed. He smiled and caught my arm as I made towards the last tub.

"My call-up papers have come and I'll be going into the air force this week. There's a chance that we may never see each other again!"

I felt stunned by the news, especially when I had thought the war would end soon. I could find nothing to say as I looked up at him. My first thoughts were, that I should miss him; I had become so accustomed to his sudden appearances at the most unexpected times. What would life be like without his visits to Avonlea? All at once the world was a duller place, and then he said,

"Can I write to you when I get settled at the training base they're sending me to?"

"Yes," my voice was almost a whisper and I had to swallow before I could continue. "I expect I'll be at Avonlea until the end of the war," I said as casually as I could, but I felt my eyes brimming with unshed tears.

His arms went round me drawing me close, and as his lips gently touched mine the silver rain began falling around us. I drifted into his enchanted world enclosed in his warmth and nearness, and then he was saying softly,

"Jackie, will you wait for me?"

Suddenly I heard Matron's voice, and her feet crunching on the path as she hurried towards the woodshed.

"Jaqueline!" she called, "where are you?"

I struggled to free myself, terrified of being caught with Sean. The enchantment had vanished and I pushed against him; reluctantly he let me go as Matron called again. Then I stepped from the woodshed.

"What on earth are you doing? You know I am waiting for the last tub!" Then she caught sight of Sean. "What are you doing here?" she called. "Why are you here?" she demanded again on reaching the woodshed.

"I came to say goodbye to Jaqueline," he answered.

"Oh, yes. Of course! You are going into the services this week." Then, as an afterthought, she added, "Have you permission to come here?"

Sean picked up the tub, hoisted it onto his shoulder, and looking at her keenly through narrowed eyes, he answered,

"Do I need permission?"

Slightly flustered by his cool answer Matron turned to me.

"Bring the tub, Jaqueline!" she said, and she walked back along the path while Sean followed, carrying the tub on his shoulder. He stayed to help space the tubs across the common room floor, while Matron watched frigidly. "Jaqueline is quite capable of doing her own work!" she said, but Sean carried the water from the kitchen, helping me to fill the tubs and pour in the apples.

Matron's eye was still on us until Sean quietly left, when he looked across at me from the doorway and nodded. I stood looking after his tall, slim, retreating figure; storing in my memory the brownish-fair hair, the leather jacket, his tight, doe-skin trousers, all of them blending into a sameness in colour.

"The nuts are in my sitting-room, Jaqueline, bring them through, now! Then go to the kitchen for an early meal. I will need you later."

The excitement of the party was at its pitch when I returned to the common room, and chairs had been placed for the little ones to stand on so they could drop their fork straight into an apple as they floated round the tubs.

I left to stoke the furnaces, and when I got back the boys were ducking their heads into the tubs to catch as many nuts as they could hold in their mouths.

"Take the towel and rub as much water out of their hair as you can, Jaqueline!" said a busy Mary, and she rubbed hard at the ones who had had their turn of ducking for nuts.

Within minutes all the nuts had been caught and the tubs were carried away by the older boys. Shrieks of delight echoed through the common room when Matron switched off the lights, then Mary entered carrying a large tray of baked potatoes. Quickly I mopped up the puddles from the polished wood floor, while the turnip lanterns glowed eerily in mid-air where they were suspended on strings tied to the rafters.

Chestnuts popped in front of the glowing log fire and it was then that the eerie Hallowe'en stories began. When they had become alarming we picked up the little ones and carried them off to bed.

In the sitting-room we patched and darned listening to the squeals of the boys as they gave vent to their vivid imaginations.

"It's your turn to make the cocoa, Mary," said Bridget, "and just have a look in on the boys and tell them it's bed in fifteen minutes."

Mary put down her mending and tripped off humming a song to herself, but within seconds she was back.

"Come quickly, and listen to this!" she said.

We hurried silently to the slightly open common room door, and stood listening to the exaggerated, deep voice of one of the boys as he related a gruesome tale.

"He approached the door of the haunted room, and putting his hand forward to turn the knob he was instantly filled with dread as it slowly swung open." The speaker paused for effect, while we leaned closer to the common room door, and he continued, "He wanted to turn and run downstairs out into the fresh cool of the evening air, but he was compelled by something evil to step into the darkness of the room. Rivulets of perspiration began to trickle down his temples as the door closed behind him with a slight clicking noise, then he shuddered as an icy chill moved across his face." We all looked at each other, and hung on every word as the voice went on low and soft, "The room was covered in dust and cobwebs clung to his clothes, but his eyes picked out something on the far wall as they became accustomed to the gloom and he saw the glint of metal." The speaker paused again, and we all waited. Mary eased the door open as he continued, "Plucking up his courage the man walked across the room to the outline of a large, four poster bed, and then he gasped in horror at the sword standing straight up from its coverlet. Beneath the coverlet lay the shape of a human form." The speaker breathed quickly and then in a voice near to panic he continued, "Again he felt compelled by some evil force to wrench back the coverlet; unable to resist, he pulled it aside and the whitened bones of a long dead man gleamed up at him. Then he started back in terror as the sword rose from the coverlet, following him as he ran towards the closed door. While he pulled desperately at the handle the sword lunged and he fell to the floor writhing in agony."

There was a gasp from some of the boys, but most of them were petrified with fear. Rob was giving a vivid performance of the dying man at the peak of his death throes. He rolled on the hearth-rug gasping and clutching at his throat.

Bridget suddenly pushed open the door.

"Right, boys! Enough!" Her voice was brisk and business-like, "Time you were all in bed!"

Sheer relief showed on the faces of the boys, and they dashed out of the common room and fled upstairs to their dormitories.

"Let's all go to the kitchen, together, and make the cocoa," said a white-faced, shivering Karen.

"I should have boxed Rob's ears for telling such a story!" said Bridget, leading the way to the kitchen. "They were almost in darkness, with only one lantern still burning and the fire almost out."

"You must admit he told the story well, Bridget, and the writhing on the rug at the end was horrifying," I said in defence of Rob.

"Most of them will have nightmares," Mary replied, solemnly looking into her cup as she stirred her cocoa.

When we had finished with our mugs and rinsed them at the kitchen tap, Bridget closed the door behind us and we moved into the hall.

"Goodnight, girls," she said softly, and she and Mary turned left along the corridor to their rooms.

"Wait for me, Jaqueline!" Karen hurriedly slipped her arm through mine and we started up the wide staircase in the dark hall. "Goodnight, Jaqueline," she whispered on reaching her door.

When the door closed behind her I glanced furtively around me, then I started uneasily up the narrow, winding stairway that led to my turret bedroom. I had never been too keen on Hallowe'en with its ghosts and witches.

Busying myself in the bathroom brushing my teeth and splashing my face with water, I found I was still thinking about Rob's horror story when I slipped into bed. But when I closed my eyes it was Sean's nearness I could feel and all the emotions he had stirred. Still wondering what it was all about, I drifted into sleep caressed by the enchantment Sean had created, and wondered if he had shared it. Or was it just something that happened in a woman's world?

Chapter Fifty-Five

I barely felt the cold as November passed mistily into December. Perhaps it was because I was always on the move working up heat. While Tam pruned his fruit bushes and roses, I trudged back and forth through the back gate piling up the cuttings and setting them alight on the first blowy day. The garden was trimmed and tidy, and because I liked things that way my labours seemed light.

The dahlia tubers had been neatly stored in a dark corner of the garden shed, placed upside down on mesh trays ready for planting out the following year. I picked icy sprouts, and dug up leeks that were usually heavy with frost; and all the time I prayed for the war to end.

It was when the poultry began to huddle inside the hen house that I noticed a real coldness in the air. Until then it had been mostly heavy, grey skies and scurrying winds, with a touch of frost in the early mornings. A few yellowed leaves still clung to the oaks, but most of the deciduous trees stood naked throughout the estate, deep in their winter sleep as the cold air crept silently down on Avonlea.

In the mornings it was dark when I rose, and although the frost glistened on the grass at night roses still bloomed on the bush outside Matron's sitting-room window. Tam had not yet pruned her roses. As the days passed it became bitterly cold with temperatures dropping well below zero on the garden thermometer. I knew there would be no Sean appearing, as if by magic, to brighten my days. It was now six weeks since he had left and his promised letter had not come.

The sacks of potatoes seemed to be getting heavier and I stood leaning over the barrow after lifting one, gasping with the effort. With so much to do and think about in the past few weeks I had almost forgotten the duckling. Tears suddenly stung my eyes wondering what he would do in this cold, wintry world of leafless trees and earth that clanged against my shovel like stone.

I had started to cry over nothing at all, and even in the busy kitchen there was a loneliness inside me. Trying to analyse why I was no longer the light-hearted teenager I had been before my nineteenth birthday was difficult. It had become a cold, sad world, but pushing the barrow up the short, steep slope and along the path, I felt comforted by the rich, dark green of the fir plantation.

The pointed tops of the tightly packed silver-frosted conifers were etched into the sky, and stopping to beat my gloved hands together I drew the zip of my padded jacket right up to my neck. The watery sun cast a pink glow over Avonlea; and if it had not been so bitterly cold it really would be a beautiful world, just like a scene on a Christmas card.

Becoming aware of the cold seeping into me while I stood there, I gripped the handles of the barrow and started along the path. Bridget would have the teapot sitting on the hob at the side of the glowing range, and my mug would be waiting on the well-scrubbed, pinewood table; the thought of the warm kitchen made me hurry towards the house.

The sack of potatoes was too heavy to lift, so I cut the string at the top and carried them into the kitchen in basketfuls; the mere thought of trying to lift the sack from the barrow made my legs go weak.

"It's as cold as it ever will be, so I made you a cup of hot chocolate, and have a biscuit with it," said Bridget, her eyes peering through the bottom half of her spectacles while she measured ingredients into a large baking bowl.

I heard Tam's boots stamping outside the kitchen door just as I drained my mug, so I left Bridget in her warm, aroma-filled haven to concentrate on her baking. Tam pushed the barrow in silence and we made our way to the fir plantation. He started to speak as our boots sank into the thick carpet of pine needles in the firebreak,

"This one here will do!" He had selected a tall slim fir tree just at the edge of the break, and marking it with a piece of chalk, he muttered, more or less to himself, "I'll take it down a week before Christmas, the top's a fine shape for a Christmas tree; Matron should be pleased with that." He then lifted the two-handled saw from beneath a piece of sacking and he placed it across the tree trunk that lay along the trestles. "Right!" he said, spitting on his hands and rubbing them together.

Back and forth we pulled and pushed getting faster with every cut; I no longer thought about the cold and only hoped he would tire before

I became exhausted. Suddenly, the sound of voices coming through the densely packed trees reached Tam's ears.

"Buggers, it's them buggers!" he hissed, and three evacuees called out as they approached:

"Matron sent us to collect the Christmas tree, Tam!"

Tam glared, and answered:

"I'll cut it down a week from now, plenty of time!"

"But Matron said we were to put it on the side lawn!"

His glare fell on the boys and they hung their heads, scuffling their feet in the pine needles.

"Get off with you, I'm busy!" The boys retreated a few yards, then stood waiting. "Are you deaf !" bawled Tam, "Get off with you!"

Unexpectedly, Matron's voice spoke from behind us.

"The boys have told you I want the tree on the side lawn today. It will stay perfectly fresh outside! Which one have you selected?"

Tam walked over to the tree with the chalk mark and put his hand on the trunk.

"Rather scraggy looking, is it not?" I felt myself cringe at the tone of her voice.

Stifling his anger, Tam made no answer.

"Jaqueline, come with me along the firebreak and help select a tree with a pretty top!" Her mouth smiled, but her eyes did not.

Holding her hand above her eyes Matron walked along scanning the tops of the fir trees towering some twenty to thirty feet in the crisp air. We had gone almost fifty yards before she stopped.

"I can never understand the gardener's choice, utterly miserable I would call it! Let's have a beautiful one. What do you think of that tree, Jaqueline?"

Tam had chosen a thin trunk, but the trunk of this tree was twice as thick.

"The trunk will make it too heavy, Matron." Then I looked along the line of trees and saw several more suitable. I pointed them out, and Matron stood pensively for a few moments.

"Yes, perhaps a thinner trunk would be better, although we just use the top twelve feet," she paused. "That one will do!" she said decisively, pointing to the tree of her choice.

The boys had been trailing behind us and when the choice was made they dashed back along the firebreak to tell Tam. He came grudgingly carrying an axe, and with a few well-aimed blows he notched the tree.

"Better get the boys out of here before we bring it down!" Tam looked mean as he spoke.

"I want it on the side lawn before five p.m.!" I had noticed that Matron never thanked him. "That will be before my guests leave!" she called over her shoulder, and she walked away with the boys as Tam smouldered.

Lifting one end of the saw Tam glared, and said,

"You heard Matron, take the other handle!"

We cut into the tree and as the saw bit deeper the graceful pine creaked, and slowly swayed and toppled, falling neatly along the firebreak.

"That was nicely judged!" I said, as it settled. I had let the words escape my lips without thinking.

"Humph!" Tam said. "Bring the axe!" And he walked with the saw to the middle of the fallen tree. Feeding out a steel rule he gave me the end to hold. "Stand where you are until I take the measurement from here to the top of the tree. Right, forward a bit!" I stepped forward with the rule and he took up the slack. "Enough!" he shouted, "We'll cut right where you're standing!"

By four thirty the Christmas tree was on the side lawn for the guests to admire.

The days were flying past, and with less than a week to go before Christmas Eve Bridget had caught the imagination of the boys. Each evening they made their way to the staff sitting-room clad in their pyjamas, where their scrubbed, shiny faces and plastered down damp hair were scrutinised. Then each pair of hands were inspected before they were allowed to enter the sitting-room.

The tallest boys took their places at the back of the room, and the little ones lined up in front near to the open fireplace. When all were assembled they sat down on the carpeted floor, and there was a sudden hush when Bridget took a large paper bag. Putting her hands inside she opened it out until it could stand easily on the stone hearth. In the two corners sticking up she put a twist, and the moment they had been waiting for arrived.

Bridget had become the entertainer and now held the rapt attention of her audience. At this point she folded a sheet of newspaper into a long taper.

"Who is to be first?" she said, looking at the little ones, and they shyly raised their hands. "And what is it you'll be asking Santa Claus for?" Her wide open, blue eyes sparkled behind her glasses as she continued, "Let's all hear what you want to say before we burn the bag. And remember, once it disappears up the chimney you can't ask for anything else!"

All eyes were glued on Bridget's face as she spoke; then she took the long taper and pushed it into the glowing embers of the fire. When it started to burn she applied it to the corners of the bag, and one little voice was heard,

"A teddy bear!" said our youngest.

The others, so awed by the burning bag drifting up the chimney, had remained speechless. Bridget looked at them in mock amazement, saying,

"Tut, tut, tut! You'll have to do better than that!"

Another bag was puffed out and the corners carefully twisted, then Bridget gently placed it on the hearth; given a second chance they all chorused,

"A teddy bear!" And the thumbs went back into their mouths.

With the ceremony over the boys ran upstairs to the dormitories and climbed into bed. In the nursery we hugged the very thoughtful little ones, tucked them in and listened to their prayers.

In the dormitory of the nine year olds and over prayers were a difficult business. These bashful, fast-growing boys would climb into bed and no prayer could be coaxed from their lips until we put the lights out; hugs were an embarrassment to this age group. We then listened by the door as a gruff mumbling of voices, from below the sheets, could be heard. When the mumbling stopped we called goodnight and closed the dormitory door.

On the following evening they all queued up to enter the staff sitting-room. Hands were checked with the same thoroughness, and one or two boys were sent to scrub their nails. While we all waited I glanced around the well-scrubbed boys sitting patiently in front of the glowing fire.

They all belonged to someone. And I wondered how they could bear being separated from their families at this time of the year. The little ones sleepily sucked their thumbs. Wet hair was scored down the middle, or to the side, and combed flat onto their heads; but as the warmth from the fire filled the room it dried, and curls started to tumble over a forehead, or stood straight up on end, if it was short.

Bridget had been carefully folding the page of newspaper into a long taper, and when everyone was in their place the ritual began. The bag was pushed out until it could stand, and the corners neatly twisted. Bridget placed it on the hearth, and asked,

"Whose turn is it tonight?" Her eyes roamed over the five to eight year olds and their hands went up.

There was a noted difference in each age group when their turn came. With the five- to eight year olds they managed to say at least three items and, as the burning bag drifted out of sight, add a further request for an apple and a penny.

On the following evening it was the nine to eleven group; this time we came up against the doubting and unbelievers. However, their ability to read out long lists of demands before the bag took off up the chimney staggered us. Even Bridget was slightly breathless.

From twelve years and upwards it was the knowledgeable sceptic who played the part to please the small boys.

The smell of mince pies filled every corner of the house, and a large white cloth covered the royal icing and decorations on the Christmas cake. Bridget was very possessive towards her beautiful cake and chased any boys from the kitchen who might have been tempted to nibble the edges. There had been a glow of pleasure on Matron's face as she studied this work of art, and while fumbling with the back of her hair she had sniffed.

"It's very nice, Bridget, very nice, if it tastes as good as it looks!"

Earlier on we had been worried about enough toys for all of the boys, but a request was made from the church pulpit and toys flowed in from the village to surprise us; among them were four battered teddy bears. The teenage boys proved helpful, taking wooden and metal toys to be repaired in the school workshop.

Finally Matron was satisfied that every boy had one gift that was important to him. The staff, however, were anxious to find games and odds and ends to fill stockings. We collected near perfect pennies and spent time bringing them up to a bright gold with brass polish.

In the meantime a large wooden crate had arrived at Avonlea. The three men who delivered it had used belts to guide it down the sloping planks of wood from their lorry, and having managed to lower the crate to the ground, the next step of opening the double main doors and trundling it into the hall was comparatively simple.

Matron was hovering in the background, insisting that I should help if necessary. But the brawny males only smiled, and the obscene language flowing freely from their mouths drove Matron into her sitting-room, where she remained behind closed doors until they had gone.

Once the crate was inside the main hall, where it took up quite a large area, Bridget insisted that the three men come into the kitchen for tea and home-made scones. The swearing was replaced by grunts of satisfaction, and wide grins spread over their faces at the sight and smell of home baking.

The kitchen was large, but the men seemed to fill the place, as they sat at the pinewood table devouring the scones and emptying large mugs of tea. I felt overwhelmed sipping my tea at the end of the table; but I watched with interest while Bridget kept the men amused with a witty flow of conversation. The inability of the men to answer without one obscene word in three left Bridget unperturbed. She pushed her hands into the pockets of her white starched apron and her wit flowed easily with a quickness that made me feel immature.

The men were dressed exactly as I was, in open-necked shirt, sweater, dungarees and boots. I was a complete miniature of them and they found it amusing to tease me. I wanted to stand up and shout out that I could shovel a ton of coal, but I remained tongue-tied and silent and would never have been able to explain why.

When the boys arrived on the school bus they seemed to know the crate was there and headed for it like a column of ants; crowding round they chanted out the words written on the gift that had crossed the Atlantic to end up in our hall.

"From the people of the USA!" they shouted, "from the people of the USA!"

Having read out the large, block letters over and over again, they made their way upstairs discussing what the crate might contain and marvelling at how far it must have travelled through the submarine-infested waters of the Atlantic Ocean.

When Bridget's ritual had been gone through that evening, and the boys had lingered on their way upstairs, all eyes glued on the large crate, we made sure all were in bed and then turned our thoughts to the mysterious gift.

Under Matron's guidance the crate was opened, and as the boxes it contained were unpacked we realised our gift problems were over. There were more than enough luxuries we had been deprived of during the long years of war. The boys would have sufficient stocking fillers and toys to test their skill and imagination throughout the winter evenings that lay ahead.

For the female staff there were luxury toilet items, and beauty soaps such as we had never seen before, with full instructions on how to use them. Mary and Karen's eyes glowed with anticipation, but Bridget sniffed as she gave her opinion,

"There's nothing like a handful of oatmeal in warm water, 'tis as fine a beauty treatment as you'll find!" she said.

While we busied ourselves emptying the crate the full realisation that we were no longer alone with our war dawned in our hearts. The resigned feeling of hopelessness, to which we would never have admitted, was gradually replaced by a deep sense of relief; and as the contents of the boxes unfolded before our eyes there seemed to be something more. Perhaps it was an aura of peace and goodwill from the loving hands that had filled the crate, not only with gifts, but with hope for the future. Whatever it was, the hall glowed with magic, bringing a calm, deep happiness to us all.

"Aren't people kind!" said the emotional Mary, dabbing at the silent tears trickling down her cheeks.

Chapter Fifty-Six

It was on Christmas Eve that the boys lined up to attend a special carol service in the local church.   Dressed in their best they were looking quite different from the rowdy bunch that clambered out of the school bus every day.

The little church where the service was to be held lay halfway between Avonlea and Burnsyde, so Mary and I, with Karen at the head of the column, marched with the boys along the path and through the firebreak to the stile.   From there we could see the wooden bridge that spanned the narrow winding river on the opposite side of the road.   The morning was crisp and clear.

On reaching the stile the big boys took charge of the column, herding us across the road and waving down any oncoming traffic, while we held on to the little ones.   We crossed the wooden bridge that led to the small, stone church, and on entering, the first thing to catch the eye was the glittering Christmas tree glowing with fairy lights by the side of the altar, a brilliant star poised on top reaching into the rafters.

Matron and the Warden, who had gone by car, were already seated on the left at the front of the church with their friends, and the boys filed into the empty pews behind them.   We had barely settled down when the sound of the organ rang out, breaking the silence and causing the whole congregation to rise to their feet.

After a short introduction from the minister the carol singing began and the well-known words flowed from every throat; but sounding clearly above the loud singing of the boys I could hear two voices, that of Mary and the Warden.   They sang in a key of their own, one that was pitched slightly higher than all the other voices and one that sounded very rich and low.

During the singing of the carols about a dozen people moved into the empty pews on the right at the front of the church, and a young couple took their place by the christening font.   The pale-faced mother carried her baby in its long, white, lacy christening gown and shawl. Calmly attentive to its needs she tucked the delicate shawl over its tiny hands. Beside her stood the rosy-cheeked young husband looking uncomfortable in a suit that had not grown with him. The carols died away to the ringing cords of the organ and the minister approached the font.

There was the odd clunk of a shoe kicking against a pew as the boys fidgeted, causing Matron to turn round and frown disapprovingly at all of us. Then everyone's attention turned to the minister when he took the sleeping infant in his arms, and as he spoke, dipped his hand into the font and touched the baby's forehead with wet fingers.

A ripple of amusement ran through the boys when the small chin of the baby quivered and its tiny bottom lip pouted; again Matron turned and frowned disapprovingly. But the adoring parents glowed with happiness as they gazed on their first-born child.

Chip sat beside me with his head hanging dejectedly and a little puddle was growing below his dangling legs. But the minister talked on in his clear, cold voice. He suddenly said three words that had a shattering effect on me; I was appalled by the phrase that seemed to come from some dark, unholy dimension of the minister's mind,

"Born in sin!" he repeated, his eyes cold and vacant.

The words appeared to tarnish the beautiful, sleeping child he held, and banish the adoring parents to the realm of evil. I had witnessed several christenings and our minister, who had children of his own, had never used these words. I felt angry. Why should he say something ominous, when all was perfectly pure and natural to the young married couple on this happy day?

The minister's face was just as it had been when he took afternoon tea with the family at Burnsyde: the grey complexion above the white collar, the bleak, red-rimmed eyes that held no light of pleasure in the Christmas mood of his congregation. It was as if he stood alone and aloof, conscious of superiority, and had no contact with the happy, humble people who were his congregation. On the way back through the fir plantation to Avonlea my mind dwelt on the evil injected into a perfectly normal relationship between two married people.

The boys were already running across the lawns chasing a football when I walked into Bridget's kitchen, and I turned to her thoughtfully.

"Bridget, why didn't you come to the carol service?" I asked, but she made no answer, so I continued, "A baby was christened just after the carols and it was beautiful to watch."

"It wouldn't be right for me to enter one of your churches," Bridget replied suddenly, then went on, "Matron has asked if you would take a Christmas hamper down to Jenny's house in the village this afternoon."

"Why yes, of course! It will be like playing Santa Claus!" I answered, delighted to have been asked.

"This is the day the minister gives her a call," said Bridget, turning from her pots, "so you can cheer her up when he leaves." I looked at her inquiringly, and she heaved a sigh before saying, "Yes, he visits once a month to lecture on the shame of poverty, and the pitfalls of bringing up five children without the firm hand of a God-fearing father."

"Why that's absurd! Jenny's not to blame if her husband was killed in the war. As far as I can see she works very hard to support her children. And she won't have time to put her feet up when she gets home with five mouths to feed!" I said heatedly, feeling concern for the hard-working woman.

It was afternoon when I dressed and took the bus to Jenny's house in the village, feeling full of the happy Christmas spirit; but Bridget's words, regarding the attitude of the minister towards Jenny, niggled at the back of my mind, as did her refusal to enter our church. I had eagerly asked to be invited into Bridget's church,

The hamper of food put aside by Matron and the Christmas cake made by Bridget's loving hands were on their way to a family who lived on the bare necessities of life.

Jenny lived in a terraced house, and the small boy who opened the door when I knocked asked me to come into the sitting-room. My entrance interrupted the minister in full flow, but he only hesitated for an instant before continuing in his voice of doom.

He glared as I took a seat by the door where I could watch the scene to advantage while studying the impact of his words on the unfortunate family before him. Jenny sat stiffly on the edge of her chair with the children standing on either side, and for the first time I saw the short, brown hair curling round her head; at Avonlea it was always covered with a head scarf. Then I noticed how thin she was without her overall.

Having achieved the desired effect of making the family before him utterly miserable, the minister turned to me.

"You are the land-girl from Burnsyde Farm, are you not?"

"Yes," I replied, "but I am now employed at Avonlea."

"I am aware of that circumstance!" he replied stuffily. "Your infamous behaviour while at Burnsyde is known throughout the parish, and yet you wear the face of innocence!"

I studied this man as I listened, fascinated, and answered,

"Perhaps I am innocent of what you accuse me, or had you not thought of that?"

He looked startled, and replied,

"My information came from the best authority, I assure you!"

I was beginning to feel angry with the empty head that rattled before me, and said deliberately,

"Your authority judged me wrongly and must be as bigoted as yourself."

He stared, and seemed to be stuck for an answer, so I gave vent to the outrage I felt,

"There is no doubt in my mind that you would have me burned at the stake if we were not living in the twentieth century!"

He rose suddenly and hurried into the small, unlit hall, and as he turned, he lifted his black hat and put it on, pulling it down to just above his eyes. He said loftily,

"I will report this to your employer!"

In the dim light of the small hall his silhouette in the black clothes and hat made me start, and I felt the fear I had experienced on that dreadful night at the gates of Burnsyde. There was the smell of camphor from his clothes in the room, and I was filled with utter contempt for this evil creature who posed as a messenger of God.

Before he could take another step, I felt my eyes blaze and I answered loudly,

"My private life has nothing to do with Matron or anyone else who may have employed me! And do you ever question your own behaviour?"

The coldness of my words startled me, I glared at him and wondered for an instant if I had really said them; but their impact made the minister slip hurriedly out of the door.

Having come face to face with the man who tried to rape me, I saw him for what he was and had only contempt for such an evil and unholy creature. He didn't look back, or answer me, and the outside door stood open as he had left it.

I rose and closed the door against the cold outside air, while Jenny fussed nervously with the table cloth before she turned to look at me. The children stood quite still, just looking.

"I wouldn't have dared to speak to the minister like that," she said, her face as white as a sheet.

"Then it's time you learned! I spoke the truth, Jenny," I answered, laughing as I did so, because all the tension had gone from the room. "I've brought your Christmas hamper from Matron, don't you want to see what's in it, children?"

The children crowded round while Jenny opened the hamper and placed every item it contained carefully on the table. Thoroughly examined, the luxuries were replaced in the hamper, and only Bridget's Christmas cake, and a round, red cheese that brought squeals of delight from the children were left on display.

I glowed with pleasure as the bus wound its way back to Avonlea on that memorable Christmas Eve.

"Goodnight, Miss! And a Merry Christmas!" the conductor said, and his Rs rolled softly as I stepped down from the bus.

"Goodnight! And a Merry Christmas to you!" I replied, smiling.

Then he swept off his hat and made a lavish bow from the platform as the bus moved off into the darkness. I laughed at the extravagant gesture and hurried down the drive.

Excitement was at its pitch when I raced upstairs to change into my dungarees after the visit to Jenny's house. This was the night when the furnaces were to be extra well stoked to ensure a good supply of hot water for the washing-up on Christmas Day.

Even the little ones were rubbing themselves with soap and a cloth when I walked into the bathroom.

"I'm washed clean, look!" said Martin, trying to pull on his pyjama trousers, letting out a squeal of excitement.

"Yes, you're clean, but you're very wet!" I answered, picking up a towel and giving him a good rub down. "Now, you can get into your pyjamas."

"I'm getting a great big stocking from the big boys to hang on the end of my bed for Santa!" Martin went on excitedly, and he continued to struggle with his pyjama trousers while I slipped on his jacket.

"Off you go then!" I watched as he ran from the bathroom, stooping to clutch at his trousers when they dropped to his ankles.

"Can we have a great big stocking, Jaqueline?" The two youngest, still sitting in the bath, looked at me with wide open eyes and waited for my reply.

"Yes!" I said. "When you are all clean and in your pyjamas we'll go and ask Rob because he has the biggest feet!"

I dried our youngest in the bath while they watched the water spinning round as it ran down the plug-hole. They stood patiently as I tied the cord in their pyjama trousers and buttoned up their jackets. Matron was there when I walked into the big boys' dormitory with a little one on each hand. She looked up irritably from where she knelt on the floor, and through tight lips she said,

"Can't you see to it that the boys are dressed in their pyjamas before they leave the bathroom!" and her hands trembled as she tied the cord in Martin's pyjama trousers.

Then she stood up and glanced round the boys in the dormitory. Turning to three of the doubting and unbelievers age group, whose beds filled the large area of a bay window, she said with authority,

"Take these pillow slips down and hang up a stocking at the end of your beds like all the others!"

I controlled the urge to smile as the doubting and unbelievers ran to the cupboard and hastily replaced the pillow slips with stockings.

It was not the usual practice for Matron to come round the dormitories in the evening, but it was Christmas Eve and even she was stirred by the excitement in the air, until she looked at me.

"This is not the nursery, Jaqueline!" she said with contempt. "Why are you here?"

"The little ones would like to borrow larger stockings, Matron."

"Oh, all right! Collect what you need, and take the children to bed!" And she walked out of the dormitory.

I managed to find some striped football stockings in the cupboard, but as I left the dormitory with the little ones the three pillow slips appeared once more on the beds of the doubting and unbelievers.

When all the boys were in bed, determined to keep their eyes open for the arrival of Santa, I walked to the landing with Mary, Karen and the three big boys who were to help once all were asleep; there was still a lot of work to be done.

The Christmas tree reached past the landing at the top of the polished staircase, its fairy lights reflecting on the oak panelling as they winked their elusive colours. Crowning the tree was the fairy in freshly starched lace, the star on her wand sparkling beside her dainty, glittering tiara.

We started down the wide, polished staircase discussing our plans for the evening in subdued whispers. The crate had been taken apart and cleared from the hall leaving the Christmas tree to dominate the scene with its sparkling glow. The feeling that only Christmas brings was all around us. The boys were quiet with expectancy, and the ancient house was full of peace and plenty, some given by the quiet, suspicious people from the village, and some sent across the dangerous waters of the Atlantic from strangers we would never see.

Chapter Fifty-Seven

Unusually restless during the night, I awoke from a troubled sleep. Rising from my bed, I walked towards the whiteness of the net curtains in my turret window and stood there in the warm air of the ventilators, my disturbing dream and the cause of it filling my mind.

The smell of camphor in Jenny's sitting-room had made me uneasy when I took my seat near the door, but I had shrugged it off. But the sight of the black hat shading the eyes of the minister, and his silhouette in the dim hall, had brought back the events of that terrifying night at the gates of Burnsyde.

What woke me from my dream had been Belle's barking breaking the spell that held me petrified as my attacker leaned over, the smell of camphor strong from his clothes, his cold fingers fumbling beneath my skirts; I wanted to scream in protest!

I felt again the terror that had given me wings when I swung my parcel and raced up the drive to safety. Turning from my turret window, I shuddered in the warmth of my cosy room and wandered back to bed. But sleep refused to come.

My mind went back to a particular weekend at home, when I had broken all the unspoken rules on what girls should know only after marriage. Alone in the house, I had looked up plates one and two of the male and female form in volume one of my mother's Household Physician. But what was referred to as the frontal view of the male form had nothing more on the lower part of the body than that of the female form.

In my school books the big secret had always been covered by a fig leaf, and in the Household Physician it had been omitted, or ignored completely. It had taken over an hour of furtive research in the main branch of the public library to educate me on the subject of the male penis; and if the name of that organ had been mentioned in my hearing before my visit to the library, I would have been completely ignorant of what it referred to.

On my way home from the central library I felt myself grow in stature and maturity. At nineteen years of age I realised I had been too obedient a daughter, and too good a Girl Guide. I smiled at the thought of my parents protecting me so well and dozed off into a dreamless sleep.

At five in the morning I was wide awake, and unable to lie in bed any longer I rose and made my way to the bathroom. The sound of bare feet pattering along the polished wood floors of the corridors on the floor below made me hurry. I dressed as the whispering voices of the boys grew louder, then walked silently down to the top of the main staircase and stood listening to the buzz of voices coming from the dormitories.

The softly glowing Christmas tree cast its winking colours on the polished wood, and I could reach out and touch its branches from where I stood looking down into the ancient hall. I could see the heavy, gold frame of an ancient portrait, and the white marble bust on its pillar by the sitting-room door was almost luminous in the glow of the tree.

The kitchen door opened, and the peace of the house was shattered by Bridget's toneless voice murdering *The Twelve Days of Christmas*. Then Mary joined in and it was like a peal of silver drifting across the hall and rising through the warm house that smelled of furniture polish.

I hurried down to the kitchen, where Bridget stood cutting toast into small triangles at the end of the long, pinewood table.

"Merry Christmas, Bridget!" I said brightly, all my fears of the night forgotten.

"And the same to you, Jaqueline!" she replied, dipping a knife into the large tin that stood on the table beside her. "Come and try some of this. It's some new-fangled, American concoction that came in the crate. I'd say it was the greatest invention since bread. And it took a war to bring it to us!"

She spread the doubtful looking, light brown butter on a piece of toast and handed it to me, I nibbled at the corner and as the creamy flavour of peanuts spread across my tongue I smiled.

"Oh, it's delicious, Bridget! What is it?"

"'Peanut butter' the Americans call it, here, read the label for yourself!" and Bridget turned the seven pound tin round as she said,

"I'll bet the boys won't be able to get enough of this, we'll have to ration it!"

The little ones from the nursery were already looking round the kitchen door waiting for Bridget to notice them; their four teddy bears had been held up at least twice.

"Oh, Bridget! How can you keep them waiting?" I asked.

"When you come from a large family you have to learn to wait." Pretending not to notice them Bridget went on sipping her tea, and then she turned towards the door and said, "Oh, my goodness! If it's not a teddy come to visit us!"

Shyly Chip, our youngest, stepped from behind the door still holding up his teddy.

"It's me, Bridget," he said.

She put out a hand beckoning him to her.

"Come on then! Let's see teddy!"

Within a flash Chip was on her knee and the others followed bringing their precious teddy bears.

"Mine is a pirate!" said Martin, climbing on to the bench beside me. "Look! He's got a black patch over one eye. And I got this big box of games!" Then he paused. "But I don't know what this is – it was in my stocking with this gold penny and an apple."

I took the small, oblong box of chocolate and ran my knife along the top edge, where there was a lid concealed by the wrapper.

"Now open it, Martin, and see what's inside."

He opened the box with chubby hands and took out a piece of chocolate.

"Can I eat it, Bridget?" he asked, looking across the table.

"Yes," she replied. "Christmas day is special for little children like you, but don't be making yourself sick!"

"But I'm not a little children, I'm a big boy!" he replied instantly.

Martin, who had had his fourth birthday just a month before, looked quite indignant.

"Yes, of course you are, but Santa Claus is bigger!"

Bridget's answer pleased him, and after showing their presents to each of us in turn the little ones rushed off to the big boys' dormitory to surprise them.

"I don't think I would like to part with my little boy at that age, if I had one," I said.

Then I looked at Mary and Karen; after all the chatter with the children they seemed quiet. It was Bridget who spoke as she refilled our cups,

"Martin is an orphan; his parents were blown to smithereens in Coventry."

Bridget's voice had been quiet, but when the tears stung my eyes I realised we were all feeling the same way.

"Poor little lamb," said Mary, rising from her chair.

"Time I started breakfast, and if any of you have a minute to spare come and lend a hand!" said Bridget briskly.

Mary wandered out of the kitchen in her pink quilted housecoat, one hand stifling large yawns, while the other ruffled through her thick, wavy hair.

Outside the windows the snowflakes drifted down soundlessly on the still air. Karen flounced across the kitchen, immaculate in her pert table-maid's attire. The snowy-white of her cap and apron reflected the perfect white Christmas that lay outside the tall kitchen windows. With a toss of her head Karen cast a look of disdain after the sleepy-headed Mary.

It may have been Christmas morning, but Tam was outside the kitchen door early. He had said nothing about it being Christmas Day, and I spent it chopping kindling in the woodshed, feeding the hens, piling logs on the open fires and stoking the furnaces.

After lunch, I went to the boys' dining-room where the tables were set for Christmas dinner at three o'clock. Matron was adding the finishing touches with crackers and paper napkins. I placed two logs on the open fire and the sparks showered on to the hearth.

When I turned from the fire, it seemed to me that there was nothing more beautiful than the polished wood panelling reflecting the flames from the burning logs; the colours danced around the walls and lost themselves up amongst the rafters.

The Warden's large, carved chair stood in the centre of the main table and there were several crystal glasses at his place setting, and a bottle of wine in a silver holder, already uncorked. Matron's place had been set on the Warden's left; she seldom dined with the boys.

"Jaqueline, I see there are very few potatoes in the kitchen, you had better bring a sack up from the garden before the boys start dinner!"

"Yes, Matron."

Grudgingly I wheeled the barrow through the falling snow; there was no sign of Tam anywhere. On the way back from the garden the tracks I had made on my way down to collect the potatoes had almost been obliterated.

Hurrying along through the swirling snow, I turned away to the side as it blew into my face and clung to my eyelashes. Inside two pairs of gloves I felt my fingers go numb with the cold, but I pushed the barrow and doggedly plodded on. Never had the journey from the garden been so long; I kept running off the path because everything before me was one vast blanket of white.

By the time I reached the house and carried the potatoes in, a basketful at a time, the boys were eating their way through Christmas dinner. Mary and Karen slipped sideways past each other, carrying large platters of food, or stacks of empty plates; the house seethed with activity.

Not once had I thought of home as I hurried down to stoke up the furnaces; my numb hands stung with the heat when I opened the metal doors. Bridget would need plenty of hot water for the mounds of pots and dishes already piled up in the kitchen sink, and plates had been stacked high on the floor.

When I had finished my work outside, I went thankfully into the littered kitchen where there was barely a space for a mug on the table. It was groaning with steaming hot bowls of Christmas pudding, and mouth-watering trifle already served up in glass dishes. Bridget was relaxing in her chair with a cup of tea before the next onslaught of serving the Christmas pudding hot.

"Just taking the weight off my feet before helping Mary to tackle this lot!" she said, waving a languid hand at the sink area. "Jenny promised to come in and do the washing up, but with her brood of five and no husband she probably has her hands full."

I took off my rubber boots and slipped into my house shoes, then answered,

"The snow is quite thick, Bridget, and perhaps the buses have stopped; what's more, it's already getting dark."

I rolled up my sleeves and let the hot water run into the sink as a weary, flushed Mary came into the kitchen.

"Thank goodness Christmas only comes once a year!" she gasped, setting down another pile of empty plates on the draining board beside me. "I could fill two dustbins with the crumbs and paper littered about the dining-room floor!"

She flopped onto the bench, and Bridget rose and cut into the steaming Christmas puddings. Filling a tray with the first servings, Karen walked swiftly through the kitchen lifting the tray high and made for the dining-room. Mary followed with the next tray while Bridget emptied several more bowls.

I plunged the first of the dirty plates into the hot water and my chilblains screamed. While I washed and stacked, Karen flounced in.

"Matron will not be having Christmas pudding," she said, "but she wants coffee in her room now."

I saw Bridget's eyes flash with exasperation, but she turned immediately to fill the silver coffee pot as Karen arranged the tray.

Drying and carrying the clean plates to the sideboard, I returned each time to the sink to find the dirty dishes piled higher than ever, while Mary hurried back and forth from the dining-room. When, at last, all the empty trifle dishes were brought through, I washed and stacked them and turned to the mound of pots. Mary had collapsed into Bridget's chair still holding her dustpan and brush.

"Here, put your feet up and drink your tea!" Bridget spoke briskly, pushing a stool with her foot while she took the dustpan and brush from Mary's hands.

I listened while I scrubbed the pots to Mary relating her account of the Christmas dinner.

"I never saw the boys get through so much food!" she began, "I'd have thought the turkey with all those roast potatoes would have been enough. But no, they piled the custard onto the Christmas pudding and as soon as the plates were cleared they waded into the jelly and trifle. I refilled the water jugs a dozen times!"

"You forgot the stuffing and sprouts!" said Bridget mildly.

"Did I?" replied Mary, revived by the strong tea. "Well, there's sure to be half a dozen of them groaning all night!"

The excitement of the day had been too much for the little ones and they were nodding off as we put on their pyjamas. Prayers were forgotten as we tucked them into bed. It had been the most wonderful day of their lives!

Karen was kept busy for the rest of the evening serving the Warden and Matron's friends who came to visit. But Bridget, Mary and I sat in the sparkling kitchen sipping tea and eating a large slice of the fabulous Christmas cake being served to the guests. None of us had had any Christmas dinner; there had been no time and no inclination to eat.

Chapter Fifty-Eight

Neither a Christmas card nor letter had arrived from Sean, and in a few days it would be two calendar months since his departure; perhaps he had forgotten me. I picked up my boots and wandered slowly downstairs to the kitchen.

The Christmas tree still glowed festively in the hall, and soon it would be New Year. I wanted to be at home with my family now, but it was out of the question. The staff considered themselves fortunate if they had one weekend off in the month, and I had become like the staff. Matron's constant reminders of duty unnerved me, and yet she never lifted a hand when she could have.

The snow had been falling steadily and I had to shovel my way into the hen house. By New Year's Eve we were cut off from the outside world by more heavy falls of snow.

Nothing could move along the snow-bound roads, and so Matron's guests would not be able to come to welcome in the New Year. On that day, while the boys built snowmen and rolled along balls of snow until they became too big to roll any further, Matron decided to arrange a party in her sitting-room for the staff.

When I went to the kitchen for lunch Bridget was on her high horse.

"Matron has invited us all to her sitting-room this evening for a party!" she announced with dignity.

I looked up, smiling with pleasure at the prospect of being Matron's guest; and, at once, decided to wear my rose-pink, linen dress, with the dainty matching Cuban-heeled shoes. They were still in the wardrobe upstairs from the weekend I had spent at Bridget's home.

Mary's mouth dropped open in surprise.

"I'll be a bag of nerves!" she said, shuddering.

Karen went on eating her lunch, seemingly unmoved.

"It will make a change to be a guest," she remarked in her aloof way.

Bridget was banging things about a bit, muttering to no one in particular.

"It's only happening because her friends can't get here, otherwise she would never lower herself to invite us!" said Bridget angrily.

I smiled while I listened, watching the different reactions to Matron's invitation. It might well be an interesting evening, I thought.

Outdoors it was bitterly cold and I was wishing I could escape from an afternoon of chopping kindling in the woodshed. I still had the feeling that Sean would appear to help me with my labours, but the thought of him not writing upset me. I wiped away a tear and decided to finish chopping for the day. There was enough kindling piled up in the corner to light the fires for a week .

I had seen Tam only once, in the early morning, when he had actually brought the vegetables up from the garden and left them outside the kitchen door.

"The Christmas spirit getting through to Tam, do you think?" said Bridget, her remark filled with sarcasm. I piled the vegetables into the rack while I listened. Perhaps she was right.

I wished the day's work was over so I could dress for the party. The day had passed slowly and in the descending darkness of late afternoon I hurried to the furnace room. The door stood open, and I almost fell back with surprise to see Tam shovelling coal into the open doors of both furnaces.

"Off you go!" he grunted, barely looking up. "And I'll see to them at nine thirty!"

I was so startled at the sight of Tam doing my work that I hurried away to the kitchen without offering any thanks. The kitchen was empty; everyone would be getting ready for the party, so I ran upstairs and turned the taps on in the bath. Then I brought my dress from the wardrobe and laid out my silk stockings carefully on the bed, since my rough hands could easily ruin them. Life always seemed wonderful when I was steeping in a hot bath, which had never been the regulation five or six inches since coming to Avonlea. Sinking under the hot water I found I could think about Sean without dissolving into tears. Perhaps he was fully occupied with his training and had no time to write.

When I was dressed, with my unruly hair neat and shining, I made my way downstairs. The others were just being welcomed by Matron into her sitting-room, and she nodded as I crossed the hall.

"Just take a seat where you can find one, we're having supper buffet style, Jaqueline."

Tam was there with his wife, and it was the Warden who introduced me to her for the first time; she was small, dark, and bright-eyed.

The Warden was in a jovial mood, showering compliments on the female staff in their pretty dresses. All the anger, nerves and resentment expressed in the kitchen at lunch-time had been forgotten.

Matron sat upright and smiled primly by her desk. Her grey hair, and clothes, blended into the faded, heavy brocade curtains that belonged to a past century, as did all the other furnishings in the room.

Tam's hard, muscular body was sunk in a deeply padded armchair; he smoked his pipe and stared blankly into the fire, while his dark-haired, bright-eyed wife chattered nervously to Matron about washing her curtains every month to keep the house clean and cheery. Like the staff she wore a dress for the occasion, while Matron remained in her eternal tweed skirt and twin set. But she had made one concession to the party spirit; on her feet she wore black calf court shoes; the heels were twice the height of her usual brogues.

After a daintily served supper with wine from the Warden's cellar, Matron sat down at the piano. Mary was called upon to sing, and we all clapped to encourage her while she selected a sheet of music from the pieces Matron had offered. As soon as there was a tinkle on the piano Mary started to sing. Matron's concentration turned to a frown.

"No, no! You don't sing until I have played the introduction!" she said sharply.

I had heard Mary sing the aria note perfect at the kitchen sink, but an introduction meant nothing to her.

"This is where you come in!" continued Matron, running her skilled fingers over the keyboard, while Mary listened.

Matron started again and the sweet untrained voice came in at exactly the right note, and once Mary started it was Matron who had to follow.

We listened to the pathos of Puccini's *Oh, My Beloved Father* which had been poured out over the unfeeling vegetables in the kitchen sink on at least one day each month. As Mary stood by the piano, her eyes and voice full of pleading, I felt she was wasted on the vegetables and the dustpan. But she probably never noticed her work as her voice carried her into the magical realms of music.

For Mary, singing released the happiness or sadness she felt as she went about her duties. For Matron, it was a series of black dots on different levels, with varied measurements, that she beat out on the piano keyboard. To sing a quaver when it should have been a semi-quaver was unforgivable.

Mary's last silver notes died away to almost a whisper and we sat locked in sympathy with her. Matron finished the last bars on the piano; then there was silence. Immediately, a grin spread across the small, white face with its halo of dark, wavy hair, bringing us back to the realisation that it was our Mary, the kitchen maid, who had been pouring out her heart.

The Warden called for an encore as we clapped, but Mary was not to be lured by our show of pleasure. Instead, she suggested that the Warden should sing; I sat up with interest as he accepted the challenge and addressed his wife.

"Let's have *The Flea*, my dear, I feel in fine form!"

Matron thumbed through the sheets of music, coughed, opened the piece and set it on the piano. We waited, but the Warden remained in his chair as Matron began, and the room filled with his rich baritone voice.

Song flowed from his throat, and his body shook with melodious laughter. It was, indeed, the perfect setting for the song: the flaming log fire, the rich, red port in the crystal decanter on the rosewood table, and the man who looked just like a king with a flea. Sitting in this slightly musty, old-world setting, I listened while the music poured from his obese body sounding rich and clear and magnificent.

Chapter Fifty-Nine

Our Bridget had been quiet and unsmiling during the first week of January, but I put it all down to the long hours of work she had endured during the festive season. There was no one in the kitchen when I took my seat at the breakfast table, so I opened the letter that had come from my sister; Bridget bustled in and started to fuss over me.

"Will you be coming home with me at the weekend?" she asked, looking intently into my face as she put the toast rack on the table.

"No, Bridget," I answered quietly.

"Well, I've asked you!" she said, and her Irish accent was soft. Then she launched into a flood of words, just like her old self, and I felt my spirits rise as she raved on in her light-hearted, amusing way. "Any feelings they have are limited to their stomachs and their loins!" she said, and I felt myself smile. "I've listened, while they smoke their pipes and talk sadly about their first, second, third and even fourth wives who have died in childbirth."

Bridget stopped talking, and dipping her hand into the jar of salt she threw a handful into a large pot; the words she poured out started to penetrate through the gloom that had wrapped itself round me since the first day of the New Year, and she started again,

"There are men who won't leave their wives alone, even when they are breast-feeding, or pregnant." And she lifted the large, black pot and dumped it onto the hot range. "By God, it's nothing but dead wood they carry above their shoulders!"

Any dreams I had cherished of dashing young men fighting duels over me, or even the average, rugged male wooing me with a bunch of roses, burst like bubbles with the impact of Bridget's impassioned words. Feeling wiser, but sadder, at having been introduced to some of the more sordid realities of life over breakfast, I at last managed to get a word in,

"Then why did you ask me to go home with you at the weekend, if that is life after marriage?"

"Because my family expect it of me, and now I can go to confession with a clear conscience," Bridget replied, crossing herself with the wooden spoon still in her hand.

"Why don't you come to *my* home for the weekend, Bridget?" I asked.

"No, I couldn't do that," she replied thoughtfully. "My good mother's too near her confinement and I want to be there if she needs me."

Although Bridget's outburst had shattered any romantic illusions I might have had, it dragged me out of the apathy I had been feeling and I dashed upstairs to collect my wellington boots. When I got back to the kitchen the gloom had gone completely.

It was mild outside and I started to clear the snow from the paths again. Most of the snow on the lawns had melted, and the tips of snowdrops were pushing their way up through the wintry soil. Digging into a drift that blocked the path down to the river I scattered the slushy, icy snow. The water looked cold and grey as it moved slowly past, but nothing could stifle the mounting happiness inside me.

I had come to Avonlea the previous March when the blossom trees were starting to bloom pink and white, and after almost a year of speculation on a turn in the tide of war, it still raged throughout most of the world. Would I ever get the chance to travel and see the world? And would there be anything left to see?

Most of the low-lying garden was under a crust of melting snow, but the kitchen still needed a supply of vegetables, so I dug up leeks from the slushy ground and tossed them into the barrow.

Tam had been fixing the oven door for Bridget, and he had just gone up to the lodge when I arrived with the leeks.

"Tam's left his waistcoat, Jaqueline, would you take it up to the lodge after you've had your tea?"

"Yes, Bridget, I'll take it up later."

I picked up the waistcoat and hung it on the back of Bridget's chair so I would remember to take it, then I sat down at the table.

"The tips of the snowdrops are showing already, Bridget!" I remarked to her back as she peered into the oven.

It was at that moment Matron walked into the kitchen, and pointing at Tam's waistcoat, she said,

"Who does that garment belong to? You know I will not have clothes in the kitchen!"

She walked to the chair, picked up the waistcoat between finger and thumb, and opening the door dropped it on the step outside. Bridget had turned from the oven and her face was frigid when she answered,

"The oven door wouldn't stay closed, but Tam fixed it for me this morning; that's when he forgot his waistcoat, Matron. Jaqueline will be taking it to the lodge after her tea break."

"It's leeks and white sauce for vegetable today on the menu, I see!" said Matron, ignoring Bridget's explanation. "And we will have the potatoes mashed, Bridget! So you have decided to use the lamb chops after all," she continued, "and what is for sweet?"

"Bread pudding, Matron," replied Bridget coldly.

"Good, that should fill up their tummies and keep the cold out!" she answered with a fixed smile, then added abruptly, "Where is Mary?"

"Cleaning the staff sitting-room, Matron."

When Matron left the kitchen Bridget reminded me about Tam's waistcoat.

"Don't forget the waistcoat, Jaqueline, and bring it inside, just in case he should see where Matron dropped it."

Bridget was anxious to avoid strife between Tam and Matron, and being aware of her concern, I replied,

"I'm just going, Bridget, I'll take it up to the lodge now!"

The air had become warmer since early morning and it was pleasant strolling up the drive. I knocked on the lodge door and when it opened I handed the waistcoat to Tam's bright-eyed, little wife.

"Oh, so he didn't lose it after all!" she said cheerily. "Come in, Jaqueline, and take a glass of sherry with us, it's still the festive season."

"I don't think Matron would allow me to take sherry during working hours," I said apologetically.

"Oh, who said anything about Matron! Come into the parlour!" Then she pulled me into the vestibule of the cosy little lodge and closed the outside door. "It's my own home-made sherry," she said, "not the poison you buy in the shops!"

Tam's wife chattered on, guiding me into her parlour with both hands. The quaint-sounding name she gave to her pretty sitting-room amused me. It sounded like something from a fairy tale, and because it displayed a neat replica of the open fireplace in the sitting-room of the large ancient house, with smaller versions of the church-like windows, it looked like something out of a fairy tale.

Tam sat in an armchair with his stockinged feet on a padded stool, and the smoke rose lazily from his pipe. Lowering his newspaper a little he grunted, and I smiled. His wife placed three glasses on the table near Tam's elbow, and lifting the decanter she filled them as if she were pouring lemonade.

"Bottoms up!" she said, offering me a glass.

Before I could take a second sip she had emptied her glass and was refilling it, offering to top up mine. I put my hand over the half pint glass while the smooth, sweet sherry rolled round my mouth. Tam's wife chattered on and all I could do was smile, while Tam hid behind his newspaper,

"Thank you, that was delicious sherry, Mrs—" But before I could say her name, she replied,

"Yes, I make it myself, but I don't tell anyone how it's done, not even Tam!" and she started guiding me towards the door. "He tells me you're a grand worker," she half whispered as I misjudged the step outside the door and stumbled onto the path.

The door closed, and as I turned down the drive I was conscious of the large grin on my face. I could feel myself weaving from side to side, and I had lost the feeling in my lower jaw. Later, chopping up the kindling wood to avoid meeting anyone until the effects of the sherry wore off, I heard a distinct quack coming from behind the woodshed.

I dashed outside and there was the duckling, much more grown, waddling towards me wagging his whole body. He waddled straight into the shed and I followed. While I chopped, he told me a long story in a series of quiet little quacks, with occasional glances. I listened, nodded and agreed.

It was while we were communicating, that I realised 'he' was a 'she'; there was no glossy green head colour, no white collar at her neck; she was just plain greyish-brown all over. She had settled herself in the sawdust and I tried to think of a name, but nothing would come to mind but 'the duckling'.

The letter from my sister was still in my pocket, so I took it out and started at the paragraph I had reached at the breakfast table. It read on as follows:

Trudy has invited us to go with her when she visits Penny at the weekend. Since Penny married she has moved into a cottage on the airport road. Her baby is due in May if her calculations are right. And she is looking forward to seeing all the land-girls before the happy event takes place.

Last week three of our German prisoners made a bid for freedom while working alone in the barn. They got down to the harbour without being missed and took a motor boat, then they headed out to sea. Unfortunately, or should I say fortunately, the fuel ran out and they were picked up by the local fishing fleet in the early hours of the morning, half frozen and drifting helplessly in the icy cold sea. It amazed me; there was no punishment for the prisoners; in fact, they were welcomed back like long lost brothers. But the man who had left fuel in his motor boat engine was severely reprimanded by the police.

I often wonder what it's all about, don't you?

This invite will give you the chance to meet all the land-girls I work with, and, of course, our three lumberjills.

I hope you will be able to make it home this weekend; if you can, let me know so I can make arrangements with Trudy.

Much Love,
Margaret.

The duckling followed behind me when I left with the kindling for the kitchen, and Bridget shooed it away with her brush when it started up the two steps outside the door. For several days she turned up to feed with the poultry, then the rain came in torrents and her visits stopped.

The air had become mellow and humid, and everything that grew sprouted new shoots.

"It's too early in the year, they'll be nipped by the frost," Tam was saying to Matron. But she suddenly turned away from the side door of the kitchen leaving Tam outside in mid-sentence.

"Miserable man!" she muttered, passing Bridget and I on her way through to the hall.

"She's very rude to Tam," I said, more or less thinking out loud.

"He's spoiling the perfect little world she wants to live in, even down to controlling the weather. Just how selfish can a person be?" Bridget muttered. Then glancing in my direction she continued, "He's probably right about the frost!" Bridget prattled on while she filled pots, emptied pots and swung them from the range to the table, her face flushed with the effort.

For the whole week I plodded round in wellington boots pushing the barrow through deep, muddy puddles, but one morning the wheel of the barrow ran over thin sheets of ice that had formed in every wet area of the estate. I watched the new growth turn brown and die with a cold snap. Tam, I decided, had been right. And Matron's expectations of an early spring would have to wait. But the snowdrops would survive.

At the end of February the weather became stormy, and it was on a violent night that I woke from a deep sleep, the ancient house shaking with a terrific, thundering crash. I gripped the blankets as I lay in bed and waited for more to come. How would we manage the boys, I thought.

Had the horrors of war spread across the country to this almost empty part of Britain? As the noise subsided and the odd clattering stopped, I still waited for the next thundering crash feeling desperate for the little ones. Bombs never fell singly!

The seconds passed, and nothing more happened; there was no sound of aeroplane engines throbbing in the stillness of the night. Cautiously I rose from my bed as if the floor was about to open up under my feet. Pulling on my housecoat, I stepped behind the heavy black-out curtains that closed off the turret window in my room, but there was nothing to be seen hovering in the rain-swept sky illuminated by an invisible moon.

Cautiously I opened the bedroom door and made my way in the dark to the narrow staircase. The wind was howling through the floor below as I descended, and I pulled my housecoat tightly around myself. When I reached the top of the main staircase, I saw that the whole roof over the large hall was open to the grey night sky and the rain poured through in torrents.

The debris from the roof lay where it had fallen, piled up in the hall below and completely blocking the main staircase; I could hear whimpering from the nursery. Then Mary and Bridget called from the corridor that led to their rooms just as Matron opened the door of her bedroom. Completely cut off by heavy, wooden beams and large, jagged pieces of thick plaster, Matron stood there, a tiny figure in her nightdress.

I looked around me and down into the hall, brushing the rain from my face, while the wind tunnelled through the open roof lashing the deluge over the devastation below.

"It's all in the hall area from what I can see up here, Matron!" I shouted. "There's nothing wrong on my floor! I'm going to flick the light switch to see if we have lighting!"

"Just on and off again, Jaqueline!" Matron's voice reached me in broken sentences, "and as quickly as you can for the black-out!"

"There's no water pouring from anywhere, except the rain," Bridget shouted, "so we can't have any burst pipes! Matron, is the phone dead?" she added urgently.

Matron's frail-looking figure moved a step into the slates and plaster that lay round her bedroom door, and she knocked the debris from the small table pulling the phone into her bedroom. I saw her listen for the dialling tone and then she called out imperiously:

"Return to your rooms, everyone! I will make a report to the police! There is nothing anyone can do while it is dark, because of the blackout! Karen, stop that wailing, at once, and go with Jaqueline to settle the boys down, then go back to bed, goodnight!"

The house was humming with activity as the first signs of daylight appeared; and when I reached the top of the main staircase workmen were already clearing the mound of large, wooden beams, chunks of heavy plaster and slates from the main hall.

The boys had found a way to reach the kitchen by sliding down the broad banisters of the staircase, and as it was the safest and cleanest way through the rubble, I did the same. Excited by the devastation that had come to Avonlea during the night, with no injury to anyone, the boys were up early and rules were thrown to the wind.

Sliding down the banisters had been strictly forbidden until that morning. It was impossible to get through to the common room, or the dining-room where the boys had their meals, so everyone squeezed into the kitchen.

"Lift the table back a bit from the range, boys! I need more room to move!" Bridget was bustling round giving orders. "You two can stand at the sink-board to eat your breakfast, you can do without a seat for one morning; and Carrots, off my chair and give it to Jaqueline, she's got a hard day's work ahead of her. She won't be sitting at a desk holding a pencil. Up!" she added, and Carrots reluctantly moved to the sink-board.

The boys were all making for the school bus by the time I had raked out and stoked the furnaces, so I started brushing down the remaining rubble from the staircase while listening to Mary's deep sighs. Workmen carried out the larger pieces of debris to a waiting lorry, while others were on the roof securing large tarpaulins over the opening where the roof had once been.

The workmen were just moving off, their lorry piled high with the first load, when Tam walked into the hall.

"No use both of us working here!" he said. "You can start filling the barrow with rubble and take it down to the rubbish tip behind the garden wall. See that you dump it well back away from the compost heap."

The large double doors stood open, and I could see Matron's Persian carpet still lying under the rubble in front of her sitting-room door. The white marble bust had fallen from its pedestal and lay decapitated amidst the devastation. The Warden had not yet appeared, although Matron stood fully-dressed at her bedroom door waiting for a path to be cleared across the hall by Tam.

"Remove that mound of debris outside the main doors, Jaqueline, these ridiculous creatures didn't need to drop it right at the entrance! No thought for anyone but themselves!" she said from the cosiness of her bedroom. If the men in the lorry, now halfway up the drive with a mountainous load, had heard her remarks, I felt sure they would have turned and dumped it on her doorstep.

"They have just gone with the first load, Matron, they will be coming back to pick it up," I said, starting to fill the barrow where I stood inside the hall.

It was impossible to lift the barrow after I had piled it high, so I shovelled some of the rubble out until I could lift it easily. After the treacherous storm of the night before the weather was beautiful, and I made three trips to the tip in the warmth of the bright sunshine that streamed down from a clear, blue sky.

Just as I filled the barrow for the fourth time Tam came blustering through the main doors.

"Get a move on, and fill the barrow! You can get more than that on. Stop wasting your time!" he roared.

"But I can't lift it if it's too full, I've tried," I answered.

Cursing to himself he piled on the heavy rubble and I found it impossible to lift no matter how hard I pulled on the handles. Leaving me for a few minutes, Tam came back with a length of rope and tied one end to a handle of the barrow, then he passed the rope round the back of my neck and secured it to the other handle.

"Right, straighten up and take the weight between your hands and neck!"

I managed to stagger forward a little so he removed some of the plaster, and when he was sure I was taking as much as possible I was sent trudging down to the back of the garden while Tam stayed to clear the hall.

Negotiating the slope down to the garden gate was the most difficult part of my labours. By midday my nose bled profusely and when I complained, Tam's answer was:

"The job has to be done, get Bridget to drop a key down your back, that'll stop it!"

Lunch was on the table when I walked into the kitchen.

"I'd better change my jacket, Bridget, the blood looks awful."

"No point in doing that!" she replied harshly, then dropped a large, cold, metal key inside the back of my shirt. "Now sit down and eat your meal. You can wash the blood off your face when you're finished, your nose is still bleeding."

She turned back to her pots and started to talk between tight lips:

"Kill you he would, for the sake of an extra couple of barrow-loads, bastard that he is!" and there was no movement of her hand to make the sign of the cross. What Bridget was saying barely penetrated my mind, because I ached like toothache all over. "Wear the same jacket and stop fussing about being clean, let him and Matron see the mess you're in!"

I cleaned my face up in Mary and Bridget's bathroom to avoid climbing the stairs, then went back on the job for the afternoon in the blood-streaked jacket. Tightening my stomach muscles and bracing my legs to take the load he had waiting for me, I headed for the tip. It's only for one day, I kept saying to myself.

Matron had come into the hall with two men, but it was later when the tea break came that I learned who they had been.

"It's dry rot," Bridget told me, when I sat down at the table. "Some of the beams had crumbled into dust when they examined them. They'll be going through the whole house systematically to see how far it has spread. You're being moved into Karen's room while they do more tests. I see your nose has been bleeding again. You look a fine sight! Has Matron seen you?"

Bridget had just finished speaking, when Matron walked into the kitchen from the hall.

"You have blood on your face, Jaqueline, go and wash it off at once and change your jacket!"

"It will be pointless to change my jacket until I finish taking the rubble to the tip, because my nose will continue to bleed as long as I have the rope around my neck."

"What rope?" she said scornfully.

"The one Tam tied to the handles of the barrow so I would be able to lift it; it lies on the back of my neck," I replied, and I was annoyed with myself because my hands trembled when I picked up my mug.

"Oh, after all, it's only for one day, you should be finished by this evening." Then she turned abruptly and left the kitchen.

When Matron's sitting-room door had closed, Bridget said,

"She wants the mess cleaned up, but as my mother says, 'the last straw broke the camel's back'." She spoke slowly and deliberately, and again she didn't cross herself. It made what she had said seem foreboding.

"Is there any dry rot in my room, Bridget?"

"Yes," she replied, "that's why you have to share Karen's room. It won't be as comfortable as your own, because you'll be sleeping on a camp bed, but all your things have been moved already."

I think Bridget and I had lost track of time while we talked, because the back door swung open to reveal Tam standing there.

"We want this cleared today," he said, "so the longer you sit there the later it will be when you finish."

Without saying a word I rose stiffly from the table and rinsed my mug. I had lost all interest in my appearance, it didn't seem to matter anymore. It was almost seven o'clock when I was giving a final brush to the floor under Matron's eagle eye, and Bridget had glanced at me from the kitchen door more than once. Then, as if she could wait no longer, she called out,

"Come and eat, Jaqueline!"

Matron looked at Bridget sharply and Bridget glared back.

"It can be gone over in the morning, Jaqueline, so go and have your supper." Having agreed with Bridget, Matron walked into her sitting-room and closed the door.

"I don't feel like eating, Bridget, I would rather have a bath before I stiffen up."

"You're going to eat!" she said. "It's only a light omelette, so sit down and then you can have your bath. You can't work all day like you do and eat only enough to feed a sparrow!"

If Tam and Matron were oblivious of how wretched I felt, Bridget certainly was not. She watched like a patient mother until my plate was empty.

"Now! Upstairs with you and have your bath!" and Bridget pointed to the kitchen door.

I felt hysterical at the thought of five or six inches of water and watched the bath fill. Then I slipped shakily in and the hot water closed over me. If anyone had asked at that moment what was the greatest luxury in life, I would have answered: steeping in a hot bath after navvying from dawn till dusk.

I had to force myself to stay awake by rubbing myself with a soapy cloth, and I stood in the bath to towel myself dry while the water rushed away. Karen was lucky to have a bathroom off her bedroom like this, I thought as I stepped out of the bath with the towel around me. Suddenly, I doubled up with pain as my stomach muscles went rigid; I managed to reach the camp bed and ease myself down until it passed, but I felt shivery and damp, and an invisible band tightened round my chest as the cramp returned.

I felt sorry for myself and started to cry, but as I drew the blankets over me and warmth began to spread through me, my stomach eased so I could stretch out. Then came the strangest sensation: it was as if I was falling backwards; I felt myself spinning up and up drifting as light as a feather. I began to worry about the furnaces; I would have to stoke them before I fell asleep or they would be out in the morning because the dampers were open.

I wanted to get up, but the band tightened round my chest with the slightest effort and I fell into a sleep of utter exhaustion.

Chapter Sixty

When I woke up in Karen's talcum-scented bedroom it was morning. But all was not well, sleep had not restored my energy or refreshed me. I felt uncomfortably hot, and perspiration trickled down my neck. Suddenly I remembered the furnaces; they would be out, because I had no recollection of stoking them before falling asleep last night.

Tam would be furious. I made to rise from the camp bed and a thousand red hot needles raced through every part of me. When I tried to raise my head from the pillow the searing pain shooting across the back of my neck made me feel dizzy.

Karen was still asleep, so I waited, afraid to move. I could feel a soreness in my throat, and an invisible band kept tightening round my chest, making it difficult to breathe. The feeling passed after a while, then hoarsely I managed to say Karen's name. She was on the point of waking up and without opening her eyes, she said pleasantly,

"Good morning, Jaqueline." She stretched luxuriously, and because I was afraid to move I felt a pang of envy.

"Can you help me off this bed, Karen? I can hardly move," I croaked.

Alarm registered on her face and she sat up quickly. I was amazed at the sudden change in her; she rose from her bed whimpering and slipped on her housecoat. For as long as I could remember my father had frowned upon tears, or any sign of distress from a member of the family. As Karen ran from the room to tell Bridget, I lay helpless wondering at the sudden flood of tears rendering her incapable of coping with an emergency, and yet I had seen her intimidate the doorman at the cinema with a few well-chosen words.

Becoming restless I tried to move my legs over the bed, but the pain in my groin was excruciating. Slowly I touched the area with my fingers and found I had a large swelling stretching the length of my groin. I had no idea of what it could be, but now that I was fully awake the pain had increased.

I heard the sound of quiet cursing and whimpering at the bedroom door, and it opened wide to admit Bridget who hurried in followed by the tearful Karen.

"Take hold of her other arm," said Bridget, easing my shoulder from the pillow, "and get her into a sitting position. Now, slowly put her legs over the bed. And keep quiet!"

Between them they dressed me and I was filled with relief. Their gentleness eased the pains, and Bridget's soft curses made me realise the depth of feeling she had for the suffering of others. Her cursing was an outlet for the indignity she felt when one human being abused another.

Bridget was at her best in command of a difficult situation, and while I philosophised, I leant heavily on the strong Bridget and the immature Karen for support as they helped me downstairs to the kitchen. They eased me into Bridget's straight-backed chair and a bottle of aspirin was placed on the table. Then Bridget poured a cup of tea, saying as she did so,

"Take three aspirins, then you'll be getting yourself off home as soon as you've had this cup of tea; the bus will be passing the main gates in twenty five minutes."

Karen stood with her hands clasped in front of her, her eyes full of dread.

"Run upstairs, Karen," continued Bridget, "and throw all Jaqueline's things into her case as fast as you can, and bring it down to the kitchen. And be as quiet as a mouse."

Karen hurried into the hall, glancing back as she went, while I swallowed the aspirins. Tears of weakness were dripping into my tea, because I had never been so wracked with pain, or felt so useless. Bridget hurried off to her room and came back with her coat on, then she poured a cup of tea and sat down beside me.

"She'll be the death of us all!" she began in a hushed urgent voice. "But not if I can prevent it!" Then she started to talk hurriedly about the land-girl into whose shoes I had stepped on coming to Avonlea. "Do you remember the day we had a visitor by the name of Heather, a tall girl who spent most of her time in the staff sitting-room?"

"Yes," I replied, picturing the thin, waxen-faced girl with the pale blue eyes and lank, fair hair. Her shoulders had been slightly stooped, perhaps because she was tall. She had been quiet, as I remembered, and only spoke in answer, as if she had no conversation of her own. I had tried to strike up a conversation when we were introduced, but she had given me no encouragement.

Then Bridget continued in a hushed voice,

"Heather had been the land-girl at Avonlea for two years when she developed tuberculosis. It was Karen who found her in bed delirious with a high fever, and Matron had to send for the doctor. Heather was rushed to hospital and is now convalescing. She has been allowed to visit us twice since being moved to the convalescent home."

Karen had come quietly into the kitchen carrying my suitcase, and Bridget rose immediately to her feet.

"Now rise slowly, Jaqueline, and we'll help you into your coat." Bridget's voice was even quieter than it had been. "Close the door to the hall, Karen, I don't want Matron to hear us when we've got this far."

Softly Karen closed the door, while Bridget helped me to my feet, and then they slipped my coat on. The side door creaked when Karen opened it and they held their breath; then I was being helped down the two steps on Bridget's bony arm.

"Goodbye, Jaqueline." Karen gave a slight wave of her hand, and her whispered goodbye sounded wistful.

"Goodbye, Karen," I whispered back, and winced as the first steps on the rough path almost shattered me.

I felt secure with Bridget at my side helping me to hobble up the drive, and the fresh, morning air was stimulating. I wanted to break into a run at the thought of going home, but it was impossible.

"I only hope Tam is still in bed, it'll be easier all round if you're gone before anyone is up and about," said Bridget determinedly.

"What will you say to Matron when she finds out I've gone home without asking permission, Bridget?"

"The truth!" she replied staunchly. "I'll say you've gone to see your doctor because you're ill!"

I loved the way Bridget spoke, so definite as to what was right and what was wrong. I had always known where I stood with her, and she was good. My face was chilled and drawn, but my body felt weak and warm inside the excess of clothing Bridget had pushed me into. We passed the rambling roses still lying dormant; it would be next month before they started to show signs of life, or even April. Tam had taught me to prune them just above the bud with a sloping cut.

"I hope the bus is on time!" whispered Bridget as we approached the lodge, and she chewed on her bottom lip while her arm tightened on mine. We stood quietly listening for the bus.

Just moments after we had reached the main gates the bus swung round the curve in the road and Bridget waved it down. When I looked at the lodge windows the blackout curtains were still drawn. Bridget's face was flushed and the excitement of the chance she had taken showed in her eyes. She spoke to the conductor in a hushed voice,

"She's going all the way to Edinburgh; will you be good enough to put her into a taxi when she gets there?"

The conductor took my suitcase and swung it into the bus.

"Certainly!" he replied, helping me onto the platform.

"Goodbye, Bridget, and thanks for everything," I said, smiling down at the bespectacled, pale-cheeked face of my good friend.

"Goodbye, Jaqueline," and Bridget's blue eyes twinkled behind her thick glasses as she added, "To be sure, it was no trouble at all!" As the bus moved away she called out, "Get a doctor's note and have a week of rest before coming back! They can manage without you for a week!"

The bus moved away, and in the pale morning light I watched through the window as Bridget's slim figure faded into the distance. I was on my way home before Tam came out of the lodge, thanks to Bridget; she had defied both him and Matron for my sake.

In the warmth of the bus I dozed, and shivered every time the door opened and a cold draught of air hit me. Then I was being helped into a taxi at the square in Edinburgh and my suitcase was pushed in at my feet. By the time I reached home everything had become vague and hazy; I heard my mother pay the taxi. I was quickly carried up the garden path by the driver, my mother hurrying ahead opening doors. I was helped into bed and then all was quiet.

I must have slept for a while; for when I opened my eyes the doctor was there busy with his stethoscope, and while he examined me I groaned, and my mother waited. Then they walked to the door of my room speaking in hushed voices as they had always done; suddenly I felt irritated.

"I'm not a child any more, you don't have to whisper!" I said.

A startled look crossed my mother's face and she faltered in mid-sentence, but the doctor crossed the room and seated himself on the edge of my bed.

"You have torn the muscles in the groin of your left leg and the bowel is protruding through in three places; until the muscles are repaired you must rest as much as possible so as not to aggravate the condition." He paused and smiled. "Your work has strained your whole body, so be content to rest until it repairs itself." Then he patted my hand, just as he had done when I was a child with chicken pox. "Be patient, you have your whole life before you. Take time to get well!" he said as he left the room.

When the doctor had gone there was time to reflect on how rude I had been. I remembered the hurt look that had crossed my mother's face, and the doctor hurrying across to my bed to explain; I had been rude to them both because they had treated me like a child.

I felt empty, exhausted, and a complete failure. Hot tears rolled down my face, running into my ears and seeping into the pillow. I cried bitterly for all the months of futile effort that had not brought the war to an end, or even made the slightest bit of difference.

It was the beginning of March 1945 and for me the end of the war was as much in sight as it ever had been. I was a physical wreck at nineteen years of age, and my dreams of becoming a WREN were over. A heart murmur, the doctor had said to my mother in an undertone, but he had not said it to me. I lay steeped in despair, and wracked with pain at the slightest movement; the tears streamed down as sleep took me out of my misery.

It was evening when my mother's voice woke me out of a deep sleep, and I sighed with relief to find myself in bed at home.

"I didn't phone Matron," she said, smiling, "I thought you would want to call her yourself. Let me dial the number for you!"

It was one of the boys who answered the phone and I could hear him calling,

"Jaqueline's on the phone, Matron!"

A few seconds passed then Matron took the phone.

"Yes?" she said coldly, and remained quiet until I told her what the doctor had said, then she answered, "And how do you think we are going to manage without a land-girl! You selfish, thoughtless creature!" her offensive voice rose, "And how dare you leave without my permission! You should have waited until—"

Bridget had been very wise; Matron was not interested in anything I had to say. I pressed my fingers on the phone buttons and when the line went dead I put down the receiver. Avonlea, with all its hard, unending, thankless work, would never again be part of my life.

Part Four

Three Years After The War Has Ended

Chapter Sixty-One

My husband pushed open the door of the tailor's shop and I stepped out of its close, dry atmosphere into crisp, sunny weather.

"I'll see you on the steps of the GPO," I said, "I must get some stamps before it closes!"

Men, I thought, as the door swung shut behind me, were worse than women when it came to choosing material for a suit.

Pulling on my gloves before stepping out onto the pavement, I felt a glow of satisfaction steal over me on catching sight of my reflection in the side window of the tailor's shop. My shoulder-length hair was looking well groomed today, the sun turning it into sparkling gold, and a fashionable three inches of navy skirt was showing below my matching cape. I fastened the clasp at the neck, then smoothed the back of my kid gloves. I could feel the soft comfort of the suede court shoes that completed my outfit.

In ten minutes the post office would be closed, and through the glass door of the shop I could see Rolf still talking to the tailor, so I moved into the crowd that thronged the busy pavement. People were still in uniform and yet the war had ended three years ago; about two months after I left Avonlea.

Princes Street was always invaded at the weekends by people from the country villages, so I walked with the crowd as they crossed the road on my way to the post office. I felt pleased to have got the stamps before it closed, and sticking them on my letters I went outside to drop them in the posting box.

It was while I waited on the steps that a shadow fell across me, and I looked up into keen, blue, Scandinavian eyes. He was wearing an air force uniform and the wings on his chest that distinguished the pilot. He looked broader than I remembered him, and perhaps it was the peaked hat that made him look taller. Then his hands closed over mine and he said my name, but this time it was not abbreviated to fit into his masculine world.

The noise of the busy street faded while we stood there, as if we had been transported back in time. I could hear once more the whispering of the shimmering aspens as the sunbeams filtered through their spinning leaves and danced along the path before us. The scenes flashed through my mind's eye, and I was standing in the moonlight at the river's edge while the glistening salmon wriggled at my feet. Somehow, something that had not seemed beautiful at the time, had indeed been beautiful.

"You didn't write, Sean," I said quietly.

"I wrote just before Christmas, but you didn't answer, Jaqueline." As he spoke his eyes seemed to be searching mine for an answer.

"I didn't receive any letter from you," I replied, feeling puzzled, "and yet I got letters from my family."

"I wrote again," Sean was saying, "when my first leave was cancelled, but the letter came back with 'not known at this address' written across it. When I eventually got home on leave the ancient house of Avonlea had been boarded up, because the surveyors had found it riddled with dry rot; there was no one left to ask where you had gone."

While he spoke of Avonlea my mind travelled back. Matron had always taken the mail into her bedroom from the telephone table, where the postman left it. Then when Karen took Matron her breakfast tray she would return to the kitchen with the staff mail. Why hadn't I received Sean's letter? Only Matron could answer that.

Then Sean was smiling down at me, he took my arm and tucked it into his, still holding on to my hand.

"Let's find a coffee shop and start from where we left off in our teens; it's almost four years ago! We've grown up since those days." And then suddenly he felt the rings on my finger under my glove and his eyes clouded.

"I'm too late," he said quietly. "When were you married?"

"Eighteen months ago," I murmured.

I had been unaware of everything, except Sean, until a hand touched my shoulder and Rolf said,

"May I interrupt!"

Sean released my hand and stepped back as I said,

"This is my husband, Rolf." I paused for a moment while they sized each other up. "Rolf, this is Sean!"

They shook hands and exchanged a few polite remarks, then Sean said,

"Goodbye, Jackie," and turned abruptly, hurrying down the post office steps.

Sean vanished into the crowds thronging the busy pavements and a great sense of loss swept over me. I felt isolated and lonely.

"Well! Who was the handsome pilot?" Rolf asked, and he brushed his finger across my cheek to wipe away the single tear that rested there.

"Oh, just Sean!" I answered.

"Come, come, there must be more to tell than that!" We walked down the wide post office steps together.

"Some day," I replied thoughtfully, "when I write of my war-time experiences, I'll let you read them. Now! What's next on the shopping list?"

The brief meeting with Sean had stirred up memories of Avonlea and that sad day in my life when I had become a useless member of society. For a time I had moped and waited to get well, and then the doctor had said I could take a desk job in work of national importance and I had gratefully accepted the chance to be useful again.

The challenge of doing something useful instead of being idle was what I needed; I entered a new world of dust-proof, air-cooled surroundings where we were completely cut off from the sounds of nature.

At first, when I thought of Tam in the kaleidoscope of colour that was his well-tended garden, I missed the fresh air and the showers that fell through rainbows to refresh the earth and all that grew upon its surface. In this new world of grey electronic units, and patient men who taught me to read blueprints and test electronic equipment, I became absorbed.

Then one day a white-coated young man with dark hair had stayed by the testing cabin, resting his arm on top while I rotated a gyro until it spun to perfection.

"Do you know what they're used for?" he asked.

"No, am I supposed to know?" I answered, looking up at him.

"I'll tell you all about it in the canteen at tea break, if you can leave the harem at the top end and come to my table"

"You can't blame half a dozen girls for staying together in this virtually all-male reserve, can you?" I answered, smiling.

But the dark-haired young man had persevered; at the tea break he lifted my cup from the counter and carried it to his table by the window. With growing interest, I followed.

"I can't tell you until you sit down," he replied, pulling out a chair for me. "And introductions always come first!" He smiled. "I'm Rolf," he said.

"Jaqueline," I replied.

It had taken many tea breaks to get through the designing and development of the delicate, aircraft instrument, and before I could get the ever evasive answer the news burst upon us all. Suddenly the war was over and within a few weeks the factory had been reduced to a skeleton staff; the instruments of war were no longer needed.

I looked up at my husband as we walked along Princes Street, my arm lightly placed through his. There was a touch of arrogance in the tilt of his head, and his dark grey eyes, with just a hint of blue in their depths, were smiling.

"It hasn't been easy finding tropical weight material," Rolf said, "but one lightweight suit will be enough to arrive in. They say suits can be made up in a day once we're in Hong Kong!" Then he added, "Penny for your thoughts, Jaqueline?"

I had been listening to him, but the words that were running through my mind, as the music of the 'Warsaw Concerto' drifted up from the bandstand in the gardens below, were memories: "Would it not be better to marry and see the world together?" I could recall the tawny eyes full of mischief, and the ancient, yellowed piano in the Polish canteen that the officer played the concerto on. The nostalgic scene of that last evening filled my thoughts while we walked.

I smiled at the concern crossing my husband's face when he glanced at me waiting for my answer.

"I can still change my mind about accepting a post on the other side of the world. Are you sure you still want to go?" he said urgently, and the blue in his eyes deepened, but I remained silent with my memories.

This dark-haired young man had come boldly into my life, and it had taken courage to approach the unapproachable, which I had become since leaving Avonlea. His colouring reminded me of Reno, and I smiled at the memory of Reno's spoken words, "It is my duty as an officer of Rome!", and it seemed such a long time ago.

Still silent with my memories I glanced up at Rolf. He was tall
and straight, and he walked with the easy grace of the athlete; his
mind was the mathematical mind of the engineer. It had been the
people who had touched upon my life during the war years who had
shaped his image for me.

The castle rose dark and strong ahead of us, set against the clear
blue sky, and the sun shone on the brooding rocks on which it had
taken shape since the eleventh century. I felt a surge of pride go
through me, because this was my city. No matter how far I travelled
part of me would always be here.

"Shall we cross now," Rolf was asking, "and turn up Frederick
Street?"

"Yes," I replied and turned with him to cross the busy road.

When he first began to notice me amongst his blueprints and test
equipment I had been lifting a box of tools. "Here, let me carry that,
you couldn't lift a feather!" he had said, and I had had no inclination
to shout out that I could shovel a ton of coal.

Then, when he said, "We must get you out in the fresh air at
weekends", there had been no urge to tell him I had worked out-of-
doors every day and all day and that exposure to the weather made no
difference to the paleness of my skin. Perhaps I would tell him some
day.

I had been content to sip my tea at his table adored, and looking at
the glow in his eyes. Dark velvet skies and stars had not been
necessary to bring us together. In the almost deserted canteen, after
the war had ended, he had put his hand over mine.

"I've known you all my life," he had said softly, "and I want you
to be my wife."

At first I was reluctant to give up my freedom, but each day my
awareness grew; and when he began to ride into my dreams on a black
charger I remembered Mr William's words: 'I can see nothing else
but a prince on a white charger will do, Jaqueline!' But Mr William
had been wrong; the prince on the white charger had not been meant
to stay in my life. I had looked across the table at the sincere, dark-
haired, young man and felt I had known him for all of my life and
more.

Rousing myself from the ghosts of the past to the realities of the
present, I became acutely aware of my husband, and only he and I
were real as we walked; the future was yet to come. I was content to

wait for it.   His longing to travel was the same as mine, but his horizons were wider than I had ever dreamed of.

Having given some thought as to how I would answer him, I said,

"Being a mere woman, or should I say wife, I have no choice but to go with you, having promised to love, honour and obey."

I still looked straight ahead as I spoke, but I glanced up from the corner of my eye as he threw back his head and laughed; his teeth gleamed white against the healthy tan of his skin, and he answered,

"I know you will always do what you think is right, Jaqueline, and I wouldn't want it any other way!"

His grey-blue eyes sparkled as he squeezed my arm, and I knew in my heart that this was the man I could love and respect for the rest of my life.